OTHER SPORTS CLASSICS FROM FIRESIDE BOOKS

FIVE SEASONS, by Roger Angell
MY TURN AT BAT, by Ted Williams with John Underwood
A HANDFUL OF SUMMERS, by Gordon Forbes
A FALSE SPRING, by Pat Jordan
A DONALD HONIG READER, by Donald Honig
HEAVEN IS A PLAYGROUND, by Rick Telander
DOCK ELLIS IN THE COUNTRY OF BASEBALL,
    by Donald Hall with Dock Ellis

DOLLAR SIGN ON THE MUSCLE

THE WORLD OF BASEBALL SCOUTING

KEVIN KERRANE

A FIRESIDE BOOK · PUBLISHED BY SIMON & SCHUSTER INC.

NEW YORK   LONDON   TORONTO   SYDNEY   TOKYO

FIRESIDE

Simon & Schuster Building
Rockefeller Center
1230 Avenue of the Americas
New York, New York 10020

Designed by Kathy Kikkert
Manufactured in the United States of America

10   9   8   7   6   5   4   3   2   1

Library of Congress Cataloging in Publication Data
Kerrane, Kevin.
  Dollar sign on the muscle.

  (Fireside sports classics)
  "A Fireside book."
  Reprint. Originally published: New York : Beaufort Books, c1984.
  1. Baseball—United States—Scouting. I. Title. II. Series: Fireside
sports classic.
GV880.22.K47   1989   796.357'023'73   88-33425
ISBN 0-671-66649-5

It is indeed a risky business to put the dollar mark on the individual muscle.

—*Branch Rickey,* The American Diamond

A new column titled "Dollar Evaluation" has been added to your prospect-summary sheet. Your dollar evaluation should be the highest figure you would go in order to sign a player if he were on the open market. The figure would be based solely on the player's ability. Other factors, such as what the player is asking for, or what you think you can sign him for, would not be considered when determining a dollar evaluation. (It is likely that you would sign the player at a smaller figure.) Boiled down, it is the "dollar sign on the muscle" and no more.

—*Philadelphia Phillies'* Scouting Manual

CONTENTS

PREFACE

The Employee pledges to maintain the confidentiality of all scouting information which he acquires hereunder, and to preserve such information for the exclusive benefit of the Club. Disclosure by the Employee of any such information to any unauthorized organization or personnel will, in addition to providing grounds for termination of this contract, subject the Employee to disciplinary action.

> —*Clause 3(b), Uniform Scout's Contract, National League*

Baseball scouts take Clause 3(b) very seriously, but they also recognize the fleeting value of their secrets. Any fragment of inside baseball information has a short half-life, after which it's old news and thus potential material for a story. And baseball scouts like to talk. The job is lonely, and the essence of it is to have opinions, so that most scouts are ready to give frank answers to good questions and then to keep on going, to follow the curve of an idea from one perception of talent to another, in language shaped by a lifetime of baseball metaphors. Like cab drivers or barbers, baseball scouts often do their best work while providing a running commentary on it.

In putting some of these commentaries into print, I have edited for the ear as well as the eye in order to convey rhythms, pronunciations, and usages that make each voice distinctive. I have tried to avoid two traps: on the one hand, phony dialect spellings that would merely demean the speaker; on the other, rigid conventions of written English that would blur the individual styles of such individualistic Americans.

Six of the following chapters—the profiles of veteran

scouts—include long passages that are set off (indented without quotation marks) to indicate highly selective editing. Such passages eliminate my own questions and responses, condensing the interviewee's remarks into an extended statement. Sometimes the material is drawn from more than one interview, and often it has been transposed; a scout's concluding comment, for example, might really be a transcription of something he said early in a discussion. But at no point have I distorted what my notes and tape recordings actually contain.

The other chapters try to describe the shape of a scouting year: spring training, spring scouting, cross-checking, the June draft ("the center of the season"), a tryout camp, an amateur tournament, pro scouting in September, and the autumn season that continues even after the major-league season ends. The scouting year I followed was 1981, when a strike tore a hole in the major-league season, when ownership in baseball shifted dramatically from families to syndicates, and when most teams made new commitments to scouting as a basis of success in the 1980s. But it might have been any year. The scouts kept reminding me of the timelessness of baseball dreams.

In the period between my initial research and the publication of this book, several of the young players evaluated in these pages have matured into major leaguers. Others are still struggling through the thickets of the minors. And some are no longer in professional baseball because they were injured, or because they didn't take their talent as seriously as the scouts did, or because that talent didn't develop quickly enough to match the accelerated pace of modern minor-league systems, or because they were scouts' mistakes in the first place. In an epilogue (Chapter 15) I have included updates on many of these players and on a few scouts.

This book is based on interviews with scouts from fifteen major-league organizations. All of these men were patient even with my dullest questions, but three of them—Brandy Davis, Jack Pastore, and Jim McLaughlin—became invaluable resources by checking facts, arranging interviews with other scouts, and offering exceptionally candid advice. Most often their opinions conflicted, but even this was an advantage: some of the views I express in this book are really triangulations of theirs.

To gain perspective on one scouting system, I worked closely with the Philadelphia Phillies, demonstrably one of baseball's best talent organizations in 1981. Although the Phillies' style of scouting was more secretive than most, I had access to even the most recent scouting reports and to the frank discussions preceding the June draft. I am especially grateful to the Carpenter family, the Phillies' former owners, for opening these doors.

As an indirect result of the Carpenter family's sale of the team, several members of the 1981 Phillies' staff left the club. From that group, I extend special thanks to Hugh Alexander, Ruben Amaro, Gordon Goldsberry, Dallas Green, Moose Johnson, Lou Kahn, and especially Brandy Davis. I am also indebted to these Philadelphia scouts, coaches, secretaries, and executives for hundreds of favors, large and small: Jim Baumer, Eddie Bockman, Eileen Cifelli, Jeff Cooper, Bill Gargano, Sue Ingersoll, Arky Kraft, Dick Lawlor, Aldie Livingston, Tony Lucadello, Pidge McCarthy, Pat Morfesis, Paul Owens, Bob Reasonover, Joe Reilly, Tony Roig, Larry Rojas, Larry Shenk, Tony Taylor, Elmer Valo, Randy Waddill, and especially Jack Pastore.

Scouts and former scouts from many other clubs gave me interviews which are not recorded in this book but which provided early guidance for my work. I appreciate particularly the contributions of Hank Peters, Harding Peterson, Pat Gillick, Bobby Mattick, Al Campanis, Dee Phillips, Fred Hawn, Sheldon Bender, Tom Ferrick, Al Diez, Howie Bedell, Tony Stiel, Ed Liberatore, Tony Pacheco, Frank DeMoss, Bill Jurges, and Jim Russo.

No one has ever written a history of baseball scouting. My own brief survey (Chapter 1) owes much to the help of baseball historians like Clifford Kachline, former librarian at the Hall of Fame; Paul Mac Farlane, archivist at *The Sporting News;* and David Voigt, professor of sociology at Albright College.

It also draws heavily on oral history, especially the recollections of Kenny Blackburn, Branch Rickey's former secretary; Hugh Alexander and Ed Katalinas, who began scouting before World War II; and Paul Florence, who was signed to a New York Giants' contract by John McGraw in 1924 after having been discovered by Sinister Dick Kinsella, one of the first true baseball detectives.

From baseball biographies and from collections like Frank Graham's *Baseball Wit and Wisdom* I have drawn a few scouting stories and quotes. In Chapter 1 the scouting report on Casey Stengel is taken from *You Could Look It Up* by Maury Allen; the report on Sandy Koufax is taken from *Koufax* by Sandy Koufax and Ed Linn. At an early point in my reading I gained a more general understanding of postwar scouting from Pat Jordan's *A False Spring* and Roger Angell's essay, "Scout." *A False Spring* dramatizes the bonus era with brilliant scenes of scouts like Jeff Jones and Ray Garland trying to sign Jordan out of high school in 1959. "Scout," reprinted in *Five Seasons,* clarifies the draft era by recording several scouting trips Angell took with the late Ray Scarborough in 1975.

For their insights and encouragement I am grateful to these members of the working press: Milt Richman, Dick Young, Rod Beaton, Buzz Saidt, Frank Dolson, Harry Kalas, Richie Ashburn, Hal Bodley, Gary Mullinax, John Schulian, Tom Boswell, and Joel Oppenheimer. For their thoughtful editorial advice I am grateful to these good friends: Katharine Carter, Michael Rewa, Heyward Brock, Michael Fahey, Zack Bowen—and especially my agent, John Ware. For their unfailing support through the most difficult times I am grateful to all the members of the Kerrane and Naum families, most of all to Barry Kerrane, my brother; and to Kate, Quinn, and Sean, my children.

Sheila Naum Kerrane, my wife, died in July 1982. She was a bright spirit, and her influence on this book is evident to me on every page. She believed before anyone else did that a project on scouting would be worth doing, and she shared everything that went into my early research and drafts: the energies, the ironies, the frustrations, the jokes. She thought that the lore of scouting would help her to become a better baseball fan, but she was really more attuned to the non-baseball side of the material—the sheer human interest in distinctive personalities. She was an ideal critic and a fiercely loyal partner. In loving memory I dedicate this book to Sheila, who still is a bright spirit.

1 BASEBALL MEN: AN INTRODUCTION

Good hands, good power, runs exceptionally well, nice glove, left-handed line drive hitter. Good throwing arm. May be too damn aggressive, bad temper.

—*Larry Sutton's scouting report on Casey Stengel, 1911*

When scouts refer to themselves as "baseball men," they might as well be naming a distinct class of primates. Just before Jocko Collins retired in 1982, in his forty-third year as a scout, he defined a baseball man as "a guy who played the game as far as his talent took him, even if that was just to the low minors, and then kept hanging around ball diamonds after that, because there's no line anymore between him and the game, no point where baseball leaves off and he begins."

All coaches, most general managers, and even a few owners belong to the genus *baseball man*—but scouts constitute a species of their own, distinguished by willfulness and independence. They dislike supervision and hate bureaucracy, even as both affect their work more directly each season, and they express clear-cut opinions on any topic in or out of baseball. When they write reports, they avoid words like *but* and *however*.

However, they are wrong 92 percent of the time. Out of every hundred players they sign to professional contracts, about eight will ever appear in a major-league game.

Some critics—pro football scouts, for example—cite this statistic as evidence that baseball scouts are old-fashioned, stubborn, subjective to the point of superstition, more interested in folklore than research, and more religious than scientific in their thinking. As a group, baseball scouts *are* all those things. Most of them doubt the value of radar guns that measure the precise speed of pitches, and some old-timers have still not come to terms with stopwatches. Many talk seriously about players with "the good face" or some other outward and visible sign of having been touched by God. If their report-forms had a box marked *Aura,* most baseball scouts would be able to write something in it. Unlike football scouts, they are proud of maintaining a human connection to amateur talent. They are unable to use game films or to subject prospects to elaborate strength tests—but even if they could use such techniques, most of them wouldn't. They believe that ability in baseball is less reducible than in football to measurements of strength or to technological understanding in general.

The real meaning of that 8 percent success rate, baseball scouts say, is that they are looking so far into the future that any player who makes it to the majors will be a different person by the time he gets there. The football scout studies fully developed specimens and searches for those who can help his team within a year. The baseball scout studies raw talent, allows for more variables (poor fields, metal bats, players at the "wrong" position in terms of their major-league chances), and tries to project that talent, and that person, about four years into the future.

Being a baseball scout, according to Jack Pastore of the Philadelphia Phillies, is the next best thing to being a major-league player. "It's unique in all the world, and one of the best jobs a man could have. You're your own boss. You make your own schedule, and the front office doesn't get on your ass too much. If you're an area scout, I won't tell you how to run your area, because I don't know your area. You know the back roads and the interstates, and exactly where the ballparks are in all the little towns, and you have your own contacts and your own style of work. So you just move around and do what you have to do, like Jonathan Livingston Seagull. You drive a company car, and you go watch kids play ball, and you use your experience and insight in a way that's yours and nobody else's. And then you're home for three or four months a year, so you can make some dough in the off-season."

You'll need that dough, too, because Pastore's poetry omits the fact that local scouts are underpaid. As an established scout covering an important area, say northern California, after twenty productive years with a good organization, you might be close to $30,000. As a new full-time scout, young (thirty-five) and college-trained, you're under $20,000 and not very interested in becoming an established area scout. The bright young scouts today all talk about moving up, out of scouting and into the front office—which is where Jack Pastore himself is, as the Phillies' assistant scouting director.

The twenty-year scout has probably worked for at least three organizations so far, and been let go (the euphemism for fired) once because his club hired a new scouting director who brought in some friends. The old-boy network that gives a scouting job can also take it away. Or maybe he was let go when his club joined the Major League Scouting Bureau, substituting computer reports from a central service for what fifteen of its own people used to provide. On the bright side: as long as he can take the endless travel and the odd seasonal rhythms that disrupt family life, he will probably not be let go for getting old—because a scout at seventy is supposed to be twice as canny as a scout at thirty-five. And even if he wants to retire at seventy, he might not be able to afford it: unless he works for an organization like the Dodgers, the Cardinals, the Reds, or the Phillies, his baseball pension is likely to be under $100 a month. "The fringies," scouts like to say, "are horseshit."

But the job itself, for some people, can be almost what Jack Pastore says it is. Scouting is professional baseball's personalized way of renewing itself, from year to year and generation to generation. It reaches to the social roots of the game, to small towns and skinned infields, and to the psychological roots of the game, to seasonal optimism and persistent dreaming. The players' dreams of glory are no more compelling than the scouts' dreams of discovery, of seeing the crystal through the carbon, the future shining through the present.

In 1981, the year a strike disrupted the major-league season, I followed a scouting season, looking at amateur players and listening to baseball men put the dollar sign on the muscle. I tried to watch games the way scouts do, which must be the way theatrical agents or casting directors watch plays: with less interest in the subtleties of action or the beauties of scenery than in the talent, potential, and price tag of the individual performer. The veterans advised me to "scout the player, not the game"—which sometimes means forgetting the inning or the score, and focusing as much on what happens between innings, when that good-looking shortstop fields practice grounders and snaps his throws to first.

My own scouting was usually mediocre, because the games themselves were too interesting, or because I was really scouting the scouts, or because I simply lacked a baseball man's quality of awareness. That awareness comes mostly from experience, but it is also a matter of willed concentration, as if the scouts had been tutored by some tobacco-chewing reader of Henry James: "Try to be one of those on whom nothin' is lost."

"You married?" one old scout asked me. "Well, didja scout your wife? I hope to hell you did, because any guy gets married better scout that woman—whether she's gonna be hard to get along with or go operatin' around on him, or whether she's got potential as a partner or a mother." For him the psychology of scouting carried over to the rest of life and stayed true to the original sense of the word.

Scout is familiar as a military term, but its root refers more generally to a searcher, a sensitive recorder of information, carefully sifting out significant details. (The word is related to the French *écouter*–to listen.) What use those impressions are finally put to may be less important than having them to begin with. Scouts think of themselves as special perceivers as well as the forgotten men of baseball. Both images allow them freedom of expression and a range of individualistic styles— crude, elegant, confidential, flashy, salty, moralistic, taciturn, windy—that could easily belong to characters created by Damon Runyon.

When I looked into the history of scouting, I found that Runyon had in fact written occasionally about one of baseball's first full-time scouts, "Sinister Dick" Kinsella. I found records of other colorful characters, their theories of talent, and moments of discovery. But I also found fresh perspective on contemporary baseball and the issues behind the strike, because the history of scouting is largely a chronicle of business strategies.

As an introduction to a modern scouting season, I have sketched out this history below, dividing it into four eras based on the methods major-league teams have used to acquire young talent. The dates for these eras are fairly arbitrary, because some teams have lagged more than a decade behind others in moving from one era (or one business phase) to another.

PIONEERS: THE BIRD DOG ERA (?–1919)

In 1902 Al Bridwell, a semi-pro player, had an excellent day at shortstop in an exhibition game against Columbus of the American Association. That evening the Columbus business manager, Bobby Quinn, signed Bridwell to a minor-league contract of $900 a season. Two years later Garry Herrman, the owner of the Cincinnati Reds, happened to see one of the Columbus games, and again Bridwell starred. Herrman bought him and then signed him to a major-league contract of $2,100 a season. In Lawrence Ritter's *The Glory of Their Times* Bridwell summed up the status of scouting in the first decade of the century: "Then it was pretty much of an accident whether you got into professional ball at all, and if you did there was still a lot of luck involved in getting to the big leagues. Now they have scouts who watch a man for weeks to see what he can really do, but then there were no scouts or anything like that."

For Bridwell, Honus Wagner, Ty Cobb, Babe Ruth, and almost every other player before World War I, the normal path to the majors was: (1) to be discovered and signed by an independent minor-league team, usually local, and (2) to be sold up the ladder after being seen by a major-league representative. The problem was that there were so few of these representatives, and until about 1909 none of them was a full-time scout. Signing a player to a major-league contract meant buying him, and owners were reluctant to delegate such decisions to specialists.

Instead, they relied on an informal network of baseball friends as tipsters and on an office executive as a part-time cross-checker and negotiator. The tipsters might be "bird dogs" (commission scouts), receiving a finder's fee for each player signed. One such bird dog was Branch Rickey, the University of Michigan baseball coach from 1910 to 1913, who routinely sent scouting reports to the St. Louis Browns, the team he had once played for. Like so many scouts since, Rickey began as a catcher. His major-league career had been unimpressive (in one game in 1907 he allowed the opposing team to steal thirteen bases), but he brought to scouting a catcher's knowledge of pitchers and hitters, and a catcher's perception of the playing field, open and entire.

John McGraw of the New York Giants had the most extensive scouting network in baseball. In McGraw's thirty-one seasons as a manager, most of his stars—Larry Doyle, Travis Jackson, Frankie Frisch, Mel Ott, Bill Terry—came to the Giants because of friends like Kid Elberfield, Art Devlin, and Sinister Dick Kinsella. Kinsella was not a left-hander; he simply reminded people of a stage villain. He was tall and solid, with thick black hair, bushy eyebrows, expensive-looking dark suits, and an ominously quiet manner. In reality Kinsella was a paint-store owner (Damon Runyon called him "the varnish king of Springfield, Illinois") with a sense of style and a talent for finding talent. Shortly before World War I, McGraw made Kinsella a full-time scout.

Kinsella's greatest scouting coup came in 1928. As a prosperous businessman and an Irishman, he took a lively interest in politics, and served as a delegate for Al Smith at the Democratic National Convention in Houston. He skipped one afternoon of speeches to attend a Texas League game between Beaumont and Houston, and he watched the Beaumont pitcher, Carl Hubbell, dominate the Houston hitters with a fadeaway (today's screwball). Kinsella discovered that the Detroit Tigers owned Hubbell but were willing to sell him, because they believed that no pitcher, even a left-hander, could rely with consistent success on a fadeaway. They theorized that the unnatural arm rotation the pitch requires must inevitably lead to muscle damage. Sinister Dick Kinsella worked from no theory; his scouting reports usually consisted of different ways of saying whether a prospect had "it" or not—and he began his report to John McGraw with "Hubbell has it." McGraw needed little convincing: the best pitcher he had ever managed, Christy Matthewson, had built a brilliant career on the fadeaway. Within ten days Hubbell was pitching for McGraw in the Polo Grounds; by the end of that rookie season he chalked up the first ten of his 253 career victories.

Eddie Herr of the Cardinals and Mike Drennan of the A's were also full-time scouts before the war, but the honor of being first probably belongs to Larry Sutton. After twenty years as a bird dog Sutton became Brooklyn's scouting specialist in 1909. "His territory," Frank Graham wrote, "was limited only by his imagination and his budget for traveling expenses— which was smaller than his imagination by far." Like Kinsella, Sutton was big and solemn-looking, but his style was less intimidating. Paul Florence remembers him simply as "the guy with the umbrella." Sutton was famous for always carrying an umbrella, even in the sunniest weather. He also carried around a few scouting superstitions, such as the belief that light-haired players hold up better in summer heat.

"I liked him right away," Sutton said of Casey Stengel, an

outfielder he found in Class C ball at Aurora in 1911. Stengel was temperamental—Sutton saw him use the bat to smack an umpire who had bent over to dust off home plate—but he was a versatile player and, like most of Sutton's other discoveries, he had light hair.

Even in an era without farm systems, Sutton demonstrated the economic value of scouting. Of the players on Brooklyn's pennant-winning team of 1916, eleven had been discovered by Sutton and purchased for a total of $14,200. He was proud of his work, but he also spoke frankly about the liabilities of being a scout. Still active for the Dodgers in 1926 and acknowledged by then as "the dean of ivory hunters," Sutton reflected on occupational hazards—obscurity, exhausting travel, second guesses from management—that have continued through the subsequent eras of scouting:

"I've been combing the baseball bushes for forty years—forty years of rotten meals in hick hotels; of making connections at three o'clock in the morning for Moose Jaw or Cowtail, or missing them and sleeping in the station; of thinking up good rejoinders when the club president wires and asks if your brains are made of mush because you recommended a fellow that looked good in his home town. I've been pretty successful, and in my long trek I've discovered Dazzy Vance, Jimmy Ring, Jake Daubert, Howard Ehmke, Zach Wheat, Dots Miller, Hooks Wiltse, Doc Scanlon, Nick Altrock, Casey Stengel, Leon Cadore, Hi Myers, Maurice Rath, and a lot of others, but the average man knows more about the newest recruit than he does about me."

IVORY HUNTERS: THE RICKEY ERA (1919–1946)

By the 1920s *ivory hunter* was a familiar sportswriting synonym for *scout*, and it conveyed the essence of the job in the era between the wars. With the advent of farm systems scouts had begun to look more for amateur than minor-league talent. They explored the deep interior of American baseball—sandlot teams and town teams and mill teams—searching, as the saying went, for "an arm behind the barn."

These were scouting's most wide-open decades, the days of hard drivers and hard drinkers, when physical stamina was the key to the job. The key to third-era scouting would be salesmanship, but second-era players were relatively easy to sign. The trick was to find them. A scout's competitors were tough but not numerous: there were still fewer than two dozen full-timers in 1940 when a group of younger men (Hugh Alexander, Jocko Collins, Tony Lucadello, Ed Katalinas) were coming into the game. This meant that significant bonuses were usually unnecessary. It also meant that any one scout had to cover enormous territory. When Charlie Barrett died in 1939, one of his obituaries included this note: "In hunting ivory he traveled nearly a million miles, by railroad, bus, airplane, automobile, and even tractor, from Cuba to Canada and from California to New York."

Charlie Barrett began as a part-time scout with the St. Louis Browns. He became a full-timer with the Cardinals in 1918, when Branch Rickey took over as president, general manager, and field manager. Barrett, Rickey said, "could assay the gold content in a handful of ore." Moreover, Barrett understood Rickey's master plan and was more responsible than anyone for its masterly execution.

When Rickey himself had worked for the Browns, from 1913 to 1917, he experimented briefly with the idea of a farm system—direct control of minor-league teams by the major-league parent organization, creating a production line of talent. The farm system was a strategy for saving money: instead of bidding against other major-league teams for minor-league players, Rickey wanted to grow his own. After the war, when the minors were in a financial slump, Rickey put his strategy into effect. In 1919 the Cardinals acquired controlling interest in teams at Houston and Fort Smith; by 1939 the Cardinal empire included thirty-two minor-league teams and about 650 players.

The Cardinals bought pitcher Jess Haines in 1920, and then purchased no more players until 1945. The system did save money. But it made money too: Rickey was able to generate such a steady supply of young talent that he could sell off the excess at a nice profit, while providing the Cardinals with enough manpower to win nine pennants by 1946. The competition among so many young players in the system operated as a kind of natural selection, and it kept constant pressure on the veterans at the top. Rickey, as Enos Slaughter once said, "would go into the vault to get you a nickel change." He was able to bully and bluff major-leaguers, bound by the reserve clause, into absurd salaries. The minor-leaguers could be left on the farms until, as Rickey liked to say, they "ripened into money."

Rickey's fundamental principle, "quality out of quantity," had direct implications for scouting. Since the Cardinals would be signing droves of amateurs instead of buying a few polished minor-leaguers, Barrett and Rickey needed to project players further into the future. Scouting would now require a clear analysis of a youngster's total athletic talents, his "tools." For the Cardinals the most important tool, even in the new age of home runs, was running speed: Rickey called it the only common denominator of offense and defense, and he believed it to be the best single indicator of major-league potential. The least important tool was fielding: "We can *teach* them to field," Barrett said. In fact the system depended on teaching. In his larger vision of "player development," Rickey applied scouting insights to teaching and vice versa, and he winnowed prospects by erecting some hypotheses into laws: "The overstriding hitter cannot be corrected."

The principle of quality out of quantity also led Rickey and Barrett to devise tryout camps (they ran baseball's first ever in 1919, at Robison Field in St. Louis) and to hire more scouts: Pop Kelchner, Jack Ryan, Joe Mathes, Carl Lundgren, Fred Hunter, and Rickey's brother Frank. It remains unclear just how many of these were full-timers. Their salaries were so low that some of them may have been unsure about it too, and

Ryan continued to work for Rickey even after the Cardinals cut him from the payroll. Frank Rickey was his brother's right hand: when Branch was asked to write a letter of recommendation for him in 1942, he simply drew up a list of "Frank's players"—seventy-seven names in all, including Enos Slaughter, Marty Marion, and Preacher Roe—and noted that the Cardinals had sold off twenty-five of them for $428,500 in cash and fourteen new players.

The New York Yankees, even without a farm system, began to invest in scouting after the war by hiring Bob Connery and Paul Krichell. Connery had made his reputation in 1915 when he discovered Rogers Hornsby in the low minors and talked the Cardinals into buying the eighteen-year-old shortstop for $600; Hornsby was in the majors by the end of that season. Krichell, like Rickey, was a former catcher, sturdy and bow-legged. Lefty Gomez once remarked: "Paul would be seven feet tall if it wasn't for the two-foot bend in his legs." In the spring of 1922 Krichell attended a college game in New York and watched the Columbia pitcher, Lou Gehrig, hit a ball across 116th Street and onto the steps of the library. When Connery heard Krichell's report on "the new Babe Ruth," he immediately offered Gehrig's coach, Andy Coakley, $500 to talk his player into quitting school and signing a Yankee contract.

Over the next thirty-five years Krichell signed two hundred more prospects for the Yankees—among them were Red Rolfe, Charlie Keller, Phil Rizzuto, and Whitey Ford—but that flash of recognition at Baker Field remained the peak experience of his scouting career. "I knew then," he said, "that I'd never have another moment like it the rest of my life."

In 1929 the Yankees decided to build their own farm system, and George Weiss soon made it a rival empire to the Cardinals'. Weiss, according to Rickey, "couldn't tell a bull from a cow" when it came to judging players, but he could judge scouts well enough to hire aggressive ivory hunters like Joe Devine, Bill Essick, Gene McCann, and Johnny Nee. Devine was known as "the human divining rod." Scouting for the Pirates early in his career, he discovered Joe Cronin and the Waner brothers; with the Yankees from 1931 to 1951, he discovered Joe DiMaggio and twenty other future major-leaguers. In 1935, when DiMaggio was the property of the San Francisco Seals, most scouts lost interest in him after he injured his right knee. Devine and Essick arranged for secret tests by an orthopedist, and on the basis of his report they negotiated DiMaggio's purchase for $25,000.

More than most scouts, Devine studied a prospect's character—his personal habits, intelligence, and even diet. "I always talk to a prospect to investigate his way of living. How much he eats is important too. How many fine-looking prospects have you seen hog their way back into the minors? If a player is absolutely dumb, I won't consider him unless his tremendous ability counterbalances his mental handicaps. Usually I pass up the moron ballplayer. He is outdated." By "outdated" Devine meant that the Yankees' farm system, like the Cardinals', was based on progressive methods of instruction and close working relationships between scouts and minor-league teachers.

From 1921 to 1945, all through his tenure as commissioner of baseball, Kenesaw Mountain Landis railed against the system that Rickey and Weiss perfected. "It is intolerable and un-American," he said, "when a group of ballplayers can be boxed into a minor league and advance only at the whim of their employer." Landis saw the farm system as a monopoly thwarting the upward mobility of minor-leaguers, and on several occasions he was able to construe baseball law so as to turn "chain-gang" players into free agents. Ironically, Landis more consistently penalized teams without farm systems, teams which directed the progress of their signees by means of illegal gentlemen's agreements with minor-league clubs. The most flagrant manipulator was Cy Slapnicka of the Cleveland Indians. According to sportswriter Gordon Cobbledick, "Slap spent so much time on Judge Landis's carpet as to be practically indistinguishable from the nap."

Like many other teams between the wars, the Indians were

in effect still doing first-era scouting. Slapnicka became a scout in 1923, and for most of the next dozen years he constituted a one-man staff. Then, when he became the Indians' general manager in 1936, he began hiring scouts and showing them how to cut corners. He had once been a vaudeville juggler, and he could also juggle the contracts he issued to new prospects, leaving them undated or otherwise non-binding until the prospects proved themselves in the minors.

Slapnicka's gimmicks were illegal; Rickey's were merely manipulative. Rickey devised the "desk contract," for example, as a means of signing thousands of amateurs on a purely tentative basis. A player could be sent from one of Rickey's tryout camps to a minor-league outpost far away, there to be scouted at greater leisure—and perhaps to be released a few weeks later without money for transportation home. While exploiting players on a grander scale, Rickey maintained an air of piety that Slapnicka never affected, and a style of prose that occasionally tipped over into unintentional irony. "In a profession where the physical is dominant in the triune nature of man," Rickey wrote, "it would be surprising indeed if we did not find here and there an occasional scalawag."

By contrast Slapnicka was a plainspoken Iowan—with at least one odd theory of judging major-league potential. In Jerome Holtzman's *No Cheering in the Pressbox,* Abe Kemp recalls the day that Slapnicka decided not to buy Lefty Gomez from the San Francisco Seals. Slapnicka told Kemp: "I saw Gomez undressed in the clubhouse, and anybody who's got a prick as big as he's got can't pitch winning ball in the major leagues."

Slapnicka was eloquent, though, when describing a sixteen-year-old pitcher he saw in 1935: "He was pitching on a semi-pro diamond on the outskirts of Des Moines. I watched a couple of pitches from the first-base line, and I got the funny feeling that this was something extra. So I moved over behind the backstop and sat down on a car bumper. It must have been a hell of an uncomfortable seat, but I never noticed. All I knew was that there was a kid I had to get. I didn't know then that he was smart and that he had the heart of a lion, but I knew

I was looking at an arm the like of which you see only once in a lifetime."

In signing Bob Feller, a farmboy from Van Meter, Iowa, Slapnicka realized the ivory hunter's ultimate dream. He had found the arm behind the barn.

TRAVELING SALESMEN: THE BONUS ERA (1946–1965)

When Bob Feller signed with Cleveland in 1935, he received a bonus of one dollar and an autographed ball. When Dick Wakefield signed with Detroit in 1941, he received a bonus of $52,000 and a new car. Wish Egan, the scout who signed Wakefield, was contending against six rivals, including Slapnicka, and he persuaded the Tigers' owners, the Briggs family, to stay in the bidding war. Egan's negotiations previewed the major change in scouting after World War II.

Almost all teams hired scouts in quantity after the war and assigned them to cover smaller areas. The typical scout was no longer an ivory hunter searching for unknowns, but one territorial salesman among many, competing in something of a buyer's market. Amateur players had higher expectations, and most owners had new money to meet them. In 1945 the Philadelphia Phillies, now under the ownership of DuPont heir Bob Carpenter, signed Granny Hamner for $6,500; three years later they signed Curt Simmons for $65,000.

But, as the saying went, bonus money can't scout by itself. Baseball's postwar economics left plenty of room for the old-fashioned arts of evaluation and for new dimensions of salesmanship. If the best stories from the first two eras of scouting deal with the experience of discovery (the eerie feeling of a Krichell or a Slapnicka that he was having a once-in-a-lifetime vision), the best stories from the third era deal with outsmarting one's rivals—Ed Scott spying on prospects; Jeff Jones romancing them; Howie Haak moving in with them; Paul Owens kidnapping them; Paul Richards paying them money under the table; Leon Hamilton hiring their relatives as commission scouts; Hugh Alexander providing them with fresh interpretations of

income-tax codes; Bill Enos getting in line behind them at high
school graduation and whipping out a contract to go with the
diploma. "They're persistent people," Gaylord Perry once said.
"I heard about one scout who, to sign a prospect, got engaged
to his spinster sister."

"Watch out for those stories," Bobby Mattick told me. "After
a guy's made good in baseball, the stories about how he got
discovered and signed become better and better. I know one
old guy—you listen to him, you'll find he never signed a player
in good weather. He always had to drive down a muddy road
in a thunderstorm and beat out three other scouts who thought
they had the boy signed." Mattick himself was one of the most
productive scouts of the third era, signing players like Frank
Robinson, Vada Pinson, and Curt Flood for little or no bonus
money. He attributes his success to simple salesmanship:
"Judging a ballplayer is instinctive and so is getting the contract
signed. You can't go in with a set line, because if the mother
or father says something, you have to be ready to jump on it,
go with it."

Some scouting directors, like Buzzy Bavasi of the Dodgers
and Jim McLaughlin of the Orioles, used to stage mock signings—exercises requiring one scout to act as the prospect, two
scouts as the mother and father, and another scout as the scout.
But no such rehearsal could simulate the primary condition of
successful third-era scouting: befriending the prospect and his
family long before you offered any contract.

"That's what you had to do in those days," Hugh Alexander
says, "and it was good, because before you signed him you
got a lot better idea than you do today of what kind of boy
he really was. But it took work. I read Dale Carnegie's *How
to Win Friends and Influence People* four times. If I'd have
been a scouting director, I'd have made all my scouts buy that
book. Hell, I'd have bought it for 'em. Because I saw a lot of
scouts that went into a boy's house real quick, and they didn't
want to go into the details of their lives—they just wanted to
throw down twenty thousand or whatever it was and sign the
ballplayer. They usually got a rude awakening. The mother

and father didn't know anything about that man, or that ballclub, and they'd just back right off. . . . 'We'll think about it
and let you know.' "

Most ivory hunters adjusted naturally to the bonus era. Cy
Slapnicka remained a fixture at Cleveland and continued cutting corners whenever he thought he could get away with it.
In 1953 he signed Herb Score for a bonus of $60,000. "Scouts
weren't supposed to talk to a kid about signing until he was
out of high school," Score says, "but Slapnicka was very in-
genious about getting around the rules." And when other scouts
offered higher bonuses, Slapnicka outsold them by trading
shamelessly on his reputation as the man who discovered Bob
Feller. The Yankees' Joe Devine was also at home in the new
era. After the war, when he signed players like Gil McDougald
and Jackie Jensen, other baseball men came to regard Devine
as the archetype of the salesman-scout: tough, tireless, intensely
competitive. He was still going strong in 1951 when he suffered
a freak accident on a scouting trip. He broke his arm while
trying to fix the seat of his car, and after a month of medical
complications Devine was dead at the age of fifty-six.

Some teams tried to save money by doing second-era scouting. The Washington Senators, for example, relied on coverage
rather than bonuses to find reasonably priced players in places
no one else was looking, like Cuba. The Senators had been
importing occasional Latin talent for three decades, but after
the war they posted their own man in Havana—Joe Cambria.
In the States Cambria had signed some first-rate talent (Early
Wynn, Mickey Vernon, Eddie Yost) for less bonus money, he
boasted, "than you would pay for a hat." In Cuba Cambria
didn't even bother with the hat. He applied Rickey's principle
of quality out of quantity, signing about 400 Cubans over a
period of ten years, and sending the Senators such players as
Pedro Ramos, Camilio Pascual, and Zoilo Versalles. (At tryout
camps Cambria twice rejected a young pitcher named Fidel
Castro.) Headquartered at the American Club in Havana,
Cambria became so well-known that a cigar was named for
him. It was called Papa Joe. He was popular with the players,

too, and continued to sign the best prospects even after other teams sent scouts to the island. Operating in a buyer's market, Cambria was able to tie up many prospects with desk contracts or unfiled contracts until the players proved themselves worthy of a real commitment. In effect, Cambria was taking another page from Rickey's book: sign the prospect and *then* scout him.

Rickey's contribution to third-era scouting, and to America, was the breaking of baseball's color line. When he moved from the Cardinals to the Dodgers in 1942, he instructed scouts like Tom Greenwade and Clyde Sukeforth to search for black talent, ostensibly to form a new Negro League. If Greenwade and Sukeforth understood Rickey's scheme, they knew that in this case more than any other a ballplayer's success would depend on what scouts call makeup—intelligence, courage, and competitive pride. Jackie Robinson had an ideal makeup, and by any scout's reckoning he was also a player with great tools. He was in fact the kind of total athlete that Rickey and Charlie Barrett had originally envisioned as the paradigm of Cardinal scouting.

After Robinson's Rookie-of-the-Year season in 1947 it appeared that black talent might transform scouting, and baseball itself, by providing an alternative to bonus bidding. Black players could be signed cheaply, and usually without compensation to their Negro League teams. But their entry into major-league baseball proved agonizingly gradual. Instead of capitalizing on black speed, the game in the early 1950s was more home-run conscious than it had been in the early 1920s. And scouts whose organizations allowed them to look actively for black players were sometimes called "ebony hunters" by unfriendly rivals.

Among the few black scouts in the business, Judy Johnson— formerly an all-time all-star third baseman in the Negro Leagues—was recognized as an exceptional evaluator and teacher. As player-manager for the Homestead Grays in 1930, he had discovered and trained the young Josh Gibson. After World War II Johnson spent much of his scouting energy trying to persuade his boss, Connie Mack of the Philadelphia A's, to sign players like Larry Doby, Minnie Minoso, and Hank Aaron. "I wound up giving tips on all those players to scouts from other teams," he says. "I just wanted to make sure the kids got a chance, because I could see that Mr. Mack was gonna pass them by. Doby was versatile, as good in the infield as the outfield. Minoso was kind of a crude talent, but you knew he was worth signing because of his 'action,' the whole way he moved. It was just like *cement;* it pulled his whole game together. And Hank Aaron . . . well, if Mr. Mack had signed him and Doby and Minoso, the A's would still be in Philadelphia!"

Tom Greenwade, who had recommended both Robinson and Roy Campanella to the Dodgers, was hired away by the Yankees in 1948. He eventually signed their first black player, Elston Howard. But Greenwade's greatest moment as a scout came in 1949, when he captured Mickey Mantle for a bonus of $1,400. A famous scouting story has Greenwade taking his first look at Mantle in action and saying to himself: "Now I know how Paul Krichell felt when he first saw Lou Gehrig."

The story is true—except that Greenwade's visionary moment came when he was watching Mantle play for the third time. "Mickey had leg problems, so not too many scouts paid attention to him. I saw him in two games, but I didn't really *see* him. He looked kind of small—he hadn't filled out yet—and I just didn't recognize how coordinated he was. I didn't know he was a switch-hitter! In those first two games he'd only batted left-handed, because he was facing all right-handed pitchers. In the third game, against a left-handed pitcher, he stepped into the batter's box from the right side, and I didn't know what to make of it. Mickey's father was sitting right next to me, and I asked him how long his boy had been a switch-hitter. He said, 'Since he was about eight.' Then I looked again at Mickey, and he pulled a line-shot to left for a double, and it all came together. Finally I could see that seventeen-year-old body, how it worked like a damn baseball *machine,* and how it was gonna fill out. I understood how he'd been blessed. And I was blessed too."

In that same year, 1949, Branch Rickey left Brooklyn to reorganize the Pittsburgh Pirates, a perennial second-division club. He brought along some top scouts (Howie Haak, Clyde Sukeforth, Rex Bowen), but he lacked sufficient time or money to build a team the old way, by distilling quality out of quantity. Uncharacteristically, Rickey tried for a quick fix by entering the bonus market, and the results were disappointing. In 1950 he gave $100,000 to a left-handed pitcher named Paul Pettit, who went on to win one game in the major leagues. By 1954 Rickey had been burned so often, and his treasury was so depleted, that he decided not to give a bonus of $10,000 to a left-handed pitcher named Sandy Koufax.

The Pirates lost Koufax to the Dodgers. Three months later, they stole Roberto Clemente from the Dodgers. Both players were originally signed by Al Campanis, a Dodger scout trained by Rickey himself.

"I found Clemente in a Dominican tryout camp," Campanis says. "He ran the sixty-yard dash in 6.4, and then he threw strikes from centerfield to home plate. I said to myself: 'If this kid can just hold the bat in his hands, we've gotta sign him.' He hit one line drive after another—even on outside pitches, when that odd swing of his took both of his feet off the ground. . . . He was the greatest amateur athlete I've ever seen. But we lost him, because we gave him a bonus of ten thousand and then failed to protect him in the minor-league draft, and the Pittsburgh scouts swooped in like vultures." As soon as Branch Rickey realized the value of his prize, he dispatched one of those Pittsburgh vultures, Howie Haak, to explore the Caribbean, opening up whole countries to major-league scouting and beginning a Pirate focus on Latin talent that continues to this day.

When Campanis first saw Sandy Koufax, at a workout at Ebbets Field, he wrote this scouting report: "Athletic build, good musculature. Good poise and actions—smooth delivery—many clubs interested. Two are willing to make him a bonus player. Lad appears to possess confidence in himself. He has the tools. Whether or not to make him a bonus player is the question."

The question arose because of the same rule that affected Clemente, a rule that baseball owners had designed to discourage their own spending in the open market on amateur talent. It required a team signing a player for a bonus (defined differently from year to year during this era) to place him on its major-league roster or else risk losing him in the yearly draft of minor-leaguers. The rule was later abolished because it prevented the best young players from receiving daily work and instruction in the minor leagues, and because some teams simply cheated. In 1957 Steve Dalkowski—still regarded by many scouts as the fastest pitcher they've ever seen—was designated as a "non-bonus" signee by the Baltimore Orioles, even though Paul Richards had given Dalkowski $40,000 and a car.

The Dodgers approved a bonus of $14,000 for Koufax, possibly because of two numbers in Campanis's scouting report: 77 for Koufax's fastball and 72 for his curve. In one of his few departures from Rickey's methods Campanis had devised a style of grading that would come to typify modern scouting.

"Scouting needed a new vocabulary," Campanis says. "Most old-fashioned scouts used letter grades; some still do. Rickey's system was A for 'average'—and then he might use a plus, a double-plus, or a triple-plus. For 'below average' he used a zero, or a double-zero, or a triple-zero. I didn't like that, because zero connotes absence of ability, not a point along a continuous scale. I needed something more refined, so I went to numbers. I thought like a schoolteacher: 70 is a passing grade, so that can represent the major-league average on arm or speed or whatever, and 60 and 80 can be the extremes. Before, if you saw a high-school shortstop throw from the hole, and his arm was just a *little* weak, you'd have given a zero. Now you could give a 69, and anybody reading your report would know you were talking about a kid who could still become a major-league second baseman. A number system of *some* kind is the standard vocabulary today, because the nature of modern scouting is that you have to communicate your grades to more people."

By the end of its third era scouting was more rationalized and bureaucratized—and less of an individual accomplishment. Some salesman-scouts might still be identified by the players they won (Ed Katalinas by Al Kaline), but big bonuses required approval from the front office, which required cross-checking by other scouts. And there were more scouts. In 1964 each major-league club retained at least twenty full-time scouts, with an elaborate network of part-timers and commission scouts. Within the organization a large scouting staff meant that a successful signing was rarely the work of a lone individual. Outside the organization it meant that the "unknown" amateur phenom was now widely known, and that bonuses were certain to be forced higher by bidding wars.

INVESTMENT ANALYSTS: THE DRAFT ERA
(1965–present)

"Ownership must eliminate the bonus," Branch Rickey wrote in 1965. A year before his death at eighty-three, Rickey completed his testament, *The American Diamond,* a remarkable compilation of scouting observations, memories, and sermons. In his final chapter, "The Future of the Game," Rickey explained baseball economics in moralistic terms: "It is bad for the boy, say an eighteen-year-old youth, to come into possession of unheard-of sums of money, unearned to begin with, and probably ill-spent to end with. . . . Something for nothing may be an objective among many slothful, unthrifty segments of our people, who seem to believe that the world or the nation or the community owes them a living, but it has no place in baseball because it tends to damn the player, wreck the club, and bankrupt the owner."

Even as Rickey wrote these words, the owners were implementing the solution that he recommended: an amateur draft, modeled after those in other pro sports, which would eliminate the open market on young players by constraining their right to bargain. The first draft in 1965 had the intended effect of holding down bonus payments. Its effects on scouting were more subtle.

A scout's primary job now would be to give advice without making decisions—the way an investment analyst might pass along opinions on new properties that his corporation might or might not be able to acquire. Then the scout would try to sign draftees by persuading them that the club's offer was preferable to college or to waiting six months until the next draft, when another club could similarly constrain them. But this kind of persuasion lacked the flair and intrigue of third-era salesmanship. In the fourth era it became more important to sell the boy to your organization than to sell the organization to the boy. One corollary of the draft is greater psychological distance between scouts and amateur players. Why get to know a boy personally, why romance his family, when the odds are twenty-six to one against obtaining rights to negotiate with him?

Another corollary of the draft is an easing of competition among scouts. Because an organization's chance of drafting any one player is remote, and because most organizations receive identical preliminary reports from the Major League Scouting Bureau, scouts in the fourth era are more likely than ever to share information with friendly competitors. This rarely amounts to "industrial espionage"—most often it's Scout A telling Scout B that Player X is not worth driving three hundred miles to see—but it does signify a softening of third-era standards. In the folklore of scouting the rival scout used to be the butt of most funny stories; today that role has been taken over by the college coach.

Scouting has also become more selective. In 1950 there were 454 minor-league teams feeding 16 major-league teams: about 9,000 players supplying a top level of 400. In 1981 there were 130 minor-league teams feeding 26 major-league teams: about 2,600 players supplying a top level of 650. Farm systems are now too expensive to operate in the Rickey way, and there is little room for marginal prospects—the ones who mature late, or who might take years to find themselves in the minors, or who have something a scout can't name but would like to take a blind chance on.

Fourth-era scouting feels more centralized and bureaucratic. What used to be oral or mental must now be written in triplicate, and a local scout's top prospects must be cross-checked by another scout, or several, so that the organization can make comparative judgments before each draft.

The logical extension of centralization and bureaucracy is a central scouting bureau. Branch Rickey envisioned one in *The American Diamond,* a program of "pooled scouting" that could save major-league baseball ten million dollars a year. In 1974, after a couple of test programs, seventeen clubs put up about $120,000 each to establish the Major League Scouting Bureau. That same year they fired about 250 scouts, most of them full-timers, thereby eliminating (on paper) about seven million dollars a year in salaries and expenses. Prior to each draft the Bureau provides its subscribers with computerized reports, updated weekly, on almost every conceivable amateur prospect. From June to September the Bureau assigns most of its scouts (65 in 1981) to coverage of the minor leagues.

After its first half-dozen years of service, the Bureau was still a touchy issue among baseball men, not only because it had led to wholesale firings but also because it dramatized the extent of homogenization and anonymity in modern scouting. Scouts in the fourth era preferred to see themselves not as "investment analysts" but as the last true individualists in the game, in a line of direct descent from Cy Slapnicka and Joe Devine, Tom Greenwade and Paul Krichell, Larry Sutton and Sinister Dick Kinsella—on the go, on the road, moving targets, the freest of Americans, not yet coded onto any punch card, expressing opinions in any language, reverent or crude, that matched their maverick temperaments, while maintaining a love for the game that owners and players alike had forgotten. Many scouts, especially during the strike season, contrasted themselves to the players, whose "freedom" (free agency) was merely economic, not psychological. The more the players talked about security and securities, the more they sounded—to the scouts—almost indistinguishable from the owners. And for every truly colorful player (Dock Ellis, Mark Fidrych, Joe Charboneau) there were ten others who seemed to the scouts to be doing an apprenticeship for a later career in sports broadcasting.

If the major-league players sharpened the scouts' self-image, the Major League Scouting Bureau blurred it. Many scouts believed, with justification, that the draft system would sooner or later fall to legal challenge, and with it would fall the Bureau. In the meantime their hearts and minds would remain in the third era—not in soft nostalgia, but in the exploitation of every opportunity for initiative, intrigue, fresh and uncomputerizable insight, clear and direct self-expression.

In the early 1980s the Bureau seemed to provide a litmus test of scouting philosophies, a way of characterizing the styles and financial commitments of each of the twenty-six major-league clubs. At one extreme were organizations for whom economy was not just a watchword but an end in itself. At the other were organizations dedicated to more expensive, and generally more productive, forms of traditional scouting.

The econo-scout approach was epitomized by the Seattle Mariners, Texas Rangers, and Houston Astros. Besides subscribing to the Bureau, these three teams had formed a "combine" to pool scouting information, enabling them to make even further staff cutbacks. In 1981 the Mariners were operating with six full-time and two part-time scouts, the Rangers with eight and two. Each organization stayed within a yearly scouting budget of $900,000 or less.*

The other fourteen Bureau subscribers averaged between $1,000,000 and $1,500,000 in annual scouting expenses. In

---

*Estimated scouting budgets include all salaries, fringe benefits, travel expenses, bonuses for new signees, and Bureau membership where applicable. The analysis here is based on scouting patterns from 1981 to 1983. For an update, see "Postscript, Fall 1988," in the epilogue (Chapter 15.)

1981 many of these clubs were actively recruiting more scouts. The San Francisco Giants were trying to achieve critical mass in order to drop out of the Bureau. The Oakland A's were rebuilding from scratch: their former owner, Charles O. Finley, had fired all his scouts in 1978, and for the next two seasons Oakland draft picks were based solely on Bureau reports and "underground" information.

The Boston Red Sox and New York Yankees used Bureau membership to supplement already large scouting forces, about two dozen full-timers each. The Cincinnati Reds had tried this approach from 1974 to 1977 but then dropped out of the Bureau because, they said, the dual system produced too much conflicting information and diluted the *esprit de corps* essential to a large staff. Yankee scouting morale was problematic anyway, because the organization routinely surrendered early-round draft picks as compensation for established free agents.

Among the nine non-Bureau teams in 1981, scouting budgets ranged from about $1,400,000 to $1,800,000. Half the National League was out of the Bureau—the Cincinnati Reds, Los Angeles Dodgers, Montreal Expos, Philadelphia Phillies, St. Louis Cardinals, and San Diego Padres—and most of these clubs equated independent scouting with a whole league image of aggressive baseball. The American League non-Bureau teams were the Baltimore Orioles, Chicago White Sox, and Toronto Blue Jays. In 1977 the Orioles had left the Bureau and returned to traditional scouting. That same year the Blue Jays had been created as a new franchise, and their leaders were determined to be traditional from the outset. Bobby Mattick, the Jays' original mentor, said: "The question that divides the good scouting clubs from the ordinary ones is, 'Do you belong to the Bureau?' "

In charting the philosophies of player development, other questions were pertinent. Perhaps the most basic was, "What are you looking for?" In general, National League clubs put more of a premium on running speed, not only because NL ballparks are larger and more of them have artificial surfaces, but also because Branch Rickey's disciples continue to set the tone of player development in Los Angeles, St. Louis, Cincinnati, and Pittsburgh. In the American League, Kansas City liked to draft multi-sport prospects (Willie Wilson, Dan Marino), a risky but often profitable approach later imitated by Toronto (Danny Ainge, Lloyd Moseby). When evaluating position players, scouts for the Royals or Blue Jays looked for total *athletes,* whereas scouts for the Yankees or Red Sox looked for *hitters.*

Of course, everybody put a premium on pitching, and pitchers usually constituted half the names on each scout's draft list. The Orioles even had a specialist, Bill Werle, who spent the three months before each draft looking *only* at pitchers. But the weakest clubs tried consciously to pull themselves up from nowhere by drafting pitchers with every key pick and by searching always for the "overpowering" prospect—alleged to be the next Sandy Koufax, even if more likely to be the next Rex Barney—who might single-handedly propel a bad team into the first division. In 1981 Seattle had the first selection in the June draft, and by early March rival scouts were saying that the Mariners would pick a pitcher, probably the hardest throwing they could find.

Another fundamental question dividing scouting organizations was, "Where are you looking?" Economy-minded clubs looked mainly in the college ranks, because college players were cheaper to sign, and—if successful—provided a quicker return on investment. Traditionalist clubs focused on high school players, and accepted higher bonuses and longer training as the costs of ultimate success. Organizations like the Cardinals or Expos, in which scouting was regarded as part of a larger player-development strategy, were more likely to search for younger talent, no matter how raw, and to underwrite the operation of six or seven minor-league affiliates instead of four or five.

Some successful clubs, like the Orioles, were looking almost exclusively in the United States. Others targeted Latin America, where bonuses were low and drafting was unnecessary. For the Astros and Pirates, Latin talent was part of an ongoing economy drive. For the Dodgers and Blue Jays, it was a natural resource whose extraction required old-fashioned "aggressive" scouting: sharp competition, private intrigue, and higher bonuses for younger players. To Pat Gillick, the Blue Jays' general manager, the Caribbean basin was an emblem of the open market, a reminder of what scouting had been like in the States before the draft era, and he saw the Dominican Republic as "the new Puerto Rico," just as Puerto Rico had once been "the new Cuba."

In the 1980s, Gillick said, Toronto would be "frankly scouting harder for black and Latin athletes than for Caucasian talent." The San Francisco Giants had also made a special commitment to scouting black players, most notably in the efforts of brother scouts George and Chick Genovese. Undoubtedly, in 1981 there was still some residual and subtle racism in the world of baseball scouting. Of the 500 full-time scouts, about 480 were white. But no club would admit to being anything less than zealous in pursuit of black talent, and the most common complaint white scouts had was that too much of that talent was siphoned off by basketball and football.

Some organizations could be differentiated by another question: "How well do you pay and promote your scouts?" In terms of salaries and fringe benefits, the Dodgers were probably the most enlightened club in baseball. More importantly, they expounded a whole philosophy of scouting, a tradition that Dodger general manager Al Campanis traced back to his teacher, Branch Rickey. (In his spare time Campanis was editing a collection of Rickey's tape-recorded lectures for publication.) The Los Angeles example was followed in Montreal and Baltimore, where scouts (the Expos called them *recruteurs*) and scouting directors had become general managers and even field managers, and where "quality out of quantity" was still a working premise. In 1981 Danny Menendez, the Montreal scouting director, wrote a memo to John McHale, the club president, outlining reasons for making a large system still larger, with as many as ten farm teams and thirty full-time scouts. The memo, written during the players' strike, was conceived as an "answer" to free agency.

The owners' bargaining position in 1981 followed a different logic based on the already high costs of player development. When they argued for more effective restraints against free agency, the owners pointed to development expenses unparalleled in the other pro sports. The twenty-six major-league teams were laying out a total of about $65,000,000 a year for their scouting and farm systems. Where was the fairness, the owners asked, in spending so much money on young talent only to lose that talent to richer teams, without compensation, when it had finally begun to provide return on investment?

The owners also put player development in historical perspective. In 1961 each team had spent about $1,500,000 for its scouting and farm systems combined, and about $750,000 for the twenty-five men on its major-league roster. In 1981 those figures averaged $2,500,000 and $5,000,000 respectively—an exact reversal of the ratio between development costs and major-league salaries. A projection of this trend presented long-term problems not only in achieving balanced budgets but also in maintaining the quality of the product that the owners were marketing.

Whatever the merits of the owners' position, player development in the early 1980s still looked like the biggest bargain in baseball. To many clubs, both in and out of the Bureau, a renewed emphasis on home-grown talent—carefully scouted, efficiently trained, working at relatively low salaries during their first major-league seasons—seemed to be just common sense. As salaries for some players climbed toward $2,000,000 a year, it was even tempting to imagine what that kind of money might buy if it were reinvested. For example, George Foster's annual paycheck with the Mets would have been equivalent to *all* of the following:

- salaries, expenses, and fringe benefits for ten additional full-time scouts;
- salaries, expenses, and fringe benefits for five additional minor-league instructors;
- bonuses, salaries, and benefits for forty additional amateur signees a year;
- operating expenses for two additional farm teams.

When Foster was signed to a five-year contract, the Mets' vice president for development was Lou Gorman, a baseball man for almost a quarter century. I asked Gorman what would happen if the Mets, instead of hiring Foster, committed that money to a radical development program. Wouldn't they sign about two hundred additional prospects over five years? Wouldn't the odds favor fifteen of those prospects becoming full-fledged major-league players? And wouldn't several of those players be better bets than a thirty-two-year-old slugger who ran and threw below average?

"First of all," Gorman said, "you have to consider your market, and in New York the voices demanding *instant* improvement are louder and more persistent than anywhere else. Second, if you just jump the size of your system, you create new problems. The minors today accelerate development— and if you have a kid in your system any longer than five years, you're wasting your time—so you have to avoid bottlenecks.

"But the biggest reason we don't put more eggs in the player-development basket is the draft. Without the draft it might make sense to just *pour* money into scouting and farm teams, and then major-league salaries might automatically level off. But as is, you reach a point of diminishing returns, where the talent has been so thinned out that all your extra spending becomes a luxury. It's a good luxury, because scouting and teaching are where baseball is still more of an art form, if I can use that term. It's the fun and challenge of finding the talent, and putting the right dollar sign on it, and nurturing it. It's part of the lore, the continuity, of the game. It'd be

worth doing for its own sake. And it sure as hell beats negotiating with the agents for the major-league players."

One organization in 1981 was so dedicated to traditional
scouting that it seemed to be operating in a different time
frame. The Philadelphia Phillies, in the midst of the draft era,
were still guided by pre-draft principles. The Phillies' executives
regarded the old-fashioned approach as an investment, not a
luxury, but in their hearts they believed that it *was* worth doing
for its own sake.

The Philadelphia executives thought like scouts. In fact, they
were scouts. Paul Owens had been a legendary buccaneer of
talent in California before becoming the Phillies' scouting director in 1965 and general manager in 1972. Dallas Green had
succeeded Owens as scouting director before becoming field
manager in 1979, and he had edited a scouting manual that
was still the bible of the organization.

The Phillies' 1981 scouting budget was the biggest in baseball—about $1,860,000—and its expenditure was guided by
a sharply defined philosophy. To the major questions that differentiated scouting organizations, Philadelphia personnel gave
clear answers. No, the Phillies did not belong to the Bureau;
from the beginning they had been among the most vocal critics
of pooled scouting. The Phillies were looking for the total
athlete. Even though the only Rickey man in the organization
was national cross-checker Brandy Davis, the Phillies sub-
scribed to Branch Rickey's thinking on the primacy of footspeed and the necessity of coordinated minor-league instruction.
(In 1981 the farm system, comprising six affiliates, was also
budgeted close to $2,000,000.) In the United States the Phillies
focused mainly on high-school prospects. And, in Latin America they were one of the most aggressive organizations, often
signing (or stashing away) players as young as sixteen.

The Philadelphia scouting staff was huge—twenty-eight full-
timers, sixty part-timers, and 200 bird dogs—and its men were
among the most respected and unpopular scouts in the profession. They were unpopular because they were so competitive.
"Never pass any reliable information on a player to other

scouts," the Philadelphia *Scouting Manual* said. "They are your enemies and are out to beat you in any way possible. Be courteous but at the same time be evasive." The Phillies' scouts rarely relaxed socially with their rivals, and they never allowed those rivals to ride in their cars. "We're anti–the fraternity of scouting," said Paul Owens, "as well as anti-draft, anti-Bureau, and anti–middle of the fuckin' road."

The Philadelphia scouts were respected because they were so successful. At the beginning of the 1981 scouting season the Phillies were the new world champions of baseball. Concentrated on that team, but also scattered throughout the major leagues, were forty-four proven players originally signed by the Phillies—more than from any other talent organization in the game. And the Philadelphia farm system, according to scouts from other clubs, was loaded with blue-chip prospects.

In the course of the 1981 season some of those prospects, like pitchers Jon Reelhorn and Scott Munninghoff, proved not to be blue chips after all, and the Phillies' player-development system was haunted by the failure to find or produce genuine catchers. But the biggest shock to the system, overshadowing even the strike, came at the very beginning of the season. On March 6, 1981 the Carpenter family, owners of the Phillies since 1943, took the unprecedented step of putting a championship team up for sale. Whoever the new owners were, the scouts said, they would never give the Carpenters' kind of priority, and money, to traditional scouting. The 1981 season might be the last chance to see an old-fashioned system running on all cylinders.

I began my scouting year by using the Phillies' *Scouting Manual* as a companion volume to Branch Rickey's *The American Diamond*. Rickey's book put scouting in a historical context and led to current disciples like George Kissell of the Cardinals and Howie Haak of the Pirates. The Philadelphia manual gave vertical perspective on one productive scouting system. It reflected the values of the Phillies' owners when it branded as "socialistic" baseball's amateur draft and all other impediments to free competition in the fourth era. But the manual most clearly expressed the organization's conservative philosophy when it explained the phrase "dollar sign on the muscle."

The dollar sign on the muscle was a code, a fictional vocabulary, that turned back the clock to the third era. It invited the scout to rate each ballplayer—beyond the number grades assigned to his tools, projected skills, and makeup—by naming a final dollar figure. The figure had nothing to do with the amount of money the player expected as a signing bonus, or with the lower amount the scout would try to persuade him to accept. It was an investment-analysis figure . . . from twenty years ago. "Your dollar evaluation," the manual said, "should be the highest figure you would go in order to sign a player if he were on the open market." So when a Philadelphia scout said, "I like this boy thirty thousand dollars," what he really meant was: "*If* the draft didn't exist, and *if* we had to bid against the enemy clubs for his services the way scouts operated in 1961, then I *would* recommend risking this much capital to acquire him."

Fluent use of this code required familiarity with other vocabularies of talent. It required poker-playing instincts in a game where most of the chips change in value after you win them. But most of all it required the first skill of a baseball man: knowing how to recognize a ballplayer when you see one.

SPRING

THE
PAST

315

DATE _4/24/80_

	POS	BATS	THROWS	HGT	WGT
	RF	L	L	6/5	180

'AME _DARRYL_ _STRAWBERRY_
    FIRST   MIDDLE   LAST

HOME
ADDRESS _____
    STREET   CITY   STATE   ZIP

DOLLAR
EVALUATION _$100.000_

'TELEPHONE NUMBER _____

STATUS _SR. I_

SCHOOL _CRENSHAW H.S._
    HS   JC   4 YR.

SCHOOL
ADDRESS _Los Angeles, Calif_

DATE OF
ELIGIBILITY _6/80_

CLASS _SR. 1980_   _18 Yes Age_
                DATE OF BIRTH

TEL. NO.

GLASSES – YES NO
CONTACTS – YES NO

☐ COLLEGE ☐ JR COLLEGE ☒ HIGH SCHOOL ☐ CONNIE MACK ☐ BABE RUTH
☐ SEMI PRO ☐ AMATEUR _____ ☐ LEGION

DRAFTED BEFORE: ☐ YES ☐ NO CLUB(S) _____
                           MO./YR.

PLAYERS	P	F
HITTING	67	73
POWER	70	71
60 YARD	—	—
RUN	70	71
ARM	72	74
FIELD	68	72
RANGE	71	73

PITCHERS		P	F
ANGLE ____			
FB			
CB			
SL			
CH			
OTHER			
CON			

WORD DESCRIPTION	
COMPETITOR	EXC
INSTINCTS	EXC
AGILITY	EXC
APTITUDE	EXC
MATURITY	EXC
POISE	EXC
HEALTH PROB.	?
INJURIES	?

PHYSICAL DESCRIPTION – DELIVERY _Tall, Lanky, Long Arms & Legs, Great Body with Agility._

WEAKNESSES _____

No Weaknesses Now.

STRONG POINTS _A Complete player Arm-Speed, Field, hit & power Great Body. Will Get Better in Every Dept Just might be That Super Star of The very Near Future can do, + All good hooking hitter No Faults Great Arm Good Runner Gets out of Box slow But Then Can Run. Hard to Visulize How much he will Become_

FORM 20–10/77

2 SCOUT'S HONOR

To be a scout, or to be a baseball person, you have to have good memory. I wasn't blessed with much education, but I do have a great memory. You can name any player you want to, go back as far as you like, and immediately—now I'm not bragging—immediately I can see that player on the field. I can picture him at the plate, or at shortstop, or wherever. A pitcher, I'll tell you about his delivery.

—Hugh Alexander

Hugh counts off the talents on the fingers of his right hand. "I've only ever seen a few ballplayers who could walk onto a major-league diamond and beat you five different ways—Joe DiMaggio, Willie Mays, Roberto Clemente, Mickey Mantle before he got hurt. . . . They could beat you with the consistent base hit, with power, with fielding, with the great arm, and with footspeed."

Footspeed is Hugh's thumb, and he wiggles it for emphasis. "This one really oughta count for two. Offense and defense. Some scouts'll tell you that you can't project it, that an eighteen-year-old boy is as fast a runner as he'll ever be. You *can* project it a little bit. On that 60-to-80 scale, I graded Darryl Strawberry as a 70, already an average major-league runner. But I projected him into the future as a 71. In fact, I projected him as above major-league average on all five tools, and I liked him a hundred thousand dollars. . . . I just wish to hell I'd had a chance to sign him."

Hugh's index finger points, thumb up, and the whole hand begins to quiver. "Now, the arm is like the speed: it's God-given, so it shows up early. You could be watching a fourteen-year-old boy and not be able to tell about him as a hitter yet, but know right then that he'd been blessed with the great arm. And if he has it, he'll *show* it, even in the warm-ups before the game, because he's proud of it. He wants you to see it. And that's the way I was, too, when I was a young ballplayer."

The hand stops quivering; the point has been screwed home. This mannerism is famous in the world of baseball scouting. It is Hugh Alexander's most typical gesture—a long vibrato with the right hand, as though that hand were trying and trying to express the full force of what two hands might. Because there is no other hand. Hugh's left arm ends in a stump just above the wrist.

The story of the missing hand is also the story of how in 1938 Hugh Alexander became the youngest scout in the history of baseball, and in his telling it opens out into a story about male values, styles of salesmanship, and degrees of honesty. His voice has a resonant depth, a down-home accent (Missouri-Oklahoma), a tone of tough-mindedness, and an undertone of roguery. At times it sounds remarkably like the voice of Wilbur Mills, the former Arkansas Congressman and Washington nighthawk, but it is really the voice of an ultimate baseball man: a throwback to the first generation of major-league scouts.

At the Philadelphia Phillies' spring camp, at the beginning of his forty-fourth scouting season, Hugh found his way into the story when I asked about his first teacher, Cy Slapnicka. As a pioneer, an ivory hunter, and a traveling salesman, Slapnicka signed great talent (Bob Feller, Herb Score) by cheerfully violating most of the scouting rules. In 1935, the year he signed Feller, Slapnicka also signed a seventeen-year-old outfielder who was blessed with raw speed and major-league power. His name was Hugh Alexander.

Slapnicka looked like a scholar. You know, maybe like a college professor. He wore little horn-rimmed glasses and had thin hair. Kinda small fellow. He'd been a ballplayer, not a real good one, but he'd been a ballplayer and I guess he had a sixth sense about talent, and later on he taught me. He was—I hate to use the word—he was a little bit of a conniver.

He got hauled in front of Commissioner Landis a lot because of breaking the rules. He had to go on Bob Feller and Tommy Henrich—he'd signed 'em illegally—and later on, he and I had to go together on Dale Mitchell, who I had signed, and it was a *little* on the shady side when I signed him. See, sometimes we wouldn't date the contracts, so if a player didn't work out we could just release him with no obligation. It was a common practice in those days, and maybe Dale found out about it from another scout. Slapnicka and I were called to Chicago, but in the meantime we backdated the contract so the commissioner couldn't prove anything. He asked me about it, and I lied, and then he jumped all over Slapnicka. He said, "Slapnicka, I'm going to try my best to get you before you finish your career in baseball!"

But Slapnicka outlived him by about ten years and never did stop looking for the main chance. As a scout, all he wanted was his fair advantage.

Slapnicka even signed *me* illegally. He found me in a summer league just after I finished eleventh grade. Cleveland only had two farm clubs back then, and didn't always have places to put players, so it was supposed to look like I belonged to a minor-league club while Cleveland really directed my progress. It was the same as the Tommy Henrich deal. And when I went to my first spring training in 1936, Tommy Henrich and I had lockers right beside one another. I've always thought this was a big turning point in my career, that Tommy kept saying, "Hugh, you're in the same category I am, and you can get your free agency too." And I thought I could, but I didn't want it. The commissioner finally ruled that Tommy's contract had been manipulated, and that Cleveland had to give him up, and he could sell himself to the highest bidder. A few days after that, Slapnicka called me to the office, and he said, "Hugh, are you thinking about doing the same thing Tommy Henrich did?"

I said, "No sir, Mr. Slap"—that's what I called him— "you've been good to me, and I want to stay with you. I don't want my free agency." He said, "Oh, you're a fine boy, and here's what I'm going to do for you." He opened a drawer and pulled out a thousand dollars in cash, and he said, "I'm going to give this to you." But then, instead of handing me the money, he wrote out a little agreement: I'd get one thousand dollars if and when I got called up to the majors.

The next year, 1937, the Indians called me up late in the season. I still had that piece of paper in my wallet, and finally I got up enough nerve to go up to his office one morning. I said, "Mr. Slap, I think you owe me a thousand dollars." And he had forgotten about it—he said, "Oh no, no." I said, "I've got a little piece of paper here that you signed at spring training last year." "Oh yeah," he said, "I remember that." And then he started givin' me the poor-mouth talk—and he could do it, like Branch Rickey—about how times were tough, and the Indians' attendance was low, and all that stuff. He finally said, "I'll tell you what I'll do for you, Alex. I'll give you two hundred fifty now, and if you're still in this ballpark thirty days after the season opens next year, I'll give you the other seven hundred and fifty dollars."

What went through my mind was: well, I'm gonna be on the club; I'm a good young ballplayer and I can play, and I'll just get my seven hundred and fifty next year. So he talked me into the two hundred and fifty, and we wrote up the new agreement. And at the end of that season I went home, and that December I got my hand cut off.

About two weeks after the accident I walked out to the mailbox about a mile or so up the road from the farm, and there was an envelope from the Cleveland Indians. But when I opened it up, it wasn't a letter. There was a check in there for seven hundred and fifty dollars. So Slapnicka remembered that he had beat me out of that money the year before.

The accident didn't bother me as much as everybody thinks. See, I had been a good athlete, a great athlete, and I'd played ball with men when I was fourteen years old, and went out to professional baseball at seventeen—and I had grown up fast. I wasn't prepared for it, of course, but it didn't bother me that much. It's like the physical exam I just took from Dr. Ginsburg in the clubhouse here. He uses that big scope, you know, where they go up inside you, and it hurts, right? Well, all the big Phillies' executives bitched and moaned about that exam, and I told 'em: "Hey, it's mind over matter. It *can't* hurt you, it really can't." . . . Because when I was working on an oil rig on that day in December 1937, and when my left hand got caught in the big gears, and I was by myself—I went to a house up the

road and borrowed a pillowcase to wrap it up in, and then got
in a pickup truck and drove fifteen miles to an Indian doctor,
and he gave me two drinks of whiskey and then cut my hand
off, sawed it off with a saw—I said then, that day, nothing can
ever hurt me the rest of my life. I'm talkin' about physically.
Nothing can ever hurt me, I don't care what it is, just like Dr.
Ginsburg's exam didn't hurt me because I said in my mind:
"Hey, if I took that, I can sure take this."

In the spring of 1938 I went to the Indians' training camp in
New Orleans, and Slapnicka started me off as a scout. I sat
with him in the ballpark for two weeks, and he would point
out things, what to do. And I remember he said, before I left on
my own, "You cannot find a ballplayer in a bar. And you cannot find a ballplayer by driving up and down the highway. The
only place you can find one is in a ballpark." And all the years
since then, whenever I broke in young scouts, I've told them the
same thing: "You cannot find a ballplayer in a bar. . . ."

But when I started in to scout, at twenty years old, I ran
with a pretty fast crowd. There weren't very many scouts in
those days, and they were all older people. They were all tough
guys, you know—they drank a lot, and they'd fight among
themselves, and I kinda fit in with that crowd. Like Joe Devine
and Bill Essick, great scouts for the Yankees, or Eddie Goostree
and Bill Pierre, great scouts for Detroit. Now I'm goin' way,
way back. Those guys are all dead now, and most of 'em were
in their sixties and seventies then. But they took a liking to me,
and each one taught me individually. Eddie Herr, who'd even
scouted before the First World War, took me under his wing.

It was around this time I met Branch Rickey. He took a liking to me, too, even though I didn't work for him, and he said,
"Young fellow, I understand you're going to be a real good
baseball scout." I said, "I appreciate that, Mr. Rickey." He
said, "I want to give you one little piece of advice. I'll give you
a lot, but I want to give you one right now: the minute you get
on the fence with a prospect and don't know whether to sign
him, walk away and leave him, because it's a mistake." And
how true he was, because your first impression of a ballplayer
is the best one. It's by far the best.

I walked away from a lot of players that first year—I didn't
sign a single one. But late that season Hank Iba tipped me off
on my first sign. Iba was the great basketball coach at Okla-

homa A & M, but he was also the baseball coach, and he told me, "I'm gonna have a hell of a pitcher on my club next year." The boy was a senior but he hadn't played baseball in college, because he was a fullback on the football team and he'd always had spring practice. It was Allie Reynolds. And I saw him pitch the next spring, and he used to strike out fifteen, eighteen, twenty men a game. I got him for a thousand-dollar bonus, which was big in those days, but he jumped to the majors real quick and he led the American League in strikeouts his rookie year.

My biggest mistake, I guess, was on Mickey Mantle—but with all due respect to myself, I was one of the few scouts who even knew about him. A friend of mine gave me his name, and I wrote it on a piece of paper, and I went by Commerce, Oklahoma, that spring and talked to the principal of the high school. He told me that they didn't have a baseball team, and that Mickey had been hurt in football and had "arthritis of the legs." Hell, it's hard enough to make the majors if you're healthy, and when he told me that stuff I walked out of the school, and when I got to my car I took that piece of paper and threw it away. I can still see it blowing across the parking lot.

I scouted for the Indians for fourteen years, the White Sox for four, then the Dodgers for fifteen, and the Phillies for the last ten. That's forty-three seasons, but I couldn't ever count how many miles it is. At one point with the Dodgers I know I drove sixty thousand miles every year. I had Oklahoma, Texas, New Mexico, Louisiana, Arkansas, and Mississippi. Leon Hamilton had all the Southeast for the Dodgers, and Howie Haak did everything for the Pirates, but they were the only other scouts on the road that much. And people used to say, "You guys are crazy. You'll have a car wreck, get killed." And many a time we slept in our cars. Drive all night long—no air conditioners in automobiles in those days, so we drove at night when it would be a little cooler, plus the fact that we might have to get to a town five or six hundred miles away.

When I broke in scouts in the Southwest, I used to say— "You can't cover this territory day-by-day. You have to divide it up, and be over in West Texas four-five days, and then Southeast Texas, and so on." Because Texas is a big-ass state! El Paso to Texarkana is nine hundred miles, and it's not impossible, you could make it by drivin' day and night, but—what

the hell?—when you got there, you wouldn't know Babe Ruth
if he walked out on the field.

I was kind of a loner. I think you have to be a certain breed
to be a baseball scout, I really do. You couldn't take just anybody and put him out to it. It's a lonesome goddamn life, to
begin with. And it ruins marriages. I know for sure how many
it ruined of me—I've been married five times. And I have a
daughter, she's married now with children of her own, and I
never really got to *know* her. Sometimes a scout gets to a point
where his wife just says, "Hey, here it is. I'm gonna put the ul-
timation on you. You gotta get out of the scoutin' business and
be a father, and stay home, or I'm gonna pack my bags and
leave." And that becomes a hell of a decision for a baseball
scout. I always said, "Well, I've gotta stay in baseball,
so . . ."—what's the old saying?—*"vaya con Dios."*

Or sometimes we'd argue about money, because scouts have
never been paid enough. *I* am now, and maybe six or seven
others, but for most of my years I didn't make much—and I
never, never in my whole lifetime, took an off-season job. I
never believed in it. Other scouts'd go home for four months
and get another job: car salesman, clerk, substitute teacher. I
said, "Fine, let 'em do what they want. But while they're doin'
that, I'll sign two or three ballplayers." Like in the old days,
when you could sign boys out of college at any time, I'd make
the rounds of the campuses in November or so, and go in the
dorms and talk to prospects. One might say, "Mr. Alexander, I
want to get married so bad, but I don't have any money." Or
another one might be broke, and Christmas is comin' up. And
maybe I'd sign each of those boys for less than a thousand.
Then one of the other scouts might say, "You son of a bitch!
You went and signed my player out of college." I'd say, "I sure
did. While you was out bein' a carpenter, I was still workin'."

It was coverage plus salesmanship. In those days you had to
get tight with the family—and if you didn't do that in the off-
season, I'll guarantee you in the spring you would not get the
ballplayers. Because the scout who did his homework, he's the
one who got the ballplayers. All he had to do was get close on
the money.

Remember Tommy Dean, the little infielder who was up for
a while with the Dodgers? I had gotten so close to that boy and
his family. I started watching him when he was in the tenth

grade, and I said, "Boy, he's gonna be quite a ballplayer." So when he was in his last two years of high school, whenever I'd go by their little farm in Mississippi, I'd spend the night, and I got to know the family so well—the mamma and the daddy, and the little brother, and the twin sisters—that on the day when Paul Richards for Houston offered Tommy Dean a hundred-thousand-dollar bonus, I came right in behind him because I had the last refusal. Well, I was prepared: I had already done my homework. I whipped out the tax form, because I'd gone to the I.R.S. office in Memphis and asked about taxes on bonuses. I was ahead of everybody else, I think. Well, I know I was.

So I said, "Here's what we'll do. We'll give you thirty thousand dollars"—you, Tommy Dean—"and we'll give your brother thirty thousand dollars as an agent." And the brother wasn't married; he lived right there in the house. I said, "It's gonna stay in the same house, and here is the difference in taxes." It was fifty-six hundred dollars. And you know what the boy said? He said, "Dad, I want to sign with Mr. Alexander because he's been close to our family. I like Mr. Alexander and I like the Dodgers, and I'm ready to sign."

A few minutes later I walked out onto the porch, and Paul Richards said, "Is it my turn to go in now, Hugh?" I said, "Yeah, you can go in and congratulate him, because I just signed him." He said, "How much did you give him?" I said, "I'm not gonna tell you, Paul"—even though Paul and I were good friends, and I had worked for him with the White Sox. So he said, "I'll go in and ask the boy." I said, "Fine, if he wants to tell you, it's his money." He came back in a few minutes and said, "How in hell could you sign that ballplayer for sixty thousand when I offered him a hundred?" And I said, "Well, I'm gonna tell you a little secret about scouting. It's the tax deal."

I used to put scouts in different categories. This one might be a good "closer," like Tom Greenwade or Atley Donald or Fred Hawn, and that one might be a good worker—makes an intelligent schedule, never misses a game, finds all the players—but when it comes time for him to go in that living room, he don't have a chance against me. There's no way in the world he can combat me just by offering the same amount of money. He might out-scout me in the field, but he can't out-scout me in the living room.

Let's say I thought *you* were a good young ballplayer, and I liked you thirty thousand dollars, and I came in to talk to you and your family. At first I'm not gonna mention money; I'm gonna sell myself to you personally. I should've done some preliminary work so you know who I am, and that I'm an honest person, not a fly-by-night scout, and that my word is my bond. Because my record speaks for itself: I signed Allie Reynolds and you remind me of him. I think you have ability, enough to make the big leagues—and I'd be makin' a big mistake if I signed you and didn't think that way, with the amount of money we're fixin' to offer you, 'cause if I make enough of those mistakes I get fired. . . . And pretty soon your family will like me, and they'll believe what I say, and they'll believe in my ballclub. Then I'll pay special attention to your mother. She's losin' her boy, right? But she doesn't want to lose her boy—to have him go a thousand miles to play baseball, and not see him till September—so I have to reassure her. And *then* I get to the money.

I used to balloon money up. If I like you thirty thousand, maybe I'll start out at twenty, but I'll add in your salary for the first three years and any incentive deal that applies. And I'll write all that down in big figures—not little tiny figures like a bookkeeper uses, but *big* figures so you can damn sure see 'em. Figures this high. Very emphatic. With a curlicue on the end of each one.

So now my twenty thousand looks to you like about thirty-five, and if I need to go a little higher I can do it—or I can pretend to call the office for permission, even though I really have carte-blank. But I won't actually be dishonest. Back when baseball had those bonus limits, a lot of people thought that I cheated, that I paid money under the table. I never did. I might have gone around the *edges* once in a while, but the Dodgers had an ironclad rule about bonus limits. It was other scouts who *said* I cheated, because I was tough to beat out of a ballplayer and they just tried to get themselves off the hook. When I signed the boy, they might go back to the hotel and phone the boss, and say, "Well, I lost the ballplayer, but that goddamn Hugh Alexander cheated on him." Which was not so. I just did my homework.

I always talked to the high-school principals and the bankers in the small towns, to get a line on the family and on what

kind of *person* a prospect was. I tried to picture whether he
could stand the competition in pro ball. The high-school player
you sign is not the same player who shows up a thousand miles
away on your minor-league team. He's never been away from
home before, but now he's away from his family, his friends,
his girl friend, his church. He's not the star of the team anymore—and the first time he fails, you really got your work cut
out for you. But I didn't meddle with the minor-leaguers. I
might've told their mothers that I'd look after the boys personally, but it finally got to a point that when I signed a ballplayer
I forgot about him.

And today, with the amateur draft, you usually don't get to
know the player anyway. Most scouts don't romance prospects
anymore; they just write up a shitload of evaluations. Just like
the Phillies had a big stack of reports on Darryl Strawberry, but
no reason to get real tight with him and his family. The New
York Mets had first pick in the June draft, and Strawberry was
gone right away. So "salesmanship" nowadays is more a matter
of getting your club to draft one of your players. And some
scouts just try to protect themselves: a guy'll turn in a pile of
prospect cards and then brag, "Well, I lost the ballplayer, but I
had him in." He didn't have him graded right, though! It's like
the Bureau, because the scout says to himself: "I don't want to
miss anybody. I'll turn all of those son of a bitches in."

But scouts are still the backbone of a ballclub, just like fifty
years ago. Unless you can raise a certain amount of your own
players, in your own system, you're in a hell of a shape. If you
go to trade, you have to have enough to trade with. And if you
go too deep into the free agent market, it'll break you in the
long run. . . . Yet a lot of baseball people take scouts for
granted. An executive might say, "Let's make Joe Doakes a
scout, because he's been a good minor-league player for us."
That's easy to say, but can the guy *scout?*

For me, the job still comes down to hard work and good
judgment. It's still a *human* science. So I don't rely on mechanical aids, like stopwatches and radar guns. I can be accurate on
my own. The gun registers the low pitch faster than the high
pitch, and it fixes your mind on speed. But I want to see movement on the fastball—not just speed. I want to see, period. Because to project a boy into the future, the first thing you have
to do is see him in the present the way he really is. And if you

say a boy has a major-league arm, he better *have* a major-league arm—or else you better be pretty damn tight with management.

Hugh Alexander was pretty damn tight with management. In 1981 he was working for an organization that credited its own overhauled scouting staff and farm system for the team's evolution into a consistent National League power, and within that organization he had the status of "special-assignment scout." This meant that he routinely evaluated professional rather than amateur players, either as future opponents or as possible acquisitions through trade. It also meant that he had one of the best jobs in scouting.

Special-assignment scouts are among the few baseball scouts making more than $30,000 a year, and they receive major-league accommodations as well as occasional public recognition (sports-writers usually call them superscouts). In contrast to the evaluation of amateur players, special-assignment work involves less intuition and projection and more detailed analysis and strategic thinking. Some of these scouts, like Jim Russo of the Orioles, are often cited by their colleagues as the sharpest observers in the business.

One phase of special assignment scouting is typified by the Philadelphia Phillies' 1980 World Series "book" on the Kansas City Royals, a sixty-page analysis prepared by Hugh Alexander and two other senior scouts, Jim Baumer and Moose Johnson. The report outlined the patterns and preferences of each Kansas City pitcher, graded the range and arm of each Kansas City fielder, and suggested defensive alignments and pitching strategy against each Kansas City hitter. The notes on how to pitch to George Brett were understandably vague ("Outstanding high fastball hitter; don't let him beat you"). The scouts had no hope of isolating a weakness that had eluded American League pitchers all season but were simply trying to limit the damage Brett could do, which meant "keeping the rabbits off the bases." The rabbits were Willie Wilson, U. L. Washington, and Frank White—all blindingly fast, capable of distracting pitchers and flustering fielders by stealing a base or taking an extra one with apparent ease, setting the stage for the big hits by Brett. On White, for example, the report was quite specific: "Likes to pull when ahead of count; may go opposite field when behind. First-ball, fastball, high-ball hitter—pitch down. Can change speeds on him; has trouble with breaking balls. Will bunt for base hits to 1st or 3b side." The analysis of every hitter was followed by a detailed chart for positioning each fielder. Through the six games of that World Series the three rabbits hit 12 for 73 (.164) with only 5 walks and 3 stolen bases; they struck out 23 times. And George Brett came to bat with a total of 14 runners on base.

During the regular season Alexander stayed about five days ahead of the Phillies, providing advance reports on the team they were scheduled to play next. "If I'm in the same town with the team when they start a series, I go into the clubhouse before the game and talk to the team myself. I go over all the other team's players—who's hot, who's hurt, who's playing even though he's hurt, who can take the extra base, who can throw from the outfield. How we're gonna position our out-fielders is a big thing. And I talk to the pitchers—I might say, 'Bull Durham is a wild-swingin' guy, won't draw too many walks'—but I *never* tell 'em how to pitch to a hitter. Who the hell am I to tell Steve Carlton how to pitch? I just say, 'Hey, I've watched this club play four games this week, and this is what I saw other pitchers get their hitters out with.' Because if I was Steve Carlton, and some old guy told me 'You have to throw this hitter exactly this way,' I'd say, 'Go fuck yourself.' He's gonna pitch his own game anyway, and I admire him for that."

Alexander also sized up each opposing player as a potential Phillie and he consulted with Paul Owens on every trade. It was Owens, his one-time scouting rival, who lured him away from the Dodgers in 1971 and made him a kind of baseball *consigliere*. The rapport between these men was a shared philosophy of old-fashioned scouting that really amounted to a philosophy of life. When Owens characterized the Philadelphia system at the start of the 1981 season, he defined it in terms of Hugh Alexander's style of rugged individualism: "We want guys who aren't afraid to dent a fender, take a chance, put their names out. Aggressive scouts—they're the ones who find you aggressive players."

Owens's prime example of aggressive scouting was the signing of pitcher Marty Bystrom. In 1976 Bystrom, just out of high school, was ignored in the June draft. That fall, at Miami-Dade Community College South on a baseball scholarship, he pitched four straight shutouts. Then the scouts came sniffing around, because Bystrom, as an undrafted junior-college student, was eligible to sign a pro contract at any time. A Philadelphia scout, the late Catfish Smith, asked Miami-Dade coach Charlie Greene for a special workout for Bystrom so that two other scouts, Hugh Alexander and Gust Poulos, could see him.

"At this workout," according to Greene, "Alexander assured me that he wanted a chance to see Marty to make recommendations for the January draft, and that he would never sign one of our players until the season was over." Two days later Bystrom's father phoned Greene with the news that Hugh Alexander was at the house trying to sign Marty. Greene rushed over, joined the talks, and—when he heard the bonus figure of $35,000—finally encouraged the Bystroms to accept it. Gust Poulos, who had opposed the signing because it would mean breaking his promise to Greene, was subsequently fired by the Phillies.

Charlie Greene told this story as a tale of treachery. The Phillies (including Marty Bystrom) interpreted it as an example of the kind of initiative still possible in modern scouting. A scout's job is to get the good player, not to find ways not to. And if your first teacher was Cy Slapnicka, and if you've just written up a pitcher in a report like this—

Tall, lean, long arms and young, good body. Good delivery, high ¾, except he hooks his arm some behind his back, but not bad, and his control with this delivery is real good. Workouts with pitchers are deceiving, I realize. However, this boy showed an outstanding fastball at times, with good life and velocity, fair curveball but good sweeping-type slider. Threw some straight changes. Good hard worker in workout.

—the rest comes naturally.

"I told Poulos, 'Our chances of getting Bystrom in the draft are *remote*. I have a job to do.' And I don't care about that coach—how horseshit he says I am or whatever—because he had a gentlemen's agreement among scouts that they wouldn't sign his players, that they'd wait and draft 'em. That agreement was an easy way out for the scouts: they didn't have to make the big decision or try to outbid one another, and they said, 'Let's don't break this bond we have with the school. Let's all take our chances, and we'll all do pretty well.' I'm not criticizing scouts, because I love scouts, but they took the easy way out.

"Today a scout's toughest competitors might be college coaches instead of other scouts. At the four-year schools, when they offer a scholarship, they usually don't tell the boy that it's not guaranteed, that it can be taken away for *athletic* reasons. It's not a four-year deal; it's one-one-one-one. But they're not gonna say that. The college coaches go around the edges a little bit.

"Course, if *I* was a college coach, I'd probably do the same thing. . . . It's like the survival of the fittest. Right?"

Hugh and I are sitting behind a backstop at the Carpenter Complex in Clearwater, Florida. From around us, on the four fields extending like cloverleaves from the central clubhouse, come the sounds of spring training, a soft waterfall of thwocks and thuds in the morning sun. In front of us Keith Moreland is taking batting practice.

"A pure hitter," Hugh says. "Look how he keeps the front shoulder closed and takes the whole body into the pitch . . ." (Moreland cracks a line drive to left) "with a nice short stride."

"Do you use things like that to project? Could you tell from his mechanics that a high-school hitter was a good one, even if he went o-for-four when you saw him?"

"Maybe. But on a one-game look I might be more confident to say that he was a *bad* one—you know, if he was an over-strider or had a big hitch in his swing."

"Branch Rickey said that overstriding can't be corrected, that a scout should just forget about a prospect who's a chronic over-strider."

"Rickey was right, he sure was. But he meant more than just taking too big a step. Look."

Hugh stands up and assumes a right-handed batting-stance. In slow-motion he mimes a bad swing. What I notice right away is less the big stride than the upper body already opening out—the left shoulder turning to the left and up, the right shoulder dropping, and the swing becoming snarled as the right elbow swivels down. "Tell me what I'm doing wrong," he says.

"You look like a golfer about to hit a slice. You're all opened up before the bat even crosses the plate."

"Yeah, and see how my arms are *not* extended. They should be, but I've jammed myself."

"And that's all because of your stride?"

Hugh shrugs, as if to say that cause and effect can't be so easily disentangled. "The big stride is usually a tip-off that a guy's whole *system* of hitting a ball is wrong. That's why it's not a matter of simple correction. It means his lower body's not coordinated with his upper half. It goes together with a slow bat, because the big stride takes more time, and it goes together with committing himself too soon, so he opens his body or gives up his hands when he should keep 'em back."

He slowly repeats the same mistakes, and then takes the swing farther through. "Here's another tip-off. When the bat crosses the plate, the top hand should stay on top. But if I do *this*" (Hugh's lowered right shoulder and elbow now lead his right hand below the plane of the imaginary bat), "I'll never be a good hitter as long as my ass points down. Now look at this."

Hugh takes his stance again, but something is different. It might be that he glares out at the imaginary pitcher—or that he really seems to visualize a ball and sets to attack it the way a hungry player named Hugh Alexander did in 1937 when he hit his way to the major leagues. The slow-motion stride is short, led by the front shoulder. The body stays closed as the arms extend fully, and . . . "Look at my hands! See?"

The right hand is above the plane of the imaginary bat and the imaginary left hand. "Look," he says again at the moment of impact, and I can feel a real ball jumping off a real bat and shooting toward the left-centerfield gap for sure extra bases.

3 SEEING IS BELIEVING

In a profession where the physical is dominant in the triune nature of man, it would be surprising indeed if we did not find here and there an occasional scalawag.

—*Branch Rickey,* The American Diamond

Ed Dunn, a scout for the Twins, liked to say that if you took all the minor-league coaches and teachers and put them out to scout, they'd never sign anybody. And if you took all the scouts and put them out to manage the minor-leaguers, they'd never release anybody. Dunn's was a common view in the world of player development. It pointed up the contrasts between two kinds of gifts, between finding talent and nurturing it, between idealistic vision and realistic analysis, between short-term evaluation of a dozen or less performances and long-term testing through the daily grind of a professional season. And it hinted at the kind of friction that can develop between two kinds of baseball men. According to Leon Hamilton, "A minor-league manager might say, 'This kid don't want to play. Send him home.' Us scouts'll be more lenient. Whenever they run off one of mine, man, I'm on that phone, wantin' to know *why*. And they've let some get away that we've lost for nothin'."

However, you don't have to look far for scouts who used to teach (Ellis Clary, Brandy Davis) or teachers who used to scout (Bobby Mattick, Billy Martin). Some baseball men, like

Paul Richards, take special pride in being "double-barreled." Their model is Branch Rickey. The scout who began making professional recommendations in 1906, who discovered George Sisler, who invented tryout camps, and who assembled the first all-star scouting staff was also the teacher who devised baseball's first all-purpose spring camp (St. Petersburg, 1914) and first mass camp (Vero Beach, 1949), and who initiated the use of sliding pits and batting cages and cinematic aids and special drills and his own classic chalk talks.

One day at spring training I wandered through two minor-league camps, the Phillies' at Clearwater and the Cardinals' at St. Petersburg, and I learned that in the baseball mind of Branch Rickey there was really no dividing line between being a scout and a teacher . . . or between being a genius and a sharpie.

8:30: SCOUTING BAD PLACES

Four mornings a week the younger prospects, those with two years or less of spring training experience, came early to the clubhouse for "Phillies' Warm-Up Time." This was not a set of exercises but a set of lectures and discussions on "what they're gonna run into in baseball." The sessions were organized by Lou Kahn, coordinator of the Phillies' minor-league camp, and also a scout—so old-fashioned a scout, or just so stubborn, that his reports were rarely written on paper but were usually phoned in long-distance and typed up by a secretary in Philadelphia.

The Phillies had borrowed the idea for "Warm-Up Time" from Branch Rickey. At Vero Beach in 1949, when the Dodgers ran the first modern mass camp, Rickey himself supervised the teaching. And every morning at 8:30 the players began their workday by listening to commandments and warnings about baseball morality, delivered in the style of classroom oratory that Rickey had polished at the University of Michigan. Some days he lectured to all five hundred players on such lessons as "The Cure Is Sweat" or "Leisure Time Is the Anathema of

Youth." One member of the audience was Lou Kahn, then a Triple-A catcher.

"Dodgertown had a lecture every goddamn morning for everyone in the goddamn camp. I'd been playin' ball for fourteen years. You know, you don't like to have to listen to that shit. You've been through it. You know it.

"But our classes here are outstanding! So far this spring we've covered things like 'Living Away from Home'—situations you'll run into, people you associate with, how to know who your good friends are and who your good friends aren't, people that'll try to mislead you or give you dope, and about how some people hate you because you're a ballplayer, how other kids are jealous and they want to fight you, and how you gotta protect yourself by steerin' away from bad places: *scout* a place where you're liable to get in scraps.

"It's about what it is to be a real professional. Like how to handle the media—you've gotta be courteous to those guys, even if you don't like some of the stuff they write, but you've gotta be very careful about what you say. You can't say, 'Don't print this'—because most of 'em *will* print it. And if a guy uses you, you don't want to fight him, but you face him face-to-face and tell him. And the next time that guy comes to you, . . . 'See ya later.' And some of these goddamn guys will sooner or later run out of people to interview."

9:30: FLIP

After all the prospects had weighed in, put on uniforms, and finished their own stretching exercises, there was always extra time for goofing around. The favorite diversion was a game called Flip, played just outside the clubhouse doors in circles of about fifteen prospects each. The players kept a ball moving without touching it with the throwing hand, simply using the glove to catch and flip in one motion, or to swat the ball without catching it, propelling it anywhere in the circle with added speed. If a player mistouched the ball, missed it, allowed it to hit the ground, or swatted it too wildly for anyone else

to flip, he dropped out of the game, and the circle tightened—
until only two players were left to smack the ball furiously at
each other. Don Carman, a stringbean left-hander, was a consistent winner.

The game demanded sharp reflexes. Maybe it honed them,
too, but nobody played Flip with such a practical result in
mind. Baseball had once been play to these kids; now it was
their work. Before the grind of the day began, they could still
turn it into play again, frisking like puppies. But Lou Kahn
was not amused.

"I don't like it. The managers don't like it. You could get
hurt doin' it—lose a tooth, or break a nose or a finger. I told
'em if they want to play that game, all right. But if you get
hurt and can't do a practice or play in a game, it'll cost you
a hundred dollars! . . . They kept playin'."

10:30: CIRCLE JERK

Continuous Motion Exercise was its official name, but everyone—including the officials—called it the Circle Jerk. On each
of the complex's four diamonds, a coach stood near second
base and hit fungoes toward deep centerfield. Two dozen prospects ran in a big circle from rightfield to second base to leftfield
to deep center—at which point each prospect fielded one of
the fungoes, keeping the ball with him until he arrived at the
coach's side of the circle, where he dropped it in a bucket
without breaking stride.

To Jeff Cooper, the Phillies' major-league trainer, the Circle
Jerk really was a circle jerk, without any scientifically demonstrable value for baseball. But most minor-league instructors,
like Larry Rojas, defended it. "Is good," Rojas said, "if you
run it and don' loaf, if you do it the Phillie way." The Phillie
Way was the organization's term for the right way—the professional, technically correct, cool but hustling way. Rojas looked
at the Circle Jerk on diamond number one to see if there were
any stragglers; he was wearing mirror sunglasses. "They cannot see my eyes, so they never know if I might be lookin' at

them. But if I talk to a boy, I always take the glasses off and make him look me in the eye.

"We tell the kids: 'In the Circle Jerk, run with all the speed you can stand. Don' let the guy in front of you slow you down. Pass him. If you get tired, walk a half lap.' We want them runnin' on their toes, on the balls of their feet. You want to get in shape for baseball? Sprint! Sprint, walk, and sprint again. Don' jog. If you jog, you hit with the heel; it hit the back and everything will hurt."

Lou Kahn didn't care about the Circle Jerk one way or the other, but he was impressed by the off-season conditioning most of the prospects had done, and he contrasted it to that first mass camp at Dodgertown. "I know myself, personally, it just shows you how horseshit you can think. I went to that camp tryin' to make a big-league ballclub, and I hadn't thrown a ball all winter, and I hadn't run from here to the clubhouse. And even a few years ago, we ran the pitchers and catchers in a conditionin' drill on the first day, and we had guys fallin' out and pukin' and comin' into the clubhouse gaspin' and all that stuff. But these kids today show up *ready*. A lot of 'em swim in the off-season, and that's good for your whole body, but I think too many of 'em try to build theirselves up with weights."

Larry Rojas agreed. "Remember Jerry Martin? When I firs' saw him, he was such a quick bat that when he swung you could hear the ball say: 'I don' want to stay in the park!' And then he build himself up, look like Superman—lotta bulk, but I don't think it help him. Is okay to build up the forearms— is good for *those* muscles to be tight—and you have to have strong hands. But the rest of the body mus' be loose. You goin' to hit, your hips have to whip."

11:30: KOOKY GUYS

Lou Kahn had been in charge of Phillies' minor-league camps even before the Carpenter Complex was constructed in 1968. "I remember the camp we had in 1966 at Leesburg, Florida—

one hundred fifty kids and one ball diamond. That was Larry Bowa's first spring in the pros, and you could just *tell* he was gonna find a way to the big leagues. A lot of organizations would have missed him. In fact a lot of organizations did miss him: he didn't get drafted in 1965, and if it hadn't been for our north California scout, Eddie Bockman, Bowa wouldn't have got signed. You looked at him the way a scout does, and you saw three tools—the speed, the glove, the arm. No bat. But you also had to see he had the determination. Somehow or other he was gonna *will* himself into the majors, become a switch-hitter, do whatever it took.

"One other kid, before that, that I knew on right away was Richie Allen, because his tools were outstanding! He had tools runnin' out of his ass. He could've been in the Hall of Fame if he had Bowa's kind of grit. But I remember his first spring, and how that ball just *jumped* off his bat—maybe the quickest bat I ever saw.

"We've had our share of flakes, too—but there's not as many today as there used to be. The last big one at this camp was Joe Charboneau, kinda a kooky guy. I never saw him do any of that shit myself. You know, he pulled one of his teeth out with pliers, and he ate raw eggs in the shells, and drank beer through his nose, stuff like that. I never saw it, but I wouldn't hold it against him if I had. In fact I always felt that's why some of those kooky guys make good ballplayers, because they don't worry about nothin'. They don't take the game home with 'em at night. Joe had some problems with us, he even quit one year, but he could always hit—and I figure as long as he don't go pullin' someone *else's* teeth, more power to him."

12:30: PSYCHIC FORCE

While the minor-leaguers were eating lunch at the Carpenter Complex, the major-leaguers were doing their pre-pregame exercises at Jack Russell Stadium. Herm Starrette, the pitching coach, was working with Scott Munninghoff, once the top

prospect in the Phillies' farm system. A year earlier Munninghoff had been scheduled to pitch a season in Triple A at Oklahoma City, but at the end of spring training he was a surprise
pick for the major-league roster, part of Dallas Green's program to "promote the kids." In April and early May of 1980
he had pitched in relief in four games and looked terrible each
time. Then he *was* shipped to Oklahoma City, where he had
a mediocre year.

Some of the Philadelphia scouts, like Brandy Davis, said that
Munninghoff had been rushed through the system. Most of
the Philadelphia coaches, like Starrette, said that Munninghoff
had always had a problematic delivery: "The scouts who saw
him in high school must have noticed it. He's always thrown
too much across his body and opened up his hips too soon.
He could get away with it when he was a teenager. But you
keep throwin' like that, you're gonna have arm problems."

I tried to watch Munninghoff clinically, but even warming
up he looked so impressive that I abandoned any hope of
deciding who was right, the scouts or the coaches. What struck
me, though, was how Starrette's instructions to Munninghoff
sounded just like batting coach Billy DeMars's instructions to
hitters. . . . Rotate the hips back and then propel forward without opening them too soon. Keep your front shoulder closed,
coordinating it with the hips, so that the body doesn't "fly"
open but instead gains maximum torque. Move against some
point of resistance that you supply yourself. And yet, through
that firmness, be loose. Flow. Work from a still point at the
center of your own body image.

Of course neither Starrette nor DeMars spoke this last sentence. Few professional instructors use terms that might sound
too subjective or summon up images of t'aï chi. Steve Carlton
had once talked this way, and the Philadelphia press corps had
made him look so foolish (he thought) that he no longer talked
to the press at all. Teachers relied on a one-two-three mechanical breakdown, and players, when they felt the energy
between these points, had trouble talking about it directly.

Standing next to the batting cage, Mike Schmidt took a mean

practice swing. I was hoping he could tell me how that swing had become so clean—how all hitches and twitches had been subtracted, so that any muscle not integral to that sweet execution simply remained uncontracted. Somewhere in the middle of my question, I used the phrase "psychic force," which put him off; he thought I might be intruding into his private religious beliefs. But he was agreeable about explaining, for the umpteenth time, why he had begun standing so far away from the plate.

"I can step *into* any pitch and not get handcuffed by an inside strike. I can still reach anything on the outside corner and hit it hard to the opposite field. Middle of the plate and in, I can go long-ball. But the same reflexes that allow me to do that—I have to count on them to keep me from getting beaned, because I might step *into* a fastball coming at my head."

Schmidt was interrupted by Carlton, who ignored the writers near the batting cage. "When you see the slider," asked the owner of probably the best slider in baseball, "what do you see? Do you read the spin or what?"

"Naw," Schmidt said, "I don't know what it is. I think it's the different speed or the different *plane*. It depends on who the pitcher is—how much I've seen him to read his release fast enough."

"Like Rick Reuschel," Carlton said.

Schmidt grinned and took another mean practice swing. "Man, I *kill* him."

1:30: THE SCOUT AS TEACHER

Back at the Carpenter Complex, where minor-leaguers were taking turns in batting cages, I found a scout, doubling as a hitting instructor, who supplemented American vernacular with Oriental terms to answer the question I had tried to ask Mike Schmidt.

"In the first place," Tony Roig said, "hittin' a baseball and throwin' one are so much alike it ain't even funny. You gotta go back" (and here his meaty right forearm, representing a whole body, moved gracefully in slow motion) "to come forward. You have to wind the spring. But there's a part of you that's not the spring, that stays still, and you work from that. It's like the Japanese idea of *wa*—harmony. They say it carries out in everything you do, from the way you walk to the way you live. Somewhere in between those two is the way you hit or pitch. If a hitter or pitcher lets his body fly open, that's the opposite of *wa;* it's kind of a body-panic. Before he can straighten it out with a step-by-step technique, he has to learn how to relax.

"I think we're too mechanical in the way we teach things. Twenty, thirty years ago, when I played, everything was fluid coordination. Everybody seemed to be a lot more loosy-goosy; they didn't tense up. Hands on the bat were a little looser, and your whole structure was looser. You have to be relaxed to hit—and you watch the great hitters, they make it look like fallin' off a log. They flow into the ball real easy, and they stay fluid in the swing. But the kids I work with now are tighter. They're in great shape, their muscles are well developed, but they lack that looseness, that . . ." Roig let his forearm complete the sentence: it moved back, then forward, like a stalk of wheat in the wind.

"In Japan they teach hitters style patterns—one style for power hitters, another style for contact hitters. Their concept is, we're gonna get the most outa what *you* have, your own individual abilities, and so they vary their instruction. Some teachers talk about *hara,* the belly, the center, the still point. But for me, it comes outa the head. The still point is what you're believin' up here. If you got a lot of confidence, if you really feel like you can hit, that's half the battle. You should know in your mind 'Man, I'm gonna hit this ball. I'm gonna hit it hard somewhere.' So when the Japanese talk about *hara,* I think of that more as the courage to stand in there on inside fastballs. That comes from the belly, all right. We call it guts."

After thirteen years of pro baseball in America, including parts of three seasons in the majors, Tony Roig played for six years in Japan. He was the second baseman for the Fukuoka Lions; Jim Baumer was the shortstop. At the end of every season Baumer returned to the States, but Roig took his family on tours all over Asia. He had fallen in love with the Orient, especially Japanese culture ("Work, tradition, the family—what the hell more do you want?"), and he learned the Japanese language well enough to negotiate his own contracts. When he finally returned to America, he stayed in pro ball as a combination scout and teacher. One of Jim Baumer's first moves as the Phillies' new director of the scouting and farm systems was to hire Roig in both roles. After spring training and until the June draft, Roig would be a cross-checker, looking at top amateur prospects; then he would become a roving minor-league instructor for the rest of the season. He thought that the two jobs reinforced each other, that they required the same quality of consciousness.

"If you're a coach, the first thing you have to do is *look* at the hitter the way a scout does. Let him show you what he can do, instead of tryin' right away to make him fit some cookie cutter in your mind. So before I instruct anybody on what to do, he has to prove to me that he can't do it his way. Seein' is believin'.

"And if you're a scout sizin' up some high-school hitter for the draft, you might see a problem in his swing—but your experience as a teacher tells you: 'That's correctable. All this bwah needs is a little help.' "

Bwah was Roig's pronunciation of *boy,* meaning a prospect. His New Orleans accent was one reason people sometimes called him Cajun; another was his extroverted style. Tony Roig was like the secret demonstrative side of Jim Baumer. Both were big men, 6′ 2″, who typically defined ballplayers in terms of courage, aggressiveness, and determination—or guts, balls, and heart. But Roig made it sound less military, more an expression of life-energy itself.

He wasn't Cajun. But a Spanish father and French mother and a childhood in mixed neighborhoods and six years in Japan and his own swarthy complexion and kinky gray hair and that

accent all enabled him to work well with prospects from anywhere. He claimed that the Phillies' minor-leaguers were the
best group he'd ever seen assembled in one camp, and his
favorite *bwah* was Juan Samuel, a twenty-year-old infielder
from the Dominican.

"Today that mother ran a sixty-yard dash in 6.2! Other
black players just standin' there, watchin' him with their mouths
open, goin' 'Whoooooo-eee!' He's got it all. There's not much
I'm gonna teach him about hittin'. . . . But I don't think you
can teach anybody how to hit. You might *suggest* it. A real
hitter has to have the bat speed, and the guts to stand in there—
and you don't teach those. Maybe you watch the plane of his
bat, or you see whether he might open up his body too soon
like a pitcher.

"I started when I was seventeen, and I've stayed with baseball all my life, and I wasn't a real gifted player so I helped
myself by trying things. And I think that instruction work is
trial and error. I tried enough things myself that, if a hitter's
in trouble, I can usually suggest something—and if it doesn't
work, to hell with it and let's go back to where he was. People
think it's funny that teachers like me batted about .220 when
they were in the majors, what little time they *were* there. But
the great hitters usually don't know how they did what they
did; we're the ones who had to work at it and try different
things. We can pass that along, and maybe we teach with a
little more compassion. When I say *compassion,* I don't mean
softness. I mean you feel your way, scout your way, to where
the bwah is, and you teach from the inside out."

2:30: BASEBALL FACTORIES

Lou Kahn watched the minor-league instructors teach and re-
teach the fundamentals of each position. A young coach named
P. J. Carey gave the catchers a crisp demonstration of how to
block pitches in the dirt by keeping the head down and ("to
prevent the biggest danger") the hands between the legs. On
dirt pitches to the right and left Carey showed how to shift in

an imaginary semicircle, not laterally, so that the ball was always kept in front. He told the catchers to anticipate on any breaking pitches they called, to get ready to move to the right on a right-hander's curve—and he ended with a reminder that "a good pitcher, like Carlton, may *need* to throw an occasional pitch in the dirt, even with men on base, to keep the hitters honest."

Lou Kahn had been a catcher himself: eighteen years in the minors, none in the majors. He began in the Cardinal system—signed personally, according to the Phillies' personnel guide-book, by Branch Rickey. When I asked about Rickey, Kahn propelled a giant wad of tobacco juice so hard that it kicked up dust.

"I was just a number to Branch Rickey. He ran baseball *factories,* and he screwed his players every way but right-side-up. He'd sign kids and never turn in their contracts, and watch how they did for a month in Class D, and if they didn't look too good they'd get cut with no obligation. My high-school buddy got cut that way: his ass was stranded five hundred miles from home. No fare home or nothin'. Rickey didn't give a shit.

"My first year out was Mitchell in the Nebraska State League. Rickey owned eighty percent of the players in the whole league! I hit .363 and couldn't hardly get a raise. See, he knocked down everyone's salary and he put the difference, between what they got and what they should've got, in his own pocket. You had guys comin' up to the major leagues, like Mickey Owens, makin' two hundred fifty bucks a month—and nothin' in the off-season. I tried to tell Bob Carpenter about this one time. He said, 'Oh no, Mr. Rickey was never like that.' I said, 'Don't tell me, Mr. Carpenter. I was *there!*' Seeing is believing.

"That's why I say the baseball owners brought all this union shit on theirselves. . . . Curt Flood—you can't tell me the Cardinals couldn't have enough consideration to tell him about tradin' him, after he'd worked for that club for eight or ten years. He found out about it on the fuckin' radio! Nobody can deny that the coal mines and the steel mills didn't need unions years ago, and that's what baseball finally got. It was more like factories than the owners thought."

3:30: DRIVE AND INITIATIVE

The Phillies' owner, Bob Carpenter, was an eloquent defender of laissez-faire capitalism. Of all its benefits, he said, the greatest was its openness to fresh talent and hard work—and that was why in 1946 he had hired Edith Houghton, the only female scout in the history of major-league baseball. "She just kept pestering me, and I've always had a weakness for anyone with drive and initiative. She said, 'Just give me a chance.' So I finally did. She was about thirty-three, just out of the service—the Waves—and she'd been a star on women's softball teams. And then she went out and signed some players for us. None of 'em made the big leagues, but they were okay. She knew a ballplayer when she saw one.

"There's no reason a woman couldn't scout today. She'd have to be free enough to travel all the time, because scouting's a lonely job for anyone. But it wouldn't matter if some of the veteran guys didn't like her. Plenty of scouts don't like each other, and it's not the kind of job where success depends on popularity. It depends more on drive and initiative. About twenty-five percent of the scouts don't have that; they don't exert themselves—they travel around with their golf clubs in the car, and at the games they spend most of the time talking with their friends. Another twenty-five percent does the real work. That leaves fifty percent somewhere in the middle. It's kind of like life."

Carpenter was squinting into the sun to watch the action on diamond number four, where a right-handed pitcher named Richie Gaynor was trying to prove the scouts wrong. At 5'10" and 170 pounds Gaynor qualified as a *little* right-handed pitcher, and scouts are fond of saying "Little righties are no prospects" as if quoting from some timeless scouting manual, maybe the notes of an ancient Egyptian priest in charge of picking the players for the ritual ball games in honor of the sun. Bob

Carpenter agreed with the scouts, and in fact had always felt that little players in general—either-handed, at any position—were suspects rather than prospects. As the owner of the team, he was able to make size a determining factor in Philadelphia scouting for over twenty years, until Paul Owens became scouting director. Bob Carpenter's real weakness was for mooses.

"But I like this kid," he said. "He's aggressive, comes right at the hitters, and his fastball has a nice little tail on it. He was signed as an outfielder last June, but he couldn't hit professional pitching and now the coaches want to convert him. Sometimes they think they can help a kid beyond what these scouts say is possible. I'd love to see Gaynor make it, though. It'd be fun to follow his development, if I was gonna stick around."

Richie Gaynor's first spring training was Bob Carpenter's last. Bob's son Ruly, speaking for the family, had made the stunning announcement on March 6, less than five months after the Phillies won the first world's championship in the history of the franchise, that the ballclub was up for sale. He offered a grab bag of economic reasons. Because of skyrocketing players' salaries and an unfavorable stadium contract with the city of Philadelphia, he said, the Phillies now needed to draw 2,700,000 in home attendance every year just to break even. "We could lose a few million dollars so fast it'd make your head spin." Moreover, the tax structure for baseball franchises encouraged syndicate rather than family ownership, which meant that the game in the 1980s was coming under the control of flashy high-rollers. The Carpenters were angry at the players for threatening to strike, but their deepest anger was reserved for owners like Ted Turner of the Braves, who had recently given free agent Claudell Washington a five-year contract worth more than $3,500,000. "Some of the other owners," Ruly Carpenter said, "are just nouveaux riches as far as baseball is concerned. They have a hell of a lot of money, and it could be an ego trip for them. Or they just want to buy instant success—they don't want to do it through development in the minor leagues or scouting."

All this could have been said in four simple words: It isn't fun anymore. The economic arguments were hard to take at face value, because the Carpenter family resources were estimated by *Fortune* magazine at about $330,000,000. True, most of that money was tied up in DuPont company stock—but whatever the commandments of inherited wealth are, surely there must be a rider that says it's no longer a mortal sin to dip into your capital when your personal assets are in nine figures. One of the Phillies' executives said that Ruly would have kept the team if the decision had been solely his, and that Bob, whose own father had given him the ballclub as a present in 1943, was now like a rich kid who breaks his favorite toy in a fit of temper. At the age of forty-one Ruly had already been running the franchise, and running it well, for nine years. "It's what he loves and what he was trained to do," the executive said. "What else is he going to find that lets him use his best talents? Clip coupons? Go on vacation every other week? Not much drive and initiative in that." When such questions were put to Ruly Carpenter directly, he said simply: "My father is more adamant about all this than I am."

His father hadn't arrived at spring training until the minor-league camp opened. Ever since turning the club presidency over to Ruly in 1972, Bob had kept his distance from the major-league team; he simply liked to hang out at the Carpenter Complex and watch the kids. "This is what I'll miss," he said as he pointed toward Richie Gaynor. "This has been my fun and enjoyment. You see these country-lookin' kids come down here. They look lost; they don't know where they are. Four years later they're major leaguers: all dressed up, able to converse with people, confident, smooth. Of course, some of the best ones stay a little rough around the edges. There aren't many milkshake drinkers in the Hall of Fame.

"Last year some sportswriter drew up a chart that listed all the current major-league ballplayers and showed which organizations first signed them. The Pirates were way up there; the Dodgers were way up there—but the Phillies were first, with forty-four players who got their start in this system, and

I'm prouder of that than of anything else we've done with this franchise. It means more than winning the World Series. It says we've put something back into the game.

"The guy that buys the Phillies is also gonna buy the best farm system I've ever seen, and that means he's gonna save a hell of a lot of money. Because when you have to build up a farm system, it's a nightmare. At the time Daddy bought the Phillies in 1943, our system only had two teams. Our only legitimate prospect was Del Ennis. But Herb Pennock built an organization for us. He hired Johnny Nee and a lot of other scouts, and he added minor-league teams right and left. After the war every little town wanted one. So by the time the Phillies won the pennant in 1950, we had a twelve-team system. We were following Rickey's theory of quality out of quantity."

The contrasts between Carpenter and Rickey were more striking than the similarities. Unlike Rickey, Carpenter spent bonus money freely and continued to focus on size rather than speed as the hallmark of the true baseball prospect. But the biggest difference was that Rickey had the imagination and daring—or the drive and initiative—to break baseball's color line by signing Jackie Robinson in 1946, whereas Carpenter waited another whole decade to sign the Phillies' first black player. Bob Carpenter was one of several aristocratic owners (Tom Yawkey in Boston was another) whose traditional, almost feudal, values prevented them from scouting black talent until that talent was beating them with Christian regularity. The Phillies started looking seriously for black players in 1958 when John Quinn came over from the Braves as general manager, bringing with him a couple of black scouts, Bill Yancey and William "Judy" Johnson, and a readiness to spend Carpenter money on good athletes of any color. A few years later Johnson was helping to sign Richie Allen for a bonus of $60,000.

Judy Johnson was at spring training, too—nominally as a teacher of infield defense to minor-leaguers but really as a guest of the Carpenters. At the age of eighty-one he was expected to do no more than dignify the camp with his presence as a Hall-of-Fame player with a half-century of scouting experience. From 1918 to 1936 Johnson was a stellar third baseman in the Negro Leagues; fragmentary records credit him with a lifetime batting average of .349. But as a Negro League manager he also discovered and developed whole teams of players, including the great Josh Gibson. Later Johnson scouted for the Philadelphia A's under Connie Mack but was never allowed to sign the black talent he found. The A's would still be in Philadelphia, Johnson liked to say, if only Connie Mack had allowed him to grab Larry Doby, Minnie Minoso, and Hank Aaron—each obtainable for less than $5,000.

"I have a good eye for talent," Johnson said, "and a lot of ex-ballplayers don't. Not just anybody can be a scout. But I also love to teach, and I wish they'd let me coach some of the kids this year on how to steal bases. Most of these kids think it's only a matter of speed; they don't bother to study the pitchers' patterns. Once you solve a guy's pattern, you can make your break as soon as he turns his head the last time. Old as I am, I believe I could steal on some of the pitchers here. Just let me practice a few days."

Johnson stood near the backstop of diamond number four, next to Bob Carpenter and Lou Kahn, and studied Richie Gaynor's pattern. "This kid kind of rushes himself," he said. "When he checks the baserunner, he really doesn't *check* the baserunner."

"Maybe somebody can teach him that," Carpenter said. "But what about the other stuff? Does he have a future?"

"Little righties," Kahn said. He didn't need to complete the sentence.

"I see a live arm," Johnson said, "so I wouldn't hold his size against him. He'd have to show me that he couldn't make it."

"Why do scouts want a *right*-handed pitcher to be big?" I asked.

"Tall," Johnson said. "Tall and lanky so he can get more whip action on the ball, because he won't have the *natural* action a lefty does. But this kid's fastball moves enough. The problem I see is that you're gonna have to change his motion so he gets more control, and then maybe his fastball will lose that nice tail. But control's more important. Satchel Paige's fastball hardly moved at all. It was as straight as a string. When I warmed him up I could take one of those boxes that the ball comes in and put it down for a plate, and I could just give him a target and not have to move my glove that far."

"Was he the fastest you saw?" Carpenter asked.

"I think Smokey Joe Williams was a lot faster than Satchel. Great big right-hander. His father was a full-blooded Indian, and a lot of guys told Smokey Joe he should try to pass for Cuban to play in the big leagues. But he wouldn't do it. He was too proud."

"Did you know any players who did pass?" I asked.

"Babe Ruth was part black," Johnson said. "I can't prove it, but everybody in our league used to talk about it. You could see it in his facial features. And the body build—you know, the thin legs and high rump. I don't want to sound racial, but some things are just the way they are. You can see them. Like it wouldn't be racial to say the Negroes can run, because most of us can. And I've often thought that one reason Mr. Rickey broke the color line is that he was already in love with running. I know that he had a great vision of blacks and whites playing together, but maybe he wouldn't have had that vision unless he looked at the strategy of baseball in a certain way. He even wanted every *white* boy he signed to be able to run like a deer."

"What I remember best about him," Carpenter said, "is that he had me calling him Mr. Rickey, just like everybody else. He had that personality, you know, that eloquence, and he *used* it. He was the best salesman I've ever seen. One time, just after the war, he came to see me and spent about two hours analyzing my whole team, position by position, and he had some amazing insights. He'd really scouted us. He said the Phillies were like a painting of a beautiful woman, but her beauty didn't really show because one of her eyes was slightly cocked. We needed to retouch that face so her true beauty could shine through. That meant we needed a first baseman with power—and it just so happened that he had the right player for me.

"It was Howie Schultz. He was called Steeple Schultz because he was so tall, about 6' 7", and Rickey knew I liked big guys, see, because he'd scouted *me*. At the end of two hours I was making out a check to him for seventy-five thousand dollars for Steeple Schultz. Well, in the first game Steeple played for us he hit a tremendous home run, and that was the last big hit he ever got. At first base he was clumsy. He fell down in sections. He didn't have the all-around physical coordination, which is what Rickey scouted by. He was what Rickey used to call an anesthesia ballplayer—the kind of guy who looks like he might do it but never does. He almost does it. You stick with an anesthesia ballplayer and he'll put you right in the second division. And Rickey was able to get rid of one for seventy-five thousand dollars! He hypnotized me. That was the thing about Rickey. With that voice of his, and the way he used the language, he could absolutely *hypnotize* people."

"Branch Rickey," Lou Kahn said, "is still hypnotizin' people even though he's dead."

4:30: HOW TO WALK TO THE MOUND

Branch Rickey wasn't dead at all. He was there as soon as you started talking with anyone who knew anything about scouting or teaching, and his presence was more complex and compelling, more pertinent to baseball in the 1980s, than the popular images of Rickey as saint or genius that most of his disciples and biographers still promote. The nearest Rickey man was in St. Petersburg, just a short drive away, and so before the afternoon was over I was talking with George Kissell about Rickey's many-sidedness.

In his forty years with the Cardinals, Kissell had been an official scout only from 1958 to 1962. His real vocation was teaching, and he was famous for it. But the way he did his work—running the spring minor-league camp, providing roving instruction during the season, making decisions on promoting or releasing prospects—was close in spirit to scouting and influential on younger scouts. According to Carmen Fusco, a Mets' scout who began his career with the Cardinals, "Kissell shows you how to look at talent. I even studied his playbook, because it's like a bible of baseball. He's worth his weight in gold to the Cardinals—and George is a heavy guy."

Working an intra-squad game on one of the diamonds at the Busch Complex, Kissell looked like the director of a play in rehearsal. He trundled all over the field, stepping forward to put a finger on a prospect's chest while delivering quiet personal advice, stepping back to act out for everyone's benefit exactly what he wanted to see. He felt free to interrupt the action at any point to correct a stance, reposition a fielder, or replay a relay. At the start of one "inning" (a very fluid concept in this drama) a tall black pitcher named Ed Sanford walked out to the mound with what Kissell thought was too loose a shuffle. "Stop! Wait! C'mon back." Kissell retrieved Sanford and put an arm on his shoulder. "You have to *stride* to that mound like you mean business. You're the *boss*. Here, watch me." Kissell scowled his way into the role and set out for the mound, his body projecting pure purpose—from his full-handed grip on the ball to his deep spike-marks in the dirt. "Now," he shouted, "*that's* how to walk out to the mound."

Sanford tried it, but his new style lasted for about ten feet before shifting back to a kind of cakewalk, loose-hipped and splay-footed. "No! Stop! C'mon back." Again Kissell took the ball as a prop and demonstrated the kind of body language he wanted: firm, brisk, commanding. Then he returned the ball to Sanford and followed him stride for stride to the mound. Finally satisfied with a minor breakthrough, he allowed the action to continue.

Later, after the prospects had left, Kissell talked with some young boys who were scouring the diamonds for cracked bats and discarded balls. He directed them to a treasure trove, checked out their swings, and then hopped in a golf cart and drove back to the clubhouse.

5:30: THE TEACHER AS SCOUT

When Kissell spoke quietly, in his finger-on-the-chest style, his resonant voice took on a slight lisp. "Oh, yeah," he said, "I knew Branch Rickey real well. In fact, I got the last ball he ever autographed. I was one of his boyth." And when Kissell stepped back and raised his voice, it was always to act out the story he was telling—to *become* Branch Rickey at eighty-five, returning to the Cardinals in 1964 in the ill-defined and ill-fated role of "consultant."

"He walked like this," Kissell said, pushing his spikes along the concrete floor. "And the cigar in his mouth would bounce up and down like this. He was really too old then. He was still tryin' to go hard, to look at the whole minor-league system, and his mind wanted to do it, but his body was like a car with bad plugs. And the cigar would start to shake. . . . He was starting to get senile, you know, the memory was starting to go, and he'd lose track or repeat. It was a shame that a mind like that went. If you could have preserved it in alcohol or something, like in a science-fiction movie, you could run a baseball club with it today."

Kissell seemed embarrassed even to be hinting at Rickey's fallibility. I reminded him that Rickey had been sharp enough near the end to give the world one of the best descriptions ever framed of the declining ages of man. "First you forget names," Rickey had said, "then you forget faces; then you forget to zip your fly; then you forget to unzip your fly."

"Yeah," Kissell said, "he was always a very fluent man." But for the rest of that hour I was hypnotized by Kissell's own fluency. I was listening to one great teacher characterize another, which was the best line on Branch Rickey I was likely to get. It was like having a round-trip ticket to the other side of scouting.

"He could talk you into almost bein' a noncitizen, that's how persuasive he was. And he could always make people understand and remember his points because he knew how to *demonstrate*. . . . You're married, right? If I said to you, 'I just saw your wife in the clubhouse kissin' another man,' you'd question it, right? But if I took you in there and *showed* you, you'd believe it. Well, that was Rickey's way. 'Seeing is believing'—he used to say that all the time.

"At the spring camps he'd be out there on the field, and he'd say, 'Okay, *you*. You're the second baseman. The ball's hit here. Now where do you go?' And then he'd *show* 'em. And he'd say, 'All the second basemen, get your hand up'— and he'd have about eight in the whole big group—and he'd say, 'Now this is the way we're gonna do it. And we're all gonna do it the same."

"And then he'd take one of his coaches, and he'd say, 'Okay, George, now I want you to go down to diamond four and teach this to the D clubs.' And we had about eight D clubs. And he'd go down with you and watch you teach, and later on he'd give you pointers on your teaching.

"Another saying he had was 'Over the Horizon.' When you're eighteen, you start out; twenty-five, and you're in the big leagues. So there's an arc there. When you're eighteen, you can run faster than you will at twenty-five, and you probably throw harder, hit the ball harder, and have more range in the field. All right, what happens in between? Your range—you learn how to play the hitters; at eighteen you might've played Manny Trillo the same way you played Dave Kingman. All right, hittin'—you won't hit the ball any harder at twenty-five, but you've got a better strike zone, and you're gonna make a guy *pitch*. Or if you're a pitcher—you know how to change speeds now; you got a better curveball; you got better control . . . even though your fastball may be a foot shorter, 'cause there's only so many in that arm.

"And, oh, we didn't cover running. You may not be as fast at twenty-five, but you'll get better leads. You might get on first base and notice that the leftfielder is playin' the hitter deep; so if the hitter lays one over third, you're off! Before, at eighteen, you didn't pay much attention. All you did was look at the coach, and then you'd get thrown out by this much. Now you don't. So that's Over the Horizon.

"Rickey had another expression: 'Quickie.' That was a player who moved up fast—D, C, Double A, Triple A, Big Leagues—a kid with maybe four tools and good potential. Rickey wanted to *push* a guy like that; he wanted all the coaches to swoop on that guy, like eagles. Well, when Rickey came back as a consultant in 1964, he thought this one kid was a Quickie; but Johnny Keane, the manager, didn't think he was. And Rickey got mad enough to swear. He said, 'Goddamn it, I say he *is* a Quickie, and I'm a son of a bitch if he's not.' Everybody backed off! Because they'd never heard Rickey swear before. But around the other corner Johnny Keane says, 'I don't like the kid. I don't think he can play. But the old guy thinks he's a Quickie, and he wants to stick him down my throat.'

"My job then was kind of a go-between, and I tried to soften all the conflicts, keep both sides happy. But at the end of the season Johnny Keane quit—after winning the World Series. And then in 1965 at the Winter Instruction League, Rickey got fired. And he swore that day too.

"During that time he was here, he used the same ideas that he always had and most of 'em were good. But I'd changed *sliding*. His way was to have a big old sandpit, with a rope on one end you were supposed to slide underneath. So in 1964, at camp, he says one day, 'George, you got 'em ready to slide? Where are they? I want 'em over here at the pit.' I says, 'I want to show you something,' and I brought out the kids in *football* pants. I says, 'It protects the uniform, keeps it from gettin' dirty, so we don't have to dry-clean . . .'

" 'EXCELLENT I-DE-A,' he says. He saw how it saved money, see. He says, 'Kenny, write that down!'—Kenny Blackburn was the secretary who used to follow him all around. 'Now,' I says, 'I want to show you something else,' and I had the kids slide on the *grass;* it was hosed down, so it worked great. Rickey says, 'Judas Priest, that's an excellent i-de-a. I think you've got something there. Kenny, are you writing this down?'

"Eighty-five years old and he could still learn something new in this game. But you had to really *show* him where his ideas were old. . . . We still use a lot of his drills here—like makin' kids field bushels of balls a day; literally, they have to tote a whole basket. But my main theory is a little different from Rickey's. He believed that kids tend to practice the things they already do well, and he wanted to work out a balanced program to fill in the holes in everybody's game. My philosophy is: work from a kid's talent, push him harder on the things that you think he does well. So I scout the ten fastest kids in camp and make 'em bunt an extra hundred balls a day when everybody else is through. And I scout the ten best hitters in camp, and over ten days each one'll hit maybe seven hundred balls more than the other kids. Now, I'm not gonna forget about all these other kids, but I believe that a coach has to scout—and I think that's why the Cardinals put kids in the big leagues so quick.

"And I have a theory of switch-hitting. We've developed a lot of good switch-hitters—Simmons, Templeton, Mumphrey, Scott, Ramsey, Herr—and I always claim it's because the atmosphere is right. I do this: I scout around the camp, and I listen to the managers, and I might hear one say, 'This kid can run, field, and throw, but he can't hit.' Is he a right-hand hitter? 'Yeah.' Okay, I want to turn him around, so a right-hand pitcher's curve is always comin' *to* him. I just take the ones who can fly pretty good, and I get about four a year and take 'em to the Winter Instruction League. I have three guys who come down to help me: Dave Ricketts, who was a punch-and-judy switch-hitter; and Hal Lanier, who was a leg switch-hitter; and Ted Simmons, who's a power switch-hitter—he always comes with me, 'cause he's like a son of mine.

"Every day in the Winter Instruction League, two of my switch-hit prospects play in games while Ricketts and Lanier pitch to the other two—and Ricketts and Lanier can throw by the hour. Next day the two who played stay back and hit; the two who hit play in a game. And so on. . . . What's your name? Kevin? I'd say, 'Okay, Kevin, you're gonna play in at least half the games in the Winter Instruction League, and I don't care if you hit .100. I just want you to work on switch-hitting.' See, if I wasn't the boss, I couldn't say that. Bein' the boss, I can say, 'Okay, let's go, this is for you not for me.' And that's what I mean about an *atmosphere* where switch-hitters can develop.

"If you don't count pitchers, about eighty percent of the guys who make the majors play a different position there than they played when the scouts first saw them. Most get converted because of what the organization needs. Say you're low on shortstops. Okay, you scout up the prospects and you find a centerfielder or rightfielder who can run like hell, got a good arm, not much bat. So you put him at shortstop, where he won't have to hit too much, and then you work and work with him. Russell—I remember Bill Russell when he was an out-fielder in the Dodgers' system. Walter Alston said, 'Goddamn, I need a shortstop.' They put him in there, and he took enough ground balls. We converted Ramsey from centerfield to the infield, and he took enough ground balls. . . . Look, you got good hands, a good arm, and you take enough ground balls, you *gotta* get better. It's like if you sharpened knives, and you sharpened two thousand this year, and two thousand next year, by God by the third year you oughta be able to sharpen knives!

"Now with the infield. Sometimes you see a kid who doesn't have the real good hands, but he's got speed and arm and bat, so you think: 'I'll try him in centerfield or rightfield.' Or you see a kid at second base or shortstop who's a step slow, maybe because he's built big. So you think: 'If he can hit with a little power, I'll try him at third base.' That's what happened to Graig Nettles when he was with the Twins—Carew was ahead of him at second base, and they saw that Nettles didn't have the range for the middle of the infield but they didn't want to lose his bat. So they made him a third baseman, because third base equals power plus arm plus glove. Nettles is fast with his *upper* body, but he can't get his *feet* goin' as fast.

"You don't see too many big-legged second basemen or big-legged shortstops. Why? Any scout could tell you. Range! The ones with range have little tiny legs. Concepcion, Ozzie Smith, Bud Harrelson—little tiny legs. Gary Templeton—little tiny legs. Okay, what about Chris Speier? *Big* legs, no range. He's got good *hands*, a good *arm*, hits the ball—but no range. Bucky Dent? Big legs, no range. But Willy Randolph, what's he got? Little tiny legs. Burleson? Little ones. Doug Flynn? Little tiny legs. Ken Boyer? He had big legs and wound up playin' third base. Graig Nettles? Big legs, third base. Pete Rose? *Great* big legs! But remember, he started out as a second baseman 'cause he knew what to do with any ball he could get to. Manny Trillo? Little tiny legs."

It sounded like a poem. And every time I heard the refrain, "little tiny legs," I imagined some insect stationed at second or short. Kissell was referring, of course, to thin calves—at least I think that's why he kept making a circle with his thumb and forefinger—and so I took a look at *his* calves. They were massive. He noticed my attention and said, "I used to play third base."

George Kissell was a minor-leaguer in the Cardinal system from 1940 to 1952. For the first three of those seasons his boss was Branch Rickey. "Money—he was bad that way. One year I made seventy-five dollars a month, which was ridiculous even in those days, and I hit .373 that year. Next spring I held out for a hundred-fifty a month—this was just for the months of the season!—and he let me sit a few weeks, and then he offered a hundred twenty-five, said he wanted to be generous 'cause I was one of his boyth. When he signed new kids, he didn't send the contracts in. So if it turned out you could play, he kept you and paid you a little. If you couldn't play, boom!—your contract's in the wastebasket. He was a sharpie."

"What happened," I asked, "to the money the players *weren't* getting?"

Kissell said nothing, but made a grand gesture of a man stuffing a wad into his right front pocket. Charlie Chaplin couldn't have acted out the point any better.

6:30: THE RICKEY WAY

Before I left the Busch Complex, I asked Paul Fauks, the Cardinals' director of player development, about a special report the organization commissioned in 1976. Arnold Reisman and William Cox, two professors of operations research at the Case-Western Reserve School of Management, had produced a "cost-benefit analysis of the player procurement and development program of the Cardinals."

"The whole report was written in that style," Fauks said, "and I doubt whether many people in our office could understand it all. What we *could* understand seemed to be what we were already doing—like hiring more scouts and instructors, staying out of the Bureau, concentrating on growing our own talent as a way of dealing with high major-league salaries. The report said we should add another minor-league affiliate. The irony was that the report cost us almost a hundred thousand dollars—about what it would have taken to add another minor-league affiliate."

"In essence," the report said, "we are recommending a program that will resemble the system that Branch Rickey developed many years ago for the St. Louis Cardinals. The Cardinals' farm system will produce an excess of young, talented players: the Cardinals will keep the best and sell or trade the others. Note: what was good in Rickey's time is even better now that many major-league clubs are reducing their minor-league systems to the bare minimum allowed."

The report seemed to assume that the Rickey way was a game strategy expressible in mathematical terms. It left out Branch Rickey himself; in fact, it left out both Branch Rickeys.

On the one hand it ignored his exploitive methods and the historical circumstances that made them possible—a huge pool of cheap labor, un-unionized and relatively docile, and a small-town America able to support a minor-league baseball empire three times the size of the present system. If the Cardinals really wanted to revive Rickey's principle of quality out of quantity, they would have to add fifteen or eighteen affiliates instead of just one.

On the other hand the report ignored Rickey's innovative baseball mind, which defined teaching and scouting as two sides of the same activity, and his dynamic personality, which survives in the work of the very *boyth* he exploited. Rickey's legacy is experiential—less likely to be seen in the pages of a systems-analysis report than in clubhouses, batting cages, and the dust of diamond number four. At least that's where I had seen it. And seeing is believing.

4 BIG DADDY

For the seventh consecutive year, the Pirates are one of the seventeen participating members in the Major League Scouting Bureau, headed by Jim Wilson, former general manager of the Milwaukee Brewers. A staff of sixty-one scouts in the United States will do the field work for the Pirates and the other sixteen clubs. The information they gather for the semi-annual baseball drafts is fed into a computer in Newport Beach, California, and relayed by a computer system to the member clubs.

—*Pittsburgh Pirates'* Media Guide, *1981*

In the bottom of the first inning Lee Mazzilli slammed a curveball deep to the gap in right-center. "Oooohs" from the St. Petersburg crowd, mostly Met fans: they read the trajectory as a sure extra-base hit, failing to factor in the speed of Omar Moreno, the Pirates' centerfielder. Moreno accelerated over the last thirty yards as if jets had kicked in, and without breaking stride he extended his glove and allowed the ball to catch him. I could only imagine that a stop-action photo sequence, even with sophisticated equipment, would still have registered Moreno as a blur.

"Best defensive centerfielder in baseball," said the Pittsburgh scout sitting next to me. "Andre Dawson's a better all-around player, but Moreno saves our ballclub fifty doubles and twenty triples a year that'd go by most fielders. He's pure speed. I grade on a scale of zero to sixty, with thirty as a major-league average, and I'd say that Moreno is a sixty runner—the same way I'd say that Nolan Ryan throws a sixty fastball."

Then, in a thought process he's made into a habit, this scout's expression of love for individual skill led quickly to a

statement of hatred for the organization he believed was ru-
ining the Pirates and the scouting profession itself. "Moreno
was a sixty runner the first time I ever saw him. Herb Raybourn
and I signed him in 1969, out of a tryout camp in Panama.
He was just a little skinny-ass kid, sixteen years old, but he
was as fast then as he is now. See, I don't project on running
or throwing: a kid either has those abilities or he doesn't. But
the Scouting Bureau likes to project. One of their reports on
a twenty-year-old college boy might say that his arm and speed
are below average but will eventually be above average. That's
goofy! It's just one more way that the Scouting Bureau is fucked
up."

Howie Haak (pronounced Hake) was taking no notes on the
game. His only scouting prop was a large popcorn cup that
served as his spittoon all through the afternoon. Generally
regarded as the champion tobacco-chewer in baseball (i.e., the
world), Haak has averaged between one and two packs of Red
Man a day since 1928. He even has a spittoon in his Cadillac,
hooked up with a brass ring so it won't tip over when he puts
on the brakes. The bad news is that Haak doesn't always hit
the spittoon. Other scouts, serious chewers among them, had
told me in wonderment about dinners with Howie: watching
him drink cocktails and devour soup, salad, shrimp, and the
rest—all with a plug of tobacco still bulging his cheek.

"That's true. I don't have to spit; I can swallow a little of
the juice. I learned to do that in the minors when I played for
a guy named Specs Toporcer. He had a ten-dollar fine if you
ate anything in the clubhouse. We played a doubleheader one
time, and after the first game I got a hot dog and hid it in my
glove between bites. He saw me chewin' and said, 'Whattaya
got?'—and I was able to slide the cud over to the front and
show him that. But tobacco really keeps me from eatin' so
much: it's sweet and it keeps my appetite down. Good laxative,
too. If I didn't chew, I'd probably be twice as big as I am."

Howie Haak *was* big, even at the age of seventy. He still
had the body of a catcher, thick-limbed and solid. His waist

had become more barrellike than his chest, and he walked with a bad limp (the result of an old knee injury), but he looked strong enough to maintain the schedule that had been his standard until 1979—forty-five weeks a year on the road. Multiplying by thirty-six years as a scout, and translating it all into lonely space: Howie Haak had covered more miles than anyone in the history of scouting.

Among his colleagues, men who themselves see life as one long road trip, Haak was honored for this durability—and for his perceptiveness and versatility and the kind of power he wielded within the Pirate organization. But he was most famous for his work in Latin America, where he had opened up whole countries for major-league scouting. For three decades, ever since Haak helped to steal Roberto Clemente from the Dodgers, the Pirates' roster had been peppered with names like Mejias, Javier, Sanguillen, Moreno, Peña, DeLeon, and Guante. And thousands of players and coaches throughout Latin America had come to know Haak simply as Grandfather or Big Daddy. "We thank God for him," Manny Sanguillen said. "He's opened the door for us, and he's cared for us."

Latin America is the setting for most of the stories that other baseball men tell about Haak—like the time he signed a player out of a Mexican whorehouse. Or the time he sent Branch Rickey a scouting report on a Latin pitcher with *good PHFB* underlined; when the frugal Rickey phoned him in Cuba or Venezuela (or somewhere else it cost a lot to phone), Howie deciphered the code: "pecker-high fastball."

In real life Haak was an unreconstructed Rickey man—like George Kissell at St. Louis, Rex Bowen at Cincinnati, Al Campanis at Los Angeles, Rosey Gilhousen at Kansas City, or Walter Shannon at Milwaukee. Rickey men were trained in scouting by the master himself, and they still subscribe to his theories of pitching, hitting, and the primacy of speed. They still believe in the principle of quality out of quantity, even if quantity in Rickey's sense is not possible in the 1980s. They still regard Rickey as a visionary, even if his vision included forms of centralization in baseball that they now detest. And they still excuse Rickey's business practices, even if he sometimes practiced on them.

It was with Rickey that Haak's commentary began—a commentary, punctuated by spits, that ambled through a meaningless spring training game with a Canterbury pilgrim's pace and style.

The big thing about the major leagues today is that so many of these guys make so much money, they don't give a shit. They get a hangnail, they don't wanta play. Back when I was in the Cardinals' system, you couldn't afford to get hurt, because some guy'd come into the lineup and you might never get to play again. The Cardinals had twenty-some farm clubs, and one year—1933, I think it was—they had nine catchers in Double-A ball, which was the highest classification then. So Rickey was in a position where if a major-leaguer demanded too much money, he'd just get rid of him and bring somebody up from the farm system to take his place.

I look back over those days, and I think how we had to travel by train all the time—and today these bastards argue about flyin' to California. Geez, they gotta have a day off to go and another day off to come back. We'd get on a train in New York at six at night and get to Chicago at eleven the next morning. Your baseball clothes might be all wet and there was no way to dry 'em. You just put the fuckers *on* wet.

I was an infielder when I first started out but I couldn't even make the high-school team. Quit school in the tenth grade and joined the Navy. I lied about my age, and my old man lied for me, too, because he was real religious and he couldn't take the stuff I used to do. I'd skip school, sing dirty words to the hymns in church—that kind of stuff. I was still an infielder when I got signed out of the Navy, but I didn't run too good and Rickey said, "I'm gonna make a catcher out of you." And he did, but I never got to the majors. That Cardinal system was just too deep. So then he made a scout out of me.

I think one reason he did it is that in 1941, after our season was over in Rochester, I was around the clubhouse when he called up. The manager had already taken off, so I got on the phone, and Rickey said, "I need an outfielder right now. Is there anyone in Rochester who can help me?" I said, "Yeah,

there is. You oughta take Musial and get him right up there."
Musial hit .425 for the Cardinals the rest of that season. And I
said, "You should take Kurowski." He said, "I've already got a
third baseman." I said, "Take him up there. He'll play next
year for you." Kurowski had that bad wrist from osteomyeli-
tis—but he could pull any son of a bitch in the world, I don't
care how fast he was, because his right hand was already
turned like that. The harder you threw the ball, the harder he
hit it. And then I said, "Take Dusak." Well, Dusak never developed, but he had the best natural ability of all of them. Out-run
Musial, out-throw Musial, hit the ball farther than Musial . . .
but not as often.

I went in the Navy again during the war, and while I was
out at sea I got traded to Brooklyn. Rickey had moved out
there, see. On the day the war ended I was just about to ship
out, and I called Rickey and said, "What're you gonna do with
me? I don't think I can play. I can get Lieutenant Commander
now," which was pretty good money, about five thousand. He
said, "How much you gotta have?" I said four thousand, and
he said, "Okay, don't go out. I can use you as a scout." And so
he took me to games to show me the ropes, and I got to sit
beside probably the greatest baseball scout in history. He taught
me to concentrate just on part of the field. It's natural to follow
the flight of the ball, but he showed me how to focus on one
side of the diamond—so if the pitcher doesn't follow through,
or the catcher doesn't shift, or someone doesn't break on the
ball, or the batter gets out of the box slow, I can pick all that
up at once.

One game we went to that August was between two Negro
League teams, the Kansas City Monarchs and the New York
Cubans. After the game Rickey said, "Who was the best player
you saw out there today?" I said, "Jackie Robinson, but he
shouldn't be at shortshop." Rickey just nodded. I didn't realize
that he wanted to break the color line in baseball the next year.
I thought we went to that game so he could check *me* out.

Rickey had been a teacher in college and he really never quit.
One year I traveled around with him to all twenty-four clubs in
the Dodger system, and I warmed up every single pitcher in the
organization. He'd stand behind me and dictate notes to his
secretary. He knew more about pitchers than anyone I ever
met, and he might've missed on two guys—said one would

make it to the majors who didn't, and said one wouldn't make it who did. He loved to teach the change-up: he'd take his hat and set it on home plate, and say, "You throw a change and hit that hat and I'll give you ten dollars." The way he taught the change was to keep a stiff wrist and draw the hand straight down, the way you pull a window shade. The first time you try that, the ball usually sails over the catcher's head. But when these kids aimed at the hat, they could bring the ball in for a good low strike. None of 'em ever hit the hat and he never had to pay any money.

You can teach the change; you can teach the curve; you can teach better mechanics—like how to shove off the rubber, or how not to open up the body too soon. So when I scout an amateur pitcher, I don't worry too much about that stuff. I look for the live arm and the good fastball. I stay away from wrist-wrappers, the guys who hook the ball in toward wrist when they start their delivery. Hookers—that's what I call 'em—usually don't have control, or they'll have it one day and three days later they won't have it. They're .500 or below pitchers. And short-armers: stay away from 'em. Guys who short-arm the ball, who don't get extension, usually came up with a bad arm.

I think Rickey was generally right about hitting. You write off the over-strider because you can't correct him. And you really can't correct a hitch in a guy's swing. I remember when Bill Mazeroski came up, Rickey said, "Too bad this boy has a hitch. He'll never be a good hitter." Well, Maz became an average major-league hitter: .270, .275. But he might've been greater if he'd just had a quiet bat. That's what Rickey wanted—a bat you could set a quarter on and not have it fall off while the hitter waited for the pitch.

But I don't really don't believe in scouting hitters. That's what the Yankees do, and that's why I could never work for them and be successful. I start with the footspeed and the arm, but they just go out and look for young guys who can hit. Now if all the kid can do is hit, and then he fails, what do you do with him? You might've wasted fifty thousand on him. And how many kids in the last ten years have come up to the majors through the Yankee system? Very few. Steinbrenner just signs the established players he wants, and he doesn't give a shit what it costs or who it hurts.

You should start with a kid who can run and throw above
average. If he doesn't hit, you can always use him on defense or
as a pinch-runner. But if he's that good an athlete, and if your
ballclub can afford to be patient, he'll usually learn to hit—not
with power maybe, but he'll learn to hit. Like Moreno. He was
in the minors for seven years, which was normal back in Rickey's time but today hardly anybody's there that long. Danny
Murtaugh wanted to release him, but I wouldn't let the Pirates
do it. Moreno just improved every year and now he's a fair offensive player—stole ninety-six bases last year. There's that
speed again.

Rickey was a fanatic about speed, and I guess I am, too. And
you can see for yourself: the Pirates are built on speed, the Cardinals are built on speed, the Dodgers are built on speed—and
they win. I like to get a stopwatch time on a kid in a sixty-yard
dash, because in baseball you run sixty yards more than you do
anything: first to third, second to home, centerfield to right-center. But I never time a hitter from home to first. What good
does it do you? Clemente—I don't think he ever ran to first
base under 4.4 or 4.5. That follow-through of his brought him
up and toward third base, so it took him three tenths of a second just to get out of the batter's box, but he was still the fastest man on our ballclub.

Clemente's the reason I started in to scout in Latin America.
I went with Rickey when he took over in Pittsburgh, and one
day he called me and said, "I want you to go up to Montreal
and look at a prospect for the minor-league draft. But I'm not
gonna tell you his name." I knew who it was, though. Another
Pirate scout, Clyde Sukeforth, had already been up to Montreal,
and he'd raved to me about this kid the Dodgers had hid out
there. The Dodgers knew Clemente was great but they hadn't
protected him on their major-league roster, so they didn't let
him play in Montreal: they were afraid another club would notice him and draft him away. When I walked into the Montreal
clubhouse, I said hello to Max Macon, the manager, and he
said, "You son of a bitch, what're you doin' here?" I said, "I
came to talk to you." He said, "You're fulla shit. You're here
to look at Clemente. Well, you aren't gonna see him play!"

I did see Clemente play in Puerto Rico after the season was
over, and my eyes almost popped out. I told Rickey: "We gotta
draft him. He's better than anything we have." So the next year

at spring training Clemente just tore up the Pirate camp with his speed and his arm and his bat, and I said, "What do you think of Clemente now?" Rickey said, "You're goin' to Cuba and the Dominican this summer. If there's any more of those creatures down there, I want 'em!"

That first year I got Bauta and Jiminez and Mejeias from Cuba, and Javier from the Dominican, for about a thousand dollars of bonus money—total. This was when bonuses for American players had gone through the roof. To get four guys that good in the States might've cost a hundred thousand, and the Pirates didn't have that kind of money. For example, right around this time I could've bought Ernie Banks from the Kansas City Monarchs for seventy-five hundred dollars, but Rickey vetoed the deal—said it was too much money. That's another thing about scouting, you can say this: that a scout can only be as good as his ballclub lets him.

The next year I went to Venezuela and Panama, and then I started to spend three or four months a year in Latin America. I was the first scout who went in all the countries. The Senators had been signing Cuban ballplayers for years, and they got into Latin talent for the same reason we did—to save money. Their big scout was Joe Cambria and he sent dozens of good ballplayers up here, but sometimes he'd just sign a kid and not turn the contract in; he wanted to tie up all the players. I found out about that and stole some of those kids. But Cambria never went out of Cuba, and I went everywhere. I could probably draw you a roadmap of Latin America—at least where they play baseball—and I went lots of places where there weren't any roads. Had to take a plane or a boat through the jungle.

That story about me signin' a guy out of a Mexican whorehouse is true. It was Lino Donoso in 1953—he pitched for Mazatlán in the Mexican League and he lived there with a madam. But the funny thing about that was that back in the spring of 1947, when the Dodgers trained in Cuba, Donoso and Minoso—Minnie—showed up at the ballpark in Havana for a tryout and Rickey told them to try somewhere else. See, they were both black, and this was Jackie Robinson's rookie year, and Rickey didn't want the Dodgers to be the only team with black players. Hell, Rickey had Monte Irvin signed and then turned him over to the Giants so he could get a black guy on another club. By the time I signed Donoso in the whorehouse, he was over thirty years old. He pitched all right for a couple more years and then he was through.

You know, I took Latin and French in high school, and I went to college in the off-seasons and took German, and I've never been able to use any of them. And I just picked up Spanish by scouting. I'm not fluent. I don't conjugate the verbs: I can do the *ar* verbs but not the *er* or the *ir*. I know enough Spanish to run tryout camps and get the good guys' signatures on contracts. You have to use tryout camps down there, because most of the league games are on Sundays and you could go to fifty games and not see any prospects, unless someone had tipped you off. So I conduct these camps, like the camps the Cardinals had in the States back in the 1930s, with maybe four hundred kids. First I make the kids run, and anyone who can run the sixty-yard dash in seven seconds or less gets to throw. Then the ones who can throw get to hit. And then the ones who can hit, or who at least have bat speed, get signed.

They've tightened up restrictions in Mexico and Puerto Rico, but everywhere else down there you can still sign 'em real young. I got Tony Peña when he was sixteen, Moreno when he was sixteen—and I *could* have had Juan Marichal when he was sixteen. Saw him at a tryout camp in the Dominican and just thought he was too little, not worth the risk of three hundred dollars.

Most of the Latin kids who play baseball come from poorer families. The middle-class families won't let their kids sign; they expect them to go to the universities, which're usually free, and become doctors or lawyers or engineers. And today the kids you do sign want more money. Where you used to give a hundred dollar bonus, now you have go to fifteen hundred. I went to fifteen *thousand* on Alfredo Edmead. I saw him and Alberto Lois at the Pan-American Games in 1975, and about fifteen scouts were there from other clubs and the Pirates just knocked 'em out of the box. I guess they were waitin' to see something else. Hell, you see a guy run, you see him throw, you see him hit—you don't need to see any more. Lois would be in the major leagues right now, except that he had a car accident a year ago and lost an eye. And get this: Edmead in his first year of pro ball hit .331, and by August 15 he had sixty stolen bases, thirty-one doubles, fifteen triples, and eight home runs—and that night he runs in from the outfield for a fly ball, dives for it, hits his head on the second baseman's knee, and it kills him! He may have been the best ballplayer I ever signed.

I still go to Latin America in the off-season, but I've slowed down. Up to two years ago, here's what I did. I'd come down here in the spring and cover the fifteen clubs that trained in Florida, and while I was down here I'd scout amateurs in night games. When we broke camp, I'd drive straight across the south—Alabama, Louisiana, Texas—and I'd check out amateurs all the way to California and then up the coast. Before the June draft I'd cross-check the top forty or so prospects, and then I'd make up the Pirates' draft list. Then I'd go to Latin America for a couple of months. When I got back to the States, I covered major-league and minor-league games till the end of the season. Then I'd go down to Latin America again.

My wife used to travel with me in Latin America during the summer, but otherwise it's been a pretty lonely deal—never home for more than seven weeks in any one year. And frustrating. One time—think of this—I'm in Los Angeles and I get a call from Rochester to hustle in and see a high-school kid; the guy there says the weather is beautiful. I fly all night, get into Rochester about seven in the morning, go to bed for a few hours, wake up, and drive to the high school. I'm about a mile from the ballpark and here comes the goddamnedest rain you ever saw. Ballpark's underwater. Drive back to the motel, and then the sun comes out just like today. Hurry out to the airport and get on a plane to Portland, Oregon. Get to Portland, and I'm rained out. Get back on a plane, go back to Rochester— rainout! So now I've flown eight thousand miles, mostly at night, and I haven't gotten to see one inning of baseball.

I'll tell you how things go. We're in New York for the draft meeting in 1973, and the day before the draft a scout from California calls up and says, "I've got an outstanding prospect. Send someone out here to look at him 'cause I want to put him up on the draft list." So nobody wanted to go; they all just sat there, and I said, "Oh, hell, I'll go. Don't make that much difference to me." I got on a plane at eight in the morning, and before noon I was in L.A. workin' out Mitchell Page and Eddie Murray. Page could run like a son of a bitch—did the sixty in 6.4, and that's really pickin' 'em up and puttin' 'em down. I got on a plane, got back to New York at two in the morning, and then got up at seven to tell those guys to put Page right here in the draft list with Murray right behind him. So we got Page in the third round and were gonna take Murray in the fourth, but Baltimore grabbed Murray before it was our turn.

The draft has more or less made every club equal, and maybe it's made baseball better, but I think it's changed scouting for the worse. There isn't that much you can do to help yourself. Say that you scout in California, and there's eight top prospects there, and your team drafts twenty-third. They're all gone, and your whole year is gone. And the draft has taken a lot of the fun away. Let me tell you what I did on Gino Cimoli.

Gino's mother didn't want him to leave home. And Joe Devine, the Yankee scout, figured he had Cimoli locked because he told her the Yankees would let Gino start out right there in San Francisco. So in December of 1948 I called Rickey to let him know all this, and he said, "Can you strengthen his father's backbone through his stomach?" I said, "You want me to get Mr. Cimoli drunk?" He said, "I didn't say that." I said, "Well, when you get my expense report there's gonna be some entries on there for Ancient Age."

Gino's father worked from four to midnight, and for four days I went over to their house every morning at eight o'clock with two bottles of Ancient Age. I'd sit there and drink with him—because coffee kills me; I can't drink coffee—and then I'd drive him to work. Then Gino and I would go to a show, and then I'd go back to the house with him and wait till his father got home, and I'd stay till the last scout's car had left—about three in the morning. I knew I couldn't sell Mrs. Cimoli, so I bore down on the father.

After the fourth day I said, "Mr. Cimoli, who wears the pants in your family?" He said, "*I* do." I said, "I don't believe it. Gino wants to sign with Brooklyn for twelve thousand dollars, and you want him to sign, and your wife's holdin' up the whole deal." He said, "She's not holdin' it up another minute!" So he staggered up and got her out of bed—she was wearin' one of those old nightcaps women used to wear and a great big kimono—and he said, "Go wake Gino up. We're gonna sign this contract right now!"

The next day I signed a kid named Wayne Belardi out of Bellarmine Prep. He said, "If you give me fifteen thousand, I'll sign." I said okay. He said, "But I want to talk to Joe Devine first." I said, "No, if you call Joe Devine, the deal's off." So he signed, and Devine was really pissed off. He said, "You son of a bitch, I worked on Cimoli and Belardi for three years and you just came in and signed 'em." I said, "Joe, you wasted too fuckin' much time." But he liked me, see. He'd kid me after that.

Now at that same time I wanted to sign a third Italian kid from California, a boy named Rodini out of Sacramento, and I was lucky not to get him. His father remembered that Rickey had the Sacramento ballclub when the Cardinals pulled that franchise out in 1943. He was wrong: Rickey was with the Dodgers in 1943, and Sam Breadon was the guy who took the team out of Sacramento. But he blamed Rickey and he wouldn't let his kid sign with us. Rodini signed with the Red Sox, and it turned out he had hammer toes. No one knew it— he could play once a week and look great—but when he went to his first spring training, he was crippled. They operated on his toes, and it didn't come out right, and he played about five games the rest of his career.

Nowadays it's even harder to know about medical problems, because if your club belongs to the Scouting Bureau you're not gonna have the local manpower to check a kid out thoroughly. And the Bureau itself usually doesn't find out about disabilities, because their scouts go for coverage instead of depth. Four years ago we signed a pitcher who'd had a sore arm since his sophomore year in high school. I didn't have the time to see him more than once, so I didn't know that every two weeks he could throw the shit outa the ball but the rest of the time his arm was dead. Two years ago we wasted a first-round draft choice on a bad diabetic. He didn't let the Pirates know, and at his first spring training he went into shock. He fell down out there in the field and laid out there and puked and everything else. He also had a bad knee, and when they gave him some antibiotic it swelled his prick up that big! They had to cut it open to drain it. He almost died. He's back again this year, but I'd say he isn't gonna play.

It's even trickier to know what a kid's mentally—how teachable he is, or how he's gonna mature as a man. But I usually give a young guy the benefit of the doubt, because the Pirates are more tolerant than most teams, less tight about black or Latin style. Our big question is: can the kid play ball? Dave Parker, for example. He was drafted in the fourteenth round,

but he shouldn'ta been. He got kicked off his high-school baseball team, and you'd hear scouts spread the rumor that he used
dope—which wasn't true. They all talked about his bad attitude. Parker was from Cincinnati, and after the draft Joe
Bowen, the Reds' scouting director, said, "Geez, you guys really
picked a dandy." Well, we did, but not the way Joe meant.

Listen, I'd take my chances any day on guys like Parker instead of college kids. You start goin' after these college ballplayers and you go right down the drain. You pay good money,
and then if they're not in the major leagues in two years they
quit on you. And if you look on the field right now, I don't
think the Pirates have a college player out there—except for
Garner, who we didn't sign, and Tekulve. The Yankees and
Cubs go for college players, and they stock their lower minor-
league teams with twenty-two-year-olds. In the rookie leagues
the Pirates have all seventeen- and eighteen-year-olds, and we're
probably last every year. Sure, those Cub and Yankee prospects
beat your ass, but then they don't go anywhere.

The whole point is to bring a kid along slowly and train him
your way. Hire more scouts, get more minor-league clubs, sign
more players—and then when a major-league player threatens
to become a free agent, you bring up a guy to take his place so
you don't have to pay a million dollars a year to one player.
That's the Rickey way. The problem is that it takes money for
long-term investment, and the Pirates don't have it or won't
commit it. In 1979 we won the pennant and the World Series
and still lost one million-two. In 1980 we lost two million-one.
And now we have one *less* farm club than we used to, and
we're locked into that Scouting Bureau, and in another few
years we could be down like the Mariners or the Cubs. Once
the real effect of the Bureau shows up, it'll be so fuckin' bad
the Pirates won't know what hit 'em.

We got into the Bureau to save money. Joe Brown was our
general manager, and he was one of the founders of the Bureau
in 1974, and so we paid a hundred-twenty thousand to join
and then we fired twelve guys. We went from seventeen scouts
to five. And get this: the Bureau was supposed to assemble a
staff of good scouts from the individual clubs, but mostly they
wound up with scouts that the clubs didn't care about. Joe
Brown told the Bureau they could have any scout but me, and
then he got ahold of three or four other Pirate scouts and said,

"If the Bureau talks to you, let me know and I'll tell them they can't have you."

Maybe the Pirates screwed the Bureau, but now the Bureau scouts screw us. They turn in anything that moves. Their whole scouting system is based on fear: they're afraid they're gonna miss someone, so they send out a stack of reports that high. And those reports are faceless, because our scouting director doesn't have a feel for the grades or the habits of whoever wrote the report, the way he would for someone on his own staff. So you arrange the reports in order of their grades, and you just don't have time to check the players on the bottom. You try to follow up on the top ones, and that means that all your scouts are cross-checkers now—they have to look at a kid once and say whether he's a prospect or not, and not everyone can do that.

The irony is that the Bureau has cost us money. It takes eight hundred thousand dollars to develop a ballplayer—that's if you divide your total budget for the scouting and farm systems by the number of major-leaguers you produce. And I figure that belonging to the Bureau has cost the Pirates two fewer legitimate prospects a year. That's one-million-six-hundred-thousand dollars a year, and over six years that's nine million dollars! That's how much we've *lost* by joining the Bureau.

I was puzzled by Howie Haak's computations, but I hesitated to pursue the Bureau issue any further. For one thing, I realized that his opposition came from the marrow of his bones—the instinctive response of a die-hard individualist, in his fiftieth year in pro baseball, to a system he saw as anonymous, collectivist, and above all bureaucratic. (To date no Major League Scouting Bureau computer has relayed a report on a pitcher's PHFB.) For another thing I could sense his angry perception that for all his clout, as much clout as any scout ever had, he didn't have enough to contend against impersonal economic forces. He knew that decisions about talent, training, and the quality of scouting life are determined these days by the owners' tax breaks and stadium deals, and by the players' spiraling salaries and fringe benefits. That feeling of futility explained Haak's use of everything from rhetorical prayers ("Thank God

the Bureau doesn't try to scout in Latin America") to ad hom-
inem attacks ("The guy who runs the Bureau is a big donkey—
never did know how to scout") to wishful thinking ("I don't
know for sure, but I think the Pirates may get out of the Bureau
pretty soon").

The game was almost over. It had long since become a
laugher for the Pirates, mostly because of errors by the Mets,
and half the fans had already left the park. In the bottom of
the ninth Bob Bailor, the Mets' lead-off man, slashed a one-
hopper over third base, and Dale Berra made a fine backhand
stab and a strong off-balance throw to beat Bailor by a step
at first base. The whole play was more grist for Howie Haak's
mill. "There's an example right there. We took Berra in the
first round of the draft, and that year I only saw a few guys
better than him in the whole country. But the Bureau had him
in as number ninety on their preferential list, and on that
twenty-to-eighty scale I think they gave him a grade of forty-
five. A scout'd have to be blind to do that! Berra ran above
average, threw above average, had good bat speed, could hit
the ball out of any ballpark, so what the hell are they lookin'
for? . . . Paul Moskau at Cincinnati—now just think of this—
was in the big leagues before he'd been in pro baseball for a
full year. The Bureau had graded him as a twenty-two. That's
two points above your grandmother."

I decided then to try one last question. How would this
ultra-loyal Rickey man reconcile his damnation of the Scouting
Bureau with the fact that Rickey himself had been a proponent
of pooled scouting, had envisioned a Bureau ten years before
one existed, had worked out in the 1960s the ruthless cost-
cutting logic used by the Bureau's founders in the 1970s? "Each
club would get more dependable information," Rickey claimed
in *The American Diamond*, "from fifty nonpartisan institu-
tionalized scouts than they are now receiving from the present
fifteen per club, one man to a spot, covering the entire country."

I phrased the question as tactfully as I could and received
for an answer: silence. Or maybe Haak spat an expletive into

the cup. I couldn't be sure because of the crowd noise that followed the last out of the game, a weak fly ball to Moreno. But it didn't matter. Everybody lives with contradictions, and baseball men live with more than most. If Howie Haak had played in any other farm system than Rickey's, he almost certainly would have made it to the major leagues—but that only deepened his respect for Rickey's brilliance. And Rickey apparently reserved his greatest affection for characters like Howie Haak, whose Chaucerian crudity contrasted so perfectly with Rickey's own straitlaced style. Kenny Blackburn, Rickey's former secretary, tried to explain this paradox for me: "Rickey loved Howie the way that Vince Lombardi loved Paul Hornung and Max McGee, the very guys who used their imagination to break his training rules. It was like Howie was Rickey's secret self—the one that ducked out of church to go drink and chew tobacco and say 'fuck' all the time. Because what they had in common was enough: an incredible eye for talent."

Howie's cup was overflowing, tobacco juice oozing over the top—a real treat for some guy in the ballpark's clean-up crew. He got ready to leave, then said something about going to another game that night after he and the Pirates got back to Bradenton. Good-looking young pitcher. And the whole drive would only be a couple of hours each way.

5 THE LANGUAGE OF SCOUTING

Language is not an abstract construction of the learned, of the dictionary-makers, but is something arising out of the work, needs, ties, joys, affections, tastes of long generations of humanity, and has its bases broad and low, close to the ground.

—Walt Whitman, "Slang in America"

The language of scouting is really several vocabularies: numbers or letter grades project a player's skills into a possible future; psychological catchwords describe his makeup; and a money code expresses an ultimate evaluation, the dollar sign on the muscle. But most basic is a vocabulary sharpened by slang, superlative, and metaphor—a descriptive catalogue of tools and talents, bodies and body parts.

Quickie, anesthesia ballplayer, quiet bat, wrist wrapper (what Howie Haak calls a "hooker"): these were some of Branch Rickey's contributions to the word-hoard of scouting. In the 1980s many scouts still use these coinages and others that go back just as far. On a spring Sunday in Lakeland, Florida, as I watched a player touted as the best amateur pitcher in America in 1981, I listened to the language of scouting and caught a sense of the oral tradition behind it.

BOY: ANY AMATEUR PLAYER

At the age of twenty years and seven months Ron Darling was 6'3", 205 pounds, strong, poised, articulate—all in all, "a

mature-looking prospect." But until he signed his first professional contract, he would remain a *boy* or even a *lad*.

Pitching for Yale in the first game of a doubleheader against
Purdue on Charlie Gehringer Field at Tigertown, Darling had
an audience of twenty-four, of whom twenty were major-league
scouts. Ed Katalinas, who had helped to design this training
complex, held court next to the small observation tower behind
the backstop. Dick Gernert of the Rangers was there, and so
were Al LaMacchia of the Blue Jays, Frank DeMoss of the
Cubs, Tony Stiel of the Braves, Dick Teed and Regie Otero of
the Dodgers. Three Phillies' scouts were sitting off by themselves instead of socializing with their colleagues.

"They sent three? I'd call that *over*-scoutin'."

"Nah, one's there just to check up on the other two, to make
sure they don't say hello. Loose lips sink ships."

"Loose lips sink draft picks."

"Hey, how ya been? Feelin' better now?"

"Oh, fine, fine. It wasn't serious. I'm rested up and ready."

"Well, you know, at your age you got to start cuttin' down
on pussy. No more than once a day from now on."

"Hey, that's a prescription I can follow. Every Saturday
night my wife and I hold it up and bet which way it's gonna
fall."

Over near the Yale bench Bill Kearns of the Mariners was
studying Ron Darling's warm-up pitches. Seattle would have
first pick in the June draft and would almost certainly choose
a pitcher. On the basis of Kearns's reports they might make
Ron Darling the number one boy in the country.

SNOWBIRD: A NORTHERN SCOUT ASSIGNED TO FLORIDA IN EARLY SPRING

While baseball lies dormant in the north, the snowbird flies
south where there are too many games for local scouts to cover.
Florida is patched with baseball fields, more per square mile
than in any other state, and in the spring every one of them
seems to be in use every day. Dozens of northern colleges come

down for early season games, so the snowbird may be able to get a line on players to follow next month, back home.

Dick Lawlor, the Phillies' scout for New England, had already followed Darling for a year. He had watched through the spring of 1980 as Darling, in his first season as a pitcher, compiled a record of 11–2 with two saves and a 1.31 earned-run average. And he had watched through that summer, as Darling competed against top amateur talent in the Cape Cod League, where he was named Most Valuable Player. Now Lawlor sat on the observation tower steps with two other Philadelphia scouts, Joe Reilly and Randy Waddill. He was easy to identify as a snowbird, because his face was newly sunburned.

"I sunburn easy. My father's Irish and my mother's Italian, born in Florence. I got his coloring and her features. But look at Ronny. His father's Irish and his mother's Chinese-Hawaiian, and he got the Irish features and the darker coloring. Handsome kid. And just a *great* body."

Whenever possible, Lawlor said, he tried to "project bodies into the future." And sometimes that meant taking account of "ethnic factors"—like the tendency of Italian boys to gain weight in their twenties, at the very time that Polish boys tend to shed the last of their baby fat. But Lawlor knew of no ethnic factor, other than hybrid vigor in general, to help project an Irish and Chinese-Hawaiian body. Instead, he relied on "power, proportion, and energy. Especially energy. Ronny's quick, agile, . . . springy. He's wound tight."

WOUND-TIGHTNESS: THE POTENTIAL ENERGY VISIBLY PRESENT IN AN ATHLETIC BODY

Wound tight doesn't mean nervous. It may mean high-strung, but only in the way that racehorses are high-strung—the long hamstring muscles tapering to high gluteals, the whole body at rest still vibrating with power. This scouting metaphor may have originated, in fact, at the racetrack rather than the ballpark: sometimes a horse is said to be "wound tight" when in the starting gate it seems doubly poised, both relaxed and cocked.

Ultimately the comparison is either to the coils in the armature of a motor or (more likely) to a spring mechanism like a watch. Either way, the scout is talking about potential energy, in firm control but ready to become kinetic in an instant. "If a boy is wound tight, he lets you imagine him running when he's just walking. He has a live body."

DEAD BODY: ATHLETIC INERTIA, AS MANIFESTED BY SLOW REFLEXES, HEAVY FEET, OR BAD HANDS

Scouts associate one kind of dead body specifically with football, and many of them resent the sport for beefing up, and then banging up, baseball talent. After football season, they say, the player is less likely to be loose or extended than to be short-muscled, literally muscle-*bound*. "Bulk as in hulk" is Brandy Davis's contribution to this lore of dead bodies.

Rich Diana, the Yale first baseman, was also a star running back in football. In the first inning, with a big stride and an uppercut swing, he struck out on a fastball. In the third he lifted a long fly to left field. In the language of scouting Diana looked like a "good uppercutter," who tends to meet the ball at an upward angle and thus loft it for fence power—as opposed to a "bad uppercutter," who collapses his back elbow in toward the chest and fails to extend his arms. But some scouts surmised that Diana was a "one-tool player," with little baseball potential beyond the power swing.

At first base, for example, Diana seemed to lack "the soft hands." Soft hands are good; they are, in fact, prerequisites for a catcher or infielder at the professional level, allowing their owner to accept the ball rather than fearing it or fighting it. Of a fielder without soft hands it's sometimes said: "He couldn't catch a two-hopper eye-high."

In the sixth inning, when Diana hit a ground ball and was slow getting out of the box, the scouts began to sort out their impressions of his body.

"This boy runs like he's waitin' for his blockers."

"I got 4.6 on the watch."

"I got 4.7. Horseshit either way."

"It's only a *slightly* dead body. You know he has good athletic ability. Another week in Florida, he gets those muscles stretched out, he won't be so sluggish."

"Looks like Tarzan. Runs like Jane."

HORSESHIT: UNIVERSAL TERM OF DISPARAGEMENT IN BASEBALL

Any baseball talent, body, body part, effort, action, player, team, city, or scouting assignment can be *horseshit*. The term covers everything but the world of words—the world of stories, explanations, and scouting reports—at which point *bullshit* takes over.

A real sentence spoken by a scout discussing a former colleague: "His written report was all bullshit, and that's when I knew he was a horseshit guy."

Bullshit can be a verb; *horseshit* can't. (A sentence like "Don't horseshit me" would make no more sense to a scout than to a nonscout.) Novices sometimes elide the word into *horshit*, but the veterans get the first *s* down deep in the throat, with the tongue at the back of the palate, lots of air whistling past the lower teeth, and then they follow through for full emphasis. *Horsse-shit!*

The word is popular throughout baseball—with players, managers, umpires, and executives. And it's clear enough why scouts, whose business is evaluation, would find it a handy label for anything deserving a low grade. What remains unclear, though, is the *horse,* which is far more prevalent here than in the lingo of any other subculture or occupational group in America, even cowboys. It's absent from baseball talk in Latin America: scouts down there rely on the all-purpose *mierda,* with no animal prefix.

Is *horseshit* an image from the country days of baseball, like *bullpen* or *outfield pastures?* Probably not. Only a generation ago any American living in a city could see horseshit every day, and older scouts say that the word's baseball popularity is relatively recent. It might be that *horseshit* is really a modern scouting term that has the merit of *sounding* old-fashioned, allowing its user to think of himself as a traditional baseball man rather than an investment analyst constrained by bureaucratic procedures.

NEGATIVE SCOUTING: BEING RIGHT 92 PERCENT OF THE TIME

"If you just focus on a boy's faults," Al LaMacchia said, "you'll become certain that he's not a major-league prospect—and you'll almost always be right. But negative scouting can kill you, because you'll write off some boys who are *gonna* be great. Positive scouting means projecting a player into the future, and that means when you go to a game you focus more on tools than performance. Skills can be taught; talents can't.

"You see Ron Darling pitch a weak first inning. His delivery and follow-through are too straight up. He chokes the curveball. But those are just *skills*. And right away you see that he's blessed with the *talents:* the good live arm, the good low fastball, control on the mound, control on his pitches. So already you say 'prospect.' And then he retires the next twelve men in a row, and strikes out six of 'em."

CHOKING THE CURVEBALL: GRIPPING THE BALL TOO TIGHTLY OR TOO FAR BACK IN THE HAND

If you choke the curveball, your pitch will lack "bite." Instead of breaking sharply downward ("falling off the table"), it will usually be flat and slow, and easier to hit. Ron Darling's curve was a "lollipop," according to Dick Lawlor. "It needs less choke and faster arm action. As is, professional hitters could tee off on it."

But the Purdue hitters couldn't tee off, because Darling disrupted their timing by using his curve like a change-up, mixing it effectively with the fastball and slider. Purdue's few fair balls were either grounders or pop-ups. In the first inning Darling gave up two runs on a walk, two ground singles, and a key error by the shortstop. Hanging or breaking, the curves were out of the strike zone, and he fell behind hitters on the count. But from the second inning on, Darling threw the curveball for good slow strikes, even a few strike-threes, while establishing the fastball as his real out pitch.

ADDING A FOOT TO THE FASTBALL: GAINING PHYSICAL MATURITY AND THUS GREATER VELOCITY

Darling had filled out a little since last season, Lawlor said, and had become "that much" faster. (He held out his hands as if describing a prize trout.) The extra foot was a translation of velocity into distance, a way of saying how it might *feel* to bat against a good pitcher if the mound were moved closer.

Darling's fastball did not look overpowering. The scouts weren't disappointed, though, because they knew he had pitched an inning in relief the day before and a complete game three days before that, and because his pitch had such good "life" or "run." He threw it from a high three-quarter arm angle, instead of straight over the top, and the result was a sinking fastball that tailed in sharply to right-handed batters. In order to describe this pitch some scouts abandoned words in favor of shorthand (⌐), but my own notes incorporated one of Moose Johnson's coinages—"wicky fastball."

I also wrote down this idle computation: if a boy really added a foot to his fastball, it would be roughly equivalent to an extra 1.5 miles per hour. An 86 fastball, for example, would become 87.44. "In that case," one scout said, "I can tell you that I've seen high-school pitchers add *five* feet to their fastball between junior and senior year."

86 FASTBALL: THE AVERAGE MAJOR-LEAGUE FASTBALL, AS CLOCKED BY RADAR GUN

Darling's fastball hovered right around 86, and in the middle innings a half dozen scouts hovered right around the gun, looking over shoulders to see if Darling might be slowing down. If anything, he was getting stronger.

Most scouts consider radar guns awkward to carry around and use, useless at gauging what they really want to see ("life"), untrustworthy in making fine discriminations of speed, and truly valuable only in night games when the fastball is harder to read. Nevertheless, they don't mind craning their necks to check the numbers on somebody else's gun. As a result, the scouts who do carry guns sometimes have them adjusted to give phony readings, so that an 86 fastball might flash up as 80. But if the distortion is more than a couple of miles per hour, it usually takes less than an inning for the magpies behind the gun to begin muttering "Bullshit" or "Add six."

Ed Katalinas, a big teddy bear of a man, was amused by the radar game and its pseudo-scientific language. "The old-fashioned scouts, like me, we used to say: 'He can throw hard.' That meant he could throw hard. 'He's got smoke,' we used that expression. The eye sees it; the brain tells you. Ability is naked to the eye. But some of these scouts don't trust their own eyes, and the modern way is: 'He throws 86,' or 'He has a 76 curve.' It's a number thing, just like scoutin' is a number game now.

"You only get one out of twenty-six in the draft, and you don't get the boys you want, because everybody's seen them and the big number-wheel turns around. Or you're a scout director, like me, and you tell your area guy: 'Offer George eight thousand dollars, and if he don't want it to hell with him.' Because of the number that he got.

"Back when Billy Pierre was on his last legs as a Tigers' scout, he used to call me up and say, 'Ed, I got a boy who can play.' I'd say, 'What's his name? Where's he from?'—address and all that, and we'd do everything on the phone—and then

Billy'd go out and sign him. Or I'd call him and say, 'I hear Johnny Jones is pretty good.' 'Ed, he can't play.' That was it—that was the old-time way.

"But you wanta hear a story about a fastball? Okay. Back in 1962 I happened to be in Clinton, Iowa, one day. I'm scoutin' the Midwest League to look at other clubs' first-year players, and when I arrive in Clinton I run into a guy name of Rich Kolsch. He says, 'Ed, I know why you're here. *He's* gonna pitch tonight.' I say, 'Right, that's why I came.' And meanwhile I'm wonderin' who the hell *he* is.

"Turns out it's Denny McLain, who the White Sox had signed that June, and I've never seen him. In Clinton the bullpen was up on a sort of hill, and if you sat near home plate and looked up you could see the pitcher warm up in the distance. So here's this McLain before the game throwin' with a beautiful delivery, and here's the catcher bobbin' up from his crouch whenever McLain throws the fastball. I say to myself: 'He must have a *riser!*' Then the game starts, and McLain throws what today you'd call maybe a 90 fastball, and besides that his ball just *jumps,* and he strikes out about twelve guys. Now my wheels are turnin'. Are the White Sox gonna protect McLain in the minor-league draft? And then I figure it out—they can't.

"That year the Sox had signed four pitchers, McLain and . . . I need three names. DeBusschere, the great basketball player—they gave him seventy thousand and put him on the major-league roster, so he was frozen. Then a boy name of Mike Joyce out of the University of Michigan—they gave him thirty-five thousand. Then a boy out of Villanova—can't remember his name, but he was a right-hander with a good slider. So I realized there's no way the Sox can protect four first-year men on their roster. And at the end of that season here comes McLain through waivers, and the Tigers claim him for eight thousand.

"Now that's what you call bein' in the right place at the right time. And it was luck. Because to add to the story: I wound up in Clinton because I'd come to this fork in the road, and a sign said Burlington this way and Clinton that way, and it didn't matter which one because I had to see all eight clubs in the league, and I just said, 'Oh, what the hell, I'll go to Clinton.' No reason. . . . So who sent me there to see that catcher bobbin' up for those risin' fastballs? My guardian angel!''

TWO-WAY SHOT: A PLAYER WITH MAJOR-LEAGUE POTENTIAL BOTH AS A PITCHER AND A HITTER

Dave Winfield, Fred Lynn, and Cal Ripken, Jr. were once two-way shots, but shortly after each turned pro he abandoned pitching to become an everyday player. It was conceivable that Ron Darling would do the same. As a college hitter he averaged about .380 with home-run power, and he usually played centerfield when he wasn't pitching. He had intelligence, baseball instincts, catlike reflexes, and that arm.

Throughout the game Darling showed all-around baseball talent. In the bottom of the sixth, with the score tied 2–2, one out, and Purdue runners on first and third, Darling foiled a suicide squeeze by pouncing off the mound to snare the bunt just before it hit the ground. The runner from third was still moving toward home—still sure, even after the bunt was caught, that it was uncatchable. Darling glanced at him, then trotted easily to third for the final out.

The score was still tied after the regulation seven innings, but Yale rallied in the top of the eighth. With a man on third, no outs, Rich Diana hit a sacrifice fly to left for a 3–2 lead. Then Darling came to bat for the last time. In three previous at-bats he had shown good whip in his swing, and in the third inning he had lined a ground-rule double to left. Now in the eighth he stepped into an outside curveball: his stride was long and maybe a tenth of a second early, but he kept his hands back and then used his hips to spring a swing worthy of a major-league hitter—head down, arms extended, front leg straightened into a fulcrum, and back leg bent into a perfect L with the toe-spike still dug in and pushing for power. The ball carried deep to right-center, between the fielders, and Darling was in high gear before he'd turned first base. He made third base standing up, and some of the scouts were panting harder than he was.

As the very next pitch became a ground ball toward short-stop, Darling broke for home. He slid in head first, twisting away from the bat near the plate while shoving his right arm ahead of the tag and between the catcher's feet. Breaths were sucked in all around me.

"Holy shit!"

"No, he's okay."

"Yeah, look at him bounce back up."

"Holy shit . . . he coulda broke that arm."

"And lost himself a hundred and fifty thousand."

"Only a hundred thousand if Seattle drafts him. Right, Bill?"

Bill Kearns said nothing. Signability was no joke.

LOUNGE HITTER: LATE-NITE BAR CRUISER (WORDPLAY ON *LUNGE HITTER*)

In the bottom of the eighth inning, working with a two-run lead, Darling struck out the first Purdue hitter on a low and wicky fastball, maybe his best pitch of the day. The second hitter lined out to the second baseman. The third hitter looked at three killer pitches: another beautiful low fastball, a curve with real bite, and then a *high* fastball—the only one Darl-ing threw all afternoon—that sailed in on the fists to end the game.

In eight innings Darling had given up three walks and four hits, none big, and had struck out ten. And his command and composure had been at least as impressive as his physical per-formance. Dick Lawlor said that wasn't all, that Darling was "a good boy off the field, too—serious, earnest, well behaved." But the consensus among the scouts was that if Darling wanted to be a lounge hitter, just for tonight, he deserved it . . . as long as he kept Casey Stengel's adage in mind: "It ain't sex that's troublesome; it's stayin' up all night lookin' for it."

SIGNABILITY PROBLEM: THE GAP BETWEEN (A) WHAT A BOY THINKS HE'S WORTH AND (B) THE SCOUT'S EVALUATION

At the water fountain near the observation tower Tony Stiel introduced himself and gave Ron Darling a business card.

"I enjoyed watchin' you pitch today."

"Thank you. I didn't have the good heater."

"Well, when was the last time you pitched?"

"I did an inning yesterday."

"Yeah? Well, you looked fine today. You know when you might pitch again?"

"Right now I'm scheduled against East Carolina on Thursday."

"I'll try and catch that game. Anyhow, you got my card—Tony Stiel of the Braves. Real nice to meet you. And take it easy now."

Once upon a time Tony Stiel would have tried to ingratiate himself with a prospect like Darling, jockeying for position among the other scouts. Now, because of the amateur draft system, Stiel simply had to put the dollar sign on the muscle and check to see if the boy had "unrealistic" bonus expectations beyond that figure. And since the Braves would have the twelfth selection in the June draft, and since Darling was almost certain to be chosen before that, there was really not much point in romancing him.

Some boys create signability problems by hiring an agent. Ron Darling would later exercise that option on the eve of the draft. But right now he was less interested in money than in proving his abilities to the scouts.

"No, I don't mind this many at a game. I think it helps me bear down, because I want to show them. Of course, I don't *know* many of them, except for Dick Lawlor, and I don't have any preference about ballclubs. It doesn't matter; it doesn't matter to me. I just want to *get there*, you know? Sometimes people say if you get drafted by a lower club, you have a better chance of gettin' to the majors, but I'm not sure that's true.

If you have good talent, and you're in a good system, they'll get you up there somehow—or trade you to someone that's gonna get you up there. I want to get drafted as high as I can. Not just for the money, but because the ballclub would be givin' me a high priority, and they'd have a big stake in my progress."

Up close Darling was even more strikingly tall, dark, handsome, and wound tight. In a relaxed voice he spoke modestly about his repertoire of pitches. "I've been workin' on my curveball, and I've worked so much on my curveball that now my slider's dropped off a little, because I had a good slider last year. So I've gotta make sure I work on each pitch the same and not give one a preference over the others."

MILEAGE: MILES PER HOUR, AS EXPLAINED BY REGIE OTERO

"For me," Regie Otero said, "I consider that this boy throws a curveball. And in the minors he can really improve that curveball to become a real curveball. If I had anything to do with him, I would tell him: 'Stop throwing the slider! You keep on throwing the slider, you will lose your curveball.' Because the slider is thrown with the, what do you call, stiff wrist, and then the curveball with the break of the wrist.

"Now, his fastball. He's gonna strike out many people because it *moves*—see? Sails, sinks, tails—see? With my experience and knowledge to see a boy, and I don't care the mileage that he throws or anything like that, because if today we didn't have the radar gun or anything like that and you see a Steve Ho pitch, and I get behind the plate, I say, 'I think that boy's right on,' and no questions asked. See, so the radar gun doesn't mean anything."

Somewhere in there was a bias, or insight, typical of Dodger scouting—distrust of the slider. It was another of Branch Rickey's precepts, by way of Al Campanis. But if you looked at Ron Darling through that lens, wouldn't you then have to project a third pitch for him?

"Exactly. The chonge! The straight chonge is the most dongerous pitch in baseball, because the hitter's timing throws it off. Andy Messersmith had the best. Messersmith had a pretty good curveball, pretty good fastball, and an *outstanding* chonge, and the Do-yer coaches teach it right on. So when Mr. Darling gets all three pitches, he is in the big leagues.

"If the boss says, 'How much you give this kid?' I would have to said, 'Sixty thousand.' If he says, 'They don't want sixty: they want eighty,' I would said, 'Give it to them!' Because if I'm gonna give sixty, I give eighty. Otherwise, why draft him? You might say, 'Ron Darling, no way will he be available when the Do-yers' turn to draft comes.' But you could say the same thing two years ago about Steve Ho."

Steve Ho was Steve Howe, who had been drafted by the Dodgers in June of 1979, as the sixteenth player selected in the first round, and who had become the National League Rookie of the Year in 1980. And Regie Otero was Casey Stengel, as performed by Desi Arnaz. He had come to the States thirty-five years earlier, after being signed out of Havana as part of Joe Cambria's first wave of Latin talent, but he still handled the English language as if playing a tricky bunt. He remembered Cambria as "Papa Joe, a man with a big cigar in a white linen suit—a good scout, and could see the tools, the five talents."

"And did Cambria tutor you as a scout?"

"What?"

"Who broke you in? Who taught you to scout?"

"God. He was my teacher. He give me the grace to see the diamond in the raw. To *see* the talents is as much a gift as to *have* the talents. I do not say as great a gift, but is as much a gift. Like this boy today, the way he plays there is a light shining through him. Every scout might tell you something different about how bright or how long's gonna burn. But Darling has it. Mark Fidrych had it; Willie Mays had it: the grace, the heart, the what they let you see. Fidrych was a meteor—blazes, comes down, hits the ground. But then here comes along a new boy with a gift from God. Same as we had Caruso and then Mario Lanza and now we have Pavarotti."

THE FIVE TALENTS: RUNNING, THROWING, FIELDING, HITTING, HITTING WITH POWER

These are the five talents for position players. For pitchers the five talents are usually stated as fastball, breaking pitch, delivery, control, and poise. Control and poise are two sides of the same talent, and most scouts would say that with pitchers you have to forget about distinguishing sharply between tools and makeup, the physical and the psychical—if you ever really separate them in the first place.

Because whatever else the language of scouting is, it is not scientific. Baseball scouts are men who think they're being technical when they describe a pitch in terms of miles per hour. That the ball also travels in feet per second, or that key reaction times like bat speed can be computed in tenths or hundredths of a second, simply does not interest most of them. Their language is impressionistic, based on four generations of oral tradition. Regie Otero's "Darling has it" echoed one of Sinister Dick Kinsella's scouting reports from 1928: "Hubbell has it." And now, just as then and always, the *it* names a mystery beyond the reach of technology.

The business of baseball scouts is to describe the future, and, despite occasional exceptions like Steve Howe, that future is generally four years away. Consequently, their vocabulary emphasizes energies—the live fastball, the live arm, the live body (wound tight)—rather than static quantities. This is Al LaMacchia's "positive scouting," genial in spirit, more vitally expressed by "holy shit" than "horseshit." Sometimes it's even aesthetic scouting, because in the modern era scouts are able to look at a player like Ron Darling without plotting how to steal him from other scouts; they have to be resigned, as a fact of life and as a basis of pure appreciation, to losing him in the draft. "Will never be there when we pick," read one of Dick

Lawlor's many reports on Darling—and yet there Lawlor was: enjoying this great performance, proud of it, and oddly protective of a boy his organization would have no chance to acquire.

The language of scouting is also religious. To have a talent is to be "blessed" with it—and scouting itineraries can sometimes be planned by guardian angels. And if you really want to know about the five talents, there are scouts who will tell you to read the Gospel of Matthew, chapter twenty-five, where *talent* means a unit of wealth. After receiving talents from their master, two servants invest the money and double it, but one servant just buries his talent in the ground. As a moral parable, the story ends with weeping and the gnashing of teeth. As a baseball parable, it ends with some scout telling you about a lounge hitter who never developed his God-given potential.

At the end of the spring I talked with Al Campanis, the Dodgers' general manager. He was a Rickey man and thus more of a rationalist in scouting. It was Campanis who had refined number grades as the new language of evaluation, and his 60-to-80 scale was the most popular grading system outside the Major League Scouting Bureau.

"Regie told you that God taught him to scout? Well, I'll just say that he wasn't speaking for the Dodger organization on that point. Scouting's a lot more than intuition. . . . It does take *some* intuition in baseball, though—more than in football and basketball—because you have to look further ahead. You watch a boy and you try to see him as a pro. Can he make the transition? Will he quit on you?

"You ever hear of 'the good face'? Well, I never used to sign a boy unless I could look in his face and see what I wanted to see: drive, determination, maturity, whatever. And when I was the Dodgers' scouting director, we used to have a real thing about that. Some scout would give me a report on a boy, and I'd say 'Tell me about his face,' or 'Does he have the good face?' "

The good face? What the hell could that mean? Certainly

nothing you could define in one snappy entry. It was the strangest way I could imagine of judging major-league potential, aside from Cy Slapnicka's clubhouse inspection of Lefty Gomez. But it was also one of the most resonant terms in the language of scouting. And as it turned out, I would spend much of the scouting year learning what "the good face" was all about.

6 A PIECE OF WORK

In one of his expense reports a scout includes an entry of $11.50—"for a hat, to prevent sunburn at ballgames." But the scout isn't reimbursed: his scouting director, as ruthless as any I.R.S. auditor, disallows the expense and sends a memo warning against such frivolous entries. The scout's next expense report is a model of nonfrivolity, neatness, and apparent accuracy. Everything looks the way it should. Paper-clipped to the report is a small note that says: "See if you can find the hat."

—Scouting folktale

That's one version, probably the best, of a story I heard from five different scouts. One of them said that it was just a fable and that its moral was really about sunburn. (As a hazard of scouting, skin cancer ranks a close second to divorce.) The other four guessed that if the hat story were really true, the scout in question must be Leon Hamilton of the Cleveland Indians.

I talked with Leon Hamilton just after he came home from the hospital in the spring. A rumor among the other scouts was that it was a serious deal, that old Leon would finally be slowing down. Other rumors were more crude, involving nicknames like "K-55" (the biggest model of Louisville Slugger) and "John Dillinger." But the Dillinger tag was also a way of describing Hamilton's personality: his outlaw accounting, his love of intrigue, his need for attention, and his sense of his own destiny as a scout. That sense of destiny is what leads him to talk about himself in the third person—and even, just to let the world know he's there, to have himself paged over PA systems in ballparks.

"Like they told you, I'm pretty much of a loner. I go out with the other scouts, eat with them, drink with them, cruise the streets with them. But at the ballparks I always sit by myself, because I don't care what anybody else thinks about a guy. Nobody gets me on or off a ballplayer but Leon Hamilton.

"I've made a pretty good career out of guys that other scouts didn't like. I'm known as a gambler. Don Sutton—nobody wanted him, but I discovered him in 1965 and he made the big leagues in one year. I don't know what it is. I see a guy, and I like what I see, and I'm not afraid to gamble, so I go get him. Maybe it's somethin' in his face or maybe in the way he *acts* out on the field. I feel thisaway: a ballplayer's not a number to me; he's a ballplayer, or else he's nothin'. A guy can either play or he can't play. There ain't no in-between. And I got a little mad one time about the numbers. There was a big meeting in our organization about how to grade, and I got up and left the room and got a phone book, and come back and says, 'There's all the names and numbers you want, right there.' Big thick phone book. Big city.

"Mel Durslag, the sportswriter, he did a story on me one time called 'The Backwoods Scout.' And that's what I was. I stayed in the backwoods scoutin' up them farmboys, and I come up with some pretty good ones. But today with the draft unless I've got somebody stashed out in the backwoods, like Doyle Alexander, then I won't get the guy. The draft has been a bad deal for the solid backwoods scout. So to offset that, I've had to go deeper into the backwoods. And take a sharper axe.

"Nobody was interested in Doyle Alexander, but I just saw him and liked him. I had a fella who was workin' for me in Alabama, and the scouts in the area didn't like Doyle—Jack Sanford didn't; Hugh East didn't. A lot of scouts work over in that Birmingham area, because Birmingham has always been productive for baseball talent, and . . ."

*   *   *

The story never concludes. It just becomes another story and another, wandering through Birmingham's baseball history, circling back through Hugh East to Leon's own career as a basketball player for the House of David, and then shooting off toward an interesting punchline that has no discernible relation to anything that's come before: "I couldn't scout football, because I know you could take the dumbest son of a bitch in the world and put a helmet on him and he could be a good football player. But I'll be damned if you can take the dumbest son of a bitch and put him on the mound and have a pitcher. He's gotta have a mentality. I've never seen a dumb guy be a good pitcher. I've seen some *illiterate* ones, but dumb and illiterate is two different things."

To interview Leon Hamilton is to enter the tall-tale world of Mark Twain—to become the traveler in Calaveras County who asks a native about a Reverend Leonidas Smiley, only to be treated to a long series of free associations on the career of someone named Jim Smiley who owned a celebrated jumping frog. An old baseball cliché says: if you ask so-and-so what time it is, he'll tell you how to build a watch. "In Leon's case," says his friend Ellis Clary, "it's a watch factory."

"This is my fiftieth year in baseball," Leon Hamilton said. "The first club I ever signed with—what the hell was it? Kinston, North Carolina? Was that it? I believe it was. I remember lookin' not long ago at my original contract and saw where I had signed with the Kinston . . . no! It was Greenville—Greenville, North Carolina—in the Coast Plain League, which had Greenville, Tarboro, Kinston, all them towns. No, it *was* Kinston where I started out. And I played there and moved around the minors, and never was a very good ballplayer but I studied the game. So that's how I got to be a baseball person—at Kinston. No. It was Greenville, North Carolina."

Forewarned by other scouts, I was ready to divide everything Leon said by twenty-five. This is the man, they said admiringly, who raised expense-account writing to the level of imaginative art, even obtaining a pad of receipts from a motel that had

burned down and then using those pages for three years' worth
of good creative material. That story proved to be as elusive
as one of Leon's own: it had simply become part of the lore
of baseball scouting. Whether or not it really happened, it
should have. It was like Leon's driveway—"the longest in organized baseball," the scouts said, meaning that they pictured
him driving back and forth on it to boost his expense-account
mileage.

I stood in Leon's short driveway in Lutz, Florida, on a day
when he and his family were packing up to move to Kenesaw
Mountain, Georgia. Leon pointed out that Judge Kenesaw
Mountain Landis, baseball's first commissioner, got his name
from that place. Then he launched into a description of the
region's natural beauty, its good farmland, its stately houses
(I visualized their nice long driveways). Then he segued into
a summary of his life as a scout. He was wearing a hot
pink sweater and tight black gabardines, and he projected a
thin, angular intensity as he spoke. And "all through the in-
terminable narrative," as Mark Twain wrote in the Calaveras
County story, "there ran a vein of impressive earnestness and
sincerity."

> I was tellin' another scout a true fact the other day, and he
> looked up and says, "Leon, you'd lie with a mouthful of fish-
> hooks." People don't believe me sometimes, but that's because
> they forget how strange this world really is. And everything I'm
> tellin' you is God's honest truth.
>
> I played pro basketball seventeen years, all over the country
> and out of it, with the House of David. We were a better team
> than the House of David baseball team. We barnstormed every-
> where and packed in as many as four games a day—booked as
> many as we could 'cause it was all on percentage. I used to be
> good at passin' the basketball behind me. I was a guard and I
> could shoot from out—two-hand set, very accurate. And I
> could run, too; I could run with the black ones at the time.
>
> I wasn't as good at baseball. I played second base, but I was
> just a warmed-over shortstop—didn't have an arm. Johnny
> Nee, the old Yankee scout, signed me. And then later when I
> broke in as a scout, I was a leg man for Nee and Paul Krichell

and some of those old son of a bitches. For the first couple of
years those scouts'd say "hey, boy" or "hey, punk, go get the
lineup." And I would. But that's all the attention they paid to
me. Wasn't none of 'em too damn friendly. Those old-time
scouts might tell you something, help you a *little*, but they'd
only tell you once. And if you didn't take it, they wouldn't tell
you again. They figured "fuck you."

I remember the time that Billy Pierre, who was scoutin' with
the Giants, went up to North Carolina. No, it was *South* Carolina. He wanted to sign this pitcher—I can't think of the boy's
name, but he made the big leagues quick—I mean right now!
The boy's daddy was a sharecropper, and when Billy Pierre
went out to the fields, him and the daddy got to drinkin' some
of that branch water and moonshine. So he got the old man to
sign the contract, but when they got back to the house the boy
wouldn't sign it, and he never did sign with the Giants. All the
other scouts knew about the contract, though, and they was
sayin' to Billy: "Goddamn, Billy, things must be gettin' tough
when you go out and sign a sixty-three-year-old pitcher."

See, it was competitive then. And when I started out, I had
one hand tied behind my back, because the Yankees wouldn't
let me sign black ballplayers. Then in 1949 I went with the
Dodgers and the problem was just the opposite. Man, you talk
about tough times for Leon Hamilton! I was the Dodgers'
southern scout, the only one they had between Baltimore and El
Paso, Texas. No, to the Mississippi River. I had about seventeen states. But anyway, here I was in the middle of all that ani-
mosity, because people would say, "He's with the nigger
ballclub." There are scouts still livin' who called me that or
who told a boy's parents: "Do you want your son to play with
the Dodgers? They're a nigger team."

To give you a concrete example, I lost Bobby Richardson. He
was from Sumter, South Carolina, and a very religious boy, a
nice boy. And I liked Bobby Richardson, and other scouts
didn't, and I *had* him—bought him his first good glove, used to
loan him my car, and he wanted to sign with me. His father
sold tombstones, worked on 'em in the back of their yard, and
I can still tell you the address of their house: number three
Washington Street, Sumter, South Carolina.

Bobby was the only ballplayer in my life that I *really* wanted
and didn't get. What caused me not to get him was the local

politics. High officials come over and told his daddy: "If your boy signs with that nigger ballclub, you'll never sell another tombstone in South Carolina." Mr. Richardson was a poor man; if he made four thousand dollars a year to feed his family on, he was lucky. So Bobby told me what those officials said and I got mad, boy, and I've got a short fuse. I went *after* those guys, and then they give me an hour to leave town.

We wound up with Jim Gilliam instead of Richardson, so the good Lord kindly evened things out. What a man Gilliam was. Can you imagine all those years he was hittin' behind Maury Wills, and Wills on first base always goin' for the stolen base, and all those times Gilliam gave up a base hit to protect the runner? If he could've taken his swing at all those strikes, he would've had hundreds of more hits in his lifetime.

When I worked for the Dodgers, Branch Rickey had already gone over to the Pirates, so I never did work for him. But I knew him real good. Him and I were sittin' in the same box one time, just the two of us, at this major-league game and he says, "Leon, how much baseball do you think you know?" and I says, "Mr. Rickey, how much baseball do you think *you* know?" He says, "Young man, I question whether I know fifty-five percent of baseball."

And before I knew it I said, "Hell, Mr. Rickey." See, you didn't use strong language around him—people were afraid to—but I said, "Hell, Mr. Rickey, I think I know that much." He said, "Leon, you're a fine scout and gonna be a better one. You have a fine future in this field. But you *don't* know fifty-five percent." And then he asked me five questions, and I couldn't answer a one of 'em. Questions like "Why does a championship team never have a left-hand hittin' shortstop?" I didn't know. He said, "The reason is that the ballclub is gonna have to win a lot of tight games in the late innings, and if you have a left-hand hittin' shortstop, the other teams are gonna bring in left-hand relievers to pitch to him a lot. And you can't pinch-hit for him, because he's too valuable on defense: nobody on your bench can really take his place in the field."

My baseball knowledge is more intuition. I've never organized it like Rickey did. For instance, I've never scouted catchers too good, because all I'm seein' is their backsides. If I could see a catcher as a straight-up ballplayer, like a shortstop—I'm good with shortstops—then I might be a better judge of catchers. But I have to go down the first-base line or the third-base line to see how he moves his mitt, and when I do, I'm missin' a lot of other things in the game. So I've signed very few catchers in my scouting life.

I did sign Mike Ivie for the Padres, and I thought he was the best young catcher I ever saw. But he didn't stay one for long. He got some kind of mental block about throwin' the ball back to the pitcher. Couldn't even lob it back—the goddamn ball always went in the dirt or into centerfield. What it was, I think some of his friends told him that he'd last longer as a first baseman, or die later or something. But, what the hell, he caught in the big leagues at eighteen years old, and in fact I signed a fella that same year named Franklin out of Alexandria, Virginia, and he pitched in the big leagues at seventeen, and Ivie was his catcher. So it was probably the youngest battery ever to appear in a big-league game.

Howie Haak and I, I guess, have signed more players than anybody in baseball. And I've traveled with Howie, and he's a wild Indian. We could've got killed down in them fuckin' Latin countries. Ridin' them old-timery planes. Out hellin' around. You know, any woman who marries a man in this business and then stays around, she's gotta be crazy. Because we have no *hours*. I put in more hours than a man who don't sleep could ever put in. Man, five hundred miles ain't nothin' to me. And there's been times when I didn't even know what home was. If I went home, the dog would bite me; he didn't know me. And I've stayed in places you wouldn't believe, like those old shotgun hotels in little southern towns. I've slept in the same bed with another man, a total stranger! And it's a wonder I'm alive, what with all the shit ballpark food I've eat—nine thousand hot dogs and then still hungry.

But I know this. I know a baseball game is like a train or a plane or a bus. That thing is gonna leave at a certain time, and if you're not there, you've missed it—and you might sit there ten more times and never see what you *would* have seen. So any time I miss a game, I'm hurt. And sometimes, like at the Wichita tournament, I've watched eight games in one day. And if jackasses played baseball, I'd be out watchin' them, too.

You travel like I do, you gotta know how to operate, how to promote, which is a whole side of the scout business in itself— promotin'. I don't mean dickin' around with your expense account; I mean how to find a decent place to sleep or how to talk yourself into a home-cooked meal. First you've gotta get known throughout your territory. Anytime I went into a town to see a game and had a few hours, I'd walk those streets and shop in stores, maybe buy a pair of britches, talk to people—talk to them farmers and chew tobacco with them and whittle with them and get *along* with them, because I speak the southern language pretty good. And I'd pick up tips on everything, ballplayers included. That's why I've never been a scout that had to have bird dogs: I didn't need a local contact, because I made my own. And when I signed a ballplayer, that was promotin', too. I learned this early on: that when you go in there, the father will talk a lot, but he'll be the boss maybe two out of ten times. So the percentage is—play the mother! Let her know her son's gonna be all right. Get her believin' in you. Try to come across as a down-to-earth sort of guy. After you eat the chicken dinner, offer to help her wash the dishes.

Most of this advice is obsolete, because the draft's speeded everything up. In the old days you'd go into a town till you either won a guy or lost him, and I've sat on front porches with other scouts when we drew straws to see who got to talk to a family first. Nowadays scouts are a little bit like the ticket sellers at the racetrack, where it's more of a computer deal. You have to do broader coverage, travel even more than before, so you don't see as much. You don't know if a boy smokes pot because you're not around town long enough to find out. You can't tell if he has heart. You don't even get to know his mother.

You take this boy Vance Lovelace, just comin' out of high school in Tampa. Big black left-hand pitcher. Well, he's really a *thrower*, but that's what you want a high-school boy to be—somebody that can blow like hell, got the good fastball, the good live arm, the great size. But he's gotta have the mentality, the makeup, and I don't have the time to find out if Lovelace does. I'm behind schedule this season as it is. So my report just talks about his pitches, except that something makes me say *no*. I don't know what it is. He's on the same American Legion team with another black pitcher name of Dwight Gooden, who's a year younger but for my money a better prospect. The difference is hard to put your finger on. When I watched Lovelace pitch, I didn't get that good feeling. That's all. Because if you asked me what makes a ballplayer, I'd have to say I don't know. It's just like what makes one woman different from another, what makes one a good wife and one a bad wife—I don't mean bad in operatin' around but just hard to get along with.

I got that good feeling on Don Sutton. I got it on Herb Score—and, man, you talk about a thrower! He was wild as a march hare, but he could throw. God a-mighty, he could throw. And I was the first scout to come up with him. He was in high school right here in Florida, and I was the only scout at that time who lived in Florida. Now there's about fifty full-time, and I think I brought a lot of 'em down here when I signed some ballplayers for the Dodgers. Like Craig and Bessent—and Pee Wee Oliver, who could've been a great infielder except he turned out to be gun-shy at second base, wouldn't hold his ground when the runner came right at him. But I didn't sign Herb Score. Cy Slapnicka for the Indians come down and offered him about sixty thousand dollars in bonus money, and the Dodgers couldn't come close to that. Not when we were playin' in Brooklyn. Time we got through with the ward heelers up there, even if we had a packed house, there wouldn't be but twenty-two thousand paid attendance, because they all got tickets. So we didn't have a lot of bonus money to give out, and in those days we had to stock about two dozen minor-league teams.

But the big farm systems made sense; this shit today don't make sense at all. I wouldn't own a ballclub today. If you give it to me, I'd sell it, because I wouldn't go through all that stuff. When I look at the fellas I've signed that are millionaires and gonna get more, when I look at them kind of guys, you know, I think: "Well, I remember when you was just farm boys. And if it wasn't for baseball, you'd never have done nothin' but look at a mule in the rear end for the rest of your lives. And yet you don't *love* baseball."

I love baseball. I hope to die, when my time comes, in a ballpark. And I just hope that I don't fall on the guy next to me while the tyin' or winnin' run is on base and keep him from seein' it. . . .

Leon didn't stop there. He went on to digress from his digressions until he wound up, somehow, with Hank Aaron ("Could've signed him. Turned him down. Said he'd never make it as a second baseman—and I was right!") and the new psychological tests for amateur players ("If the Indians used them things to veto a boy I wanted to sign, I'd quit!"). But I'd really stopped listening when he got to the death scene. It was his ultimate scouting fantasy: getting paged at the ballpark by God. To make it a better story you'd only have to add a few minor touches, like having him clutch a piece of paper that, when his hand is pried open, is found to contain a single sentence: maybe "Home-team shortstop is destined for greatness," or "Add $34.25 to expense report—for new radio to listen to ball-games."

As spring turned into summer I learned to do some promotin' of my own, and I sometimes used my scouting project to talk PR directors of major-league clubs into issuing press passes for me. One evening I stood in the Houston Astros' dugout before a game and saw Don Sutton walk in from the clubhouse. "I understand Leon Hamilton originally signed you for the Dodgers," I said, "and I wondered if you'd mind telling me about that."

"Leon Hamilton didn't sign me," Sutton said. "The Dodgers had to send in Monte Basgall to do it. My parents threw Leon out of the house!"

"Why?"

"I don't want to talk about it."

Neither did Leon, except to remind me that he'd never said he had signed Don Sutton but only that he had "discovered" him. And discovery was what scouting was really about—the experience of recognizing talent, of having "that good feeling" when he projected a ballplayer into the future. It was a business of intuitions. He might brag about being "the best signing scout in baseball," but he was most animated when discussing the players he failed to sign, like Bobby Richardson or Herb Score. Like any practiced storyteller, he gave most attention to the ones that got away.

Other scouts might invent or repeat stories about him: having him win a bar bet by covering a row of silver dollars, or having him drive from Tampa to Lakeland via the Great Circle Route. But the joke was really on them, because Leon Hamilton was still the scout other scouts talked about most. He had used them to promote himself into the realm of American folklore. His own peers saw him as the archetype of the old-time scout, a man from another time (his persona of "backwoods scout" was a version of the traditional "ivory hunter") who was still doing pretty well in this one. Most of the scouts were underpaid and unnoticed and so took special delight in the exploits of their John Dillinger—ready to drive from hell to Texas to see a ballplayer, while beating the ballclub out of more expense money than anyone else would have the courage to claim. Most of them operated by intuition, too, and Leon took that unscientific style to its anti-scientific conclusion. He was hostile not only to psychological testing and radar-gun technology but even to the concept of number. And all of them agreed that Leon knew a ballplayer when he saw one, that he was perceptive or persuasive enough to impress baseball executives like Buzzy Bavasi and Phil Seghi, so that he'd always have a good job in scouting and probably *would* die in a ballpark. In the spring of 1981, after his surgery and his trip to Kenesaw Mountain, Leon Hamilton resumed full duties as the Indians' scout for Florida, Georgia, Tennessee, North Carolina, South Carolina, Alabama, and Mississippi.

The other scouts saw him as an exaggeration of themselves. But even that didn't exhaust their preoccupation with him, because there was also that quirky individual living inside the legend. Leon was just unabashedly himself—"a different guy," the scouts said again and again, "a piece of work."

I'd heard "a piece of work" as a baseball expression many times before, but I never understood what it meant until I stood in a driveway in Lutz, Florida. To say that Leon Hamilton is a piece of work is to accept his own vision of how strange this world really is. It means that when God made him, He took a good long time to do it, and that He probably rested all the next day.

SUMMER

THE PRESENT

The Whole Ball Player

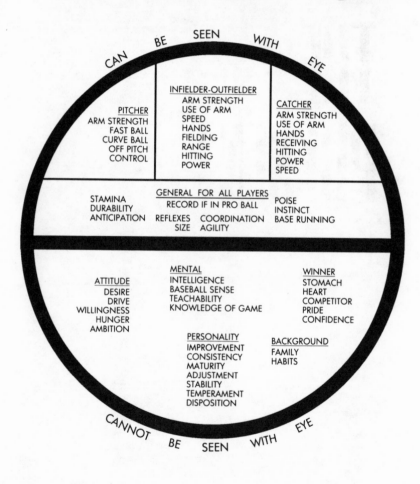

CAN   BE   SEEN   WITH   EYE

INFIELDER-OUTFIELDER
ARM STRENGTH
USE OF ARM
SPEED
HANDS
FIELDING
RANGE
HITTING
POWER

PITCHER
ARM STRENGTH
FAST BALL
CURVE BALL
OFF PITCH
CONTROL

CATCHER
ARM STRENGTH
USE OF ARM
HANDS
RECEIVING
HITTING
POWER
SPEED

STAMINA
DURABILITY
ANTICIPATION

GENERAL FOR ALL PLAYERS
RECORD IF IN PRO BALL

REFLEXES   COORDINATION
SIZE   AGILITY

POISE
INSTINCT
BASE RUNNING

ATTITUDE
DESIRE
DRIVE
WILLINGNESS
HUNGER
AMBITION

MENTAL
INTELLIGENCE
BASEBALL SENSE
TEACHABILITY
KNOWLEDGE OF GAME

WINNER
STOMACH
HEART
COMPETITOR
PRIDE
CONFIDENCE

PERSONALITY
IMPROVEMENT
CONSISTENCY
MATURITY
ADJUSTMENT
STABILITY
TEMPERAMENT
DISPOSITION

BACKGROUND
FAMILY
HABITS

CANNOT   BE   SEEN   WITH   EYE

7 ARTS AND SCIENCES

There's no art
To find the mind's construction in the face.

—Macbeth: *I, iv, 12–13*

The chart entitled "The Whole Ball Player" has become a familiar icon in the world of baseball scouting over the last twenty years, and is now included as a page in almost every club's staff manual. Its creator, Jim McLaughlin, presided as scouting director of the Baltimore Orioles and Cincinnati Reds during some of their greatest talent-producing seasons. He explains the chart by recalling how one of his scouts found a future Hall-of-Fame third baseman.

"When Fred Hoffman scouted Brooks Robinson, he saw the whole ballplayer. Brooks was just an average runner, he didn't have a great arm, his frame was still kind of frail, his hitting was still a question mark, and he was playing at second base. But Fred visualized him as a third baseman. He said, 'This boy's *quick* even though he's not *fast*, and he's gonna be just like a vacuum cleaner in the infield.' Fred saw the soft hands, the live body, the great reflexes that allow you to project hitters. He was able to break the player down into individual tools, and he was also able to see the masterpiece in its entirety. Not just the total coordination in that body, but the total coordination in that *person*—beyond what could be seen with the eye."

Jim McLaughlin mapped the strategies of draft-era scouting a decade before the draft era began, and he is still regarded as a mentor by some of the sharpest scouts in the profession. But when he came to the end of a brilliant forty-year career in the scouting business, he was still hesitant to call himself a baseball man. "Baseball was never my life. It was just a life that I lived."

In retirement Jim McLaughlin expresses far less interest in baseball than in Shakespearean plays, Renaissance paintings, or various forms of the Faust legend. He has become a serious student of the humanities. But on the subject of scouting, once you're able to turn his attention back to it, he remains committed to a scientific ideal.

"I think I went a lot further than other people in taking the scientific viewpoint on acquiring talent. And that's another reason I wasn't a real baseball man. Baseball men are like a tribe. And if you don't think the way the tribe thinks, if you think on your own and ignore the conventional wisdom, then you spend half your time bucking complaints from scouts who say, 'That's not the way I learned it,' or 'You never played a day of pro baseball in your life.'

"I used to hear scouts talk about 'the good face'—as if they could tell about a kid's makeup just by looking at him, instead of taking the trouble to get to know him, or studying the results of a psychological test. I used to hear those 'good face' stories and they'd drive me up the wall. Scouts can be so damn unscientific! At one time it was the conventional wisdom that a black kid couldn't become a successful big-league pitcher, because he wouldn't have any guts when he walked out to the mound, because he'd be only sixty feet, six inches from home plate. There was no basis for that. It was just prejudice—or fantasy, or myth, whatever you want to call it. I was the scouting director and I had to listen to this bullshit. I said, 'I don't have the time to reeducate you guys diplomatically.' I was dictatorial. I was opinionated. I said, 'This is the way it's gonna be.' I wanted to inculcate basic principles, like with that chart. I wanted rationality. I wanted science."

Science in baseball scouting? Might as well aim for science, I thought, in racetrack touting, or poetry writing, or loving. At the end of the spring season, after weeks of going to games with veteran scouts, I still found their work mysterious. The talents they studied seemed so resistant to measurement, and needed to be projected so far into the future, that subjectivity was inevitable and maybe desirable. Let pro football scouts be proud of their objectivity; they could afford it. The football scouts were able to survey a smaller crop of prospects, more mature and already naturally selected by college competition, in a setting comparable to a Double-A farm system. They took uniform playing conditions for granted and had easy access to game films whose slow-motion isolations provided significant re-vision. They enjoyed plenty of lead time between the end of the scholastic season and the football draft in April, so that all major prospects could be subjected to thorough physical tests. They dealt with prospects who were agreeable (or inured) to being so tested and with numerical results that could be directly correlated with success or failure in a highly specialized athletic role.

Baseball scouting could never be this objective. So could it be made scientific, in any serious sense of that word? Yes, Jim McLaughlin said, yes, it could—in three ways:

- By substituting centralized management for old-fashioned individualism: computerizing player data, rationalizing draft procedures, and applying consistent policies to hire scouts, train them, and grade them the way they grade ballplayers.
- By psychological testing: securing professional analysis of the makeup of each prospect, by means of an exam like the "Athletic Motivation Inventory."
- By physical testing: insisting on thorough tests of eyesight and general health, and using new technology to quantify information on bat speed, reflexes, or ratios of muscle strength.

McLaughlin's career was a case study in the first option: he brought baseball scouting into the modern era by exercising rigorous bureaucratic control. He began employing cross-checkers in 1955, ten years before the draft, to provide multiple, layered views of top prospects. He reorganized scouting territories for more extensive fishing where the fish were biting.

He held scouting seminars, staged mock signings, and barraged his staff with memos on the difference between skills and talents, or between performance and tools. And, when possible, he got rid of the old-fashioned individualists.

"I was trying to weed out the free spirits, the ones who think God taught 'em how to scout. I hired younger guys, new scouts I might be able to indoctrinate before they went on the road and got . . . contaminated by the old-timers." Among those younger guys were Bob Engle (now with the Blue Jays), Joe McIlvaine (Mets), Tony Stiel (Braves), and Jim Russo (Orioles). Paradoxically, all of them still regard as their mentor a man who rarely left the office to look at ballplayers. "I scouted scouts," McLaughlin says.

"You know what makes the best scouting director? You ever read the Nero Wolfe detective novels? Well, I used to think of myself as Nero Wolfe. The scouts were like Archie, out doing legwork, getting details, while I sat back and analyzed. I went out occasionally—I went out on Boog Powell, not so much to evaluate him as to help sign him—but mostly I was in the office, so that somebody could remain objective. And the scouts couldn't bullshit me, because I used to run surveys on everything—the progress of players each guy had recommended, the progress of players he *hadn't* recommended, the amounts of money he was ready to risk, the amounts he ran up for expenses in a year. I tried to open the scouts' minds to what they were really doing, to make them apply something outside of baseball so that they could see themselves as more than just 'baseball men.' That's why we had all those seminars, rehearsals for signing, and lectures by psychologists and insurance salesmen and F.B.I. agents.

"An F.B.I. agent would tell them how to get background information on a 'subject,' how to compile a dossier by subtle investigation. In our case the 'subject' was any given ballplayer. The scouts didn't see the F.B.I. the way we do now, as raising questions about the suppression of American liberties. They could compare themselves to a government agent, and it made them feel important, and maybe they could grasp how being a baseball scout had meaning to it, and logic.

"In one way all of that was picking up where Branch Rickey left off . . . even though I never liked Rickey. I thought he was an ethical fraud, the way he manipulated people and then made those pious speeches. There was no substance. I couldn't have worked for him two minutes, because of my Jesuit education. I could see through him. But when it came to producing talent, the man had real intelligence, real imagination, because he could change his thinking—like a good novelist who doesn't just keep repeating himself after the first novel. And near the end of his career, he was ready for scientific scouting.

"Up to that time, see, Rickey was a Darwinist. 'Quality out of quantity' is really a version of natural selection. The other baseball men didn't even know who the hell Darwin was, so Rickey could operate like one of these companies that gets a monopoly on the market. Then, when farm systems got too expensive, and when bonuses went sky-high, Rickey changed. He went after quality only, to the extent that he could. He was trying *conscious* selection—even though the tools weren't very precise. But if he were alive today, he'd be experimenting with *new* tools: tests, special equipment, computers. He wouldn't be bound by the conventional wisdom, because he was the guy who invented the conventional wisdom.

"Most ballclubs have computers now, but they use them in a dull way. They just make them a memory for written scouting reports—and sometimes that's garbage in, garbage out. The scouting director better have a great memory of his own, because he's gonna get most of the good stuff in phone calls. A scout calls up, and maybe he's excited, and he gives his whole sense of a player. A few days later, his report comes in the mail, and the player sounds like John Doe or six other guys. Most scouts don't express themselves that well on paper. Or they'll use grades inconsistently, maybe suggest that this college pitcher will develop a fastball, which is a perfect example of confusing a talent with a skill. So on the subject of written reports I'm a little cynical. In fact I'm kind of a cynic in general. You probably shouldn't even be talking to me."

Jim McLaughlin is a skeptic, not a cynic. He expresses no smug, reductive views of human behavior; he merely uses doubt as a method and enjoys playing the role of devil's advocate. He's a rationalist who has spent forty years supervising romantics— and a realist who has learned that the greatest obstacle to pure scientific management in scouting is the impure nature of baseball politics.

How was it possible, I asked, for the Oakland A's to make intelligent draft picks from 1978 to 1980, after their owner, Charles O. Finley, fired all of his scouts? And why had Finley fired them in the first place?

"Well, when you talk about Finley, you might as well talk about the whimsy and petulance of King Lear. See, Shakespeare knew all about Charlie Finley. Except he wouldn't have taken him seriously enough for a tragedy. He might have made him a minor character in a comedy—maybe to showcase that talent for scheming. Because there was a pipeline. After Finley fired all his own scouts he used to phone up scouts on other ballclubs, flatter them, hint that he wanted to hire them. Then he'd ask their opinions on ballplayers. The funny thing was, I'd hear one scout say to another: 'You know who called me today? Finley.' And I'd think: 'You dumb son of a bitch, he's just picking your brains.' I mean, he'd *seduce* people—and they either didn't know it or didn't care. . . . In that way Finley was a little like Rickey.

"But there's a ton of information that gets traded, all through the scouting business. I used to talk with my friends in other organizations: 'Who've you got on your list? Who's exciting?' And maybe you give a little here, get a little there, like with Johnny Bench. I was with Cincinnati in 1965, the first year of the draft, and a friend of mine with another club said, 'You better send someone down to Binger, Oklahoma, to look at this kid Bench. We're not gonna draft him, because the general manager's seen another catcher he likes up in New England.'

Which is unscientific scouting again, because what the hell was a general manager doing interfering in the chain of command? They took that New England catcher on the first round, and the kid never got above Double A. And we took Bench on the second round. It was kind of a poker game. Nobody else knew much about him; his team hadn't played many games, and our scout was usually the only one there, so we could wait. After the draft Bill DeWitt, my boss, said, 'I've never heard of him.' I said, 'I know you haven't, but you will. And that's why you hired *me*—to hear about kids like this one.'

"I'd worked for DeWitt when I first broke into baseball, with the old St. Louis Browns, and I stayed with the team when they became the Baltimore Orioles—until Paul Richards bounced me out in 1962. He wanted to fire me sooner. When he first came in as general manager, he had some intermediary tell me to show up at a breakfast meeting; it was supposed to be my last meal. When I got there, he must have expected me to defend the farm system, but I told him the truth: it was horseshit. We didn't have anything, because we hadn't been able to spend enough money. But I showed him how we might turn things around, and so he kept me on—and a few weeks later at a sports banquet I heard Richards give this speech about the farm system, and it was word-for-word what I'd told him. He just left out 'horseshit.' I knew I had him then: he didn't know any more than what I'd said.

"Where Richards and I saw eye-to-eye was on pitching, the priority it ought to have in building a farm system. He was more interested in the training of young pitchers—and when it came to how many pitches young prospects should throw, he laid down numbers as laws. It wasn't just pseudo-science, but it was another case of plagiarism: he took all his theories verbatim from an orthopedist, Dr. Bennett. I was more interested in finding pitchers in the first place. And I always believed, if you take the scientific approach, that pitching is the easiest area to perfect your scouting techniques, because pitchers show so much of themselves in a game. If you send a scout to look at a hitter, maybe the kid gets walked three times, or maybe he gets two good pitches to swing at the whole game, or maybe he's in a slump and then the scout writes him off forever. But pitchers are more consistent, in terms of *showing* you tools and makeup. There's more to see. And if you find enough good ones, which we did, you can turn a poor team into a consistent winner.

"But one of those pitchers, Dave McNally, was the reason I got fired. There were two separate factions in the Baltimore organization. Richards and I each had our own people, like the king and Richelieu. And then I authorized a bonus of eighty thousand for McNally—without Richards' approval—and I was gone.

"I'd overstepped myself. I wasn't simon pure. At that point in my career I was probably a little greedy for power, and in my own way I'd played some of Rickey's themes—thinking of ballplayers as chattel and just focusing on results at the top. I don't think I was as much of a phony as Rickey, but maybe my kind of scientific scouting led to the same result, where you wind up talking about players as shadow and shade. I studied him, and I guess something rubbed off. That's why I get so interested in Shakespeare or the Faust stories, these plays about people who want too much or who study the devil and then find out there's a devil in them. And that's why I think it would be interesting to do psychological tests not just on the players, but on baseball men themselves."

The second option in scientific scouting, psychological testing, is best represented by the Athletic Motivation Inventory (AMI) administered to about 550 amateur baseball prospects each year. Like the Minnesota Multiphasic Personality Index, and the five thousand other tests modeled after the MMPI, the AMI poses a series of statements with multiple-choice responses ("always, sometimes, never" or "true, false, in-between") so that the participant's answers can be gridded quickly on a separate sheet and then graded by machine. Unlike all the other tests, the AMI is "sports specific," aiming to describe such qualities as leadership or trust solely in athletic terms. It was devised in 1969 by three psychologists—Bruce Ogilvie, Thomas Tutko, and Leland Lyon—who incorporated themselves as the Institute of Athletic Motivation, under the parentage of the Winslow Research Institute, and began selling their program to high-school and college athletic departments and professional scouting systems. Baseball clubs that belong to the Major League Scouting Bureau receive AMI results on the year's top prospects as part of the package; the rest may spend $3,500 for profiles of prospects their own scouts choose for testing.

"Answer honestly," the directions say. "Mark the answer that describes you as you are now, not what you would like to be or what you think the coach wants you to be. It is best to say what you really think." But in order to gauge the prospect's real test-taking attitude, the AMI's 190 statements juxtapose the clear-headed, the ambiguous, and the bizarre:

> I always do exactly what the coach tells me to do.
> In athletics one must "either push or be shoved."
> I can put up with a conceited fellow athlete fairly well.
> During competition it's easy for me to really hate my opponent.
> I get tired just thinking about a long, hard practice session.
> Athletic competition started just ten years ago.
> I enjoy getting into arguments about athletics.
> I turn in my equipment in the same condition I got it.
> I would like to become a coach.
> The youngest athlete I know is eighty-five years old.
> I feel humble when I face really great athletes.
> I rarely swear during competition.
> Most athletes do not wear uniforms.
> I believe in "pain, torture, and agony" for a winner.
> This country is not the only one that has athletic competition.
> There are things happening among my fellow athletes that I
>   don't know about.

The resulting motivational profile, as supplied to a major-league scouting director, is preceded by indications of accuracy—that is, whether the prospect had trouble comprehending the questions, or whether he tried to present a falsely positive or negative image of himself. (If all questions like the first one are answered with a pious "true," the test is flagged as unreliable.) The profile itself then gives percentile rankings in eleven categories: drive, aggressiveness, determination, leadership, self-confidence, emotional control, mental toughness, coachability, conscientiousness, trust, and guilt proneness (recently redefined as "responsibility").

The significance of each percentile grade may vary from interpreter to interpreter, sport to sport, level to level. William Winslow, president of Winslow Research, thinks that the AMI is often more valuable as a coaching tool than a scouting tool: "If a coach discusses the profile with the athlete himself, then they both have a basis for more productive practice and better counseling, to help the kid realize his full potential. Some of the categories, like emotional control or mental toughness, are not very modifiable; others, like drive or coachability, can be improved more directly. Of course the AMI can be a great scouting tool too. But, for some reason, professional baseball has been the slowest of all major sports to respond to the scouting value of our program."

Dave Ritterpusch, one of Jim McLaughlin's protégés, believes he knows what that "some reason" is. "Pro football and basketball scouts are college-trained and college-oriented people, and they're comfortable with the language of testing and scientific measurement. Baseball scouts are baseball men, and they speak their own language.

"A lot of baseball scouts feel threatened by a tool like the AMI, because they like to believe that they 'just know' about a kid's makeup. Sometimes they do—and when they talk about 'the good face,' they may be on to something, by intuition, that's fundamentally important, like honesty or aggressiveness. But how do you make very fine distinctions? What kind of number-system would you use to grade good faces?"

Like McLaughlin, Ritterpusch is now out of baseball. After the Orioles replaced him as scouting director in 1976, he re-enlisted as an army officer and is currently stationed at Fort Sheridan, Illinois. "I think I loved baseball more than Jim did," he says, "and I'd love to get back in it . . . but this time as an owner! If I had Steinbrenner's kind of money, I wouldn't have to argue with all the baseball men; I'd just make radical changes from the top down. Because baseball spends about sixty million a year on development and almost nothing on research. So those scouts just tend to repeat the same process, season after season, decade after decade, century after century. In a line of work where there's so much emotion and hearsay and folklore, the scientific opportunities are tremendous. Even simple objectivity is rare and valuable. How else could teams like the Orioles, who have to draft from the twenty-second or twenty-fourth position every year, keep coming up with better players?"

One answer might be that the Orioles have also been coming up with better scouting and managerial talent: McLaughlin himself hired Jim Russo, Earl Weaver, Harry Dalton, and Hank Peters. Another might be that the organization has maintained most of McLaughlin's procedural innovations and added new ones. (Baltimore's is the only scouting system with specialist cross-checkers; Bill Werle, for example, focuses almost exclusively on amateur pitchers.) Still another might be that the Orioles, sooner and to a greater extent than more teams, have made tools like the AMI integral to the scouting process. According to Dave Ritterpusch, psychological profiles have been crucial in preventing the draft selection of some players (especially pitchers with low scores in aggressiveness and emotional control) and in insuring the selection of others—like Mike Flanagan, Rich Dauer, and Eddie Murray.

"All the scouting reports I'd seen on Murray stereotyped him as a big, lazy power hitter. I think most scouts, when they judge makeup, tend to value kids who remind them of *themselves* when they were players—and that's why you run into problems when white scouts look at black prospects. Here was Eddie Murray, younger than most of his classmates, and extremely composed, cool—to the point that the scouts called him 'lackadaisical.' But then I read his motivational profile, which said his drive was well above professional average, and his emotional control was off the charts. And it hit me that the emotional control was really *masking* the drive, and that the scouts who talked about his laziness must have an unconscious ethnic bias. In the meantime I sent Bill Werle in to cross-check Murray, and he said, 'This kid's got more than power. He drives the ball.' So now I could see Murray in still another dimension, as more than a double-or-nothing kind of hitter. And we were able to draft him on the third round in 1973—and if you look at Murray's record for every season since then, *every* season, you'll see that he's probably the most consistent player in baseball, because slumps don't bother him, nothing bothers him, and that emotional control keeps him on a steady keel.

"I used to study the old files of psychological tests and correlate them with a kid's later achievement, and I started to see real patterns. I got to the point, for example, of not taking anyone seriously as a starting pitcher unless he had high scores in aggressiveness and emotional control. I didn't go looking for this: it was empirical. But now I can see why it *ought* to be true.

"The pitcher is the player who, just within the definition of baseball, has the potential to determine the most things: when the ball is thrown, how fast it moves, where it goes, the sequence of pitches. All the hitter can do is select from the pitches that are thrown. And the fielder, in turn, is the most passive, because he has to go to the hit ball. So the pitcher's role is the most aggressive in function, and it demands a tough attitude, the belief that he *owns* home plate. That's why the scouts, instinctively, give a kid higher marks if he's willing to knock hitters down—even though they know he won't be able to get away with much of that in pro ball. The psychologists are really pointing to the same thing when they define aggressiveness as 'ability to channel hostility.'

"The starting pitcher's problem is to sustain that aggressive role, and that's where emotional control comes in. It may not be so crucial for relief pitchers—when a guy like Gossage or McGraw or Hrabosky comes into a game in the late innings, he's usually on an emotional *high,* really pumped up. But the starter needs *low* emotionality, because his job is really more mechanistic than we usually think. Guys like Carlton, Seaver, Palmer, Valenzuela—when they're on the mound, they're inside their own bubble. And in some science-fiction future, if you could ever program a robot to play baseball, the position you'd pick for him, or it, is starting pitcher. . . . Out there on the mound: a perfect machine that throws strike after strike to the corners of the plate—with an occasional brushback to keep those human hitters honest.

"Back in the early 1970s we had Jim Palmer take the AMI. He had a real low score on coachability, and he came across as a total perfectionist—too much for his own good. But he was up in the 90's on aggressiveness and emotional control. That's when I started to see this pattern, and that's when we decided to take a chance on Mike Flanagan. We got him in the seventh round of the draft, because he'd had arm problems, and because a lot of scouts said he had a bad attitude. We had him checked thoroughly by an orthopedist, and we studied his AMI results, which showed us what we wanted to see. So would you call that scientific scouting or just common sense?

"But there's one thing I haven't told you about psychological tests. Most of them are administered by *scouts*. And it happens, it happened to us, that a scout really likes a boy, and the AMI test looks to him like a hurdle, something that might keep us from drafting his player. So he coaches the kid on filling in the answers, or maybe he even fills them in himself! And we kept getting these flagged reports on players from one geographical area, where this one scout was working. It's like any other application of science. Your instruments are only as good as the people who use them. And you have to watch out for the fudge factor."

Physical testing, the third option in scientific scouting, would seem in principle to be the most definitive. In fact it's the most nebulous.

Dave Ritterpusch was once an engineering student at Lehigh, and he's able to use engineers' terms to explain how "rising" fastballs are optical illusions (whereas curveballs really do curve), or how major-league baseball could profit from a scouting program based on technological analysis. "You could measure the movement on a fastball, not just the velocity. You could measure balance and agility, or reaction times for outfielders, or infielders' ability to transfer the ball to the throwing hand— which is one reason Brooks Robinson was so great, because his arm wasn't that strong, but with his quick release he could nail any runner. But most of all, you could measure different aspects of *hitting*.

"Jim McLaughlin's right: when scouts look at a pitcher, it's easier for them to see the kid's physical strengths and weaknesses. Hitting is less consistent—and if I were a general manager today, I'd draft pitchers, acquire defensive players, and trade selectively for hitters. *Unless* I had some scientific way of preselecting the hitters, by testing things like reflexes, eyesight, and bat speed.

"The technical capability is there to run all these tests right now. The initial costs would be enormous—but in the process of doing measurements, you'd start coming up with findings you hadn't counted on, answers to questions you hadn't even asked yet. The logistics would be tricky, because if you wanted this information on all the top prospects before the draft, you'd have to test kids in high school as well as college. There may be sixteen thousand high schools with baseball programs, and those kids are just coming of age, and you can't possibly scout them in volume till they're seniors. So there's a short window there—especially in the North, where a kid may only play in April and May, and then the draft comes up in early June. But, frankly, the logistics would be a minor problem, compared to the problem of changing the mind-set of baseball men, and convincing them that all of this meant something.

"In pro football a lot of the technical tests are run by scouting combines. In baseball the Scouting Bureau just administers the psychological test and an eye test that only spots medical weaknesses. The Bureau could do more, but their clients don't particularly want technical information. And if there's nobody in the marketplace to buy the product, you're not gonna build it. The baseball industry has no history of providing a marketplace for sophisticated information, so any move toward technical testing would have to come from an individual club that has an inspired and enlightened owner."

From 1963 to 1972 one owner—Bob Carpenter of the Phillies—underwrote a "Research Program for Baseball," a series of tests of bat speed and eyesight, conceived and administered by a team of University of Delaware professors and DuPont scientists. Despite some provocative findings the Research Program was generally ignored or mocked by baseball men.

From 1971 to 1975 another owner—Ewing Kauffman of the Royals—underwrote a more ambitious project, an "academy" whose goal was nothing less than the *creation* of baseball players. When the academy folded, however, none of its scientific innovations was integrated into the Kansas City scouting system. And in the current folklore of scouting the academy's only legacy is thought to be one ballplayer, Frank White. Some scouts have nicknamed White "The Six Million Dollar Man."

"The basic assumption underlying this study," said the first (1963) report of the Research Program for Baseball, "is that valid and reliable measuring devices and instruments can be constructed that will be useful in the selection and training of professional baseball players." Over the course of the following decade the Research Program focused more on training and less on selection—partly because of the resistance of scouts to the technological analysis of talent.

In a series of experiments with major-league, minor-league, and college hitters, the researchers studied bat velocity, bat acceleration, total force, and smoothness of swing. In 1968, for example, they found that the average major-league hitter took .15 seconds to complete his swing, and that a few superior hitters—like Dick Allen, or Peter Rose from the right side—took less than .10 seconds. The superior hitters also waited longer before swinging (Allen and Rose began their swings when the ball was less than 20 feet from home plate), achieved peak bat acceleration closer to impact time, and had later, quicker strides.

But what was the cause, and what was the effect? Perhaps the good hitter waited longer because he *could* wait longer, because he possessed the reflexes and eye skills to take a "late read" on a pitch before committing himself. Concurrent with the bat experiments, the researchers conducted a series of tests with the Bausch and Lomb Ortho-Rater, the kind of machine used by school nurses to check the visual aptitudes of children. The complete test measured near acuity, distance acuity, depth perception, and lens convergence. This last aptitude, put scientifically, was the "A.C.A. score" and was expressed as the "ratio of accommodative convergence per diopter, as derived from a measurement of lateral phoria." In laymen's terms (i.e., scouts' terms) it meant that the good hitter easily adjusts his binocular focus as the pitch approaches the plate, achieving a sequence of visual "locks" that the average hitter may be incapable of. The vision scores, when coupled with results of the bat tests, enabled the researchers to make some impressively accurate predictions each spring about the offensive production of young hitters in the Philadelphia farm system.

Other test results indicated that successful pitchers had, relatively speaking, average to poor scores on depth perception and lens convergence. Their near acuity was usually good, but the demands of their role might as well have been understood as two-dimensional: seeing the catcher's glove as if through a tunnel and blocking out peripheral distraction. As might have been expected, the players with keenest depth perception were usually outfielders.

Robert Hannah, the leader of the Research Program, and now head baseball coach and chairman of the Physical Education department at the University of Delaware, regards his ten years of testing with mixed feelings. "The importance of our research wasn't so much the conclusions as the *numbers*. And if we'd been allowed to continue, it would have been possible, in several categories of physical ability, to establish cut-off levels for amateur players or at least to flag the poorer performers for close scrutiny before they were drafted or signed. In the years since we stopped our work, there've been so many technical advances—in telemetry, cinematic analysis, the portability of equipment—and if you used them systematically, in a year-to-year program, you could save yourself a lot of money in the long run by eliminating some expensive scouting mistakes. The spin-off value would be that you could check every player in your own organization every year, mark his progress or regress, and make trades on a more scientific basis.

"But the scouts don't see it that way. It's too much work. It's too technical for them. They don't want to open another category where they'd have to relearn. As baseball people they're forever steeped in that tradition that says, 'Look, I've got all the information I need. Don't give me any more.' In all the tests and in all the years I've coached college ball, I've met a lot of scouts—and I can tell you the favorite expression most of them fall back on. 'For me.' As in 'This boy didn't do it for me.' Or 'For me, this boy shows real potential as a power hitter.' These words 'for me' are like a badge: scouts are *proud* of being subjective. So if you wanted to apply technical testing to scouting, you'd have to hire someone more qualified than scouts to do the testing. The whole Ortho-Rater eye test only takes five minutes or so, but it's still something that the average scout would just be anxious to get out of the way.

"So we began to direct our research work away from scouting, away from the original selection process, and more toward evaluation of professional players in the Phillies' system. The tests for eyesight were especially valuable, because we could spot weaknesses and recommend corrections—glasses, or sets of muscle exercises, or at least a thorough follow-up by an ophthalmologist. It was as a result of our tests that Dick Allen started wearing glasses. But with some players the problems we found—in focusing, for example—couldn't be corrected at all. At one time, I'll never forget it, we tested Don Hoak, who was trying to hang on with the Phillies at the end of his career. He had several poor scores, and the bottom line was that eyeglasses or muscle exercises weren't going to help him as a hitter or a third baseman. We turned those results in, and later I was sitting in one of the Phillies' offices when Hoak saw me—his eyes were *that* good—and he rushed in and tried to lift me up against the wall. He said, 'You sonsabitches want to take my job away from me, and I'm not gonna let you do it!' "

The researchers turned out to be right. Hoak's career was almost over, through no fault of theirs or his. But to be lifted off the ground and against the wall by one of the fiercest players in the game, a man whose nickname was Tiger and whose hometown was Roulette, Pennsylvania, must have been a test in itself, of one's own commitment to science.

In the middle of my scouting season I asked Jack Pastore, the Phillies' assistant scouting director, what had ever happened to the test results from the Research Program. He didn't know and barely cared. The Philadelphia system, as he saw it, operated from the premise that scouting would always be more art than science. And he had already decided that the organization didn't need to spend the few thousand dollars it would take every year to obtain AMI profiles of top amateur prospects.

"One reason we discontinued the psychological tests is that we don't belong to the Bureau, and so if we wanted a profile on a kid we had to have one of our own scouts go test him, which might have been the fifth time in the season that the kid was being asked to fill out one of those questionnaires, and he was naturally resistant. But another reason is that we expect our own scouts to get off their seat cushions behind home plate, to find out about the whole ballplayer. I can show you an old psychological profile on Larry Bowa, where his 'guilt proneness' is rated above ninety and his 'emotional control' is below ten. That's interesting information, but how would you use it today if you were thinking about drafting or signing a kid like that? Our first question is: 'How bad does this kid want to play professional ball?' And our scouts get paid to have an informed answer to that question.

"As for physical tests, I just don't believe they give enough of the picture. There are too many intangibles. When you say that the modern scout is like an investment analyst, that rings true—kind of like Paul Newman in that movie about Philadelphia lawyers, where he traveled around and evaluated properties. But baseball scouting is really much tougher, because you're dealing with the human individual, and you're looking so far in the future. The kid might get injured after you sign him, or he might come out the other side of adolescence as a different guy.

"And when you build a scouting staff, you have to give your people plenty of leeway. A scout has to be his own man. He's under *some* supervision, but if you try to impose too much or play too much by the percentages, you undercut effectiveness and morale. Scouts don't scout in order to get rich. They scout because they know baseball—from direct experience, not tests— and because they're opinionated men. You could fire them all tomorrow and hire scientists and buy machines, and you'd wind up with lots of numbers and not too many clear recommendations, where a guy is ready to put his own individual ass on the line. It's a unique job. Sometimes I think scouts are like the last real Americans."

For me, as a scout might say, Jack Pastore's comments raised an immediate question: if scouting is such a psychologically rewarding profession, what are you doing in the office? Why are you a scouting director instead of a scout?

The answer was that Pastore, unlike Jim McLaughlin or Dave Ritterpusch, *did* scout whenever he got the chance— sometimes to the chagrin of the Phillies' national cross-checker, Brandy Davis. And if the money were just a little better, Pastore said, and if the right territory opened up, he'd leave the office as a happy man, ready "like Jonathan Livingston Seagull" to express himself more fully and truly as an individual.

Jack Pastore's apprenticeship as a baseball man began in Baltimore. He was hired in 1967 by Lou Gorman, who had been hired by Harry Dalton, who had been hired by Jim Mc-

Laughlin. In 1969 Gorman left for Kansas City, first as the director of player development and later as the administrator of the most grandiose development program in the history of baseball—the Royals' Academy. This project, Gorman hastens to say, was not his idea; it was the dream of Ewing Kauffman, the Kansas City owner, whose experience and vast fortune came from pharmaceuticals (Marion Laboratories) not baseball.

"Ewing Kauffman used to say: 'We have to be more definitive. Scouting has always been just an inexact science.' Well, it has. And it probably always will be. You can try to make it a science, but it's really more of an art form.

"He said, 'But why can't you scout more like the football people do? They do all these work-ups, strength tests, and all that.' I said, 'Mr. Kauffman, we can use a Cybex to measure ratios of muscle strength, even get a computer to graph them, but what that spots is physical flaws not physical abilities.' Look at Ernie Banks. Shit, he was weak. But he could hit the ball as far as anyone in the game. Good hitters depend more on bat speed than strength.

"So Kauffman said, 'You tell me bat speed's important. All right, let's get a goddamn machine to measure bat speed.' I said, 'Bat speed *is* important, but what's more important is when the bat speed occurs.' He said, 'Then we can do reflex tests and eye tests.' I said, 'Fine, Mr. Kauffman, but there's so many skills involved here that you'll never have the machines to isolate them all and tell you everything you need to know. Because so much of baseball is psychological, like lack of fear at the plate.'

"He said, 'Then we'll do psychological tests too.'

"And we did. And we did everything we could think of with machines: slow-motion analysis, bat speed, balance and agility, and especially reflexes. We had some guy come in who'd done this marvelous process photography for Walt Disney productions, and he put together stop-action sequences so our kids could sit and watch the rotation of a pitched ball, and we could check out their patterns of recognition.

"By the time the academy folded, though, most of that testing just wasn't very useful; we couldn't translate it back into our regular scouting program. But Ewing Kauffman loved that kind of thing. He loved anything that would be science. He has a very empirical mind. Two and two will always make four to him."

What do two and two make to Lou Gorman? The same thing they make to most baseball men: something between three and five. "There are so many variables," Gorman says. "I remember when Don Gutteridge, in his first year as a scout, went to Sioux City to look at a pitcher named Paul Splittorff. He watched him warm up, and then it started to rain, so he never saw him in a game. But he said, 'Splittorff looks like he has a good arm, and he looks intelligent.' So I had his card on file during the draft that June—and in Round twenty-two I was looking for a left-handed pitcher, just to fill out the roster of a rookie club. I found this card, and I said, 'Oh, what the hell, let's draft *him*. We did, and then we brought him to Kansas City for a tryout, and he showed us a great arm, and we signed him right there. And Splittorff became the winningest left-hander in Royal's history. The variables in scouting, and the luck, prevent you from ever trusting numbers too much."

And the variables in baseball economics prevent you from applying the same principles everywhere you go. After Gorman left the Royals he worked four years for the Seattle Mariners, an organization so poor (or tight-fisted) that its scouting staff consisted of five full-timers. "You do what you have to do when you have to do it," Gorman says. Then, as a vice-president with the New York Mets (serving under Frank Cashen, another product of the Baltimore executive system), Gorman oversaw a much larger talent network—while contending with the realities of the New York market, where the fans and the media demand immediate improvement.

"We didn't have those pressures in Kansas City. Ewing Kauffman could underwrite a program like the academy without hearing a lot of complaints about how he was spending his money. He could simply try something daring. His idea was to find good young *athletes,* even if they didn't have much baseball experience, and try to turn them into whole ballplayers. To get into the program a kid had to meet three criteria: good results on a psychological test, above-average running speed, and excellent eyesight—not just 20/20, but 20/15 or 20/10. In the five years we ran the academy we looked at about 40,000 kids, and we took the best 140 specimens.

"We built the academy complex in Sarasota. I bought the property, 121 acres for $121,000. And then we spent about a few million for construction—housing, offices, classrooms, a swimming pool, basketball courts, and baseball diamonds. The kids were there for 350 days a year. In the mornings we bussed them back and forth to Manatee Junior College; in the afternoons they played baseball, took instruction, or went through tests. We had technicians there, and we had an eye doctor and a clinical psychologist—and in fact Dr. Ogilvie himself, the sports psychologist, came in early on to do evaluations. At one of our staff meetings he presented work-ups on eighteen players, and sixteen were so accurate that they staggered us. I think *that* kind of testing has real merit, as one more tool to give you insight into the whole player, because my experience is that in baseball the makeup is just as important as the physical skills. Maybe more important. What I always loved about George Brett was his makeup. At seventeen he was a man!

"But the psychological tests created a problem on one player, U. L. Washington. His brother, who worked at Royals' Stadium, came to me one day and asked about tryouts for the academy, so we had him bring U. L. to one of the camps, where we had about three hundred other kids, and this kid had a toothpick in his mouth even then and a pair of old jeans on. We had him take some ground balls at shortstop, and he was one of the worst fielders I've ever seen. The ball went through him, under him, by him—and we almost had to *roll* it to him so that he could pick it up and throw. But when he did throw, he had rifle arm across the infield. Great arm. The ball just took off.

"We had him hit, and he was terrible at that. But his eyesight was well above average, and his running speed was outstanding. The other test he struggled with, the psychological thing. He didn't have a good educational background. When the camp was over, we met with the psychologists and the regular staff, and they recommended two kids, but I wanted to keep Washington too. The doctor said, 'No, he didn't pass the test.' I said, 'Fine, I appreciate your position, but I'm gonna put him in the program. He can run and throw and see, and we'll find out if we can make a ballplayer out of this kid.'

"So we took him down to the academy, with his psychological profile still in his folder. And about a week later Ewing Kauffman called me up at the office, and said, 'Why'd you put him in the program? I don't like him bein' there.' I said, 'Well, unless you order me to take him out, Mr. Kauffman, he's gonna stay.' And he did stay, and I kept my eye on him, and his drive was remarkable. You could put him out there four or five hours fielding ground balls, and he wouldn't leave. He began to pick the ball well after a while, and his hitting showed real improvement too. At the end of his second year we put him in the regular farm system. So be sure you count U. L. as an academy product, along with Frank White.

"All along I tried to convince Kauffman that we should take the better players we already had in our farm system and expose *them* to that kind of training. But he wanted the regular program plus this program. Well, it was a noble effort, but its effect on scouting today is almost nil. Scouts don't see themselves as scientists; they see themselves as artists. Of course a lot are neither one, but the best really do have a gift.

"Rosey Gilhousen loved Randy Jones. He took me to see him five different times, and I never saw Randy get past the fifth inning of a game. I said, 'Rosey, this kid's never gonna pitch in the big leagues. He can't even get college hitters out. He's too slow. His pitches come up to the plate in stages.' Rosey said, 'I know he's gonna pitch in the majors. He has a good motion; he can *change* speeds.' Four years later Randy won the Cy Young Award. All he did was get hitter out after hitter out, and he made the best ones look awful.

"And then there was the time we got Willie Wilson, when we had no right to get him. We were drafting from the eighteenth position in Round one, and he should have gone as one of the top three in the country. He was worked out by the Phillies, the Yankees, the Mets, the Pirates, and the Orioles—and all of them were convinced that he'd go to the University of Maryland to play football. He was one of the greatest football players to come out of the East; I think he scored fifty-two touchdowns in his junior year of high school in Summit, New Jersey. Our scout in that area, Al Diez, liked Willie so much that we sent in Tom Ferrick, and Ferrick liked him so much that we sent in Lilly and Blaylock. Willie was a catcher, but Diez said he should be in the outfield. We worked him out and with that speed he had . . . Christ, he was awesome.

"I said, 'Al, I just want you to tell me that this kid will sign. I don't care what it costs. Have we got a chance? Does he want to play baseball?' So Diez just *lived* with the family, and the parents were divorced, so he got to be like a second father, got to know Willie so well. And before the draft, Al said, 'I swear to you that this kid will sign.' After we drafted Willie a lot of baseball people from other clubs said, 'We loved him too, but we knew he'd never sign. You just wasted your draft.' But we hadn't—because it was a case of a scout doing, literally, his homework. It was individual initiative, and salesmanship, and friendship: the human touch. And if you ever hear of any machine, or any test, that can simulate *that,* please call me collect at my office."

My interviews with all the ex-Oriole scouting executives had finally become a survey of the two sides of baseball intelligence. McLaughlin and Ritterpusch were left-hemisphere critics, believers in rigorous quantitative analysis. Pastore and Gorman were right-hemisphere poets, attracted more to the exception than the rule, more to qualities (personality, intuition) than numbers. Both sides meant to study "the whole ballplayer."

I came away convinced that major-league organizations could, and ought to, sponsor more testing—but on a fairly modest scale. It seemed obvious, for example, that top amateur prospects should at least be subjected to thorough medical exams, to prevent the kind of expensive mistakes described by Howie Haak (e.g., unwittingly taking a bad diabetic as a first-round draft choice). Underwriting those physicals might cost any one organization less than $10,000 each spring—along with the cost of having to listen to local scouts complain about all the new paperwork. In addition, given the technology now easily available, it would make sense for every team to obtain more precise readings of the skills of its own successful players. These measurements might or might not influence decisions about trades or long-term contracts, but they would at least constitute an initial data base, from which (as Dave Ritterpusch observes) serendipitous discoveries might follow.

"Even that's not enough," Jim McLaughlin insisted. So I decided to let him have the last word. Even though McLaughlin was at the furthest remove, in time and feeling, from the current business of scouting, his attitudes were the most sharply defined, and he expressed them with the energy of a true devil's advocate.

"You could run all kinds of tests on amateur prospects too. A football prospect knows he's not gonna play unless he goes through that testing. Pro football says to them: 'We're like Harvard. If you want to get in, the first thing you have to do is pass some tests.' Baseball could say the same thing, but the local scouts pamper the prospects. Face it. As long as you have scouts who think it's a big deal to ask a kid to run a sixty-yard dash, as long as you have scouts who don't even trust stopwatches, you're gonna have prospects who don't care either, who begrudge the hour it takes to do a simple eye exam and fill out one of the psychological tests—much less undergo a total medical or get wired up like an astronaut plugged into a computer.

"And Jack Pastore's theory is in the Middle Ages. Those local scouts have to be *controlled* from the office, and you can't do that if you're a frustrated scout yourself. It's not a scouting director's job to go scout; if he tries it, he gets subjective. But I think Pastore has romanticized scouting . . . and maybe you have too.

"As for the Kansas City Academy, the original idea was good. It was the kind of thing Branch Rickey might have tried. The fallacy came in starting on such a large scale. The initial investment was too high. They should have begun with twenty or twenty-five kids, taken 'em to spring training, and then found a small facility where they could continue the program. But Kauffman started with this beautiful physical plant, and then his people said, 'We've gotta go out there and fill it for him.' So they reverted back to the old baseball way of doing things, without scientific standards. I don't think Kauffman got a fair deal: Gorman and the rest of those guys didn't believe in the initial concept.

"When Gorman says that scouting is really an art, I don't see why he can't accept that it's a *combination* of art and science. Rosey Gilhousen's belief in Randy Jones wasn't intuition. It was experience—that of all the left-handed pitchers he'd ever seen, there'd been guys like Randy Jones before, and Gilhousen's mental computer was automatically separating the differences between Randy and all the other kids who don't throw hard. So even that is more scientific than it is an art form.

"There are some things that you can't answer in words. Right now I'm reading Karl Rahner's *Lessons in the Faith,* and it occurs to me how much of our lives we live that we can't give explicit answers for in language, as to what we do and why. But that's no sign that within our minds and within our spirits, we're not giving answers. It's just that we're not capable of expounding those answers in a verbal form. When I was a scouting director, I'd listen to the scouts tell me about intuition, and I saw that there was no use in getting into battles all the time, so I just said to myself: 'This is what's really happening in this man's mind.' Where I got into arguments was after I'd had a few drinks, and I'd try to convert scouts to my way of thinking. And there's no way in the world you can convince a scout that he doesn't have intuition, especially when you're on your fourth drink.

"But in my rational moments—in my non-drinking moments—I did a lot of thinking about what happens when a scout sees the whole ballplayer. He can't make the recognition unless he already has some structures in his mind—or if you think in terms of computers, some program. That's what I was trying to provide, to direct their experience and memory. And at one time I had as good a memory as any of them. When it started to go, I just started to get tired of all the hassles. I was ready to get out of baseball."

8 CROSS-CHECKER

Ohio Univ., Athens. This boy is wiry, strong, raw-boned. Has good features—good voice, poise; looks like a ballplayer. Is a competitor. Reminds me of Fregosi. At bat has square stance, back in box, body fairly erect, bat high. Can drive the ball: quick bat, consistent contact. Has idea of strike zone but is aggressive. Fielding—soft hands; good, open glove; A + arm. Good range—glides, is effortless in actions. This boy's running speed to first base will sour a lot of people, but he is agile, quick otherwise; can do the other things and star in big leagues. Will not survive first round in the draft.

> *—Brandy Davis's report on Mike Schmidt, May 5, 1971*

From the end of February to the beginning of June, Brandy Davis traveled over one hundred thousand miles in search of more Mike Schmidts. He was looking only at blue-chip prospects, the ones rated at $20,000 or more by the Phillies' area scouts, and he saw most of them only one time. To be a cross-checker, he said, is to focus the whole scouting process toward a single point, so that the job requires tricky logistics even while offering a special kind of freedom.

"The Phillies give me an airline charge card, and a credit card for hotels and rental cars and phone calls, and then they turn me loose! I follow the sun north—in early March I'm usually in the Southwest, and I may not get to New England until May, but it's really more complicated than that because I keep criss-crossing the whole continent. I couldn't ever plan my spring schedule more than a week in advance.

"I'm always trying to catch a break on the variables. If possible, I want to see a hitter in an *away* game, because his team will bat in the last inning even if they're ahead, and I might get to see him hit an extra time. And I always want to see a pitcher in a *day* game, so I can really tell what his pitches do. Fastballs look faster at night, and you can't just rely on a radar gun. I also try to have a back-up game in case I'm rained out, even if that game is five hundred miles away. If I get a rainout in the East, see, I've got the time zones going my way, so I might be able to make it to Chicago for a game that afternoon. And I try to see a prospect against a good team, not just anybody—and if I schedule it right, I might even see two top boys in the same game."

Davis's favorite game of the 1981 scouting season came in early May in Joliet, Illinois, when he watched a matchup between Mark Grant and Dick Schofield. Davis saw it as a confrontation between the best high school pitcher and the best high school hitter in America. Grant pitched a one-hitter, Schofield got the only hit, a single off a breaking pitch. But to a cross-checker the hit was actually less important than one foul ball. When Schofield pulled one deep down the leftfield line, he proved that he could get around on a major-league fastball and drive it with major-league power.

"Usually I'm only looking at one prospect," Davis said, "so I just focus on him for the whole game, because I have to assume that I won't see him again before the draft. I watch everything he does, even on the sidelines, and even in the practice before the game. If I have an off day, I might go to a high school workout. I flew from L.A. to San Diego one time just to see Alan Trammell practice bunts and infield plays with his team. So it all adds up. You have to stay awake! It's ironic, but occasionally a cross-checker will travel a thousand miles to see a boy play, and the game starts and he's not sure who he's supposed to be watching because he forgot to check the uniform numbers of the players."

Whenever Davis cross-checked fielders, he took it for granted that most of them would be playing a different position if and

when they succeeded in pro ball. He pointed out that shortstop
Bill Russell began as a centerfielder, centerfielder Dale Murphy
began as a catcher, catcher Bob Boone began as a third baseman, and third baseman Mike Schmidt began as a shortstop.
When Davis first saw Schmidt in 1971, he noted then that this
college shortstop had size instead of range. When he factored
in Schmidt's great reflexes, A+ arm and soft hands, he said:
"Third base."

It was a matter of checking the player's tools against the
specifications of the game of baseball. The logic of such scouting might look like this:

	SS, 2b	3b	C	1b	OF
SOFT HANDS	√	√	√	√	
QUICK FEET	√	√	√	√	
STRONG ARM	√	√	√		√
RANGE, SPEED	√				√
SIZE		√	√	√	

Some problems of cross-checking were not so amenable to
logic. They were political. "One conflict," Davis said, "is that
a lot of area scouts won't commit themselves soon enough. In
any given region our area scout is about three weeks ahead of
me, seeing which good-looking prospects survived the winter
and passing the top names on to me. But the average area scout
doesn't want to get too high on a boy too soon and then have
to backtrack on his opinion. And yet he doesn't want to discover a great player out of the blue in late spring, because if
a boy's that good he should have shown traces of it earlier.
So the scout might protect himself by pacing his reports, which
makes my job trickier.

"But I guess, to the area scout, *I'm* the problem. Maybe he's
nursed a boy along, seen him develop through high school,
watched him in a dozen games or so, gotten to know him as

a person—and then I come in for one game, and I say, 'Compared to the rest of the year's crop, this boy has to be low on my list.' Sometimes I like a prospect better than the area scout does; that happened with Dale Murphy and Robin Yount. But with Mike Scioscia or Keith Moreland, and this Lebo Powell case, area scouts got upset at my recommendations, and I'm sure some'll be upset this year too. Because I've trained myself to be more critical than benevolent."

I first met Brandy Davis in 1976, when he began showing up at a lecture series I organized at the University of Delaware, featuring historians and journalists on the theme of "Baseball in American Life." The last visitor was the sports journalist Pat Jordan, who fielded ninety minutes of questions and answered them all with his usual frankness—but he seemed distracted by a man in the third row.

The man was in his late forties, a stocky six-footer, his graying hair in a short brush cut. He wore a blue golf sweater. He asked no questions, but frowned often—as when Jordan mentioned by name some major-leaguers who smoked dope, or when he alluded to his own descriptions of scouts in *The Suitors of Spring* and *A False Spring*. In both books Jordan, a high-school pitching sensation in 1959, recalls being "romanced" by such scouts as Ray Garland of the Yankees and Jeff Jones of the Braves. Although the Braves won the bidding war with a bonus of $40,000, Jordan never advanced above Class C in the minors. His memories of scouts, like his memories of his own baseball career, consist of precise unromantic images:

> Their conversation seldom touched on what was happening before their eyes. They paused only infrequently to pull out a stopwatch and time a runner to first base, or maybe to ask a neighbor about the last putout, which they then recorded in the notebooks they had to turn in to the front office as proof they were doing their job. But these pauses were mere interruptions in their perpetual talk about good restaurants nearby where they would meet after this, their third game of the afternoon; or about too much bourbon consumed last night in a motel

room in Naugatuck, Connecticut, and how they couldn't handle it like they used to, or women either for that matter, and they'd all laugh; or finally about that good Polack boy they'd given a $40,000 bonus a few years ago and was now hitting .227 in the Three-I League, but was still saving their hide with the front office by showing a little power, and thank God for small blessings. . . . As long as they didn't do anything foolish, they would never be out of baseball. They would never have to join that "lunch bucket brigade" which they feared and which they joked about behind the homeplate screen.

In response to one question Jordan professed nostalgia for the days when scouts had to win prospects instead of drafting them—but this only led him to characterize modern scouting as relatively lifeless, now more than ever the domain of "company men" who survive by keeping their noses clean. The man in the blue sweater frowned again, and then as the session ended he unwrapped and lit a cigar before strolling out with the rest of the audience.

Jordan asked me if I knew the man, and I identified him as Brandy Davis, chief scout for the Phillies. "I knew it! I knew he was a scout. The whole time I was talking, I felt like a hooker being stared at by a cop."

It's not that Davis looks especially stern; it's that his whole demeanor projects his sense of himself as a serious critic. The very nature of his work defines a new bureaucratic element in scouting: centralized comparative judgment prior to each draft. "As a result of the draft system," the Philadelphia *Scouting Manual* says, "the cross-check scout has become a necessary evil. In short, scouting is no longer strictly an individual accomplishment."

But Davis belies Pat Jordan's stereotype of the company man. He sees himself as an enemy of bureaucracy and imagines that his constant travel keeps him always one step ahead of it. In 1981 his supervisors, Jim Baumer and Jack Pastore, were complaining that Davis needed to be "reined in"—made to phone the office for more frequent instructions instead of flying all over the country on his own—and they introduced a new program that made him only one of several Philadephia cross-checkers. Davis's face, the same one that distracted Pat Jordan, told you that he wouldn't be easily reined in by any program. And if you scouted scouts the way that Brandy Davis scouts ballplayers, you might decide that he has "the good face" for an individualistic baseball man.

I had read through enough of Davis's old reports to be amused at the recurrence of the phrase "good face, good voice." Some version of the formula appeared, almost as a headline, in his original reports on Mike Schmidt, Dale Murphy, Mike Ivie, Mark Clear, and dozens of other players he liked at first sight. It seemed incredibly subjective, one cut below phrenology. It also made me self-conscious, when I interviewed him, about my own face and voice.

"It's not subjective. Subjective would be if you wanted to sign a boy because you were swayed by the enthusiasm of his coach. Or if you put the dollar sign on the muscle and then raised it just because you thought he was such a nice kid—we call that 'falling in love' with a boy, seeing more than what's really there. But 'good face' is *ob*jective: it means he impresses you as an athlete—not a pretty boy. He's not withdrawn. He projects strength, virility, maturity. Sometimes you see that in the face, the same way you can hear in the voice that he has presence or competitiveness. Out of baseball, in real life, we all do these kinds of readings all the time when we first meet someone.

"And besides, I bet if you really looked through the reports on boys I've liked, you'd find a word that shows up a lot more often than *good face*. That word is *durable*. Baseball is a more physically demanding game than most fans realize, and the season is *long*. It's hard enough to make the majors if you're healthy, and a brittle player just doesn't have too much future. That's why I couldn't get too interested in this boy named Ricky Nelson, the outfielder at Arizona State. He has all the tools but also a long-term problem with shin splints. I put twenty-five thousand on him, less than most scouts did; he's only number thirty-one on my draft list. On the other hand the number one player on my list needs a knee operation, but we've had detailed medical reports and they're all good. And he's so strong that I think he *will* be durable."

By the end of the spring Davis sometimes said "my list" in the same way that a writer might say "my novel." It was a highly personal construct and an exercise in continuous comparative judgment. The season's prospects were like a deck of cards that the cross-checker kept shuffling, constantly re-examining each player's ability in relation to all the others. Davis's list was fifty names long, and he gave me thumbnail descriptions of his top ten prospects.

1. KEVIN MCREYNOLDS: CENTERFIELDER; UNIVERSITY OF ARKANSAS—$100,000

"Whoever drafts this boy won't be able to use him for the next six months, because he'll need rehabilitation on the knee, but he's worth the wait. Before he got hurt, he ran a sixty-yard dash in 6.6; right now he's running at about eighty percent efficiency. If not for that, I'd say he has all five tools, and the best is home-run power to all fields. He's just *strong*—6′1″, 200 pounds—and he's poised, doesn't get rattled, can pace himself down. Sometimes he seems too nonchalant, but he'll dive for balls in the outfield, and he has the good hands."

2. DICK SCHOFIELD: SHORTSTOP; HIGH SCHOOL, SPRINGFIELD, ILLINOIS—$90,000

"A baby face, but he's mature for his age. His dad played in the major leagues, and this boy's game shows that background. He knows what he's doing on the field—always gets a good jump on the ball and doesn't rush himself or panic on the short hop. He'll be a shortstop in pro ball until he plays himself to second base or third base. His bat's quick—it drives the ball—and he can jump on mistakes for fence power."

3. RON DARLING: RIGHT-HANDED PITCHER; YALE UNIVERSITY—$90,000

"In the last few weeks of the season he was carrying the Yale team all by himself. I don't take him seriously as a hitter and outfielder, but the way he performs there shows you he's agile, coordinated, and he's an excellent *fielding* pitcher. His fastball and slider are above major-league average, but his curve is slow and flat, almost a change-up. He still needs a consistent groove for his arm angle—he wanders around three-quarters—and a better follow-through, because he tends to finish straight up, using a lot of just arm. But he's still my number one pitcher this year."

4. JAMES WINN: RIGHT-HANDED PITCHER; JOHN BROWN UNIVERSITY—$85,000

"This is a power arm, with a consistent three-quarter release point for low fastball strikes, and a great slider. He comes overhand for his curveball, but it doesn't break much, and he should just forget this angle pitch. If he can develop a straight change off the fastball, he should pitch in the majors. He has a towering strong build—6'4", 215 pounds—and plenty of poise. You watch him on the mound, and you know he just *loves* to be there."

5. MARK GRANT: RIGHT-HANDED PITCHER; HIGH SCHOOL, JOLIET, ILLINOIS—$85,000

"When I saw Grant head-to-head against Schofield, he got a strikeout off the fastball. It's a live fastball, and he's not afraid to bring it inside, to back hitters off the plate. But his curve is like Winn's: straight overhand with not much break. On all his pitches he needs the consistent three-quarter arm angle for his release, but at his age there's already a good base to work from. And he has a durable body."

6. JOE CARTER: RIGHTFIELDER; WICHITA STATE UNIVERSITY—$80,000

"Also durable—a tall and strong black body. He may have the best all-around tools of any player I saw this spring. He shows a fine arm from rightfield, runs with a powerful stride, steals bases, has good power. The only hole in his game is lack of discipline at the plate: he needs a better idea of the strike zone, and he has to extend his arms to swing. Right now, with that long swing, he can be jammed. But he could make fast progress, because he has a great makeup—competitive and loose at the same time."

7. JON ABREGO: RIGHT-HANDED PITCHER; HIGH SCHOOL, MISSION SAN JOSE, CALIFORNIA—$75,000

"Both his upper body and legs are strong, and he has a live arm. He has the *spin* for a good curveball, but he needs to work on it—instead of fooling around with knucklers and forkballs. He's mature at eighteen and very coachable, and again you'd want to find a consistent pitching angle for him— probably straight overhand. With that nice compact delivery his fastball can be overpowering."

8. VANCE LOVELACE: LEFT-HANDED PITCHER; HIGH SCHOOL, TAMPA, FLORIDA—$70,000

"He's tall and rangy—6'5", 190 pounds—an ideal build for a pitcher. He has a live breaking pitch, kind of a running slider, and he really intimidates left-handed hitters. His follow-through's inconsistent: sometimes he drags his back foot or doesn't bring it forward at all, so he almost seems to fall backward. Right now he's more of a pure thrower than some of these other pitchers, but he has good rhythm on the mound, and I like his potential."

9. TERRY BLOCKER: CENTERFIELDER; TENNESSEE STATE UNIVERSITY—$65,000

"If you compare Blocker with Joe Carter, you might give him an edge for being left-handed, because hitting from that side of the plate he can almost steal first base. He runs the sixty in 6.5 and he's a *gliding* runner: he eats up the ground with his stride. But he's not as good all-around. His arm's just okay, and at the plate he has trouble with any pitches but fastballs. On the breaking pitch he commits himself too soon, and then he just swings with his arms. His build reminds you of Garry Maddox—lanky and trim with good power."

10. MIKE MOORE: RIGHT-HANDED PITCHER; ORAL ROBERTS UNIVERSITY—$60,000

"His low fastball is terrific. It's also too true, without much movement. For me his breaking pitches are a long way off: when I saw him, he looked like a one-pitch thrower. He has the inconsistent release point, he doesn't use his legs for advantage, and his follow-through is off-balance. Still, he has fine arm, and he'll definitely be among the first fifteen taken in the draft."

Listening to Davis's sketches, I began to make some generalizations. That six of his top ten prospects were pitchers illustrated his belief that a real pitching find can get to the majors faster than a position player and make a bigger difference once he's there. That so few of these pitchers had good curveballs suggested that kids today are favoring the slider, even in high school. That arm angle was such a problem implied that one of the scout's first questions must be: What's correctable and what isn't?

"Yeah, especially if you're a cross-checker. That's why I try extra hard to see the top pitching prospects in more than one game. You focus on what can be smoothed out, what might be taught, because so few of these boys have had good coaches. In half the high schools it's the social studies teacher."

But Davis was really working on a different set of generalizations. The first was that the Phillies, even drafting from
the twentieth position, would still have a shot at one or more
of those top ten players. The second was that the value of
Philadelphia's thoroughness in scouting ought to show up in
the later rounds of the draft: "We don't just cross-check the
outstanding boys—whereas a Bureau club, with maybe ten
scouts, might have to start guessing by the eighth round." The
third was that "Scouting is like baseball itself"—an observation that opened out into a discussion of a way of life, a way
of seeing.

Scouting is like baseball itself. The game is a game of errors
and bad pitches, and if you make fewer mistakes, and less
costly ones, than the other team . . . you should prevail. We all
make big mistakes as scouts, but the idea is to be right more
often than you're wrong. I could be wrong about some of those
ten prospects. Or I could be wrong about players I left off my
draft list—like David Leeper, a left-handed outfielder, a senior
at Southern Cal. He looked fine last year, but this season he
really tailed off, and I'm wary of amateur players who don't get
better each year, the way Mike Schmidt did. Especially if
they're from California. The kids out there play so many games
that they mature early as ballplayers, but a lot reach a certain
plateau and that's it. So I've crossed this boy off, but I'm also
remembering that in 1974, for exactly the same reason, I
crossed off another Southern Cal. outfielder named Fred Lynn.
    Another way scouting is like baseball is that every player is
already a scout. You learn as you go along, as you play with or
against certain guys, that this one has intangibles that win ballgames, or that one has a slow bat, or another one has a 75
arm.
    I say 75, because I learned to use that 60-to-80 system that
Campanis developed for the Dodgers. In old-time scouting any
system that worked for you was good—and I knew one old
scout who used to draw a parachute next to a player's name if
he was a bail-out hitter. But today you have to communicate
your grades to a lot more people, so there has to be some code
that everybody tries to apply the same way. I like the 60-to-80

system; in fact I helped get the Phillies to adopt it. But I never forget that it's just a code.

I learned the mechanics of evaluation when I was a manager in the Dodger chain, because Fresco Thompson, the farm director, made us file scouting cards on all our own minor-leaguers, and all their best opponents, all the time. But I'd learned how to be objective when I was still a player, when I had to take a hard look at my own abilities.

I had two major-league tools—running and throwing. And two fair tools—fielding and hitting for average. Speed was the big thing. On the track team, at Duke, I did the 100, the 440, and a leg of the mile relay. The baseball coach, Jack Combs, put me in the outfield to take advantage of that speed, and I hit for a good average. No power, though—and that was the era in baseball when most scouts rated power way ahead of speed; the top base stealer in the American League in 1950 only had fifteen. But Branch Rickey was in love with speed, and so were his scouts. One of them was Rex Bowen, who wanted to sign me to a Brooklyn contract, and I was all set to do it because I was loyal to Rex. But then Rickey moved over from Brooklyn to Pittsburgh, and Rex was loyal to *him* and went to Pittsburgh too, and I wound up signing a Pirates' contract. I guess if Rex had been a scout for the Cubs, I would have ended up in the Cubs' system. But that's a kind of bond that's vanished from scouting now, and from all of baseball.

One year in the minors I stole eighty-two bases in eighty-five attempts. And I hit for a decent average, but when I was up for part of two seasons with the Pirates I hit about .220. Now if a player like me came along today, they'd try to get him to switch-hit. That's what's got a lot of light hitters to the majors—Larry Bowa, Maury Wills at age twenty-six, and all those kids that George Kissell hatches for the Cardinals. But when I came up, nobody experimented much with switch-hitting, so I was just a weak bat in the outfield. If you don't hit for power out there, then you have to hit for percentage, like Richie Ashburn, and if you don't hit for power or percentage you're not going to make it. Even on the Pirates of 1952 and 1953, which was a bad ballclub. That's the team that Joe Garagiola still makes jokes about—and Rickey himself said that we "achieved last place on merit."

Mr. Rickey liked to smoke Antonio and Cleopatra cigars,

and the one time he got me to try one it kept going out. They have too much green stuff in them. Anyway, while he held the cigar in one hand, he used the other hand to imitate a big steam shovel. He kept dipping down with it, and he said, "If you scoop up enough talent, you can develop quality out of quantity." In those days a major-league team might have as many as fifteen farm clubs. That meant that on a given day you had fifteen shortstops in your system, forty-five outfielders, and maybe a hundred-fifty pitchers. If you got in trouble, you could just reach down with that scoop and move bodies up.

All that's changed. No organization now has more than seven affiliates, and most have five or less. Now you have maybe five shortstops in your whole system! You have a narrow talent base, and you can't afford to broaden it by signing a lot of marginal prospects. So the point is that now you have to develop quality out of *quality*. And if you fail, there's nothing to fall back on.

In most other ways, though, I'm still a Rickey man, and when it finally dawned on me that I wouldn't make it as a player, I was able to apply his ideas to coaching and scouting. I mean everything from teaching baserunning to avoiding the overstriding hitter and the shortarm pitcher, to little observations on prospects. I remember him saying: "Never sign a medical student—he's already dedicated to another vocation. And never sign a divinity student—the world's in bad enough shape that we don't want to take anyone away from the Lord's work."

It isn't just divinity students. A couple of years ago the Orioles had one of their top draft choices quit, after he'd spent just a couple of weeks on their Bluefield team. He didn't know that ballplayers and managers cuss and drink and play cards, and he was shocked. I'm like Rickey: I'm a realistic man, but I try not to swear. You know, one time when I was managing a minor-league team for the Astros, I was out on the field arguing a call with an umpire, and I *wanted* him to throw me out of the game because I thought it might fire up my kids. But he wouldn't do it. See, all I could think to do was wave my arms and say stuff like, "That was a terrible call. You're one of the darnedest umpires I've ever seen." I had to stay in the game.

I was with the Houston Astros because of Bobby Bragan, another Rickey man, when it was a new franchise in the early sixties. We got it off the ground fast through aggressive scouting—people like Paul Florence, Jim Baumer, Jim Wilson, Pat Gillick; Tal Smith was the scouting director. But some of us, like Baumer and me, resigned after Spec Richardson became the general manager, because he started trading away our best prospects—Joe Morgan, Mike Cuellar—for not very much. Our young talent wasn't being realized. So I went with the A's for a year, before this job opened up in Philly. And at that time, late season of 1969, I saw this good-looking prospect named Manny Trillo that the Phillies had with their farm team at Spartanburg, and I found out that they weren't protecting him in the minor-league draft. So I got Phil Seghi of the A's to steal him for four thousand dollars. And then a few months later I went to work for the Phillies, and we started scheming how to get Trillo back.

Before I went with the Phillies, they didn't do any real cross-checking. The draft had come in in 1965, and every year they were making subjective choices—like having to select between two top prospects without any advice from a scout who'd seen *both* of them. If an area scout wasn't that highly thought of by the office, or if he couldn't flower his descriptions, or if he wasn't that outgoing to push a certain boy, then the Phillies wouldn't draft his ballplayer. So the older scouts who were closer to ownership would be favored. One of them, from South Carolina, was especially close to Bob Carpenter, and for two years in a row the Phillies' first pick in the draft had come from his area. That scout said to me in 1971, "This black player will get drafted high, but I don't want anything to do with him. If the Phillies draft him, I don't want my name involved." He didn't sign black players. Period. In this case the player was Jim Rice. Another scout in Louisiana had never turned in a recommendation on Vida Blue. These scouts, on their own, were doing what they wanted to do, but the organization was suffering, and that's one reason we hit rock bottom in 1972.

The turnaround came when Ruly Carpenter took over from his father, and Paul Owens became general manager. Owens had been the scouting director, and he was kind of a mentor to Ruly, so they started pumping money into player development—and it paid off. We hired more minor-league coaches and instructors. We added another farm club. We started drafting differently: doing cross-checking and going in more for black players and high-school prospects. College guys can make your minor-league teams look good, but a lot of them have already reached their full potential and don't stand a chance of getting to the big leagues. If you take enough of the younger players, they keep on going. It costs more money, but you develop more genuine prospects.

The money for scouting and player development is the best money a ballclub can spend—and the Phillies spent the money. We hired away aggressive scouts from other teams, we added new scouts to go fish where the fish were biting, like California or Latin America, and we laid out dollars to sign more of the players we drafted. It wasn't just money, though; it was organization. From 1972 to 1979 Dallas Green was the farm director, but he really considered scouting to be more intriguing, more of a challenge, a fun thing, than the 120-game schedule of a minor-league team or the spring training bit. He led the fight against the Bureau, and he made Philadelphia scouting very self-contained. He's proud that we're not popular. When we're with scouts from other clubs, we don't share information, we don't get into this stuff about the "fraternity" of scouting, and we don't even let 'em ride in our cars! Dallas also set up a kind of pyramid—bird dogs and part-time scouts at the bottom, then area scouts, then three regional supervisors for the whole country, then me, and then Dallas himself at the top. All the roles were clear-cut. But now it seems like everybody's doing a little bit of everything.

When Dallas left the job and went back down on the field as manager, there was a power vacuum. Jack Pastore ran the scouting in 1980, and this year he's Baumer's assistant. He was supposed to be an office coordinator, but he's seen fit to go out and make scouting judgments on his own, and he's replaced the pyramid with a committee system. And I don't think you can scout by committee.

It's not objective. If you make up your draft list by consensus, and everybody gets a vote, it throws the whole thing off, because some people are voting between one player and another, and they haven't seen either one. So it might come down to who can sell a player better, verbally. You have too much input, too many cooks. And that's what happened last year, on the Lebo Powell deal.

In spring 1980 Henry Lee "Lebo" Powell was a high-school catcher in Pensacola, Florida. Andy Seminick, the Phillies' area scout, put $40,000 on him; Randy Waddill, the Eastern regional supervisor, put $75,000; Joe Reilly, a snowbird in Florida that March, put $100,000. Hugh Alexander, providing free-lance advice, said $40,000; Lou Kahn, just helping out, said $25,000. Brandy Davis said that Lebo Powell was not a prospect at all.

Joe Reilly had written that Powell was a "definite major-leaguer," noting only one weakness: "Has every girl in town tied down." As Reilly saw him, Powell was an ideal specimen, "built like Double X—Jimmie Foxx." Looking at the same physique (6', 205 pounds), Brandy Davis wrote: "Big, thick body. Bulk as in hulk. Lower body somewhat dead." And then, as an apparent afterthought, he added: "Good voice."

"I stopped in Pensacola that April," he said later, "and this boy looked so far from what they told me about that, just to be fair, I stayed over an extra day to watch him in another game. In all I saw him take two long batting practices and hit six times in games. He was a high-ball hitter, but not with a home-run swing—he one-handed the bat. On low pitches he chopped at the ball. His swing didn't coordinate his hips and legs. As a catcher he showed too much effort, poor instincts, bad hands. His throws to second weren't accurate, and they were all shoulder: no strong forearm or wrist action. So after that second game I red-carded him—'No prospect.'

"But Reilly and Waddill and Pastore had fallen in love with him. Comes the draft in June, and by the time that committee was through we wound up taking Lebo Powell as our number one pick. Then we used up our number three pick on another catcher named Maggio, who has a giant hitch in his swing. And this year they're talking about how we still need more catchers. You wait and see if they don't use a high draft-pick on one."

I waited and saw, and Davis's prediction proved accurate— as did his characterization of the Philadelphia draft meetings as an exercise in committee consensus. But the whole draft process was much more than that. It also included exercises in the art of rhetoric, the luck of lotteries, and the honest difficulties of putting the dollar sign on the muscle. And it featured an irony that Brandy Davis had trouble accepting: his frustration at having his professional advice ignored was a perfect mirror of the frustration of an area scout who contends with a cross-checker.

But when the draft was all over, his reaction was just as stoic, as "objective," as it had been when the Phillies signed Lebo Powell for $55,000. "This may still pan out. We'll know in about four years."

9 THE CENTER OF THE SEASON

Although the Philadelphia National League Club is fundamentally opposed to the amateur draft and its inherent socialistic qualities, our scouting personnel must make the best of the situation.

—Philadelphia Phillies' Scouting Manual

The Los Angeles Dodgers' executives gave practical reasons for their dislike of the amateur draft. "We have money," Al Campanis told me, "and we're already committed to growing our own talent. And besides, California would be an ideal area to sign amateurs on the open market." When the Philadelphia Phillies' executives stated their opposition to the draft, they sounded more philosophical. Their language reflected the conservative beliefs of the Carpenter family, Paul Owens, and Dallas Green: individual freedom, laissez-faire capitalism, and the survival of the fittest.

But in characterizing the draft as "socialistic," the Phillies were rewriting the economics of baseball. Team owners designed the draft to save money after bonuses began spiraling in the early 1960s. The owners had been using new money from television and league expansion to bid against each other in the open market on amateur talent, and the result was a bonus inflation that reached its peak when the California Angels, a new franchise underwritten with Gene Autry's fortune, secured the services of a college outfielder—Rick Reichardt— for $175,000. In establishing the draft in 1965, just as in bargaining against the major-league players in 1981, the owners wanted a structure to discourage their own spending in a market that was *too* open. I asked Paul Owens: "Isn't *capitalistic* a better word for the draft?"

"The draft is socialistic," Owens said. "For one thing, it gives the teams with the poorest records the earliest selections in each round. It's part of a push to equalize talent from team to team—but there never has been equalization of talent in baseball, and there never will be. The draft rewards mediocrity. It stifles initiative in scouting. Eleven days after the draft came into baseball in 1965, the Phillies made me scouting director, and the whole time I was in that job I felt like a race-car driver with a governor on his engine. The best thing I can say about the draft is that it's a bad way of keeping a ceiling on bonuses."

Joe Reilly, one of the Phillies' area scouts, argued that the draft also puts a "floor" on bonuses, and he expressed the feelings all traditional scouts have about the draft's bureaucratic by-products. "Today if you draft a kid in an early round, he knows he's an early round choice. Right away he wants big money. You could sign a lot of players cheaper without the draft. The Dodgers and Yankees wouldn't get all the talent: they'd still have to *find out* who was the best, and that would take real scoutin'—with heart and soul in it. Scouts would have to get to know the amateur players better, inside and out, like in the old days. And remember . . . no draft would mean no Bureau, no cross-checkers to second-guess everybody, and a hell of a lot less paperwork. Because ninety-five percent of the talent you report now, you don't get anyway."

But the June draft, like it or not, was the center of the scouting season. And the Phillies, selecting twentieth on each round, believed that the quality and quantity of their information would enable them to out-draft most of the teams ahead of them. Jack Pastore made it sound like a computer game. When I attended the Phillies' pre-draft meetings, and the draft itself, I found that the whole process was really more like an old-fashioned game-show . . . on the radio. To the Phillies, and to me, the printouts of scouting reports and the collation of cross-checkers' lists were less important than the images and impressions of young talent that the scouts summoned up for one another.

The draft was to begin on Monday, June 8. On the morning of Friday, June 5, at Veterans Stadium, ten scouts supervised twenty prospects in last-look workouts: sixty-yard dashes, fungoes, throwing, and batting practice. Nobody looked great at the plate, but two prospects caught my attention. One had a classic athletic body, 6'4" and 215 pounds, with speed, fluid movement, and a forearm tattoo that said UCLA. "His name's Charles Faucette," Tony Roig said, "which might mean he's a New Jersey Cajun. He looks hellacious. I put forty-five thousand on him last month, but I think that horseshit tattoo means he'd rather play football." The other player was Jerry Holtz, who ran a 6.6 sixty and showed a rifle arm at shortstop. He was the "find" from Atlantic City that Joe Reilly had been talking about for the last two weeks. As it turned out, Joe Reilly would also spend much of the summer talking about Jerry Holtz.

Brandy Davis introduced me to Ben Marmo, a scout from New Jersey, and for the next five minutes they commiserated with each other by describing for me what had happened at another such workout, just before the June draft in 1974. "We had Dale Murphy in here," Davis said.

"And Willie Wilson!"

"Right. And they were both catchers in high school—and in fact, I liked Murphy as a catcher. He had about a 72 arm with a quick release and good instincts on pitches in the dirt."

"But Wilson," Marmo said. "I knew early on that he had to be an outfielder. Speed! Well, he was a natural athlete, played four sports in high school, and most scouts thought he'd go play college football."

"So they came in here," Davis continued. "And at the workout the pitching coach, Ripplemeyer, threw batting practice. He just overmatched those eighteen-year-old kids. He gave Murphy a lot of sliders and made him look stiff and—"

"And he kept pitching Wilson inside, and you know Willie has kind of a long swing, so he got jammed."

"Right. So neither one of them hit any balls into the stands. And some people were seeing Murphy for the first time—like Ruly Carpenter, who wanted to help scout—and they questioned his power, which is one of the best things he does. He has the big bat you're looking for. Just imagine if we had Murphy in the Phillies' outfield today."

"We could've had either Murphy *or* Wilson, because we drafted high that year."

"Yeah, and we took Lonnie Smith. Not a bad draft by any means, but he has more holes in his game than the other two. He certainly doesn't have Murphy's power."

"Or Wilson's coordination."

"I had Wilson as number two," Davis said, "behind Murphy and ahead of Smith. But that one workout made both of their stocks fall. . . . It would've been smarter not to bring 'em here." He shook his head.

Marmo's head shook in tempo. But behind them, in right-field, Tony Roig was moving to a tempo of his own. The prospects had left, so Roig had the astroturf and the 65,484 empty seats all to himself. He became a drum major, marching into the infield with his knees high, strutting back at the waist, his right arm moving a Louisville Slugger baton up and down in perfect rhythm with the strange noises he was making with his mouth. "That's a ragin' Cajun," Jack Pastore said. "And not from New Jersey either."

For the rest of the day the joint chiefs of the Philadelphia scouting staff discussed forty-two of the best amateur players in the country. The first fourteen, which included Brandy Davis's top ten, had been categorized as "Group One," designating players whose evaluations averaged out to more than $51,000—designating, in turn, players with "all the tools." Some of these prospects received surprisingly little comment. Ron Darling, Jim Baumer said, "will be the number one pitcher to go, and Seattle may use its first position in the draft to take him, so there's no point even talking about him."

Baumer sat at the end of a U of long tables in the Phillies' executive dining room. Jack Pastore was to his left. In front of them was a speaker-phone, stacks of reports and notebooks, a big ashtray, and a bottle of Rolaids. Along one side of the U sat the two national cross-checkers: Tony Roig and Brandy Davis. Along the other sat the three regional cross-checkers: Randy Waddill (East), Moose Johnson (Central), and Gordon Goldsberry (West). Bill Gargano, the executive secretary for the Phillies' minor-league system, stayed near the blackboard at the open end of the U. The discussion was frank and free-wheeling, structured only by the list of players in descending order of dollar average.

Kevin McReynolds, Davis's first choice, was at the top, and the scouts spent ten minutes reviewing medical reports on his injured knee. Moose Johnson quoted the area scout, Don Williams—"He'd be better with a cast on his leg than anyone else I've seen this year"—and concluded with a justification of Williams's $150,000 evaluation. "McReynolds could be the first college boy since Bob Horner to jump straight to the majors."

A long discussion focused on Jon Abrego, the high-school pitcher from Mission San Jose, California. Northern California scout Eddie Bockman, famous for his persistence and insight, had sent in at least ten reports on Abrego. On the Phillies' 60-to-80 scale (with 70 as a major-league average) Bockman kept projecting Abrego's fastball and curve to 74, his change-up and control to 73. Bockman emphasized Abrego's poise, determination, durability, and all-around athletic skill. "Has to be one of the top three kids in the country," read one report, "and I cannot imagine any pitchers in comparing him, unless it would be a left-hander with the same qualifications." Another reason for interest in Abrego was Gordon Goldsberry's surmise that the Phillies, even drafting from the twentieth position, might still have a shot at Abrego when their turn came. "For me," he concluded, "Abrego's more of an over-thrower;

he needs to slow his motion and get more rhythm. But even now, the ball just seems to jump out of his hand. He has a live arm."

"You ain't shittin' about that," Tony Roig said. "The most consistent velocity of all the high school pitchers I saw this year. And even better is, he's a real competitor. Got a real tough makeup with men on base. Intent. Aggressive. I *like* this bwah."

Another *bwah* Roig liked was Matt Williams, a Group One pitcher from Rice University. "He pitched a couple of double-headers during the season. And in the College World Series he pitched five innings one day and fifteen the next, and didn't lose his stuff—a plus fastball, a hard slider. He's a mean son of bitch. He comes at you. He's from Clute, Texas, and that's red-neck country, man. They'd just as soon kick your ass as shake your hand."

Moose Johnson laughed. "I saw Williams pitch a game at Texas A & M, and he hit a few batters, really stirred up the fans. He loved it when they yelled at him. The last batter in the game hit one back to the mound, and Williams held the ball up to the A & M fans, and then he *kissed* the ball before he threw it to first!"

Brandy Davis said that Williams was mature ("He should be—he's twenty-two") and durable, but that his motion was stiff rather than fluid. Davis seemed subdued, more matter-of-fact here than he had been when discussing his top prospects with me. I wondered if this was his usual manner at draft meetings, or if the presence of a second national cross-checker (especially one as extroverted as Roig)—or of what he took to be a clique (Baumer-Pastore-Roig-Waddill)—made him withdraw a little. In any case he wasn't trying to sell his favorite players to the other scouts, and his role in discussions was more that of a counter-puncher. His number two player, the high-school shortstop Dick Schofield, had been averaged out to number fourteen by the other scouts: nobody else considered Schofield a Group One player. But Davis let Moose Johnson do most of the talking about him. Johnson had gone to $45,000, half Davis's evaluation. "Schofield has two fine tools," Johnson said. "His speed and his bat make him at least a strong Group Two, and he has the good hands both in the infield and at the plate. But his arm may turn him into a second baseman."

"Schofield," Davis finally said, "is the best everyday player I saw in high school this year. I have his arm at 71. And he'll be a major-league hitter. . . . But I doubt if we have a chance at him. The Angels and the Cardinals like him a lot, and they both draft before we do."

"What bothers me," Johnson said, "is that it'll probably take at least a hundred thousand to sign him. His dad signed a big-bonus contract years ago, about forty thousand, and I think the family has high expectations." Jim Baumer frowned at this news. "I think we can draft another good shortstop," he said.

Randy Waddill and Tony Roig had already touted one high-school shortstop—Matt Shumake from Hartsville, South Carolina—as not only "fast, hard-nosed, and surly," but also lightly scouted, unlikely to be drafted by anyone else in the first two rounds. One problem with Shumake was a pushy father ("He's done almost all the kid's coaching, and he's done it wrong"); a second was that he had already accepted a baseball scholarship to Clemson. So as the discussion turned to the Group Two players, the scouts isolated another shortstop: Jerry Holtz, Joe Reilly's find, one of the workout kids in Vet Stadium that morning. A Group Two player (evaluations averaging $34,000 to $50,999) was supposed to be one with "a hole in his game," but Randy Waddill didn't see any in Holtz's: "He's a Group One player for me, and a legitimate first-round pick."

Baumer shook his head. "I want to gamble with this kid, risk letting him go a few rounds. Joe Reilly says no other clubs have really seen him. And the Bureau didn't like him." Roig looked up and grunted. "That just confirms my thinkin' about the Bureau. I wouldn't let this kid go *too* many rounds. He's got good initial quickness and a hell of an arm, a quick release. I mean, today he was firin' strikes to first base from his right tit. No wind-up, hardly needed to set himself—just *shooom!*"

Roig stood up to act out Holtz's throw, the same way he mimed the motions of other players some of the scouts hadn't seen. A while later he was showing everyone the "loosy-goosy" wrist and the snap on the curve belonging to a Texas high-school pitcher, Ricky Barlow, 6' and 150 pounds, "a black man with no ass on him." And he demonstrated the stance and swing of Charles Penigar, a California high-school out-fielder: this black man had an ass, at least in Roig's version of him, and he generated power (slow-motion speeding up as Tony met the ball) from both sides of the plate. "He just started switch-hittin' this season, but he can *do* it. Only seventeen years old, 6'4" and 175. And he's got the best outfield arm I saw this season."

The only other person in the room who had seen the real Penigar was Gordon Goldsberry, but by the time Roig finished his sales pitch most scouts' eyes had lit up. Goldsberry had $41,000 on Penigar (Roig had $58,000) and described him as "aggressive, confident, and very signable." Jim Baumer was intrigued. "Can we wait till the second round on him?" "I think we can," Goldsberry said. "The White Sox and the Car-dinals and the Bureau all like him, but almost all the scouts were watching him early in the season when he was still feeling for the ball as a right-handed hitter. Spider Jorgenson kept following him, though, and he's impressed."

"I know," Jack Pastore said, "because Spider called, and he's bumped up the money he wants to put on Penigar. Right now, this kid would average out to Group One." Pastore had spent most of the week on the phone, probing for last-minute revisions from area scouts, and he made another call during the meeting to check on Lee Tunnell, a Group Two pitcher from Baylor University. Tunnell, according to Roig, was "a real religious Baptist."

"Is he bad?" Pastore asked. (In the terminology of religion rather than baseball, Pastore's question might have been "Is he good?") "Well," Roig said, "I talked with him last month about pro ball, and he said that Jesus hadn't told him yet whether he should play. I said, 'You know the draft is comin' up in June. See if you can get an answer before then.' I don't know if he did. But I like his stuff—he's got a live fastball and a bitin' hard curve."

Pastore got Don Williams on the speakerphone, and asked if Tunnell had heard from Jesus. "I'll tell you this much," the voice squawked from Texas, "he's not real religious when he pitches. He's *mean*. He'll hit you and laugh at you." By the end of the phone call Tunnell's stock had risen.

Meanness, in fact, was one of the first qualities the scouts talked about in a pitching prospect. Scouting forms have boxes for aspects of makeup—competitiveness, maturity, poise, teachability—but most written reports emphasize physical tools. In the draft meetings, as the scouts rated players with comparable physical tools, makeup became more significant. For a catcher this was brute toughness and a willingness to "sacrifice his body." For a pitcher it was grace under pressure and a readiness to "dump hitters on their asses."

"Doyle," Goldsberry said, "is an *effortless* pitcher. I mean that both ways. His delivery is easy and smooth—but he doesn't intimidate hitters and his stuff's not as good with men on base. I wouldn't say he has a lot of bulldog in him."

"Is he a puss?" Baumer asked.

Goldsberry shrugged. "He's just a high-school kid—"

"I think he *is* a puss," Roig said. "Got a weak-lookin' face. . . . I saw him spit the bit in the seventh inning. His team hustled and tied up the score, and he goes out and walks the first hitter in the bottom of the seventh, and then he's lookin' at the bench for his coach to come get him and feelin' his arm like it hurts. I can't stand that shit, and I've had to coach too many minor-leaguers like that—who everybody said would turn into men sooner or later, but they never do. Once a puss, always a puss."

One of the last prospects discussed on Friday was David Cochrane, a high-school player from Fullerton, California. "I like him thirty-eight thousand," Goldsberry said. "A switch-hitter, pretty fair from both sides. And versatile—we have him listed as shortstop and outfielder, but he can also catch. And the reason the Bureau rated him low is that they wrote him up as a pitcher! Rosey Gilhousen worked him out for the Royals, but most clubs aren't too interested. He has a good body, 6'2" and 170. And I don't know if everybody here buys this . . . but I also think he has the good face."

All the heads in the room nodded assent. I found that, unconsciously, I was nodding my head too. But what *was* the good face? Brandy Davis's explanation hadn't fully satisfied me, and so before the discussions resumed on Saturday, I asked Goldsberry to elaborate. His own face looked scholarly and relaxed, not at all like the image of Gordon Goldsberry I had as a kid. I never saw him play (you had to look fast to do that, because he was only in 217 major-league games), but I could still visualize him in a white St. Louis Browns' uniform on a 1952 Topps baseball card: he had seemed hard and resolute, like the statue of a general.

"When a scout says 'Good face,' he's not talking about what good ballplayers *ought* to look like. He's talking about what good ballplayers *do* look like. He's hung around ball diamonds most of his life, and he has the sense that when God stamps out the good players He may only be using three or four molds. You walk in any major-league clubhouse and you'll see what I mean. You're looking at the faces of athletes, not accountants. You'll see a lot of square jaws and not too many weak chins— just think of George Brett or Mike Schmidt. And you can see something in the eyes. They show strength; they look straight at you."

Goldsberry looked straight at me, and once again I was seeing the face on the 1952 baseball card. After two seconds I broke eye contact and stared at the floor.

"I go more by body build," said Moose Johnson, whose own fifty-year-old body was remarkable: about 200 pounds, most of it still muscle, packed into 5'9". His wife hated his nickname. She probably wouldn't have liked Bulldog Johnson any better; *Bulldog* might give a better impression of his physique, but it would misrepresent his genial, agreeable style. His big square face smiled often—and when it did, all you could see of his eyes were two little points of light.

"You take this kid Brister," Johnson said to me on Saturday morning. "His body's the main reason I went to sixty-five thousand on him yesterday." Walter "Bubby" Brister, a high-school shortstop from Monroe, Louisiana, had averaged out to Group Two. Davis had put only $23,000 on him, mainly because he saw a batting hitch: "Brister collapses his arms toward his chest, and that gives him trouble with inside pitches—and will continue to."

But Johnson believed he saw Brister in fuller perspective: "This kid will make it to the major leagues. He's an all-around athlete, poised, a leader. And you look at that body, you know he's *gonna* have power. He's 6'3" and 180—only eighteen years old, and you can see how he'll fill out. At twenty-two he can be as strong as Mike Schmidt. . . . Scouts talk about 'projection' like it was a mystery, which it is in a way. But when you study a prospect's body, you have a kind of *ground* for your projections."

In the Philadelphia scouting files I found an old report, dated May 27, 1970, and stamped WILBUR H. JOHNSON. It was Moose's description of Richard Gossage, a high-school pitcher from Colorado Springs, 6'2" and 175 pounds:

A tall, lanky RHP. Possesses a plus arm with a loose delivery off a good body. Delivers his FB off a low ¾ and also side-arm—with his CB from ¾ but will probably have to resort to a hard slider. His FB moves into RH-hitters and with a sinking effect. But with added weight of 20 pounds or so as he goes into manhood, he could develop a wicky FB with even more movement. His body can easily take the added weight. His potential is promising. Only a fair or borderline student—so should sign.

On Saturday and Sunday the scouts spent twelve hours discussing 175 more players who had been categorized as High A ($16,000 to $30,999), Mid A ($6,000 to $15,999), and Low

A ($300 to $5,999). Another seventy-seven players were listed on a sheet marked *WNS*, pronounced *winnis* and standing for "Would Not Select." Some were there because their skills didn't match any known position on a baseball field. A high-school outfielder named Gregory Morehardt was described in Dick Lawlor's reports as having "Pete Rose desire and a showcase arm." But he was a bean, 6' and 160 pounds, who lacked speed as well as power. Told that Morehardt's best time at sixty yards was seven seconds flat, Jim Baumer said simply, "Winnis him."

Jeffrey Carl, a college shortstop from Wisconsin, was winnised because he was twenty-two, 5'10", and wore contacts. "That's three strikes," Baumer said. Joey Meyer, a high school first baseman from Hawaii, was winnised because he weighed 270 pounds. "He's 6'4" and might slim down," Goldsberry said, "and I'd like to take a chance on him, because his home runs go halfway to the mainland." "Winnis him," Baumer said. But most players were winnised because they couldn't be signed, according to area scouts, at any figure near what the Phillies thought they were really worth. They expected a bonus commensurate with Group One talent they didn't seem to have— like Mark Gubicza, a High-A high-school pitching star in Philadelphia. Or they had their minds set on a college program whose scholarship value the Phillies weren't ready to match— like Robert Fingers, Rollie's nephew, a pitcher about to enroll at Arizona State.

Gordon Goldsberry liked player ninety-seven on the High-A list but noted that his own evaluation ($14,500) made this prospect Mid A. (Jack Pastore suggested calling him Upper Fair). The player was Joe Nemeth, a senior first baseman at California State. "He reminds me of Jason Thompson," Goldsberry said. "He's a left-hander with power, which we need, and his hands are okay. He could get drafted surprisingly high— say by Minnesota on the third or fourth round." Asked his opinion, Brandy Davis used his strongest expletive: "It was windy as heck the last time I saw him, so I'm not sure I got the best look. But I'll stick with my fifteen thousand on the power."

Davis was more animated than on Friday, perhaps feeling that his opinions on A-level players would carry more weight than his rankings of prospects in Groups One and Two, and he did a nice job of selling Mel Williams, a black outfielder from David Lipscomb College. The area scout, George Farson, had put $12,000 on Williams, and Randy Waddill had put only $8,000; Davis had Williams in for $33,000. "He can run and throw above major-league average, and that's ten thousand right there. But I also saw him hit against James Winn, and he looked fine. He's wiry and strong, 5'11" and 175, and I don't see any bad holes in him."

I was hoping that someone would give as strong a sales pitch for Leon Roberts, a black high-school shortstop I knew only from reading through a stack of computerized reports on one of the tables. The Phillies categorized Roberts as Mid A, but Eddie Bockman's reports were like messages in bottles, trying to get someone in the scouting hierarchy to take this kid seriously. The problem was Roberts's size (5'8" and 150), because the Phillies have traditionally been committed to big players. Back in 1965 Bockman had finally been allowed to sign a small, undrafted shortstop named Larry Bowa only by pestering Paul Owens, even shooting home movies of Bowa in action and making Owens watch them projected on a motel room wall. In his movie review Owens said that Bowa was too little, but just to get some peace he approved a bonus of $2,000. Now Bockman was writing editorials about Leon Roberts, noting that Roberts's *slowest* time at 60 yards was 6.5, and concluding in the style of an urgent telegram:

Little in stature but plays big. Same lines as Joe Morgan at same age. Not much to him, just a pip, but sure can play. Arm will limit him to 2b, but does have quick release from SS. Good range, no matter where you put him. Weak—suspect with bat; could make left-hand hitter out of him. Strong—can run, likes to, can steal base. Dedicated boy, is all baseball. Can play, forget size, judge on plus marks. Can run, play defense, play baseball. Don't sell him short.

Goldsberry visualized Roberts for the other scouts as a switch-hitter with bat speed from both sides and as a kid with a good attitude ("a smiling black with a motor up his ass"), but he didn't try to generate enthusiasm: "He's really a Pittsburgh-type draft." What is a typical Pittsburgh draft? "Fast, black, a high-school kid," Davis told me. "Doesn't matter much if he's small or his bat's suspect. Howie Haak would like Leon Roberts."

At the other extreme a typical Minnesota draft is big, slow, and a college senior. "This is a Twins-type player," Davis said in describing Michael Sodders to the other scouts. Sodders was a third baseman at Arizona State: he had good power but, according to Davis, was injury-prone, not durable, and would probably have to move to first base. He was player twenty-three on the Mid-A list.

Mid-A player twenty-four, outfielder Lemmie Miller, was also a senior at Arizona State. Moose Johnson put $25,000 on him: "He's looked good in the College World Series, and I like his tools—6.6 speed, a strong arm. He has a black man's swing; he's a slicer, a slasher." But Roig and Goldsberry wouldn't go over $10,000. "He's afraid of the ball," Roig said. "If he ever gets a real knock-down pitch," Goldsberry said, "he'll shit all over home plate."

For most Low-A players the discussions were brief, and at this point—Sunday afternoon—the proceedings were interrupted by frequent phone calls from area scouts. Dick Lawlor was excited by his workout of Willard Currier, a University of Vermont first baseman who wasn't on any of the lists; Lawlor said he should be at High A. Then Scott Reid called to plug James Olander, an Arizona high-school outfielder who was seventh from the bottom of the Low-A list. Olander's early season reports made him a $1,000 player—"but now," Reid said, "I like him twenty thousand."

After the phone call Davis took over. "Let's talk about Olander. I just saw him last week, and I like him *thirty* thousand. He has the tools to be a complete player, plus a loose body and good makeup. Wiry, raw-boned, mature-looking, and has Mike Schmidt mannerisms—just giving off confidence."

Roig jumped in: "I'll boost him up too. Twenty thousand. He wraps the bat and gets jammed, but I like the way he goes about his business. You won't back him down. Gets good carry on his throws too." Goldsberry agreed: "I only saw him once, and I didn't know he could run 6.7. If that's true, I'll go twenty-five." Pastore observed that Olander had just jumped from the bottom of Low A to the middle of Group Two. "Let's just call him a good High A," Baumer said, "and see if we can get him on the fifth or sixth round."

Before the draft balloting began Hugh Alexander joined the meeting. He was in town with advance reports on the Phillies' next opponents, the Astros and Reds, but he had also seen a few of the year's best amateur players. Baumer was especially interested in Alexander's assessments of catchers. "The best one I saw was Lombardi, high-school boy out of California. I put seventy thousand on him. A tough kid with a great arm— he reminds me of Bruce Benedict."

"We have Lombardi near the top of Group Two," Baumer said, "but we're concerned about his hitting."

"Hell, I'm concerned about everybody's hitting. You guys see many ballplayers this year who can *really* hit? With power? Boy, them son of a bitches are scarce, aren't they?"

What Baumer wanted was a preferential list of forty or so players, enough to cover the first two rounds of the draft on Monday and to provide a basis for regrouping after that. But the construction of this list was oddly unsystematic. Everybody voted and everybody's vote counted the same—no matter which, or how many, prospects he had seen with his own eyes. Instead of using paper ballots ("That would take too damn long"), the scouts voted orally on each slot. So for the first place on the list, Baumer looked from scout to scout and heard:

"McReynolds." "McReynolds." "Darling." "McReynolds." "Darling." "McReynolds."

"I'll say McReynolds too," Baumer said, and Bill Gargano put McReynolds's name on the blackboard. As the voting proceeded each scout simply repeated for each slot the name of his favorite player, until that player received enough other votes to go up on the board. For every slot from the second to the tenth, Brandy Davis said: "Dick Schofield."

On the one hand this procedure undercut the advantage of the national cross-checkers' broader experience during the season: Roig and Davis had each seen about twice as many top prospects as any other scout in the room. On the other it prevented Baumer from putting his own stamp on the draft or from applying his judgment of other scouts' judgments—on each vote he spoke last, as if to avoid prejudicing the others. I told Jack Pastore that the procedures seemed to incorporate the worst aspects of committee logic. "In the first place," Pastore retorted, "who we draft tomorrow will mostly be determined *for* us by who other teams take before our turn. In the second place you'll see a different method when we regroup after the first two rounds. And in the third place we've got a damn good list!" The top of it looked like this:

1. Kevin McReynolds, of, University of Arkansas
2. Ron Darling, rhp, Yale University
3. Terry Blocker, of, Tennessee State University
4. Joe Carter, of, Wichita State University
5. Mike Moore, rhp, Oral Roberts University
6. Mark Grant, rhp, Joliet, Illinois (high school)
7. Vance Lovelace, lhp, Tampa, Florida (high school)
8. Jon Abrego, rhp, Mission San Jose, California (high school)
9. Charles Penigar, of, Ontario, California (high school)
10. Dick Schofield, ss, Springfield, Illinois (high school)

Although the first five were college players, the rest of the list (twenty-four of the next thirty-six slots) was dominated by high-school prospects—like Phillip Lombardi, Hugh Alexander's $70,000 catcher (#15); Matt Shumake and Jerry Holtz, the shortstops (#16 and #17); Walter Brister, Moose Johnson's player with the good body (#26); David Cochrane, Gordon Goldsberry's player with the good face (#32); and Ricky Barlow, Tony Roig's loosy-goosy right-handed pitcher (#35).

After Bill Gargano wrote the forty-first, and last, name on the blackboard, he looked at the whole list and turned to the scouts. "Let's have a betting pool on how many of these guys we draft by Wednesday. I'll say eight."

ESPN, the cable network, had televised the National Football League draft in April. But not even ESPN, which programs just about any sports-related event, would ever televise baseball's amateur draft. The players are generally unknown to the public, and their impact on the teams that draft them is almost always several years away. There are no exciting last-minute trades involving draft-positions: in baseball a draft position cannot be traded (although it could, in 1981, figure as compensation to a team that lost an established free agent, such as Dave Winfield). But the most obvious barrier to television coverage is that the baseball draft isn't a visualizable "event." It's a gigantic phone call—a conference hook-up of the offices of the commissioner, the Scouting Bureau, and the twenty-six major-league clubs.

Until 1975 the June draft was a real meeting in New York, where baseball men could fraternize and connive, and sometimes work on deals before the June 15 trading deadline. But the same forces that originally led to the draft eventually led to its mechanization. First, economy: one club's share of a fifteen-hour conference call is considerably cheaper than the expenses a scouting director and his assistants would run up for a three-day trip to New York. Second, facelessness: the tinny voices coming over the speakerphone seemed to take the bureaucratic tendencies in modern scouting to their logical conclusion.

At 2:10 Monday afternoon such a voice announced: "The Seattle Mariners select negotiation rights to Moore, Michael Wayne; right-handed pitcher, Oral Roberts University." The choice caused no stir. Jim Baumer had already passed along the rumor that Ron Darling's signability was now a problem (Darling had soured the Mariners, and probably some other clubs too, by hiring an agent), and that the Mariners would be drafting another pitcher. "Because the Mariners had the first choice," Gary Nickels told me, "they were able to talk specific money terms with all their favorite players. But anybody drafted number one in the whole country has to expect a bonus in six figures." Nickels and Bill Harper, two area scouts, had been brought in by the Phillies as guest observers for the draft; Jack Pastore described the gesture as "a touch of class."

The first ten draft choices were slightly closer to Brandy Davis's original list than to the list on the blackboard:

1. MARINERS: Mike Moore, rhp
2. CUBS: Joe Carter, of
3. ANGELS: Dick Schofield, ss
4. METS: Terry Blocker, of
5. BLUE JAYS: Matt Williams, rhp
6. PADRES: Kevin McReynolds, of
7. WHITE SOX: Darryl Boston, of
8. CARDINALS: Robert Meacham, ss
9. RANGERS: Ron Darling, rhp
10. GIANTS: Mark Grant, rhp

Boston was no surprise: the Phillies rated him as a low Group One ($52,500) and #13 on the blackboard. Meacham was a mild surprise: the Phillies rated him as Group Two ($34,000) and #23 on the blackboard—relatively high, considering that the scouts described Meacham as having poor eyesight, a suspect bat, and a meek attitude. But a sharp surprise—for me, at least—came when the Twins, drafting eleventh, chose Michael Sodders: the Phillies rated him as Mid A ($12,000) and not on the blackboard at all. I reminded Jack Pastore that Brandy Davis had described Sodders as "a Twins-type player," and he laughed. "Oh yeah, Minnesota likes water buffaloes—corner players who have power but can't run, and who don't have any bargaining leverage. Sodders is a senior at A.S.U., and Calvin Griffith has to figure he can sign a guy like that as a real cheap first-round choice, maybe thirty-five thousand."

The Cubs, drafting sixteenth, chose Vance Lovelace. Now Abrego and Penigar were the only players left from the first ten names on the blackboard. But they were still left after the Tigers, Expos, and Red Sox had drafted. "The Philadelphia Phillies," said a voice from the commissioner's office. "The Philadelphia Phillies," Baumer answered, "select negotiating rights to Abrego, Jon Ray; right-handed pitcher, Freemont High School, Mission San Jose, California."

All the scouts seemed satisfied. They were more obviously satisfied as Rounds 1 and 2 proceeded, because few of the draftees came from the blackboard; most came from the High-A and Mid-A lists, and a few even came from the winnis list. The twenty-ninth player drafted (by the Expos) was Jeffrey Carl, the shortstop with "three strikes"—age, size, eyesight. The thirty-fourth (by the Royals) was Mark Gubicza, who wanted too much money.

In Round 2 the Pirates took Lee Tunnell, the "religious but mean" pitcher from Baylor, and then the Phillies waited through five more picks to see if Charles Penigar would still be available. He was. A few minutes later the Yankees ended the round. They'd had no pick in Round 1 (the Padres received it as compensation for the loss of Dave Winfield), and so the fifty-second choice was their first chance to draft. When they announced the selection of Stanford University outfielder John Elway, two scouts said, simultaneously, "That horse's ass!" Why, I asked Gary Nickels, was Elway a horse's ass?

"Not Elway—George Steinbrenner. You just heard a splashy draft. Elway's a star quarterback at Stanford. A great arm, but he wants a pro football career more than baseball. Scouts figure it'll take a hundred-fifty thousand to sign him to a baseball contract, and even then he might quit on you. Eddie Bockman says Elway has good tools but not worth throwing six figures at. Steinbrenner'll probably throw it, just to get more attention."

Drafting for the day ended with the secondary phase, involving players selected but unsigned in previous drafts. The Phillies picked up a left-handed pitcher, Billy Irions from Seminole Junior College in Oklahoma, who had turned down $35,000 from the Brewers but was thought to be signable now for under $30,000. Tony Roig said that Irions was his kind of pitcher: "He comes at you to beat your ass. Got a fastball that runs and sinks, and a good slider. He's strong, 6'2" and 200, and a tough son of a bitch. He's part Indian. Tell 'em how mean he is, Moose."

"He'll drop you," Moose said.

After the conference call was disconnected, the scouts regrouped by getting back on the phone. Baumer called Eddie Bockman to give instructions on negotiating with Jon Abrego. The average evaluation on Abrego had been $69,000, and Baumer wanted him signed for less than that. Before the phone conversation ended, Bockman passed along a good name for a late-round draft: Charles Kerfeld, a right-handed high school pitcher from Carson City, Nevada. "He wears big thick glasses, and he has hair down to his ass. But he's 6'5" with a *real* good arm. Plus he's mean—he'll throw at anybody. He'd even throw at the ump!"

In the constellation of Philadelphia scouts Tony Lucadello's star burned as bright as Bockman's. Covering the Ohio-Indiana-Michigan territory for forty years, twenty-five with the Phillies, he had signed forty-nine future major-leaguers—including Ferguson Jenkins, Mike Schmidt, Larry Hisle, and Toby Harrah. Lucadello was the scout Baumer phoned next, asking for advice on a left-handed pitcher. "Nine lefties got drafted in the first two rounds, but Babcock didn't, and we want your thinking on him." Bill Babcock was a high school pitcher from Grosse Point, Michigan; his average evaluation ($54,000) made him Group One, but his problem was signability.

"He's out of line," Lucadello said. "He wants at least ninety thousand, or else he'll enroll at the University of Miami. I might give that kind of money to a great position player but *never* to a pitcher." Baumer winnised Babcock, and Brandy Davis explained Lucadello's reasoning for me: "Pitchers are like race-horses. They can break down, get a sore arm. And they're just basically less predictable than everyday players. If the everyday player has the broad range of tools you're looking for, that makes him less of a gamble. He might fail in one part of his game, or get an injury, and still make it."

After two more calls Baumer opened an Express Mail en-velope, and a moment later he proposed a test for the scouts. "Okay, take a sheet of paper and write these grades down. This is a last-minute deal, a scout's one and only report on a ballplayer he just worked out. The player is 6'4", 200 pounds, white, twenty-one years old, a college first baseman who might be converted to an outfielder because of his speed. His aptitude is described as very good. Ready?

"Hitting—67 projected to 70, because of bat speed. Power— 72 projected to 73. Arm—70 projected to 71. Fielding—68 projected to 70. Range—72, not projected. At the workout this player ran a sixty in 6.6. . . . Now I want everybody to write down a dollar figure."

"Wait a minute," Davis said. "Has the scout ever seen this boy in a *game?*"

"A couple of times, but as a first baseman. He just found out how well the player runs and throws."

"Then I'm suspicious right away," Davis said. "I'd want to get his stats in college games," Goldsberry said. "I don't think the grades jibe with the verbal description," Roig said.

"Damn it, just give me a figure. Pretend. Put yourself in my place—I haven't seen the player, and it's too late to cross-check him. I have to decide what weight to give this report."

"Tell us more about the *scout*," Hugh Alexander said.

"He's conservative."

"Okay," Alexander said, "I'll play along. My answer is sixty-five thousand." Davis's was $80,000—"if those grades mean what they're supposed to." Goldsberry's was $60,000; Roig's was $45,000. "I put twenty-five," Moose Johnson said, "because the player's already twenty-one, and that's too old for a 67 hitter to be projected to a 70."

Baumer looked straight at me. "Did *you* put down a figure?" Just for fun, I had written $45,000 (thinking "high Group Two"). I said, "I'm still waiting to hear about his face."

"We can call and find out," Baumer said. The mystery player was Willard Currier from the University of Vermont; the conservative scout was Dick Lawlor. On the phone Lawlor confessed that Currier had an uppercut swing, but said it could be helped, and he reported competition on this player from the Dodgers and Blue Jays. Lawlor said nothing about "good face," but did remark that Currier had a "firm handshake." His final evaluation was $20,000.

"So what was the point?" Roig asked.

"The point," Baumer said, "is that if Currier's still there tomorrow on the sixth round, we're gonna draft him."

The new preferential list was to include about sixty names, enough to carry the Phillies through the end of the draft, and in formulating it Baumer was more assertive, less concerned with the trappings of committee democracy. From the original list of forty-one players eighteen were still on the blackboard. Baumer added Currier, Dick Lawlor's mystery man, rearranged the list, and then allowed the scouts to take turns putting more names on the board—while indicating that he wouldn't be bound by the specific sequence.

In the first two rounds there had been a single priority: drafting the best athletes available. But from Round 3 on other factors would enter in—the pacification of certain area scouts, the balancing of rookie-club rosters by position, and especially the larger needs of the organization. One of those needs, Baumer had said, was catchers, and that was how the Phillies would spend their third-round pick. Brandy Davis shot me a look that I took to mean: "Last year's draft of Lebo Powell was a bad mistake, and Jim knows it."

*   *   *

Tuesday's newspapers published the names of all draftees in Rounds 1 and 2, but for the rest of the draft there would be a one-week blackout, to prevent predatory college coaches from getting the jump on scouts. Many coaches, Pastore said, sent scholarship offers to draftees they'd never even seen. This year, though, the coaches would have fewer high-school names to work with, because the 1981 draft was characterized most clearly by college talent.

Of the fifty-two players chosen in the first two rounds, thirty-six were college players. Ten years earlier, in the 1971 draft, the twenty-four major-league teams chose *no* college players in Round 1 and only four in Round 2. According to the new conventional wisdom, the college player is cheaper to sign, and he gives you a quicker return on your investment. But the Phillies were proud to be unconventional, still ready to risk more money and more time on players like Abrego and Penigar, in hopes of a richer reward. "A lotta clubs this year are *afraid* to go for the high-school boy," Roig said. "Afraid to project. But with the college player, what you see is what you get. He ain't gonna get much better."

On Tuesday, in Rounds 3 through 18, the college trend continued: 244 out of 415 draft choices. The Twins and Mariners and Astros were expected to go for college prospects, and they did. But even wealthy clubs (Yankees, Dodgers) and development-minded clubs (Cardinals, Orioles, Expos) were taking over 75 percent of their drafts from colleges. In Round 3 the Phillies themselves passed up the high-school catcher, Phil Lombardi, in favor of a college catcher, Vince Soreca from Pace University. In Round 6, as planned, they drafted Willard Currier from the University of Vermont. In Round 10, following Brandy Davis's advice, they drafted outfielder Mel Williams from David Lipscomb College. And in Round 12 they drafted pitcher Charles Hudson, another of Tony Roig's "loosy-goosy" black players, from Prairie View A&M. (Even as Baumer announced the selection over the phone, Roig was acting out Hudson's supple delivery.)

But most of the Philadelphia drafts were interesting high-school kids: John Kanter, a second baseman with a "Don Zimmer body and cat quickness"; James Olander, the Low-A outfielder whose stock had risen in every discussion; Stephen Witt, a 6'6" pitcher Gordon Goldsberry had rescued from the winnis list; and three highly touted shortstops—Jerry Holtz, the standout from the Friday workout; Matt Shumake, a top prospect despite his father's over-coaching; and David Denny, who had "no fear at the plate even after getting drilled in the right tit." Baumer was especially happy about the shortstops because he had gambled on their availability and won, and because it ought to be cheaper to sign them than if they had been drafted on the rounds appropriate to their real abilities.

As Goldsberry had said, Leon Roberts—Eddie Bockman's pip—was a "Pittsburgh-type draft": the Pirates picked him up in Round 5. In Round 8 the Angels drafted Joey Meyer, the 270-pound Hawaiian. Charles Faucette, the New Jersey Cajun with the *UCLA* tattoo, went to the Blue Jays in Round 12. But there were only a few such moments of interest—and for an area scout like Bill Harper, to whom most of the names coming over the phone were just names, the afternoon became tedious. During Round 15 Baumer looked up from his lists to ask where Harper was. Nobody had seen Harper since Round 9, when the Phillies finally drafted a player from his Northwest territory, high-school second baseman Troy Berry.

"What the hell is this?" Baumer asked. "We bring him all the way here to sit in on the draft, and he just takes off."

Bill Harper was exactly where, given the choice, anybody not a cross-checker or a scouting director would have been. He was sitting with Hugh Alexander in the minor-league office listening to good baseball stories.

". . . So Bert Wells and I stopped at Dodgertown that spring, and we wanted to check on the boys we'd signed—really just to say, 'Hello, how are ya?'—because I never meddled with their teachers. I never got into the development stuff, and I never will: I just scout. So we looked all around for our ball-players, and you know Dodgertown is a big-ass place. We had to walk over to diamond number three to see this player, and diamond number five for that one, and the last boy we'd signed was out on diamond number seven. For about an hour we sat and watched him hit, watched him field and throw, and Bert looked at me and said, 'He can't play!'

"And that was right—he couldn't. He was clumsy and slow, had no arm, looked terrible at the plate. I said, 'Why did we ever sign him? What did we *see* in him?' Bert said, 'I don't remember.' At that time, the Dodgers had us signin' ballplayers by the carload, because Buzzy Bavasi wanted to rebuild the farm system by goin' back to *quantity*. But this boy was so bad, he still stuck out like a hard-on. How two experienced scouts like us could ever've signed him, I don't know. Bert said, 'They're bound to release him in three weeks. But from now till then, every evening, his name's gonna come up in those coaches' meetings. And every goddamn evening they're gonna be reminded that you and I were the scouts that signed him.' Which was true. So we got the Assistant Farm Director in the bar late that night and kept buyin' him drinks, and we talked him into releasin' that boy the very next day! . . . Buzzy and the rest of those guys never found out about it."

When Bill Harper stopped laughing, he stood up. "I guess I better get back to the draft."

"What for?" Alexander asked. "Well, I guess it's kind of intriguing, all those lists. But every so often you hear a name you know, and you realize you've just lost a ballplayer. Maybe you worked your ass off on him since he was a little boy, and now you don't even have a shot at him. Tony Lucadello, good ol' a scout as he is, may not get *anyone* this year. . . . I think baseball got suckered by the draft."

On Wednesday, in Round 22, Baumer finally drafted a ballplayer for Lucadello: Robert Davisson, a righthanded pitcher from Eastern Michigan University. Movement on the blackboard was slow now. The Phillies were losing only one or two names a round to other teams, and other teams were drafting some players the Phillies had never heard of. On Round 23

Bill Gargano said, "The Red Sox just drafted Todd Sylvester Zacher. That has a kind of ring to it—Todd Zacher! It could be a big-league name someday." I saw more potential in the name Arby Oswell, the Phillies' draft on the same round. "You might be right," Moose Johnson said. "Tough right-hand pitcher. Flunked out of Texas Wesleyan and showed up at one of our tryout camps. Nobody else knew about him. We could've drafted him any time."

On Round 24 the Phillies selected Charles Kerfeld, the 6'5" pitcher with long hair and thick glasses and enough meanness to hit even the umps. "You can't go far wrong on one of Bockman's tips," Randy Waddill said, "and a lot of these late-round guys surprise you." Waddill had a list of major-leaguers who were once low draft-picks, like Bill Lee (Round 22), Dusty Baker (Round 25), Ken Griffey (Round 29), and Bake McBride (Round 39). "Ten years ago, at the 1971 draft, there were some great picks in the early rounds—Rice, Schmidt, Brett, Guidry—but Dave Collins didn't go till Round 23, and in Round 42 there was the Keith Hernandez thing. Everybody knew Hernandez was good, but nobody thought he was signable. The Cardinals drafted him just for the hell of it, and then they *watched* him over the summer, and by August they'd seen enough to sign him for pretty much what he wanted."

"The funny thing about 1971 was the White Sox," Brandy Davis said. "They had the number one pick in the whole country, Danny Goodwin, and couldn't sign him. In fact, out of their first ten picks they only signed three. They couldn't sign Warren Cromartie; they couldn't sign Barry Bonnell. They just didn't have the money that the Phillies—"

Baumer interrupted to tell Waddill: "Offer Coleman eight thousand plus incentive. We'll go, tops, ten thousand plus incentive." Vince Coleman was a Florida A & M outfielder evaluated at $14,000; the Phillies had drafted him in Round 20, mostly because of his 6.4 speed. *Incentive* was a bonus plan giving minor-leaguers $1,000 after ninety days in Double A, $1,500 in Triple A, and $5,000 in the major leagues. Baumer called the incentive "a hammer in bargaining."

The Phillies had already signed a couple of Tuesday's drafts—
Vince Soreca for $30,000, John Kanter for $22,500—but the
others, including Abrego and Penigar, were still dickering. Spider Jorgensen phoned to say that Penigar had received a stack
of college offers, and that his family wanted the Phillies to
provide a list of recent high school draftees with their average
money per round. "If he can be signed, I'll sign him," Jorgensen
said, "but it won't be easy."

Baumer, who had received a big bonus himself in 1949, now
looked around the room disgustedly. "Goddamn it! What ever
happened to the eight-thousand-dollar ballplayer?"

"Same thing that happened to the fifty-thousand-dollar major-
leaguer," Roig said. "They just quit makin' those guys. You
go in now to sign a ballplayer and he's read about somebody
else's big bonus, and his daddy wants to play lawyer with the
contract, and his mamma's sittin' there: 'Oh, I feel we need
some financial advice. Let's ask Coach Snobblejock.' And Coach
Snobblejock don't know shit, but he says, 'I think if this bwah
don't get more money, he should take that baseball scholarship
to Shoelace Junior College, where he can get as good an education as I did.' "

The Phillies dropped out of the draft after Round 33; they
were the eleventh team to quit. The rookie-club rosters, even
allowing for some nonsignings, were stretched to the limit. A
few interesting players were left on the board but, if no one
else drafted them, they might be signed later for a minimum
bonus. The Phillies' last selection was a "courtesy draft" of
Michael Dennis—son of Clay Dennis, who used to work in
the Phillies' farm office. "It's kind of a nice thing to do," Brandy
Davis said. "He might be able to use the fact that he was
drafted to get a baseball scholarship to someplace." For a
moment I thought Brandy had said "to Shoelace."

Shortly before the Phillies hung up the phone, an announcement from the commissioner's office came over the speaker-
phone: "This afternoon Federal Judge Henry Werker denied
a request for an injunction that would have set aside for a year
the issue of free-agent compensation." What that meant was

that the major-league players would almost certainly be on strike within forty-eight hours.

I thought that the main issue of the strike—the owners' effort to rein in their own spending in an open talent-market—should have made the existence of the draft an issue too. Back at spring training I had posed a question to Bob Boone, the National League player-representative: "If the athlete's right to bargain is as absolute as you and Marvin Miller believe it is, why hasn't the Players' Association taken a stand against the amateur draft?"

"Because we're professionals," Boone said, "and what happens with amateur prospects isn't any of our business." Which leaves the unlikely possibility that a drafted player might initiate a costly lawsuit. A few have threatened to: in 1979 Bill Bordley, a high-school pitcher drafted by the Reds, said he would go to court unless allowed to sign with a west coast team. The commissioner's office responded by publicly defending the draft, while quietly helping the Reds work out a trade sending Bordley to the San Francisco Giants. What most discourages a lawsuit by a draftee is that the proceedings would probably last longer than the drafting club's exclusive negotiating rights to him. Baseball's draft, unlike football's or basketball's, restrains a player for only six months at a time; if he chooses not to sign, he goes back into the amateur pool.

Since the restraints are so brief, the argument runs, abolishing the draft would only subject the "poorer" teams—say, the Pirates or the Twins—to bidding wars they can't win. Jim Baumer's answer was that the Pirates' and Twins' best talent, since the draft began, has come less from great early round selections than from finding ballplayers where other people weren't looking. The solution to $175,000 players like Rick Reichardt is not to institute a draft but to do better scouting.

"Bonus money can't go scout by itself. There has to be something behind it—experience in baseball, and common sense or guts or whatever to *use* the experience. If you want to know how good scouting can be, you're gonna have to get away from the draft. Without the draft, the scout would have to go out on a limb. Scouts from different teams wouldn't talk so much among themselves.

"You'd have fewer computers and more people. Joe Reilly's probably right—it might be cheaper to sign a lot of players who get drafted after the second round—so without the draft your total outlay for bonuses wouldn't be very much more than it is now. But where teams like the Pirates or the Twins would have to spend the money is on scouts. They'd have to get out of the Bureau and put their own staffs together, hire a lot of people, and maybe spend another half-million a year. Meanwhile, the centerfielder's telling 'em that's how much a year *he* wants. . . . Of course, the Phillies wouldn't have to do that much different."

At the time of the draft an issue of *Inside Sports* featured an article, "The Best Farm Systems in Baseball," highlighting the resources of the Phillies, Expos, and Orioles. It said less about the Phillies' minor-league program than about their scouting, and it quoted an unnamed rival scout: "There are three sure things in life—death, taxes, and two Phillies' scouts behind you every time you turn. They come in platoons. That organization has great scouts." Reading that quote after the draft was over, I suddenly realized that the Phillies were maintaining a noble fiction. They were scouting *as if* there were no draft!

That might mean that Philadelphia scouting was too good— so thorough that six days of committee meetings couldn't do it justice. Despite the trappings of objectivity, like computer printouts and lists of dollar averages, the whole selection process was surprisingly subjective. The composition of the final draft list was ultimately no more scientific than Gordon Goldsberry's notion of the good face or Moose Johnson's faith in the good body. Clearly, Tony Roig had sold the other scouts on a half dozen players; because of his energy and eloquence, prospects like Charles Penigar and Charles Hudson would become Philadelphia property. Just as clearly, when the Phillies selected Vince Soreca from among the top catching prospects in Round 3, they ignored the only scout in the room who had seen all those catchers: Tony Roig.

I was still skeptical about the construction of that first list of forty-one names. But I noted that the Phillies had managed to draft eight of them: Bill Gargano would have won his own betting pool. The scouts had made those eight players, and dozens of others, exciting to one another and to me. And I finally decided that drafting is bound to be tenuous, personal, and basically optimistic—like scouting itself.

10 NOTES FROM THE UNDERGROUND

You just can't keep the friendship out of scouting, because so many of these fellows have been buddies for years. A lot of us have played with each other or against each other, and we go back a long way together. It's a fraternity.

—Ray Scarborough,
quoted by Roger Angell in Five Seasons

A toothpick in Ellis Clary's mouth moves around like a conductor's baton, as if directing the subtle sequence of facial expressions. He does the prospects in different voices. And his own voice modulates a southern Georgia accent for dramatic effect—lowering into deadpan confidentiality on "trouser snake," rising into animated wonder on "prime beef"—with an energy that recreates a scout's original flash of discovery.

> Paul Florence called me up one time and says, "Why don't we drive to Live Oak, Florida"—little old town there—"and work this boy out? I hear he can play." So Paul and I drove to Live Oak, but we didn't have anyone to throw battin' practice. Says, "Don't you know somebody in town that could come and pitch to you so we could see you hit?" "No." He was an outfielder, so I took him out there in centerfield and Paul stood at the plate, and we had him throw and run, and he was pretty good. Then we just sit in the dugout with him. Says, "Don't you know anybody who could . . . ?" "No," he says, "I don't know of anyone."
> And a *kid* walked in—he just happened to pass by—and he says, "I'll pitch to him." This kid was in the tenth grade, and

we were afraid the other guy might hit one back to the mound and kill him. But we took a chance, and he had a good delivery—easy, nice control—so we got to see the hitter hit. When we finished up, I talked to the tenth-grader and found out he didn't even play high-school ball. But I wrote his name down in my little book, 'cause I liked him better'n I did the hitter.

A couple of years later Atley Donald, the Yankee scout, was with me when I stopped near Live Oak to get some gas. I went to a phone booth to call this boy. Turned out he was in Lake City at a junior college. See, his family had got him outa town, because a trouser snake had bit his girl friend in high school. He hadn't played a game of baseball since he pitched battin' practice that day. I says, "Next Wednesday I'll meet you at three o'clock on that same field." I didn't name it, 'cause Atley was hearin' me talk to him. I says, "Get somebody who can warm you up and bring him with you." He says, "I'll get this big boy on the high school team." I says, "What big boy?" He says, "Benny Prue." I says, "I've never heard of him, but bring him out to the field."

This was in June; the draft was already over. Well, I got out to the field and brought some balls and a mitt, and I put Benny Prue to catch and the other one on the mound. But Benny couldn't hold him. After a while I says, "All right, *you* catch *him*." Turned out neither one could catch the other: they both had too much good stuff. Goddamn if I didn't sign both of 'em! They were *prime beef*—seventeen years old, six-foot-three, and 195 pounds. Both of 'em. That wouldn't happen again in nine million years.

Benny Prue was a better prospect, but he was a jack-off guy and he jumped the club twice, and the Twins got tired of foolin' with him. But the other one, the one who pitched battin' practice when he was in the tenth grade, was Ray Corbin, and he pitched in the big leagues for six years. He'd still be there but he hurt his arm. Good ballplayer. But if he'da been a guy like Sandy Koufax, that'd be a hell of a story, wouldn't it?

I think it's a hell of a story anyway. The only problem is that a direct transcription onto the page can't begin to do justice to Ellis Clary's way of telling it. Clary himself has wrestled with the problem of putting his stories into print. In the off-season he writes a column for the Sunday newspaper in Valdosta. In 1981 the Peachtree Press in Atlanta wanted to publish a collection of these pieces, but Clary remained resolutely modest about his work: "A lot of people can't write and don't know it. I can't write and I know it. My favorite sportswriter is Blackie Sherrod from the paper in Dallas, but I could never be in his league. Sometimes I write up my picks in football games; other times I just put in some bullshit." Since Clary seemed shy about showing me some of his columns, I asked him to *tell* me one.

"Like the University of Georgia last year—we had something to write about. And I wrote in there about the Sugar Bowl game. They were leadin' Notre Dame, and everybody has got signs and banners, and you get sick a lookin' at 'How Bout Them Dawgs!' D-a-w-g-s. I don't go for that. But 'How Bout Them Dawgs!' is on cars, water tanks, and everything else. 'How Bout Them Dawgs!'—talkin' about the Georgia Bulldogs, see. So at the Sugar Bowl game Notre Dame was behind at the half, and this South Bend fanatic called the Pope in Rome and says: 'Pope, I'm callin' from New Orleans at the Sugar Bowl, and Notre Dame is behind, and we need help and advice.' And the Pope says, 'Who is Notre Dame playin'?' Guy says, 'The Georgia Bulldogs.' The Pope says, 'How *bout* them Dawgs!' "

Some scouts, like Leon Hamilton, always sit alone at a game, to avoid distraction—and maybe even to achieve a scouting trance, where the future seems to shine through the present. Other scouts, like Tony Lucadello, move all around during the game, changing the viewing angle in order to see all sides of each prospect. But Ellis Clary is sure to be found in the very middle of that knot of scouts behind home plate, entertaining his colleagues with stories and one-liners ("I think my scoutin' director's tryin' to tell me something—wants me to go look at a boy in the Bermuda Triangle") and providing a running commentary on the game, the players, and life itself. In his role as a raconteur and in his cultivation of lasting friendships among his fellows, Ellis Clary seems to live out Ray Scarborough's observation that scouting is a fraternity.

This easy congeniality runs counter to the image of Ellis Clary the ballplayer, a second baseman in the minor and major leagues from 1934 to 1948. In those days Clary, at 5'8" and 160 pounds, earned a reputation as a brawler. Near the end of his career one of his teammates was Tony Roig. "Ellis would come into bases spikes high," Roig says, "or he'd knock catchers on their asses—do whatever it took. He was a tough guy. He'd fight a buzz saw."

Today Clary plays down those stories and prefers to talk about the times that baserunners wiped *him* out. "Elmer Valo killed me one night in Philadelphia. You know Elmer Valo? He could kill a hoss. He could kill a mule. He hit me on a double play, and when I hit the ground I'm in short leftfield, laid out flat, and they walked out there and looked and says: 'He's dead.' I had that happen three times. That big second baseman, Ray Mack—his son played guard for the Rams for fourteen years—he was a *huge* monkey: he laid me out in Cleveland. And in St. Paul one day, same thing: ball got there late on a double play, and I couldn't jump out of the way, and I got destroyed—Duke Snider raped me!"

Clary was a member of the St. Louis Browns in 1944, the only season they ever won a pennant. But for forty-six of his first fifty years in baseball he worked for the Griffith family— owners of the Minnesota Twins, originally the Washington Senators. In 1936, when he joined the Senators' farm club at Charlotte, his manager was the twenty-five-year-old Calvin Griffith, destined to be the Twins' president and chairman of the board. Calvin, the nephew of Clark Griffith, was learning the baseball business from the bottom up; his apprenticeship would later include tours of duty with the Senators as concessionaire, traveling secretary, and farm director. Along the way Calvin absorbed a special philosophy of family ownership. Without the kind of outside income enjoyed by the Wrigleys in Chicago or the Carpenters in Philadelphia, the Griffiths were always committed to a low-budget, no-frills operation. (An exception was in finding jobs for family members. At one point, in 1973, eighteen Griffith relatives were on the Twins' payroll.)

Several key players, disgruntled with low salaries, left the Twins to become free agents; others used the threat of free agency to force the Twins to trade them. On the other hand the Twins themselves never signed a free agent under Griffith. "We run a sensible operation," Calvin said, "and we don't owe money to the banks."

In the June 1981 draft the Twins' first-round selection was Michael Sodders, a third baseman from Arizona State University. The choice followed Calvin Griffith's pattern of drafting college seniors, whose lack of bargaining leverage usually allowed them to be signed on the cheap. In late July Sodders was still unsigned and still arguing that $35,000 was an insulting offer to a player selected eleventh in the whole country. Ellis Clary was annoyed by Sodders' demands but he directed his real anger against the major-league players, who were still out on strike. "All everybody wants to talk about is money. Money, money, money. What the goddamn hell about *baseball*? Son of a bitches already got more money than they can count, but they won't be happy till they *break* some owners, drive 'em right out of business. Scout goes in and asks for a raise, the owner says: 'Raise, hell! We got to get out here and pedal faster to pay the first baseman.' "

The Griffiths had collected as much money in strike insurance as they could reasonably have expected to make from home attendance if there had been no strike. But Clary argued that the Twins were still coping with the previous year's operating deficit (over a million dollars) and he predicted the disappearance of family ownership in baseball. "As soon as the Wrigleys sell the Cubs and the Carpenters sell the Phillies, that makes ten big-league clubs sold in the last four years. And some of these new owners are just no-counts: they don't know any baseball, but they got big money and big egos . . . and big tax breaks, because they're set up as conglomerates instead of families."

This was a baseball man, ill-at-ease with the whole idea of conglomerates. The Gulf-and-Westernization he foresaw promised to do about as much for baseball as it had for the movies. Clary saw the other side of the game, the real side, summed up in the career of Zinn Beck, a scout for the Griffiths for fifty years. Beck had died in the spring at the age of ninety-five, and, amazingly, had been an active scout until just a few years before. When I first met Ellis Clary in March, he had just received a message from Calvin Griffith, who asked him to drive to Sanford, Florida, to deliver the eulogy at Beck's funeral. Clary had begun our interview in the spring with what seemed like a warm-up for the eulogy, but as he continued I sensed that he was eulogizing more than Zinn Beck.

He was a good man. Everybody that dies is a good man to hear people tell it, see, but Zinn Beck *was*. Didn't smoke, didn't drink, didn't use profane language, always had a kind word for anyone. A super guy. He was all baseball—still scouted into his nineties, and earlier on he signed guys like Cecil Travis, Buddy Lewis, Jake Early, Jimmy Bloodworth. Ray Scarborough was one of his. He got some plums.

Back yonder when he first scouted, there was less than a dozen full-time scouts in all of baseball. Nobody knew what a scout was. Fifty years ago there wasn't but a few guys like Zinn Beck, and Paul Krichell with the Yankees, Charlie Barrett with the Cardinals, Cy Slapnicka with the Indians. And Billy Pierre: he's the scout that signed me. It was wide open. You didn't have to pay bonuses; you didn't have to draft ballplayers—just go out and find 'em. Find 'em and sign 'em!

When I started in to scout, there still wasn't this draft. It was more fun then, because you were sneakin' around like a damn detective or a spy. Like when Blue Moon Odom was in high school over in Macon, and the Red Sox had a black scout named Ed Scott, from Mobile, come and rent a room in Blue Moon's house. Undercover. The door to Ed's room was made of plywood, and he says: "I can hear better with the door closed than I can with it open." He told the rest of us every word that was said, because he knew it was hopeless—Blue Moon was gonna sign with Oakland for a bonus of seventy thousand. The rest of us stopped around thirty-five, so old Charlie Finley give Blue Moon about double what he would've had to.

There was more competition back then, and some of those older scouts wouldn't even tell you how to get to the next

town. They could mess you up. They might give you some
bullshit about a player just to throw you off the track. But I
hooked up with three of the best scouts in the business, and we
had what we called "The Underground." Me and Atley Donald
of the Yankees and Paul Florence of Houston and Spud Chandler of Cleveland. We worked together. The ballclubs didn't
know it, but what the hell? We lived in different areas, so we
could help each other out. You wouldn't grade out a ballplayer
for another guy. If he asked you about him, you might say,
"Well, you better go see him." The main thing is—says, "Any
use me goin' to see that player down in Monmouth?" "No,
don't go." See, that's great—saves you a five-hundred-mile
drive. Had you not been doin' that, everybody'd be on they
own, and you run up a lot of mileage for nothin'.

If you talk to the average high-school coach, he'll tell you,
"I've got some surefire major-league prospects." He's not lyin',
but he don't know. He'll tell you how great a ballplayer is—
second baseman, and you get there and it's his sister's boy, a
hundred and ten pounds and can't do nothin', and you wasted
a trip. And I had a big territory to cover—I used to tell people
I had everything east of the Nile River.

You heard the scout's story about territory? This scout died
suddenly and his friends didn't know what he died from. All
the area scouts went to his funeral—asked, "What did he have?
What killed him?" Nobody knew, so they saw his wife come up
to take one last look before the casket was closed. Said, "What
did he have?" She said, "Georgia, Tennessee, and Mississippi."

That's enough to kill anybody. I know, because that's the
exact territory I had, and it killed me. See, I was scoutin' up
this Dillard boy, plays with the Cubs now. I saw him at a tournament in Mississippi and was gonna try to sign him. I told his
momma and daddy: "I'll be back next week for the next round
of the tournament." Then I went off and had a damn heart attack. Stayed in the hospital six weeks, and when I got to where
I could write, I just sent 'em the clip from the paper and wrote
at the bottom: "This is why I never got back. Fell dead." And I
never saw his family again until last year at Wrigley Field. They
spotted me and came down there where the scouts sit, and we
had a nice talk. They're good people—from Santillo, right out
of Tupelo.

Death's overrated. I died three days in a row, but they

brought me back with that machine. Atley Donald came to the-hospital and said, "Money is no object. I want the best of everything for this guy." I got more attention than Eisenhower did when he had a heart attack. Atley's retired now, but he was one hell of a scout. He's the guy who signed Ron Guidry.

Right now Guidry's about the only Yankee ballplayer that's come up through their own system. All their other players are stolen guys. See, me and another scout were on the radio in Chicago last year, on one of them question and answer deals, for a damn ninety minutes—that ain't easy—and some guy calls in and says, "What about the Yankees? They got a great team." I said, "I'm glad you asked that. The catcher Cerone comes from the Blue Jays; the first baseman Watson comes from the Astros; the other first baseman Spencer comes from the White Sox; the second baseman Randolph comes from the Pirates; the shortstop Dent comes from the White Sox; the third baseman Nettles comes from the Twins—he's one of *our* guys. The leftfielder Piniella comes from the Indians; the centerfielder Ruppert Jones comes from the Mariners; the rightfielder Jackson comes from the A's. The pitcher Tommy John comes from the Dodgers; Goose Gossage comes from the White Sox. . . . Don't tell me about the Yankee system. They ain't got a man!" I saved one back, see. I said, "*Name* one." He couldn't. I said, "Yeah, they got Guidry—Atley Donald's guy." I enjoyed that. I said, "I'm so glad you asked," and then I unloaded on him.

This is a crazy game. Gene Autry spent forty million to put together that 1980 Angel team, and we finished twelve games ahead of 'em. We've been lucky—there's a lot of luck in this scoutin' business, even though a lot of people don't admit it—and we've made some good lower drafts and some decent trades. We've lost a hell of a team, you know. We might have a dynasty goin' if we hadn't lost all them guys to free agency, like Hisle and Bostock. And Carew and Blyleven were *gonna* be free agents, so we went out swapped 'em first. Had to take what we could get, but we come out pretty good—got Smalley and a bunch of other guys for Blyleven. And we didn't die in the Carew deal. I do mostly special-assignment work now, and I looked real close at the Angels and their farm teams in 1978, and we wound up with Ken Landreaux and three good prospects. The one I liked best was Dave Engle.

Engle's a good case of where you try to look around a cor-

ner. I thought by now he might be a regular in the big
league. He can run; he can throw; he's got power. Well, you say
if he's got desire, what's gonna hold him back? But he's still got
to put it together. He has good tools, but some people put it
together earlier than others. Maybe he's on schedule. I don't
know. . . . You go scout a guy like Engle and you get an
impression about him. It may not be right, but you get an
impression. I like a guy with an opinion. If he's wrong, what
the hell, that's human nature. Don't you? I hate to run into a
guy, he don't have no opinion. There was a catcher in Memphis
a few years ago, got drafted in the first round. Great big old
boy. Throw like a son of a bitch. And couldn't get out of the
low minors! I would've bet my house that he'd play in the big
league. But everybody sees everything different—that's the reason everybody don't try to marry the same woman.

When you go scout amateurs, you don't just have to project
into the future: most of the time you have to imagine 'em at a
different position. Our guy John Castino may be the best third
baseman in the league, but when I saw him at Rollins College
he played leftfield. I'm still lookin' for the guy who played third
base at Rollins and made Castino play left. He must have been
a hell of a player! And if you go see a *high-school* infielder or
outfielder play, it's about two-to-one odds that he's gonna pitch
that day. Ray Knight—he was supposed to be a shortstop in
high school, but I didn't get to see that. He pitched the game I
saw. He had a pin that long in his left leg where he'd broke his
ankle, and it didn't bother him too much as a pitcher, but he
didn't run too good that day, and I couldn't picture him as a
pro shortstop, so I just walked away. That was a mistake—he
overcame the injury. But he wasn't a shortstop either; he was a
third baseman.

See, there ain't no Willie Mayses no more—guys that can do
five things. They just quit makin' players like that. You find a
guy today with *two* tools and he's probably worth a high draft.
But he's probably not real ready to learn. You could take Ted
Williams out to one of these high school diamonds and let him
sit down and talk to the kids about hittin', and in fifteen minutes they'd be tellin' *him* how to hit.

In the first place they never would have heard of Ted Williams. When I was that age, I knew everybody that had ever
played back to eighteen-and-ten. Today they don't know who

played yesterday and don't give a goddamn. That's not criticism; it's just the way it is. "Ted Williams? Who the hell's he?" We had a guy in Double-A ball, in the Sally League, a few years ago—a big-bonus guy, a shortstop—and one day I says, "You know, you got a lot of mannerisms of Lou Boudreau." He'd never heard of him! I said, "You never heard of Lou Boudreau?" That monkey didn't know who Lou Boudreau was. I didn't say anything to him, but that ruined my day right there. And he was a brilliant kid, a graduate of Vanderbilt.

Used to, I wouldn't go watch a college game unless I had a special assignment. I'd dodge it. I'd stay with the high-school guys. That was the ideal thing: get the high-school guys, put 'em in your farm system, and let 'em ripen till they were ready to play in the big league. You can't wait that long no more. If you sign a high-school guy today and take him step-by-step through the minors, soon's you get him up there and get him turned up to where he can really help you, somebody comes along and grabs him as a free agent and you've lost out on your investment. You're lookin' for the college guy now. He's cheaper to sign, because he doesn't have as much leverage to bargain. He's cheaper to train, because you can start him out in Double A. And he gives you a quicker return on your money, because he may get to the big league inside three years. If he's a pitcher, he might could get there overnight, like Steve Howe.

If you could *afford* to do it the old way, you would. Because sometimes you rush ballplayers, and you get a lot of big-leaguers today who still don't know the basics. That's why you see so many big-league coaches today. Back when I played, a team might have one coach—and he wouldn't tell you a damn thing, except what time the game started. Most people didn't know how to help anybody. I played for Rogers Hornsby, and he wouldn't fool with anybody that didn't know how to play. That wasn't part of the game then. It shouldn't be part of it today. A ballplayer, by the time he gets to the big league—hell, he hadn't oughta be taught how to hit the cut-off man, how to back up a base, how to do the rundown plays.

But it's one a them vicious circles. Today the Twins have five farm clubs; just a few years ago we had eight. Eight! If a guy couldn't make it on one club, put him on another one. Move him around—he might find himself. You could take your time and train him right. Today you've got to release him if he can't make it; you can't put him in cold storage. And you can't keep the pressure on big-league ballplayers—that was another way the big farm systems worked.

One of the best pitchers I ever saw was Nelson Potter on the Browns. He'd been a Cardinal farmhand before we got him, and he was on the Columbus Redbirds—the Cardinal farm team that played the Little World Series against Rochester, another Cardinal farm team. It went seven games, and Nelson Potter won all four games for Columbus. Next year he's with the Cardinals. They called him up to the majors and offered him a fifty dollar a month raise! And he raised hell about it. Sent the contract back, and Rickey sent the same one back to him. Said, "I don't care if you sign it or not. Don't make no difference to me. I'm offerin' you a chance to pitch in the big league. And if you don't want it, I'll just call up John Grodzicki." Well, Nelson knew that he'd never get to play if Grodzicki got up there, 'cause Grodzicki could pitch. What the hell was he gonna do? Sign.

The Cardinals had three Triple-A clubs. The Yankees had two, and Spud Chandler had to win twenty-five games at Newark just to be able to cross the river and join the Yankees. You wanta hear some shit? Go ask Spud Chandler about the Yankees, about tryin' to get a raise out of old George Weiss. Weiss was worse than Rickey. Ballplayer'd go in and ask for a raise, Weiss'd say, "Raise, my ass! You're gonna get a raise in the World Series. You're fortunate to be on this club. You're luckier'n hell to be here. Your raise'll come in November when you get your World Series check."

Says, "But, goddamn it, we *earned* that. We're the ones that got that."

Atley Donald took one of those World Series checks—about $6,000—and used it to buy a piece of Louisiana timberland that he sold a few years ago for $750,000. In 1981 Atley Donald was seventy-one. He had retired after undergoing open-heart surgery five years earlier, and now followed baseball only by reading newspapers. The players' strike made him especially angry. "I'm not a union man," he said, "and I think the players are flat-out greedy. I'm with the owners all the way. They have development costs you don't find in any other business. Look at all the minor-league players who never pan out."

No, there was nothing special about the circumstances of Ron Guidry's signing—said Atley Donald, the scout who used Guidry's coach as an intermediary in offering the young pitcher $10,000 to drop out of the University of Southwest Louisiana and become available, quietly, for the June draft in 1971. "I scouted thirty years and signed a lot more who didn't make it than did. But I got some guys like Clint Courtney, Jake Gibbs, Ron Blomberg . . . Marvelous Marv Throneberry—he was a great character; he ought to've been a great ballplayer. The Underground was a big help, because I trusted those other guys' judgment. I could trust them as friends, too, but I still kid Ellis about the fast one he pulled with Ray Corbin, that pitcher he had hid out down there in Live Oak, Florida."

In 1981 Paul Florence was eighty-one. In 1926, his only major-league season, he had been a catcher for the Giants. "Sinister Dick Kinsella, John McGraw's scout, saw me playing at Georgetown University. Kinsella was one of the few major-league scouts in existence in the 1920s. McGraw signed me himself. He was a fine man—and if he liked you, he was in your corner all the way. But in those days you had to adjust to the manager's way of thinking. Today the twenty-five players on a club all seem to go their own way.

"I retired as a player about the time that those other guys in the Underground were just breaking into pro ball. Did front-office work till 1946, then started scouting. I'm still at it, but the travel's getting tough. Of course, after fifty-eight years in the game I'm able to draw a baseball pension—seventy-five dollars a month. . . . About once a year I go to some baseball dinner where somebody stands up and says that scouts are the lifeblood of baseball, but it never goes any further than that. Whenever a club wants to economize, scouting is the first area to get cut. The Astros are spending more money this year on player development, but we also have five pitchers making five and a half million a year."

*   *   *

In 1981 Spud Chandler was seventy-three. After recent abdominal surgery he had resumed his regular scouting coverage for the Twins. His territory was northern Florida and southern Georgia. When I visited him at his home in St. Petersburg, he was still tired from his trip the day before. "I'm gettin' to where I hate to drive with these damn monkeys on the road." He stopped, checked the next room to make sure his wife couldn't overhear, and then lowered his voice: "I came so close to havin' a wreck last night. Just lucky there wasn't anybody comin' up on my right. They had a breakdown on that bridge— I was on my way back from Lakeland—and this car in front of me . . . I wasn't runnin' fast, but I took my eyes off the road for just a flash. I had to slam on my brakes and cut. I slid around it, but anybody comin' on my right side would have knocked me right into that other car.

"I thought I might retire in 1978. I worked for the Scouting Bureau then, and a couple of clubs dropped out of it, so they had to let some people go. They cut off seventeen old folks at one lick and left the younger blood in. I lost my job. But I couldn't just sit around on my ass—my baseball pension's not much, and my wife's been sick—so Ellis helped me hook on with the Twins. And I'm still out there. . . .

"I believe Ellis Clary could make a *dog* laugh. Atley Donald and I were with him when he had his heart attack, at a tournament in this small town in Alabama. They only had a clinic there, so we got an ambulance to take Ellis to the hospital in Mobile. He died on that trip, but they brought him back. In the hospital, when he was conscious again, he motioned me over to his bed and whispered—said, 'Spud, I want you to do something for me.' I said, 'Anything.' He said, 'I want you to go down and get the mileage off that ambulance so I can turn it in on my expense report.' "

"You wanta hear some shit?" Ellis Clary had asked me. "Go ask Spud Chandler about the Yankees, about tryin' to get a raise out of old George Weiss." I did, and I did.

Of all the scouts I met in the course of the scouting year, Spud Chandler had been one of the greatest major-league players—a strong and aggressive right-handed pitcher for eleven seasons, 1937 to 1947, with a lifetime earned-run average of 2.84. His lifetime winning percentage of .717 (109 wins, 43 losses) is the highest in the history of baseball. But through those seasons he had been treated so shabbily by his wealthy owners that his career might serve as a case-history explaining why major-league players eventually formed a union.

"Johnny Nee signed me in 1932, right after I finished college. He was an old smoothie—said, 'When you get with the Yankees, the money is *there*.' That year I pitched in the New York–Penn League and had a 12-and-1 record. Mr. Weiss promoted me to Newark but he sent me the same contract I already had: two hundred and fifty a month. That was for five months. I wrote him back a nice letter and told him I couldn't believe he expected me to sign that contract. He wrote back that he *did* expect me to, and got a little sarcasm in—had a little note at the bottom: 'In the event that you don't sign this contract, don't send it back. Just keep it for a souvenir.'

"By the time I worked my way through that farm system, pitched my way to the big leagues, I was almost thirty. Then after my second season with the Yankees I had three little bone chips taken out of my elbow. I'd just gone 14-and-5 but Mr. Weiss sent me a contract for only five-fifty a month, with a note to continue my running. I didn't sign the contract, just sent it back, but I did the running and that led to an accident where I broke my ankle. I had to pay all my own hospital bills, doctor bills, physical therapy—and when I joined the team in the middle of the 1939 season, he gave me the same damn contract. He said, 'Spud, we'll win the pennant with or without you. If you don't want to sign, it's fine with me.'

"Then in 1943 I was voted the Most Valuable Player—had a record of 20-and-4 with an ERA of 1.64, and won two games in the World Series—and I couldn't get a raise! He said, 'Don't you know there's a war on?' I sure as hell did, because I wound up doin' two years of service, but that war never kept him from rakin' in a lot of money at the gate. . . . That's the way they did ballplayers back then."

After listening to these stories about the arrogance of management, I expected Spud Chandler to express support for the striking major-league players, who argued that the best safeguard against economic tyranny was true free agency—without the kind of gimmicks that make free agency a joke in pro football. But Chandler, like 90 percent of the scouts I interviewed, opposed the players and rooted for the owners to reestablish firm control.

Were the scouts jealous? Had they simply become company men? Maybe both—but most of them just thought it was obvious that a larger share of the pie for players would mean a smaller share for scouts. I thought they were wrong. New television money ought to make the pie bigger—and most organizations were already responding to free agency by *increasing* their player-development budgets. "Scouting should be on the upswing in the 1980s," I said.

Chandler was unimpressed. The players were so intent on their own self-interest that none of the new money would increase pension benefits for old-timers. Atley Donald had taken care of himself. Ellis Clary, like Zinn Beck, could depend on the Griffith family for special pension provisions. But Spud Chandler and Paul Florence were most typical of the veteran scouts: after dedicating themselves decade after decade to a sport that turned into a business every time they weren't looking, they were now trying to figure out how to retire with dignity.

To all of that, Chandler simply wanted to add a criterion of fairness. "It's hard to blame the players for taking all that money, but they talk like there's no such thing as development costs. A boy in the minors is financial dead weight, and it's not fair to find him, train him, and then just lose him to some team richer than you. . . . It's not fair to the scouts, either. We ought to be able to take more lasting pleasure, and get more lasting credit, out of signing a good ballplayer."

*   *   *

In 1981 Ellis Clary was eleven. He computes his age now from
the time of his heart attack, his return from that other Underground.

When I phoned Clary at the end of July, three days before
the end of the strike, he sounded restless, as if suffering from
cabin fever. The Twins, like many other clubs, had long since
pulled their scouts off the road, restricting them to day trips
in order to save on expenses. Clary hated the strike for many
reasons, but the main one was that it kept him from fraterniz-
ing with his supposed rivals. "Leon Hamilton—he invented
scoutin', his way. He's a different guy. A good scout, but he'll
tell you he's the world's greatest. And Howie Haak—he chews
tobacco in his sleep, I think. Inside of his car looks like a hog
pen. He has to get a new Cadillac every year.

"And Hugh Alexander . . . there was a cartoon in the paper
one time that showed these two boxers meetin' in the center
of the ring with their managers and the referee to go over the
rules before the fight started. And one boxer's hand was cut
off, just exactly like Hugh's is, and he had one of them balin'
hooks on the end. And his manager is tellin' him: 'Watch out
for his left hook.' It was made for Hugh Alexander! Here he
stands: 'Watch out for his left hook.' I saw that and had a
convulsion, and I sent it to another scout and wrote *Leon
Hamilton* as one of the fighters and *Hugh Alexander* as the
guy with the hook. This other scout showed that cartoon to
Hugh. I didn't want that to happen, but he got a kick out of
it. Next time I saw him he said, 'I saw that left hook!' "

Clary asked me for news of Spud Chandler, and I said that
it seemed like a paradox when Chandler concluded his George
Weiss stories with a statement opposing the players' union.
"No mystery to it at all," Clary said. "Sure he got used as a
player. We all did. But today the players got the long end of
the pole, and this thing's so overloaded the other way that all
the older guys are ferocious. Go talk to 'em.

"I'll tell you what Paul Richards said in 1969. Nobody paid
him any mind, but I wrote it in a column not long ago. He

said, 'Turn *every* player loose at the end of *every* year. Make
'em all free agents at once.' You'd see a lot more guys runnin'
to first base, don't you reckon? They'd have a much better
time on that watch. The California Angels can't get 'em all;
they can only have twenty-five. Let the Angels take the twenty-
five they want in that warm climate, and the rest of you son
of a bitches get you a damn snowmobile and come back over
here and try to get a job. I'd like to see a player run one a
them air hammers that tears up the street, run one a them
things all day and then see if he can bellyache about jet lag.

"Outside of Pete Rose, I'm gonna give you all the rest of
them guys. He's the only one that sweats. Somebody told me
that his nickname in high school was Dump. Well, he's not a
very beautiful guy, but he's a credit to the game. He's *earned*
his money. On account of the rest of them guys just standin'
there, he shines like a diamond in a dog's ass!"

No, it was a diamond in a *dawg*'s ass. D-a-w-g-s. There was
no other way to render the sound of Ellis Clary's voice. And
now he was laughing. Whatever anger or frustration he had
been storing up had evaporated, at least for a moment, because
of his own way with words. He relaxed as he talked about
Zinn Beck's funeral.

"I kept the eulogy brief. Built it around three words: loyal,
dedicated, unselfish. I'm not sure if *The Sporting News* ever
ran an obituary on Zinn, but they sure as hell should've. He
was what the game used to be about, what it *ought* to be
about."

"Would you want to scout as long as he did?"

"I'm goin' to. I'll break his record."

11 BASEBALL DETECTIVES

Why not give every unscouted boy a chance to play base-ball?

> —Branch Rickey, "Notes on a Tryout Camp,"
> The American Diamond

Joe Reilly sat on the sidelines in his folding chair and surveyed the diamond. Sixty-five players, almost all age sixteen to nineteen, were milling around the field at Dover High School. Fifty-five of them couldn't possibly be considered pro prospects by the stretch of anybody's imagination but their own.

"I ran a tryout camp like this in New York City one time," Joe Reilly said, "and I had a brand-new pack of five hundred registration cards, and they filled every one of them out, and there were still more kids, so then they used matchbook covers, pieces of paper they were findin' in the park—anything they could write down a name, address, and phone number on. My brother, the part-time scout, was helpin' me, and we were there from nine in the morning until it got dark. Didn't even let 'em hit. All we did was have 'em run and throw, run and throw—a damn assembly line. Six hundred kids. Where would you get that in football or basketball?"

"In football or basketball," I said, "a kid knows he has to be big, and it's harder to fool yourself about how good you are." I gestured toward the players in front of us, but I was really remembering myself at seventeen. "Most kids can throw a little bit, or swing the bat a little bit, and maybe they've played a few thousand games in their minds, so it doesn't seem all that impossible that somebody's gonna suddenly *discover* them. It's like they're wondering whether God has secretly touched them."

Joe Reilly's eyes flickered at the mention of God's name, and he shifted position in his lawn chair. Later on he'd be expounding on his pet theme, a familiar one to most scouts: real ballplayers *are* touched by God. But for now he simply regarded the sixty-five would-be players. "Somewhere along the line, twenty years from now," Reilly said, "these kids can go into some bar and say, 'I once had a tryout with the Philadelphia Phillies.' It means something to them. It's good public relations. And a course, once in a while, even after all the scouting that's been done all spring, . . . you really do find a ballplayer."

In 1981 the major-league clubs and the Scouting Bureau sponsored about five hundred tryout camps in the United States, Canada, and Latin America. Every one of these was another ritual of homage to Branch Rickey.

In 1919, as the new general manager of the Cardinals, Rickey advertised and supervised baseball's first large-scale tryout, a two-day camp at Robison Field in St. Louis. Hundreds of amateur players showed up, including a twenty-two-year-old pitcher named Ray Blades from Mount Vernon, Illinois. On the first day it was clear to Rickey and chief scout Charles Barrett that Blades was no prospect on the mound. But an essential part of their tryout strategy was an evaluation of the total athlete, based first of all on his running speed. When the 5'7" Blades outran everyone else in camp, he was invited back the next day, and he showed enough promise as an outfielder and hitter to be signed to a professional contract. "Blades's speed could be built on because he was a natural athlete," Rickey said. He was right: the little outfielder batted .301 over a solid ten-year career with the Cardinals.

Rickey's idea of group trials was no less revolutionary than his emphasis on signing amateurs. In 1919 a player's normal path to the majors was still what it had been for Honus Wagner, Ty Cobb, and Babe Ruth: getting discovered and signed by an independent minor-league club, and then being sold upward. Rickey's first camp announced a new concept of acquiring talent, and it implied a new method of development—the farm system—which began to evolve from that very day Ray Blades was signed.

Because of the expanding farm system (twenty-four Cardinal affiliates by the end of the 1920s), Rickey's tryout camps encouraged the signing of marginal players who might develop slowly. But in an era when scouting staffs were still small, Rickey reasoned that there were also bound to be plenty of clear-cut prospects each year whom Cardinal scouts would miss during the regular school and semi-pro seasons: players like Jim Bottomley, Pepper Martin, Dizzy Dean, Red Schoendienst, and a dozen other future stars signed directly out of tryout camps. Martin, who arrived at a Cardinal camp on the rods of a freight in 1925, was the prototype of what the Cardinals were looking for: "Hard guys," Charlie Barrett said. "I don't care whether they can field or not. We can *teach* them to field. I want strong-armed, strong-legged guys who can hit and run and throw. Guys like, well, like Pepper Martin."

In his guidelines for conducting a camp Rickey stressed the evaluation of "tools," especially running, and the need to test some prospects—the Ray Blades type—at more than one position. But he insisted that no scout delay the proceedings for the purpose of instruction: "It is not an instructional camp in any sense and *should not* be. It is held and conducted for the purpose of observing players and evaluating their future." Rickey also ordered his personnel to supervise careful sets of warmups before and during the tryouts: "Under no circumstances should the club be at fault for a pulled tendon, either in running or throwing, and this simply must not happen, *ever!*"

The Cardinal-style camp became a model for other major-league teams, and Rickey himself later transported his methods to Brooklyn and Pittsburgh—dispatching scouts like Rex Bowen and Howie Haak to run camps in all parts of the U.S. and Latin America. Haak is famous for his Latin American camps, sifting through six hundred players in one day by using the sixty-yard dash as a strainer: any nonpitcher with a slower time than seven seconds in the sixty can go home right away. Haak points out that tryout camps are an absolute must in Latin America, where organized amateur ball is played mainly on weekends and a scout just doesn't have time to see enough games.

In the States, though, the rationale of the tryout camp has changed, because Rickey's premises—limited scouting coverage, big farm system—have been inverted. Each non-Bureau club now employs more than twenty full-time scouts, and each club in the Bureau is buying thorough (sometimes too thorough) coverage. So the odds are higher than ever against finding a previously unscouted quality player at a tryout camp. And today's smaller farm systems (an average of five affiliates) dictate against taking chances on marginal or slow-to-develop prospects. As a result most clubs admit frankly that the first value of American tryout camps is good publicity, and that the second is an opportunity to spot high-school juniors worth a "follow" the next season. In order to save on expenses all tryout camps are now one-day affairs.

And yet . . . any scout worth the name believes that ultimate bargains still exist. He can name a few major-leaguers signed directly out of camps, like Sammy Stewart, Kent Tekulve, or Art Howe. And he can tell you a tryout camp story—about Dave Parker, who was kicked off his high-school team in Cincinnati, then showed up at a 1970 Pirate camp in Columbus and performed well enough to be worth a chance draft on the fourteenth round that June. Or about Terry Puhl, a native Canadian who would have been worth a ton in PR alone to the Montreal Expos if they had recognized the potential of one skinny kid at one tryout camp in 1973. Which only proves that any camp, and especially the modern one-day camp, is bound to be even chancier than normal scouting, if there is such a thing.

*   *   *

Joe Reilly had his own tryout camp story, but he was going to take a while to get to it. He has a pure Irish love of talk for its own sake, and his baseball intelligence works by free association, so it pays just to listen well and let the stories happen where they will. For example, I knew that he had worked for fifteen years in the detective bureau of the Philadelphia police force, and I was hoping that he'd draw some interesting parallel between the roles of detective and scout— maybe about how both require intuition, or a special eye for detail, or long and patient surveillance. At the very least I expected him to tell some new version of the old scouting joke about prospects and suspects. But Reilly wanted to avoid the whole topic of police work. "I got some bad publicity one time," he said.

All he meant was that he would get to the topic the long way round. He had delegated seven assistants to organize each phase of the tryouts, and so he was able to relax in a lawn chair and be an overseer and muse about baseball. He took out his false teeth and replaced them with a plug of Red Man. Before he put the teeth in his pocket, he showed them around. "Made in Germany. Pretty nice, huh?"

"Yeah, they are. But why'd you send all that way for 'em?"

"I didn't. I got 'em *in* Germany. I go over to Europe just about every year. Got to get away from baseball for a little while, at least. . . . I love it, but it's a damn disease. Been in it since 1937. Know where I started out? Right here in Dover, in the Eastern Shore League. I signed a tremenjous bonus contract."

"Really?"

"Sure—sixty dollars a month, no down payment. Hell, that was less than I got for pitchin' semi-pro in Philly. We used to get five thousand people at our games up there. It only cost twenty-five cents, but five thousand twenty-five centses was a lot of money then, and so the Mayfair team paid me twenty dollars a week. But I thought I could get to the majors. The guy that signed me says to me, 'You're only fifteen? You gotta get your mother's signature.' I knew she wouldn't sign, so I says, 'I'll be back in an hour'—and I got some woman to sign, told her it was a petition to get a traffic light on this corner, so it was in a woman's signature, right? Went back home and told my mother, 'I'm goin' to baseball tomorrow—Dover, Delaware.' I didn't even know where the hell Dover, Delaware, was—I'd lived in Philly all my life—but I was all excited, until I got there and found out we only got seventy-five cents a day for meal money. We used to get up early in the morning to steal milk and buns off front porches.

"I played with Stan Musial the next year. He was a second-year man gettin' *eighty* dollars a month, and that was a high-paid player. He was a pitcher, but he couldn't pitch because he had a bad arm. Then somebody found out that he could hit, so they converted him to an outfielder. Same thing happened to me—except when they converted me to an outfielder, I turned out to be Joe Reilly instead of Stan Musial. And one year when I was in the Dodger farm system, stationed right up here in Trenton, I ran into the outfield wall and wound up in the hospital. That's how I got the bad publicity."

"What bad publicity?"

"That I was tellin' you about before. See, I was also in the detective bureau at the same time, and they let me work extra hours in the off-season in exchange for time off in the summer to play ball. So when I got hurt and the papers said CITY DETECTIVE INJURED, it didn't look good to some people. But, hell, I worked the same number of hours. And professional baseball then wasn't so set apart from the rest of life: every player had to have another job, and in fact Hal Kelleher had pitched for the Phillies in the late thirties while he was still technically on the police force."

"I guess it was an advantage to be Irish."

"It always is."

He had set up his chair near the finish line of the sixty-yard dash. The track itself was a semi-level swath of left-centerfield on a diamond that slants dramatically down toward home plate. And the grass, uncut for at least a week, was still wet from overnight rain. Just to add another variable, the sixty yards had been measured out with a baseball bat. Two of Reilly's assistants, Jack Purdy and Art Chapman, planted flags that made it all look official, while Aldie Livingston divided up the sixty-five players into groupings—pitchers, catchers, infielders, outfielders—and gave each a number within his group.

At the starting flags Purdy showed the players how he wanted them to run in pairs, instructing them to start with a cross-over step and to finish by running *through* the imaginary tape at the finish line. The runners were to break at the drop of Purdy's arm; but at our end Ed Wolf reminded the timers, each taking one runner, to ignore Purdy's arm, to click the watch at the runner's first forward movement. Pitcher number one, a moon-faced black kid, ran with too much side-to-side action in the hips, but he still beat pitcher number two by five yards. He grinned in triumph until Arky Kraft called out his time— 7.3. "Gotta be wrong, gotta be!" "No," Kraft said, "just a bad track. Don't worry—it's all relative."

"Straight line, straight line!" Purdy yelled at number five and number six—but number five, running with his head down, veered far outside the track before circling back to the finish line in nine seconds flat. Kraft told him he could run it again. "I'm over sixty," Reilly said, "and I bet I could beat some of these kids. See, you can evaluate a point right there: poor body control. A guy that can't run in a straight line isn't a well-coordinated athlete. Nothin' to keep you from runnin' a straight line, is there? That's not relative."

The last two pitchers, number nine and number ten, were McToast and Lee Marvin. McToast was a small left-hander I'd noticed warming up when I arrived that morning—noticed him because his mother, under the impression I was a Phillies' scout, had complained to me about taking the early ferry over from south Jersey and finding that the McDonalds on the Dover side were all out of Egg McMuffins. The son, afraid of being late for his big chance, had breakfasted only on toast and coffee to go, and she wanted us to take that into account. I said that we would. About seventeen, 5'8", wearing baggy jeans and an oversized baseball undershirt, he was dwarfed by the 6'4" Lee Marvin, in a uniform so formfitting that it should have revealed (but didn't) some muscle definition. I'd given Lee his name earlier, when Joe Reilly called all the college kids to one side to check on their professional eligibility: this guy answered in a voice so deep that I guessed he must have three testicles. It may have been a good guess, because he barely raised his knees when he ran, and he lurched to an 8.3 finish—a half-second behind McToast, who slowed up at the finish line to wave to his mother.

The next sprinters were catchers, whose times didn't figure to be any better. But one of them stood out: number two was a mature-looking black, about 6'2" and 210, with a powerful upper body and thin legs, a runner's legs. He wore a spiffy green-white-gold uniform, and the colors danced into each other as he ran. On this track, on this day, the announcement of his exact time—6.8—only confirmed what that dance already told you: "This bruiser has major-league speed."

But he was the only catcher who did, and the others might as well have been in a sack race. As soon as they finished, Ed Gradel shepherded all the pitchers and catchers across the right-field line, double-checked their registration cards and tryout numbers, and started them throwing. Joe Reilly set up his folding chair at a good vantage point, and then told me what to watch for: "The live arm. Good spin on the breakin' pitch. Good delivery—or at least the rhythm to base a delivery on. Because a guy with a good delivery usually gets better and better. A guy with a good arm, without the good delivery, usually stays about the same."

Ed Gradel was doing the numerical evaluations. He stood behind pitcher number one, the moon-faced kid, and watched six fastballs—all straight, but with pretty good pop. Throwing with a high three-quarter release, this kid put everything, including his heavy hips, into each pitch. "Now the curve," Gradel said, and the delivery shifted to a low three-quarter. The front foot also tipped it off, coming out to the left, and the result was an old-fashioned roundhouse curve: it broke a long way but with little speed and no tight spin. Gradel watched five more and then made some notes on the back of the kid's registration card: *FB 64/ CV 62/ CON 66*. Using the 60-to-80 scale, he had just written off the moon-face as no prospect, but he was polite enough to ask about other pitches. "I got a forkball and a knuckler," the kid said eagerly—and proceeded to show what amounted to two kinds of change-up, one which spun and one which didn't; neither one of them broke.

"Okay, thanks very much. I'll check with you in a while if you want to wait. . . . Or you can leave now if you want." The round black face was as easy to read as a clock: disbelief, anger, a certainty that he'd thrown well, that he *did* have a special talent which this bland guy had disregarded casually in a three-minute look. But "I'll wait" was all the kid said, and he went to fetch his jacket.

As Gradel rated each pitcher, he rarely gave any marks above 65. The number two pitcher threw fastballs that the catcher couldn't hold, but as far as Gradel was concerned they were 64s. I wondered if the catcher—it was the same bruiser who'd run a 6.8—just had bad hands. When Gradel came to pitcher number four, Reilly was finishing a mini-lesson based on free association: ". . . a curve with more spin on it. And when you bring your arm up, just imagine you're gonna comb your hair forward. I used to wear mine parted in the middle—that's comin' back in style now. And then follow through more *down*, like you're gonna hit yourself right in the jewelbox with that forearm—but you'll probably wanta stop just before that."

Using a high leg-kick, this pitcher threw a series of tailing fastballs that Gradel rated as 67, and then he bounced two curves in the dirt. "That's okay," Gradel said. "Sometimes that's the best kind of curve. We don't care about your control right now. Just show us some bite." The kid seemed puzzled about what *bite* meant, and he was nervous, breathing unevenly. Reilly stood nearby, providing steady chatter: "Just like I showed ya now. Like you were combin' your hair for a date. She's gonna wait for ya, so take your time. Get the good spin. That's it—nice pitch. But bring the arm *down* now, and remember that jewelbox."

A few more curves bit the dust but all broke sharply at the last moment, and Gradel repeated his encouragement ("Sometimes that's the best kind") as he wrote: *CV 66.* "You catch this kid's name?" Reilly asked me.

"Graves."

"Well, Graves has a nice live arm, but his delivery's in trouble. I tried to tell him about it. That high kick throws him off balance and it makes his arm late. Here, watch me."

Reilly, surprisingly loose-limbed, was able to duplicate Graves's delivery pretty closely, even pausing in mid-motion with the left leg cocked up and back. He teetered precariously on his right leg, but only as a slow-motion imitation of a pitcher forty-five years younger than himself, whose teetering had been unconscious. "Okay, when I'm off balance like this, I have to rush my lower body to keep from fallin' on my ass. And my arm's not gonna come through with it, so I've lost my juice on the pitch—it's all arm. And that's a good way to tear up a shoulder too." From his jerky follow-through Reilly sprang back into a boxing stance, so suddenly and with such a convincing fighting style that I started to raise my arms in defense. "Now suppose I was gonna give you a right cross." He stepped his left foot forward, then pantomimed the punch—but only after his right foot had come up on point. "See, my arm's late and there's nothin' behind it. No steam." He danced back, looking like a feisty leprechaun—if leprechauns chewed tobacco—and then showed me how to throw the good right cross.

We were standing twenty feet away from pitcher number seven when he broke off a major-league curve: the bottom fell out so abruptly that the catcher didn't even get the glove on it. "Oooohh. Heh-hehhh. Let's look at *this* guy."

It was a tall, heavy-set black man, not a kid, who propelled his whole body over the front leg, Bob Gibson style. Instead of a uniform, he wore sweatpants and a baseball undershirt, topped by the old-fashioned Pittsburgh Pirates' cap, black with layers of gold piping. About half of the black players at the tryout wore the same kind of cap, but this one was festooned with a dozen little ornaments—stars, badges, buttons, pins, and a green ribbon for the children in Atlanta. His next four curves were just as good as the first, and the catcher—it was the 6.8 bruiser again—was able to hold only one of them. Reilly looked at the card in Gradel's hand and saw that the pitcher's name was Hertford Gibbs, and that his fastball had already been rated as 67. "Let's see a few more fastballs. Hit the mitt—I wanta see that guy catch a ball."

In his windup Gibbs didn't hide the ball with his glove, but it was lost in his huge right hand, and any batter would have had trouble spotting it before the release point. It came almost straight overhand, exploding past that long front leg and rising from belt to letters at the plate. The catcher flinched away but somehow held the ball. Reilly watched two more rising fast-balls that were strikes until the last eye blink. "Better than 67," he said to Gradel. And then to Gibbs: "Any other pitchers you wanta show us?"

"No, sir."

"That's okay. Just come over here a minute. Put your jacket on."

"Don't have one."

"Well, you should. We're gonna have you throw to some hitters in a while, and that arm needs to be kept warm." He read aloud from the card: "Hertford Gibbs. That's a good baseball name. You're playin' semi-pro ball in Milford? Where the hell's that? I don't know my way around here anymore. I started playin' pro ball right here in Dover, but that was before you were even born. I hope! Let's see, it says here you're a Gemini."

"What?"

"Never mind. Twenty years old. This says you didn't finish high school. Play any baseball before you quit?"

"Yeah, an' ran track. Relays."

"Well, you did a 7.2 here in the sixty, so I'm hopin' it's just the high grass that threw you off. You gotta be faster than that, right?"

"Right!" This was the first time Gibbs had shown emotion. His face was chiseled into tight features, wary, with the alertness of a creature in the wild. If Joe jumps suddenly into his boxing stance, I thought, Gibbs will deck him by reflex.

"Just relax," Reilly said, "and we'll have you throw some battin' practice in about a half hour. And keep that arm warm."

As Gibbs trotted off I looked down the line at the last two pitchers—McToast and Lee Marvin. McToast didn't have anything but control and a nice compact motion that, from one angle, reminded me of Whitey Ford's. But Ford's fastball and curve, unlike McToast's, were clearly two different pitches. Lee Marvin worked hard, with an elaborate windup, all dips and fakes, but each little tic seemed to be taking something off the ball. Gradel watched him throw fifteen pitches, three of them strikes, and then conferred briefly with Reilly.

"We'd like to thank you all for coming," he said to the assembled pitchers, "and we hope you feel you got a fair chance. But there's just a few of you that we want to see throw to some hitters today . . . number 4 [Graves] . . . and number seven [Gibbs] . . . and, let's see, number nine [McToast]. The rest of you can leave now if you want. Or you can stay and help us shag balls. But we'd like to thank you very much for coming."

Most of the pitchers were looking at the ground. Lee Marvin turned to the kid next to him and said in that ocean-floor voice, "I really didn't expect anything. What the hell." He was already moving toward the parking lot. Moon-face was back, standing sullenly next to a black man whose whole body was moon-shaped—clearly his father, and himself in twenty-five years. The two of them corralled Gradel and walked him off to the side, whispering stereophonically. McToast was running over to tell his mother the good news; he seemed to be moving faster than he had in the sixty-yard dash.

But why him? What had the scouts seen that I'd missed completely? Nothing, as it turned out. McToast had been invited to stay not as a prospect, but as cannon fodder, somebody who could throw good medium-speed strikes so that the scouts could get a better look at the hitters. He didn't seem to know that, though. When I walked past him and his mother a few minutes later, she smiled and waved. I smiled back, nodding as if to say that her boy certainly was a whiz, even on an empty stomach.

Joe Reilly finally told his tryout camp story for the benefit of Keith Carpenter. Keith had heard it before, and he seemed indifferent to its moral, but he thought it was a great story anyway.

We were sitting along the first-base line, watching the prospective infielders. Art Chapman had lined up all of them well behind third base—the better to check their arms as they fielded grounders and threw across the diamond—and he kept telling them to "let it rip." Nobody seemed able to, although one older-looking guy in a Harvard T-shirt may have thought that "it" meant his right shoulder. His three throws skipped across the infield like stones across a pond, and he walked to the sidelines holding the shoulder with his glove.

"Haven't seen any cannons today," Keith said. "You find any pitchers over there?"

"Guy named Gibbs," Reilly said, "pitchin' semi-pro in Milford. You know where that is? It'll be worth a trip for you to come down and see him at work in a game."

Keith shook his head. "As soon as the family sells the team, that's it for me. I won't be a scout after July. I'll be outa baseball completely. It's too crazy."

"Well, that's one difference between you and your brother. Ruly's gonna miss baseball, but I don't think you will."

"I won't," Keith said, staring into right field. He looked ascetic, with the body of a runner who does ten miles a day, and a face that seemed much younger than thirty-two. He owned a big chunk of the franchise, but his only official role was as the Phillies' scout for the state of Delaware—and he had always devoted less attention to baseball than to falconry, dog breeding, and running. "I might open a running store," he announced. "You know, sell shoes."

"See these shoes? Bought 'em down in Florida. Most comfortable pair . . . made outa goatskin or something."

"So can I give you my area?" Keith asked.

"No, I don't want your area. I got an area. Besides, who knows what the strike'll do, or what the new owners'll be like? I might retire, or I might go with another club."

"There's not that much in my area."

Reilly leaned away and spat. "That's a fallacy, Keith, that you've heard from other scouts. You could have a postage stamp for an area, but there might be a ballplayer attached to the postage stamp. I mean, I got a big area, right? Philadelphia up to New York City, plus North Jersey. Well, in ninety-nine percent of that area there's no players. But you got to *find* the players. That's what scoutin' is all about.

"Today with the draft, it's all bullshit. The Bureau goes out, they talk to high school coaches—'This kid can play'—they put his name in. Everybody follows. You go into Philly to see a kid like Gubicza at Penn Charter High, and there's so many scouts they're knockin' each other down. But who's goin' into Spanish Harlem? Who's goin' down to Atlantic City? Atlantic City's not *supposed* to have ballplayers, so when I went to look at Jerry Holtz I never saw any other scouts. But Jerry Holtz has the best infield arm I saw this year. Speed. Swings the bat. And yet we could wait till the fourth round of the draft to pick him, because he wasn't really seen.

"Or you might run a tryout camp and find a kid like Harold Baines. I saw him before anybody knew about him. He showed up right down here in Cambridge, Maryland, when he was only fourteen years old. I told Ruly, I said—"

"You better write this down," Keith said to me. "This story is famous."

"Baines was fourteen years old, and you're not allowed to try 'em out if they're under sixteen, right? And this fella had known me since I'd played down here—an old drunk with a twenty-year-old station wagon, a white guy, and he was always on the bottle. But he was one of those guys who could drink twenty-four hours a day, and he could drive better than these kids can today cold sober. And he was a guy who was on the fringes of baseball all his life. He might fall asleep half drunk, but if he woke up with *one eye* he could spot a ballplayer.

"And he brought this fourteen-year-old black kid to the tryout camp—and we had just had a hassle in the office about insurance and all—and I says to him, 'Moony, we cannot permit this kid to try out.' We used to call him Moony 'cause he drank the moonshine, see. Down here in Delaware, back in the old days—you wouldn't know about this—they made a lot of moonshine, and he was always on that bottle. Well, he went away, and he come back about a half hour later. I told him no again, and he went away again and took the kid with him. I think every time he left he took a couple of belts of corn liquor. So he came back again, just when the tryouts were over, and he insisted we hadda see this kid. I said, 'Oh Moony, you're a pain in the ass. Get him up there.'

"So we let the kid hit, and I never saw anything like it! He was about 5'8" and 135 pounds, and he musta hit fifteen outa twenty balls over the fence—and this is in the Cambridge ballpark, where it's 425 to center field. When I came back down to earth, I said, 'Let's run him.' Well, he ran pretty good, not great, but you figure four years from now he's gonna be eighteen years old, he's gonna be able to run a little bit—black kid, right? You also gotta figure he's gonna play a little bit. We found out he was playin' in the Legion in Easton. In a sixteen-to-nineteen-year-old league!

"Now it's three in the afternoon. Camp's over. Everybody wants to get some lunch. I told Joe Roman, 'I'm goin' out to see that kid play. I'll get a hot dog at the ballpark.' Because there's nothin' interests me like a good player; if there's shit there, I wouldn't even go to a game. So Joe says, 'I'll go with ya.' We drive to Easton, and here's the kid battin' third, and the first time up he hits one over the fence. I says, 'Somethin' wrong with this kid. We gotta have him checked for an injection!' Well, in that doubleheader he hit two home runs, two triples, and a double in about eight times at bat, and he hit the hell outa the ball even when he made outs.

"So I came back and made out a blue card—first time in my life I ever made out a blue card on a fourteen-year-old kid. That's a prospect card, and I says, 'This kid's a prospect *right now!*' I told Ruly, 'I found a black kid I don't believe. And I've been in baseball forty-five years.' I says, 'Buy a private school, put him in it, lock him in a closet. Then wait four years and bring him out when he's eligible.'

"But . . . four years later, when he was a senior, everybody knew about Harold Baines. He was hittin' home runs all over Maryland. And he was about 5'11", 170 pounds, tall and slender, and he's got the wheels for runnin', right? And the White Sox drafted him number one in the whole country. Last year he made the major leagues. But I'll never forget the way that little kid swung the bat. Poom! . . . Poom! He hit the ball right in here—no waste motion."

Sitting on the ground near Joe Reilly's feet, Keith Carpenter was like a young pupil. "With a swing like that," Keith asked, "do you think somebody had coached him, or was it just natural instinct?"

"Hey. Keith. Ballplayers are *born.* I keep sayin' this and sayin' it. All these scouts and coaches and executives: 'We'll do this, we'll teach you.' Shit. You teach guys to be scientists or you teach 'em something else, but you don't teach baseball. The bat was there, you know what I mean. Scouts'll tell you that you can't scout a bat. Well, you *can* scout a bat. It's either there or it's not there."

"Well, when you look at a bat, do you look at the action of the bat or how the ball jumps off it?"

"It's a combination. You wouldn't look at a tall, slender left-handed hitter—say like a Ted Williams—in the same way that you look at a Dick Groat or a Granny Hamner, a right-handed squatty hitter that goes to the opposite field. Ted Williams violated one of the principles in that he had an uppercut swing, but most of your long-ball hitters do. You'll hear scouts:

'Oh, he can't hit. He uppercuts.' Well, shit, some of the greatest hitters that ever lived uppercut. But it's how they do it. You get an uppercutter who's way back here with a long swing, that's no good because the pitchers are gonna overpower him. But watch for the uppercutter who's in a little closer so that he can just, you know, flip the wrists. You don't see that, forget him.

"If a ballplayer has the outstanding tools right away, you *see* it right away. A course, running and throwing—anybody can see that: you don't have to be a baseball scout. God gives you good legs. God gives you the good arm. Now look at that—"

Reilly pointed to a ball in midair, a throw from one of the would-be outfielders. It looked like a weak pop-up, sailing higher than the fungo the kid had just caught, and it landed about eighty feet short of home plate. "He's gonna bring the rain with a throw like that. Look at him—he's a big strong boy. But no coach in the world could show him how to uncork a throw. You only have so much strength in that arm, and God gives it to you, and it don't take muscle.

"Keith, your father ran an experiment many years ago. At a workout at Connie Mack Stadium he brought a guy named Chuck Bednarik in, the football linebacker. That guy had muscles from his ears to his ass. And he brought a basketball player in, Tom Gola. Chuck Bednarik couldn't throw the ball back to the mound! God give him football—knock a guy down, pick him up, and knock him down again. He didn't give him no arm. God said: 'Chuck Bednarik, you don't have an arm.' When Tom Gola threw the ball, he threw like this—like a fairy. Gay guys, they call 'em now. But Larry Bowa was there, about seventeen years old. He was maybe 5'9" and 130 pounds soakin' wet, but he's got a great arm, right? We're workin' him out and he says, 'Let me throw the ball, Mr. Carpenter.' He heaves the son of a bitch from home plate to the left field fence! Now I want you to think about that. Gola was nine feet tall; Bednarik was nine feet wide; and this kid wasn't tall or wide, and his arm was about that thin. But God said: 'Larry Bowa, you're gonna have an arm.'

"So I applied that from that point on. Your father showed me something there. Scouts say, 'Gee, that kid ain't big enough; this kid ain't tall enough; he's too tall to play shortstop; he's too short to be longstop.' Too many negatives. Guy can play, he can play. Jerry Holtz can play . . . 'cause God said so. I'm gettin' religion now, see, because I done everything wrong all my life, and now He's gettin' ready to take me back, and I hope He will."

"We'd like to thank you all for coming," Ed Gradel said, "but based on your running and throwing, we've decided to keep only the following players around to bat. . . ." He designated seven. Just as before, most of the others showed little reaction, as if it had been just a lark, something to do; I didn't expect anything anyway; I never really did believe that I was maybe touched by God.

One of the rejects, the infielder with the Harvard T-shirt and the sore shoulder, was grateful to be finished for the day. He turned out to be a twenty-seven-year-old sportswriter named Al Morganti. The Philadelphia *Inquirer* had sent him down to do a participant's-eye story on the tryouts, even though hockey was the only sport he had ever played seriously. "You were definitely not the worst player here today," Reilly said. Morganti asked about the real value of tryout camps. As I walked to the backstop Reilly was telling a short version of the Harold Baines story.

The first hitter was the big, speedy, bad-handed catcher. He lined McToast's first pitch foul, right off Jack Purdy's knee, but that was the last ball he hit for a long, long time. "He's got a slow pole," Keith Carpenter said, dead right. "And a weak arm too. NP—no prospect. All he has is that body and that speed." I remembered Joe Reilly's description of Chuck Bednarik, and I wondered if God had given this kid football— "knock a guy down, pick him up, and knock him down again."

The second hitter sent McToast home to a long-delayed, well-deserved meal with Mom. He said that his arm was tired—his last five pitches had been lobs, all converted into line drives—so Ed Gradel thanked him for coming and then made a note, or pretended to, of the American Legion team McToast played for.

Graves, experimenting with a more compact delivery, pitched to two hitters. The first one had brought his own metal bat, but Ed Wolf told him not to use it, and then gave me a what's-the-world-coming-to shake of the head. "Nowadays," Wolf said, "you find kids twenty years old who've never hit with anything but metal their whole life." This hitter was clearly uncomfortable with each of the wooden bats the Phillies provided. And Graves was clearly uncomfortable with his newly shortened delivery: his control was off, and after a while he reverted to the unbalanced high kick.

By the time Hertford Gibbs took the mound, his arm had tightened up. An hour before, I'd imagined him as a young Bob Gibson; now he looked like a dart thrower, aiming the ball from his right ear instead of reaching back and turning loose. Reilly bellowed from the first-base line: "Let's see ya air it out now, Hertford! Let it go! We don't want any pantywaisters." Gibbs did air one out, with a fastball that tailed and tailed until it bit, nailing the hitter on the back of the left arm. The kid didn't cry out, but he danced around home plate for a full minute, and Reilly excused himself politely and walked out to the mound.

"I told him," he said later, "that we were fully covered by insurance. And that I knew he was tight from sittin' around for an hour. And just to relax and throw natural, because we *are* gonna send somebody down to watch him pitch semi-pro. I don't know if Keith will do it—he's already informed me that his days are numbered as a scout, gonna sell water rights or whatever, open a boutique for runners?—but somebody will, because he has a better arm than some of the pitchers in our minor-league system right now. A course, he's not in shape;

he's got a lotta roadwork to do. I guess if Keith was on top of things, he'd sell Hertford some runnin' shoes."

The last pitcher was the moon-faced kid. It didn't cost anything to let him throw, and it placated both father and son, so in the name of public relations we watched him pitch to the last hitter of the day, and the best. It was a lean kid, about 5′10″, who roped the first pitch down the left field line. Just the sound of that hit jerked two scouts' heads around. With his next swing he almost maimed the third baseman, who showed why he was NP by jumping out of the way.

This hitter had got around on two good fastballs, and you didn't need to be a scout to see that he had the quick bat. He cocked it in a classic DiMaggio stance, feet wide apart, and showed almost everything that scouts for the last four months had been telling me to look for. Quiet bat, short stride, eye (and therefore shoulder) on the ball, hands held back until the last instant, good arm extension, top hand on top, quick wrists—everything but power. He just kept shooting line drives to all fields.

"Who is this kid?" I asked Keith Carpenter.

"Named Seeney. A shortstop from Dover High. He just graduated—that's his coach over there." Keith pointed to a big handsome strapper, about thirty, who watched with pleasure as Seeney cracked another hit.

"How'd he run? How'd he throw?" Reilly asked. Keith's answers were disappointing: "7.2"—followed by a so-so gesture with the right hand. "Mmmmm. Well, let's work him out at shortstop. I wanta see him."

But nobody was in a hurry to stop that beautiful hitting. Moonface was looking over to the sidelines after each pitch now, first to his father and then to the scouts, pleading with his eyes for someone to come and get him. Everyone, even the father, was watching Seeney instead.

The Dover High infield was studded with thousands of little pebbles, what we used to call "strawberry seeds," and they imparted some nasty final hops to ground balls. But this was Seeney's home field and maybe his big chance, and he stayed down on the ball pretty well. Art Chapman didn't hit any vicious grounders, but tried to test Seeney's range and arm by hitting balls up the middle and in the third-base hole. On the first two in the hole Seeney had to wind up to get the ball to first, and even then his arm lacked authority; the throws were accurate but without real zip. Another kid was helping out at second base, giving and taking relays for imaginary double plays, and nobody was surprised at the lack of communication around the bag—but the scouts were bothered by Seeney's difficulty in unloading the ball quickly.

A few minutes later Art Chapman yelled, "Last one!"—and hit a sharp grounder to the hole. Seeney couldn't get there in time. "Last one," Chapman said again, and this time smacked a ball directly toward shortstop. For once Seeney didn't stay down on the ball and it bad-hopped him, catching him squarely in the crotch. He doubled over in pain, then did a leg squat to get his breath. "No cup?" Chapman asked. "You should be wearin' a cup." He looked around at Seeney's coach, who seemed embarrassed. Chapman finally hit another last grounder, an easy roller. Seeney charged it nicely and came up firing, but what little starch had been in his earlier throws was gone now. He floated the ball to first then shuffled toward third and off the field.

Seeney sat on the bench, looking at the ground—still in physical pain, no doubt, but perhaps also reading the symbolism of that badhop grounder. The shot to the crotch could have been a telegram, announcing to him what the scouts had already said to themselves: "No prospect." "No prospect," Joe Reilly said flatly. "He hits like a middle infielder. But is he an infielder? No. He lacks the range, the hands, the arm. Now if the arm was stronger, and if he had more speed, you might think about him as an outfielder. But you can't: he's a one-tool player. You look at a kid like this at shortstop, and then you look at a Jerry Holtz, and then you look at a Julio Franco, and then you look at a Larry Bowa—and each one gets higher, and you've got some kinda frame of reference for your scouting."

Franco would be on TV an hour later, in a special telecast out of Philadelphia, entitled "The Only Game in Town." A minor-league game, featuring the Phillies' AA farm team at Reading, would be shown as an alternative to the major-league strike. Reilly invited me to watch the game at the Holiday Inn, where the scouts had rented a room to shower, change, and play pinochle. "We'll get some ice for Purdy's knee," he said, "and get some beer and sandwiches to watch the game with. I wanta see Franco play, and Leroy Smith if he's pitchin'. I signed that kid, and oh do I like to see him throw!"

"I think Carman pitched last night," Ed Wolf said, "and that's the game they'll show today. It's on tape." I remembered someone telling me at spring training, where Don Carman was one of the most interesting prospects I saw, that the Phillies had originally signed him out of a tryout camp in rural Oklahoma.

"Everybody's gettin' interested in minor-league ball now," Reilly said, "and that's good. But it's taken a strike to get that interest. It's like an Irish wake—everyone's brought together like a family, but only because somebody's died."

On his way to the parking lot Reilly was interrupted by a man asking him to autograph a ball for his son. "We already got that young man's signature," the man said, pointing back to Hertford Gibbs, "and my boy has confidence." The ball was a veteran, dark and scuffed, and Reilly had to hunt for a good spot. He signed with a flourish, the bottom of the final y tailing back under the rest of the name, like the banner on the front of a Dodger uniform. "A pleasure," he said when the man thanked him, but he had already turned away from father and son to look around the field one last time.

There was no Harold Baines in sight. Nobody would show up at the last minute with an aura of divine grace, rescuing the day with his gift. It had been just a typical small camp: one legitimate "follow," a few interesting rejects, and five dozen others who lived in a dream world. But the scouts knew that world, had mapped it themselves, and needed it to sustain their own sense of vocation. I couldn't see how the camp, well run though it was, had any serious public relations value for the Phillies; it was PR for baseball itself, for the insistent dreaming that the game always allows.

The scouts have a dream of their own, left over from the Branch Rickey era. If not at this camp, then maybe at the next, some undiscovered boy arrives with all five tools and no bad habits—a natural athlete, eighteen years old, just out of high school (where they didn't have a baseball team, so no scouts saw him), eligible and eager to sign a low-bonus contract. The dream plays like background music at each new camp, where the scouting process is again telescoped into a few hours, without benefit of advance reports or repeated observations or actual game conditions, and where the scouts act out their dream roles as baseball detectives.

12 YOUNG SCOUTS

Baseball was here a hundred years before me, and it'll be here a hundred years after me.

—*Stubby Overmire*

"Spring is for quality," the saying goes, "but summer is for quantity." Once the June draft is over and there are no more obvious prospects to zero in on, an area scout's main duty is to provide coverage, to survey the large crop of players who might become legitimate prospects by the following spring. Hence the value of the big late-season tournaments, the August games in Wichita or Johnstown that allow hundreds of sixteen- to nineteen-year-olds to showcase their talents while dozens of thirty- to eighty-year-olds make copious notes.

More than that, the tournaments enable the scouts to fraternize easily, unconstrained by secrecy. With the draft behind them and the next set of major decisions so far away, they can relax with one another, taking off masks to share honest impressions and true stories. They are divided less by team rivalry, in fact, than by age.

At the tournaments the young scouts—college-trained, inured to bureaucracy, unthreatened by technology, fluent in the language of number—maintain a respectful distance from the more colorful and intuitive traveling salesmen, the kind of men who first trained them. They regard most of the million-mile scouts as vanishing Americans, not as career models. Their own ambitions extend far beyond a life of area scouting, of simply getting better at patrolling the same territory season after season; they talk about the rewards of jobs in the front office or in the "real" world outside baseball. But the young scouts, more than they realize, have been shaped by their teachers.

Billed as "Johnstown's greatest tourist attraction," the thirty-seventh annual tournament of the All-American Amateur Baseball Association opened quietly on Monday with noon games on the outlying fields of the city. At Roxbury Park new snow fences defined outfield boundaries for the diamonds at each end of the commons. Buffalo was playing Baltimore on the east field; Columbus was playing Detroit on the west. I decided to start by watching Baltimore because the team, better known as Johnny's Auto Sales, is a perennial amateur power. Managed by Milwaukee Brewer scout Walter Youse, Baltimore had the look and almost the talent of a minor-league team. It had won ten championships and five runner-up trophies at Johnstown, and was the clear favorite in 1981. The Baltimore lineup included seven players who had been drafted out of high school; each had chosen to go to college instead and to play for Johnny's during the summer as a sure way of maintaining the scouts' interest. John Thornton, the big catcher–first baseman, had turned down $25,000 from the Brewers in order to attend a community college. Ed Katalinas, senior scouting consultant for the Tigers, thought that Thornton should have opted for the money. "He won't get that kind of offer next time," Katalinas said.

Katalinas sat alone on the high slope above third base. The younger scouts clustered around the backstop and shared observations on each hitter's stance and swing. Carmen Fusco of the Mets, wearing a cowboy hat and boots, remarked that Thornton's swing came too much from the heels; it generated home-run power but also left Thornton off-balance, looking as if he wanted to run to third instead of first. Fusco seemed more interested in Renard Brown, an outfielder who showed both power and speed, and who moved, like most of the Baltimore players, with a confident grace. Brown hit a home run and a triple in his first two at-bats, but to Fusco the results were less impressive than the reasons: aggressive demeanor, compact stroke, quick bat. "He's gonna be a junior at Liberty Baptist. Eligible for next year's draft."

The Buffalo hitters didn't give Fusco much to see. Their first hit finally came in the fourth inning when Mark Gabriel lined a fastball into right-centerfield and then hustled it into a double. Gabriel arrived at second base with a perfect pop-up slide, defying gravity in an eye blink. "I wish that I *used* to be able to do that," Fusco said.

Like most of the new scouts, Fusco had never played an inning of professional baseball. "I went to Middle Tennessee, played ball there, and knew a guy—that's how I got to be a scout. Pro experience isn't necessary anymore. What's more important is being analytical, organized, mobile, able to do a lot of reporting. The scouting directors look for younger guys now because we can put up with all the travel, and maybe they figure we don't need money as bad. But that's why I want to work my way to the front office—less travel, more money."

After Thornton homered in the fourth to put Baltimore ahead 9–0, I walked across the park. "Scout the player, not the game," I had been told all season—but I still needed a reasonably close contest in order to feel perceptive, and I was glad to find Detroit and Columbus tied 1–1 in the fifth. Just as the inning began, two young girls hopped the snow fence and trotted across centerfield. Umpire Juergen Mathes halted play and ran out to order them off the field, and then discovered that they were his own daughters.

Detroit broke the game open in the fifth by parlaying singles and errors into five runs, and so for the next hour I had to be satisfied just to watch a pitching masterpiece by Greg Brake, the Detroit left-hander. Between the second and eighth innings Brake retired sixteen consecutive batters, most of them with a snaky curveball that seemed to float up to the plate and then to accelerate as it darted to the knees. Gary Nickels of the Phillies graded the curve as a 71—above major-league average.

"He throws it about sixty-five percent of the time," Nickels said. "It's a great curve, but he's a one-pitch pitcher. His fastball is way short for me, maybe a 67, and he's not gonna get any faster, so it's hard to see him beyond college or the low minors. The pitcher to scout on this team is Bill Shuta." In the bottom of the eighth Nickels finally decided that 68 was the right grade for Brake's control.

Nickels had chosen this game partly because he was intrigued by the size of the players on the Detroit and Columbus squads. "They have Big Ten–type bodies, very physical, so I figure there's somebody here who can play." The Detroit manager, Bud Middaugh, was head baseball coach at the University of Michigan, and he had stocked the roster with nine of his own players. One of them, Chris Sabo, had been injured early in the game in a collision at home plate. Bob Livchak, Sabo's replacement, later drilled a long home run to dead centerfield, and Nickels simply used a + to grade Livchak's power.

"The reports I make on this tournament," he said, "will mostly be names of kids worth a follow next spring. Then I'll write up a few players, but just with number grades. I think the grades are more important than the verbal part, because when I write out comments I find that I repeat myself. Like 'This boy's an above-average runner.' Well, I've already told you that if I put a 71. The written stuff is really salesmanship to the front office; I call it puttin' the mustard on the hot dog. If you want a right-hand pitcher who's under six feet tall, you better write things like 'His overhand curve is explosive!' or 'He throws the shit out of the ball!' "

Nickels was short and roundish with a quick, enthusiastic manner. He could watch a game without reacting visibly, but his conversation was frank and open, affecting no cool scouting pose. He was thirty-four and had already been in the baseball business for nine years. After pitching college ball at Illinois Wesleyan (the summit of his playing career), he landed a job in the Phillies' office as an assistant to Dallas Green, who was then the director of the scouting and farm systems. Four years later Nickels became a scout, mainly to acquire "seasoning." His real goal was to make it back to the office, this time in an executive role.

"What I thought scouting would be when I was in the office wasn't what scouting really is. In the first place you have to push yourself. It's not a job where you punch in, or where someone's always lookin' over your shoulder. You're on your own for a week, two weeks at a time, and it's up to you where you should go. It wouldn't be that hard, if you wanted to, to fool your boss with your reports and expense account, and if you weren't a self-motivated person you could slide by for a while.

"But the biggest surprise was that I had to make clear-cut decisions under tough circumstances. I'd go watch a high-school hitter, and maybe the game was on a horseshit field and he had to bat against a terrible pitcher and he got walked twice in three times up. Other sports are easier to scout because of the surroundings of the player; the pro-football guys can take uniform conditions for granted, even study movies. In baseball it's so easy to be wrong.

"You can *love* a kid and he can get drafted in the first round, and then he never gets out of Double A. And all you have to do is pick up *The Sporting News* to see how some of the players you said no on are doin' great. I missed the boat on Renie Martin, Cal Ripken, Bruce Benedict. With Benedict it was early in my career, and I put too much weight on his weakness as a runner and a hitter; I liked the way he threw and caught, but I wasn't smart enough to know that a catcher can get to the big leagues just on that. And sometimes I go back and look at my lineup cards from six or seven years ago, and I see a player on there who's in the big leagues, and I have no idea that I ever saw him! I have one card with Dan Quisenberry's name that says he threw from a *high* three-quarters angle, but I don't remember seein' him. He was just another guy, nothing special.

"So it's a humbling job. But out front, boy, you've gotta be opinionated. Your boss calls you about a player and you've gotta say yes or no; you can't sit on the fence. And that's the common thread I see in baseball scouts—they're opinionated people by nature."

*   *   *

To understand Johnstown's history of floods, you only need to look at the topography. The city is a valley surrounded by steep Allegheny ridges, and the one outlet—the gap that originally made Johnstown a prosperous gateway to the west—is at the confluence of the Conemaugh and Stony Creek rivers. The upland climate is wet (a hundred inches of rain and snow a year), and the runoffs have nowhere to go but Johnstown.

The northeast bank of the confluence, the Point, is the site of the stadium that serves every August as home field for the AAABA Tournament. Two blocks north at the courthouse a series of plaques marks the height of each major flood: twenty-one feet in 1889, when the South Fork Dam gave way and dropped twenty million tons of water down on the city; seventeen feet in 1936, when the swollen rivers tried to climb the ridges; seven feet in 1977, when the summer rain wouldn't stop and the baseball tournament had to move to Altoona.

Johnstown's prosperity has declined in a pattern matching the height of the floods. The city has rebuilt bravely after each disaster, but each time with less resilience and less economic diversity. Johnstown has become ever more dependent on the production of coal and steel—in a valley too narrow to permit cheap freight or to provide sites for industrial expansion. Air pollution, dilapidated housing, and a declining population (especially of young males) have discouraged new businesses, and the unemployment rate in Johnstown since World War II has sometimes doubled the national average. At the time of the 1981 tournament Bethlehem Steel and Bethlehem Mines had just begun a new round of layoffs.

The tournament would pump over $500,000 into the local economy in a single week, but its greatest value was psychological. It confirmed the belief that Johnstown was still the center of something, able to attract strong young men from far away. It provided a history of its own as a basis of faith, especially in the list of promising amateurs who had once played here: Al Kaline, Frank and Joe Torre, Sparky Lyle, Reggie Jackson, Rod Carew, Steve Garvey, Ken Singleton, Len Barker.

And it elicited the response of the whole community—a rich mix of Dutch, Irish, Italian, Armenian, Lithuanian, Polish, and Greek cultures—in the pageantry of a late-summer festival. On Monday evening a happy crowd paraded toward The Point, led by bands and beauty queens and the San Diego Chicken, to witness the tournament's official opening and a game between its two worst teams, Johnstown and Altoona.

Estimates of the crowd inside the ballpark ran as high as 14,000, double the attendance at Three Rivers Stadium on that very same evening. The fans at Pittsburgh, sixty miles to the west, were still angry over the players' strike; the fans at Johnstown were buoyant and optimistic, even though their entries had not won a tournament game since the last flood. They cheered Queen Gemma DelSignore and her court, cheered the Chicken's mimes of infield practice, and even cheered the president of the local chamber of commerce when he announced that Herb Hawkins, a helicopter pilot who had helped to dry off the field at last year's tournament, would be presented with a photograph of himself in action.

The dimensions of the field were surreal—foreshortened and elongated like the strange baseball space of the Los Angeles Coliseum in 1959. The leftfield line ended at a wall 270 feet from home plate, and a 50-foot screen jutted upward to turn rising line drives into singles and long pop flies into home runs. A snow fence marked the left-centerfield limit at 300 feet, and then angled sharply away from home plate so that center and right seemed to stretch out to the rivers. The Point had been built originally for football, and this felt like a football night: bands and banners and hometown pride in the cool climate of the mountains.

The bands were still playing when Randy Romagna took the mound for Johnstown. He was an eighteen-year-old right-hander, 5'10" and 180 pounds, who had twice been drafted by the Cincinnati Reds. So far he had chosen to stay in school and had completed one year at Indian River Community College in Florida. Romagna threw with a fluid motion, good rhythm, and clear command of an overhand curve and fastball.

But he hung a slider to the first Altoona batter, who lined a single to left, and he hit the second batter with a slider that got away. Then he began using the slider to set up his other pitches, and he struck out the next two batters with fastballs that tailed in on the fists. Two more fastballs became two quick strikes on the fifth batter, and behind the scouts' section the beauty queens led the crowd in rhythmic clapping (1 2, 1 2 3) as Romagna's curve came over the top and toward the hitter's belt buckle, then veered across and almost into the dirt for a swinging strike three.

Romagna said later that the energy of the crowd "juiced" him. The relation was reciprocal: as he disposed of hitters in each subsequent inning, he juiced the crowd to new levels of noise. And that sound had a clear effect on the Altoona players, who committed eight errors and ten wild pitches before the night was over. In the second inning Johnstown's Larry Green hit a grounder that skidded through the shortstop's legs and scooted under the glove of the charging leftfielder. Thousands of voices bounced off the brick walls, then echoed back from the ridges across the water to become a single continuous voice as Green made third base standing up.

"These kids must have left their gloves at the horseshoe curve outside Altoona," one scout said. A few innings later, with Johnstown leading 8–0, he stood up to leave. He didn't see any players he liked on either team. "I guess I've put in my appearance for tonight," he said.

The other scouts stayed, some to study Romagna in detail, others just to enjoy the spirit of the night. Every ticket stub in the ballpark had been put into a big bin, and the game was interrupted after the fifth inning when the bin and a new car were brought behind home plate. Gemma DelSignore brushed past the catcher to draw the winning ticket. "I knew I was right to stay," Ed Katalinas said. "I think I'm gonna win." If a supposedly tough-minded analyst was susceptible to that kind of optimism, who was I to resist? I was going to need *some* transportation out of Johnstown, and for a moment I became convinced that my need had a magic of its own. It did—just enough to match up on two of the five digits. A moment later I relaxed back into the happy noise and the excellence of Romagna's pitching.

Romagna struck out the side again in the sixth. He was spotting all three pitches low now, and Gary Nickels observed that the first-inning single had been the last Altoona ball to leave the infield. "Romagna doesn't throw hard enough to suit me, but I can't take this game away from him—or *this*," he said with a gesture to the stands.

"Have you ever thought how much Americana the old scouts have seen? The small-town ballparks? The Parade Grounds in Brooklyn? On a Saturday in May you could take a picnic lunch out to the Parade Grounds and watch a whole afternoon of amateur baseball, maybe see a kid like Lee Mazzilli in three games, and the fans and the scouts and the players and the day just kind of blend in together. To me that's really grass-roots America. Just like this tournament is—kids from all over America, all the races, and some are gonna fail and others are gonna be great. I wish we had some Russians here tonight, so they could see how deep the game goes in our society."

The Russians might not have understood Romagna's final statistics—eighteen strikeouts, three walks, a two-hit shutout—but they would probably have stood and applauded, the way everyone but scouts and Altoonians did, when he struck out the side in the ninth. The last batter swung too late at a good low fastball, and then the Johnstown players ran toward the mound as fans poured onto the field. The Chicken was accidentally trampled as he tried to take a mock bow, but bounced up right away to lead more cheers.

As the rest of the scouts filed out, Nickels stood watching the celebration. "This is special," he said. "It's why I've always liked this tournament. . . . But what do they do here the rest of the year?"

At the Monte Carlo tavern Bob Engle walked over to the scouts sitting at the big roundtable. "I just heard," he announced, "that the Scouting Bureau's gonna send out a report on the San Diego Chicken. They say he's a legitimate prospect."

"Could be true. Those guys have turned in worse than him. Maybe they think he's got the good comb."

"Sit down and get some of this pizza, and tell me how good you think Romagna is. Don't forget to subtract the crowd."

"How good do *you* think he is?"

"I think he's too small for a right-hand pitcher. If he was a lefty, I'd like him about fifty thousand dollars."

"The Reds'll never give him that—will they, Gene? They'll just keep draftin' him."

"I'll tell you who I'd like to draft," Gene Bennett said. "Sabo, the boy that got injured today. He's got 6.6 speed, good power, good hands for infield, a good arm."

"Enough power for a third baseman?"

"I say so."

"I say he ends up a second baseman. Anyway, second basemen gotta come from somewhere; they hardly ever start out there. I've never signed one."

"Me either. They're shortstops without the arm or third basemen without the power . . . who go to the minors and learn how to make the double play."

"How bad's Sabo hurt?"

"Broke his collarbone. I didn't see it, but that guy Morry told me."

Morry Moorawnick was the Detroit scorekeeper, and the very mention of his name was enough to make Ben McLure laugh. "You ever see Morry's scorebook? He designed it himself so's he can put everything in it. Everything. One time at this tournament I looked over his shoulder to get the lineup before the game, and there was a whole line there for weather conditions. And Morry had put: 'High, steely gray cumulonimbus clouds with soft gusts from the north-northwest at five to ten miles per hour."

"I oughta put stuff like that in my reports. Drive the scoutin' director up the wall."

"I met a high-school coach one time—he didn't know how

to read a scorebook. He had his assistant keep score by writin'
the game in sentences."

"I met one worse than that," Frank DeMoss said. "In So-
phia, West Virginia—near Beckley. This coach had Joe Goddard on his team. Joe wound up with the Padres, played one
season as a backup catcher, and in high school he was the best
hitter in the state. But the coach batted him eighth in the lineup!
I said, 'Why do you have Joe Goddard battin' eighth, good of
a hitter as he is?' He said, 'Because he's a catcher, and catchers
always bat eighth.' "

"The Cubs had a real nice draft," somebody told DeMoss.
"Carter and Lovelace look great."

"Thanks."

Gary Nickels was hoisting a beer in tribute to his mentor,
Tony Lucadello. "When Tony retires, if he ever does, I hope
the Phillies bring him in and hold a press conference, and hand
out a list of the players he's signed that went to the big leagues.
Schmidt, Hisle, Harrah, Alex Johnson, Fergie Jenkins, two
dozen others. If you tried to put a value on his players, it'd be
unbelievable. When the Phillies were down and out in the
sixties, Lucadello and Eddie Bockman kept the organization
alive."

"Well, Lucadello was born to be an area scout."

"That's true," Nickels said, "and I wasn't. I want to get off
the road and move up. But Lucadello just covers and covers
Ohio and Indiana and Michigan, and he never gets tired of it.
He has that whole web of information from all his friends and
part-time people, and if the weather's bad he'll work out a kid
in a barn or a gym. He has a sixth sense for ballplayers, a feel,
that you can't teach. But he showed me how to use grades, to
decide in my own mind what a 68 arm is and then to stay
consistent within that system. And what I really got from him
was—he taught me how to see."

I asked Nickels then about Lucadello's famous theory: that
every athletic body has eight sides (front-back times left-right
times upper-lower), and that a scout at a game should therefore
keep shifting his viewing angle until he's constructed a three-

dimensional memory of each player. According to Lucadello, scouting a game well requires scurrying all around the field. First, he says, he positions himself about ten feet behind home plate on the first-base side in order to see all the face reactions, the hand reactions, the footwork—all the front sides—of the pitcher, catcher, and right-handed batter. Then he moves almost parallel to first base to see the pitcher's back sides, all the infielders' throws, and the catcher's peg to second. Then he moves down the right field line to see the outfielders' movements. Then he switches over to the third-base side of the diamond to check the other fielders' back sides and the left-handed hitters' front sides. "So when I leave a ballgame I have a good picture of everybody on that field, because I saw all their sides."

Was this what Nickels meant by being taught how to see?

"No, I think Tony gets carried away sometimes, kind of spins a yarn. I want to see a hitter's front side, hands and all, but I can get almost everything I need from behind home plate. What Tony showed me was more like checking a player's extension on his swing or his throws. So when I scout a pitcher now, the first thing I look for is whether he has full arm action and whether he lands on a stiff front leg. Tony used to say: 'The pitchers who get faster are the ones who get to the big leagues.' And to get faster you have to be mechanically correct. Like Tom Seaver. When he was in high school and community college, nobody was interested in him. He went to Southern Cal and in one year the scouts were fallin' all over him. He'd gotten faster because he was so mechanically correct."

"Still is," said DeMoss, "but I don't believe any pitcher gets much faster after his nineteenth birthday."

"Who's the fastest you ever saw?" I asked.

"Dalkowski!" was the answer from three sides of the table.

"I doubt if Steve Dalkowski was ever mechanically correct," DeMoss said. "Sometimes he didn't even bring his back leg forward. But that guy, even with no follow-through, could *terrify* hitters. Terrified his catchers, too—they pictured gettin' a hand broke inside the mitt and some doctor walkin' toward them with a pair of shears."

"Sam McDowell," Pidge McCarthy said. "I mean when McDowell was at Pittsburgh Central Catholic. Because by the time he got to the majors, he'd slowed down. In high school the ball just kind of disappeared from Sam's hand and showed up in the catcher's glove."

"Fastest I ever saw was a boy named Kikla," McLure said. "I bet a radar gun would've had him at over a hundred."

McCarthy, sitting next to me, suddenly leaned over and spoke in a voice as low and confidential as a racetrack tout's. "The best *curve*ball I ever saw," he murmured, "was one I saw this season. Kid named Lloyd, from a high school near here—he got suspended and didn't play senior year, so he didn't get scouted."

"Why did he get suspended?"

"Keep your voice down. They kicked him off the baseball team after he took a shit on the rug of the school library. He won thirty dollars, had a bet goin'. He still got accepted to college. Anyway, he throws a *perfect* curveball!"

Startled by the sound of his own voice, McCarthy looked around and sat up straight again, pretending he'd been listening all along to Elmer Gray's story—the one about trying to sign Joe Namath to a baseball contract in 1960. "Joe's knees were okay in high school," Gray said. "He ran the sixty in 7.0. Had a fair bat—I thought it might improve—and an average major-league arm. But when Cy Morgan and I took the contract to his house, we found out he was out of town . . . on a football recruiting visit to Alabama. We never saw him again except on TV. And then it was another guy. It was 'Broadway Joe.' "

"Have you met Broadway *Charlie?*" Nickels asked me. "The Red Sox scout? That's him over there. You should get Charlie to talk, because he's like an elder statesman."

Broadway Charlie Wagner didn't look like an elder anything. Trim, tanned, impeccably groomed, he was wearing a blue and white seersucker sportcoat with a dark wine handkerchief in the breast pocket, a light blue button-down oxford-cloth shirt with a wine and navy rep tie, gray light-flannel slacks, and carefully buffed black Italian loafers—all this in a business where being "well-dressed" usually means wearing a golf sweater and polyester pants instead of a baseball jacket and droopy gabardines.

"The only scout I ever knew who dressed that good was old Sloppy Thurston. Hollis was his real name. He could impress the shit out of a kid's parents."

"That's not such a big deal anymore," Elmer Gray said.

Pidge McCarthy leaned over and muttered: "If you do get Broadway Charlie to talk, be sure to get his buddy Socko, too. You don't know the one guy unless you know the other. They're night and day. Socko and Charlie are like the Odd Couple."

Judy the waitress brought another pitcher of beer. "You fellas see any players you liked this evening?"

"You're the best-lookin' thing we've seen all night."

Two scouts said this at once, so I figured it must be an old line, maybe even another saying learned from their mentors.

Getting Broadway Charlie to talk was easy. The next morning I had coffee with him in his room at the Towne Manor Hotel, where the light had to angle down a steep mountain to get into his window. On Route 56, only sixty yards away, truckers shifted gears and revved their engines as they tried to climb the grade. Charlie Wagner himself did more than that *e* in *Towne* ever could to add a touch of elegance to the surroundings.

It had been over thirty years since *Esquire* cited him as one of America's best-dressed men, but he seemed to have stepped out of an ad in the magazine's latest issue. His manner was as decorous and as comfortable as his clothing. My question about his nickname led him to a relaxed meditation on baseball uniforms, the meaning of the word *class*, and the differences between old scouts and young scouts.

"Back when I was pitching for the Red Sox, a sportswriter named Johnny Droyan started calling me Broadway. It wasn't that I was a swinger or a nightclub guy. I'm a quiet man; I enjoy my peace and quiet. It was that I've always enjoyed dressing, ever since I was a kid. Other kids used to tease me about it. When I roomed with Ted Williams, *he* used to tease me. He went for the outdoor look—fishing jackets, open-necked sportshirts, baggy pants. He said, 'Why don't you dress casual like me? The only thing a tie's good for is to spill soup on.'

"I've always thought that the classiest look is simple and understated. That's why the Red Sox uniforms are so sharp— they're bold and yet they're traditional, so the players look tall and athletic but not flashy. Charlie Finley started the other trend, toward splashy colors. But the game itself supplies all the color you need.

"Right now I'm breaking in a new scout, Phil Rossi, for when I retire. And I'm trying to impress him with what to look for and how to look for it—tools, makeup, and all of that. But I'm also trying to impress him with the idea that the game is bigger than any of us, that we're major-league representatives, so the first thing a scout has to have is class. And it doesn't take money to be classy. It takes class to be classy. Class comes from the guy within himself.

"I got my education in those years before the draft, when scouting was wide open. Anything you can imagine happening *did* happen. It was a great way to learn, because being a salesman sharpened your skills as a judge of talent. You were playing poker with the company's money, so you paid attention to everything and you got to know the ballplayer and his family. Maybe you'd back off when you saw that all of his relatives were small; you'd abandon your hope that this seventeen-year-old was gonna grow any bigger. Or maybe you'd spot some flaw in character, and you'd know that a boy didn't have enough to carry on in professional ball, to make it for himself. Or maybe you'd see that he had the weak face instead of the good face.

"When a young scout breaks in today, it feels more cold and mechanical to him and pretty soon he's ambitious to move up to the office. Well, I've worked in the office, and I could tell him that it's tight there—he'll take the team's losses more heavily and be channeled into a narrower path and have less chance to develop his taste. But taste is the great thing about growing old as a scout: you become more selective, more sophisticated, so you improve with age.

"The young scouts are better organized than we were, because so much of scouting now is writing reports. But take Socko McCarey—he's here at the tournament to help me out, and he's from that era when reporting was incidental and scouts were just baseball men. He's in his seventies now and he can't stand it when I tell him that I'm his boss, that he has to do what I tell him. He gives me hell about my clothing. And then I tell him how I served in World War Two, how I suffered to make it safe for him. And he loves this *agitation*.

"But when Socko tells me about a player that he likes, I know exactly what he's talking about. And vice-versa. We understand each other with only a few words said. If Socko says, 'Ahhh, I don't like him,' that's good enough for me, because he knows a ballplayer when he sees one. The thing about Socko is . . . he has good taste."

"Yer ass," Socko growled at the Pirates' scout in the next row.

"It's true, Socko. You wait and see if they don't raise state taxes now to take up the slack. All Reagan's doin' is givin' welfare to the rich."

"YER ASS! It's all the unions' fault. The unions!"

The Pirates' scout winked at me, letting me know that this was only another round in the game known as Yank the Crank. It's an easy game to win, because getting Socko stirred up is about as difficult as prodding a pit bulldog. He's living evidence for the thesis that scouts are opinionated people by nature, and he thrives on loud contention. The problem is that once you've won the game you can forget about relaxing for a while.

"This pitcher you picked up," Socko said to the Pirates' scout, "this guy named Queen—he's doin' shit for Portland. Yeah. You were tellin' me how good he was before, just 'cause Howie Haak said—"

"You should've seen him in the workout, Socko."

"Workout? The hell with the workout! You've gotta walk across the white line. You've gotta show it in real games."

"He's crossed that line. He pitched good in the Mexican League."

"Mexican League? Who cares about the Mexican League?"

"Bevacqua batted against him and couldn't hit him."

"Bevacqua! What do you know about baseball anyway?"

Socko finally subsided back into the ballgame, part of the slow Tuesday action in the losers' bracket at The Point. He put his feet up (black brogans and white socks) on the back of the empty seat in front. Scrunching down in his own seat in his slouch hat and rumpled clothes, he looked even shorter than 5'8", heavier than 180. I tried to see some similarity between Socko and Broadway Charlie, and then realized that both of them looked fifteen years younger than they really were.

"Socko," I ventured, "how did you get the name *Socko*?"

"I used to be the clubhouse guy at Forbes Field, right after World War One, and I used to fool around with the players, try to hit 'em and all that, so Charlie Grimm started callin' me Socko and I guess it fit. I like to fight."

"What do you like to fight about?"

"Any old thing. I'm always in the heat of the arguments. I get after politicians—they're a buncha assholes. I get after the blacks—some of those guys who never even played in the big leagues got in the Hall of Fame, and Charlie Grimm still hasn't got in. I get after the labor unions."

"It ain't the blacks' fault they couldn't play in the majors," the Pirates' scout said.

"Ahhh, yer ass. I'm talkin' about labor unions. Like these major-league players, led out on strike like a buncha sheep. They don't look back. They never even send a Christmas card to the scout who got 'em started. And I'll tell you this: none of these guys who struck should ever be given a job in baseball later on. Shouldn't let any of 'em become scouts."

"Ex-major-leaguers don't seem to *want* scouting jobs anymore," I said. Socko stared at me, as if deciding whether I was playing Yank the Crank. "But," I said quickly, "I guess club-houses must've changed a lot over the years."

"They got loud music in there now. And they're like prima donnas with their hair driers and the stuff they *need* now, wrist bands and all that. They're not like the ballplayers before. Before, the players were more friendly. Today they just act smart, talkin' about women all the time and sayin' the m-f word—when they oughta talk more about baseball, because a lot of 'em don't know how to run the bases or where to throw the ball. See, I learned about baseball first-hand. I spent years workin' out with the Pirates, the Waner brothers and Pie Traynor and all those guys, so when I started in to scout I knew what to look for."

"Who broke you in? Who showed you the ropes?"

"Nobody. I just did it. In 1940, the Reds told me to cover West Virginia, western Pennsylvania, and western New York. You hadda be a scout just to drive around in those mountains. And try findin' some of those fields! There turned out to be some good prospects in that area, but most of my guys never got to the big leagues. They fell by the wayside. They got hurt, or they got married and quit baseball, or they just fizzled out. The year I signed Glenn Beckert I saw plenty of better pros-pects, and I didn't think that much of him, but he spent eleven years in the majors and made the all-star team four times. He got the opportunity, the other guys didn't, and they finally packed it in. These college kids today pack it in early. Early. Two years, some of them. College is bad for ballplayers."

"Socko's right for once," the Pirates' scout said. "That's why Pittsburgh signs a lot of high-school kids, especially blacks, and Latin kids—you can start 'em in the minors sooner. And besides that you're gettin' players that can run."

"Ahhh, you want speed, go to a track team and get it. I don't give a damn about running. If they have it with 'em, all right. But you get a guy, speed merchant, and he can't throw or can't hit—what good is he? The two most important things to me are the arm and the bat. If a ballplayer can throw and hit, you'll find a spot for him—even if he's just a slow white guy."

"Is that what you're trying to teach that new Red Sox scout?" I asked.

"Rossi? He's Charlie Wagner's apprentice. Charlie's teachin' him to change his clothes three times a day. But you're gonna see lots of young scouts added on now. Major-league clubs'll have to scout the minors up and down, because of this new compensation thing, this new pact with the players."

"Well, maybe that's one good side effect of the strike."

Socko stood up to leave, but favored me with a "yer ass" before departing. "There *aren't* any good side effects of the strike," he said as he trundled up the stadium steps.

"Don't mind him," the Pirates' scout said. "You know Pete Peterson, the general manager at Pittsburgh? Socko fights with him all the time. They play gin rummy and Socko gets pissed off and throws the cards in Peterson's face, and then they wrestle around till Socko breaks Peterson's wristwatch. So last year Peterson told Socko he could have the same break the Pirate people get from a dealer in town—a big discount on a new Oldsmobile. Then Peterson typed a notice and signed the dealer's name to it, and he was able to hide it in the trunk of the car Socko bought. The paper was dirty and balled up, so it looked like it'd been in there a long time, and it was addressed to one of the mechanics. It said: 'Before we sell this demonstrator, be sure to set the odometer near zero. And for God's sake, clean out those vomit stains in the backseat and spray some new-car smell.' Socko found that note and did everything but turn inside out. He came unglued! . . . Now that's what I call yankin' the crank."

The Tuesday night game at The Point featured Johnstown versus Reality. Another crowd in excess of 10,000 filled the stadium and waved the famous Green Weenies that announcer Bob Prince had distributed as lucky charms, but things went wrong at the very start. The Detroit lead-off hitter topped a grounder to second that squibbed out of Mike Whitcomb's glove; then he advanced to second on a wild pitch and scored on a single. Another grounder looked like a sure double play ball until Whitcomb bobbled it for his second error. Then Rich Bair golfed the next pitch over the screen in left. The ball may have landed only 300 feet away, but it had the right arc to make the score 4–0.

The Johnstown pitcher, left-hander Craig Humbert, battled well after that and gave up only one more run in the game. But Detroit's Bill Shuta was even more effective. He was a right-hander, 6'2" and 190 pounds, who threw straight over the top for maximum leverage and speed. When he struck out the side in the first inning, the popping sound in the catcher's mitt was easy to hear above the crowd noise. Most scouts thought that Shuta's fastballs were too high and straight, and that he should drop down from his overhand delivery to get more action on the ball—but they liked his speed. In the front row of the scouts' section Joe Branzell of the Rangers aimed the radar gun at each pitch, and the fastballs flashed up as 81, 80, 82.

"That's bullshit," Gary Nickels said. "No way that pitch is under 86."

Red Kephardt agreed. "Joe's had that thing doctored to throw us off, but he might as well *advertise* that it's six miles an hour slow."

"By the end of my first scouting season," Nickels said, "I could watch a kid throw and usually come within a couple miles an hour of how fast he was. But I don't mind an accurate gun at a night game—or at a tryout camp or spring training, where you see pitcher after pitcher and they all start to look alike. The Jugs Gun is too skittish, but the Ray Gun's okay. Tony Lucadello wouldn't like to hear me say this, but I think radar can be a useful tool."

Shuta breezed through the Johnstown lineup with only occasional trouble. He gave up a walk and two hits in the fourth, but a beautiful throw from leftfielder Chuck Froning cut down a runner at the plate to end the threat. In the fifth and sixth innings Shuta retired the side in order. "I don't know about these other scouts," Nickels said, "but I like Shuta's delivery. Everything comes together and the arm angle never changes, and that's why I'd project him as a good control pitcher. What's big to me is the ability to throw the ball where you want to in the strike zone. And he didn't do that at first; his fastballs were up, and the hitters made some contact. But the last couple of innings he's done better, and they haven't hit his curveball yet.

"I'd really need to see him in another game or two, though, because pitching is the hardest thing to scout. I wouldn't have believed it when I first started out. I thought that if a guy can throw hard, he's gonna throw hard all the time for you. Now I don't believe that at all. Pitchers are like a bunch of race-horses: one time they're great, the next time they're horseshit. So you have to see a pitcher a few times to get him correct."

After Shuta ended an eighth-inning threat with another strikeout, Nickels was finally ready to record some grades: 70 for the fastball, 69 for control, 69 for the change-up, and 68 for the curve. "That curve might wind up as a slider. Whoever signs him and works with him might say, 'Look, instead of babyin' that curveball, let's stiffen the wrist and throw it harder.' Anyway, they'd have good material to work with. You have to like his size—and his face."

As much as any veteran scout, Nickels believed in the good face. That scouting tradition, I now understood, is unlikely to die out as long as baseball players have faces. Baseball talent is so unspecialized and so resistant to numerical grades, and baseball scouts are so opinionated, that some such metaphor will always be tipping the balance of judgment. As Nickels and I followed the disappointed fans out of the stadium, and I listened to him articulate the same theory that older scouts had tried all summer to explain for me, I gave up struggling. The idea of the good face finally came to make some sense after all.

"You've seen for yourself that the younger scouts express themselves in technical terms, whereas the older scouts go by feel. That's partly because the younger scouts don't have as much experience to rely on, and partly because when we do have the feel we don't have the clout to make the ballclub listen to our intuitions. I can't get away with writin' reports about the good face, but I know what the good face is.

"When I first started to scout, I used to get phone calls that told me to go to such-and-such a town to look at a high-school boy. And the boy was just a name. I wouldn't even have a physical description; all I'd know was that he was supposed to be a hot prospect. I'd get to the field early, and I'd see the players come off the bus—and I could almost always spot him right away, he was so distinctive from the other players. I could see first-hand that the good face wasn't just some bullshit from the old scouts. It was a way of saying that a kid had charisma. It meant that he looked athletic, like a high stage in evolution— that he struck you right away as strong, forceful, manly, open instead of withdrawn. You might see that in his whole bearing, the way his body kind of opened out. But you might see it in his face, too: the broad features, the strong jaw, the direct eye-contact.

"Tony Lucadello won't sign a player who wears glasses. Part of that's the eyesight factor, but it's also a bias against a certain look. And with the Phillies maybe Dallas Green himself has the kind of look that we scout—the big body and the prominent features. Dallas didn't wear glasses till he was in his forties. I wore glasses when I was in the ninth grade."

On Wednesday morning a dozen scouts showed up at Franklin Field, the roughest and dustiest diamond in tournament use, to watch a losers'-bracket game between Brooklyn and Milford. Most of them came to see Brooklyn third baseman Shawon Dunston, who had turned eighteen in March and still had another year of high-school eligibility. Dunston was 6'1" and 175 pounds, but the scouts had to go beyond the numbers to do justice to his body. They said it was live, springy, wound tight, that it had the loose-limbed grace typical of so many good black athletes, and that it was obviously going to fill out for even greater strength.

The young scouts sat in rickety bleachers along the first-base line; the veterans—Ed Katalinas, Jocko Collins, Joe Caputo, Elmer Gray—sat in folding chairs directly behind the backstop. Gray was using a radar gun to time the fastballs of the Milford pitcher, and Katalinas was teasing him by guessing the speed of each pitch and never being wrong by more than one mile an hour. When Dunston came to bat in the first inning, Gray pulled out a stopwatch.

"If this kid runs too fast for the watch," Katalinas said, "maybe you can time him with the gun."

Dunston took a called strike on an 82 fastball that was almost in the dirt. He stepped out of the batter's box and made eye contact with the umpire but said nothing. His features were broad, strong, and open; in my notes I wrote "good face?"—then added "stylish," because what I really liked was the way he stepped quickly back in the box and assumed a classic right-handed stance, making that bat look like an extension of his lithe body. Dunston jumped on the next pitch and pulled it to deep left, but the fielder, playing back and toward the line, made an easy catch to end the inning.

As he watched Dunston play third base, Katalinas expressed one doubt. "He's got the reflexes and the hands, but I wonder about his arm. It may not be accurate enough for major-league third base. So you might project him in leftfield or centerfield, where he could take advantage of that speed."

What Katalinas liked best was Dunston's quick bat. In each of his later at-bats, Dunston met the ball in front of the plate and drove it with power: a single and another line-out to left, and then a triple to left-center that allowed us to see just how beautifully he ran. "If you're observant," Katalinas said, "you'll see that a lot of these kids meet the ball back here, almost behind the plate, but the aluminum bat saves them. They hit the ball off the fists and it goes for a hit to rightfield. If they come into the minors and get the pitch on the fists, now the wooden bat breaks and the ball dribbles to the pitcher instead of goin' over the second baseman's head. But Dunston should never have that problem."

It struck me then that some of the young scouts, in drawing on their own experiences as players, might be relying on memories of an aluminum-bat league. Weren't they limited as scouts by never having played professional ball?

"Oh hell," Katalinas said, "I never played pro ball either. I went to Georgetown in 1928 on a scholarship that got me out of the mines, and I played catcher and first base. But I didn't have it. Nobody offered me any money to sign."

"How did you get into scouting?"

"I was a high-school teacher and coach, but I also played county ball, and in 1938 I saw a kid named Al Simononis who I thought was a prospect, so I wrote a letter to the Tigers because I'd known Spike Briggs at Georgetown. When I recommended this kid, Spike sent a scout all the way from Kansas City—the Tigers didn't have anyone in the east then—and he took one look at Simononis and signed him. They sent him out to the Kitty League and he had a hell of a year. Then in 1939 Spike asked me to cover a tournament in Bradford, Pennsylvania. I did it, and in fact I signed a boy by the name of Marty Tabacheck. I guess I didn't have the authority to do it, but I signed him on a piece of hotel stationery. Spike called me and said, 'Who gave you the authority to sign that kid?' I said, 'What the hell did you send me up there for?'

"The next year the Tigers made me a part-time scout and I took it up from there. I learned a lot from Joe Brehany, the old scout for the Pirates. He's here at the tournament, still kickin', eighty-some years old and all pissed off that they won't let him put on a pre-game exhibition hittin' fungoes at The Point. Anyway, he taught me, then Wish Egan taught me and made me a full-time scout. And the rest was experience."

Katalinas's experience led eventually to the front office. He had been as ambitious as any of the current young scouts, and in 1956 he was promoted to scouting director on the basis of his education (a master's degree in counseling), his record as an eastern scouting supervisor, and his reputation as the man who signed Al Kaline. He held that post for twenty-five years, guiding the Tigers into the draft era, then coming to terms with the Major League Scouting Bureau (which meant firing seventeen of his twenty-two full-time scouts), and then beginning the new cycle of hiring young scouts for the 1980s.

"At first we thought that the Bureau would train scouts, but each organization must train its own. You find a bright guy, start him off part-time, then try to get him enough money to live on. We're training Johnny Young now. He's a big black kid who played for us, had a cup of coffee in the majors.

"You don't find many today who are former major-leaguers for the simple reason that there's no *money* in it. The pay is peon's pay, comparatively speaking. But scouting is a peculiar and unique occupation. It's like a coal miner: when he goes into the mines he becomes wedded to coal. A scout becomes wedded to baseball."

"You think that still happens with the young scouts?"

"Not as much, but it happens. The biggest problem for them is the travel. They're better equipped to handle it physically, but they're at a point in their lives where it hurts more. Hell, my wife raised our three daughters by herself, I was away from home so much. And when I was a scout director, I was kind of a marriage counselor, too. At first I had all my scouts phone the office every other day, so I could keep track of where they were on a big map. But then I thought: 'Why should a scout call *me*?' I just turned it around—I made all the married scouts call *home* every other night and talk with their families. Then if I needed to know where a guy was, I could just call the wife."

The slow cadence of Katalinas's bass voice emphasized his common sense and created a lulling, hypnotic effect. I could imagine him in the pre-draft era as the most persuasive of scouts—able, as they say, to talk wallpaper into coming away from the wall. I asked him to tell me about signing Al Kaline.

"Did you know," he asked, "that Kaline played right here at the Johnstown tournament?"

"Is this where you first saw him?"

"Oh, no. He was fourteen years old the first time I saw him. I was down in Baltimore to sign a shortstop named McCarthy, and the manager of McCarthy's team said, 'Ed, there's a boy that lives right around the corner, gonna be a hell of a ball-player. His name is Al Kaline.' So I put the name down in the little book. Then I found out that McCarthy's brother played second base for another team, and I thought: 'If I sign a brother combination at second and short, I'm gonna go down in the books.' I went to see the other McCarthy play, and who was at shortstop but this kid named Albert Kaline?

"He was about 5'10" and weighed maybe 140, but he hit line drives, ran beautiful, and threw the shit out of the ball. Fourteen years old. I watched him all through high school, saw him get stronger and fill out to about 180, and the amazing thing was that he had all the intangibles. Didn't lose his temper, had time for people, and just wanted to be a ballplayer. He was *oozing* with it. 'Lemme play ball!'—that was his attitude.

"All the scouts knew about him by then, but I had two advantages. I'd gotten close to his whole family—his father, his mother, his sister, his uncles—and I even stayed in Baltimore for three weeks before he graduated. The other thing was that I offered him a big bonus contract. In 1953 the bonus rule said that a boy who received more than six thousand had to stay on the major-league roster for two years, so I was really givin' a major-league slot to this eighteen-year-old kid. But I'd convinced John McHale that he could play rings around our outfield, which at that time was Nieman, Delsing, Lund, and Souchock. This boy Kaline, as time proved, could run better than them, could throw better than them, could catch the ball better than them. And he could hit better than all of them put together!

"Scouting's more of a numbers game now. These young guys won't have the chance to gamble like that or to romance a prospect the old way. They've become graders, and they can't afford to fall in love with talent. But it's like Stubby Overmire used to say: 'Baseball was here a hundred years before me, and it'll be here a hundred years after me.' Which is true."

*   *   *

I hitched a ride out of Johnstown with Bob Engle of the Blue Jays. He rarely stayed for the end of a tournament, he said. "I'm scouting the players, not the games, so I never know or care who wins."

He drove from Franklin Field back into the city, past the domes of Orthodox churches and the empty yards at Bethlehem Steel, and then up the walls of the valley and out, and south and east across the state until the land finally smoothed and opened out into Amish farm county. All this was only one sliver of Engle's territory. "My area could be measured in square miles, or in scouting miles driven per year, or in time away from home. I think the last one's the most significant. And that's one reason I don't want to make a career out of being an area scout."

Another reason was money. At the start, as a protégé of Jim McLaughlin and Dave Ritterpusch at Baltimore in 1973, Engle had committed a breach of scouting manners—simply by pointing out to management that it was hypocritical to boast about scouts being the backbone of the team and then to pay some of them a salary befitting a junior-high coach. He was reminded that there was plenty of time in the off-season for an enterprising young fellow to supplement his income. And didn't he have the use of a company car?

A few veteran scouts had agreed that the pay scale *was* a disgrace. Dee Phillips, describing himself as a victim of "combat fatigue" in the southwest area, quit Baltimore that year to join the Bureau staff. The Bureau, Phillips said, was a step toward a living wage for scouts and eventual unionization. But most older scouts had said that Engle should be grateful to have a job in baseball at a time when so many older and wiser baseball men—their friends—were being fired as their clubs joined the Bureau. The Bureau, they said, was a step toward unemployment for scouts and eventual mechanization.

Engle, like Nickels, criticized the Bureau now and expressed pride that his team didn't subscribe to it—not because it limited the number of scouting jobs, but because it undercut the image of scouting that had kept him in the game this far. The Bureau symbolized anonymity, uniformity, and caution. In the tradition that Engle's mentors had given him, scouting was really about individualism, imagination, and intrigue.

His most influential teachers, after McLaughlin, were Al LaMacchia, Bobby Mattick, and Pat Gillick—the men who built the Toronto talent system. The Blue Jays had finished in last place in every season of their short history, but they were no joke among scouts; their staff was considered one of the most aggressive in the business.

"Especially in Latin America," Engle said. "The rules down there are what they were in the States before the draft, so we can scout competitively, the good old way. But the best example of our philosophy is the way that the Blue Jays were originally put together. When the Mets and the Angels and other expansion teams first began, they were allowed to draft players from other clubs, and they picked a lot of veterans and utility men; they knew they'd finish in last place, but they wanted the fans to recognize the players as real major-leaguers. But when the Blue Jays first began, Pat Gillick picked mostly Double-A and Triple-A kids from other systems. He said if we were gonna finish last anyway, we might as well build for the future, and we came up with guys like Jim Clancy and Garth Iorg that gave us a base of young talent. And we still do heavy scouting of other teams' minor-league players. That's how LaMacchia stole George Bell."

In the spring of 1980 George Bell had been a hot outfield prospect in the Phillies' system. He was off to a fast start in his first AA season, but at the end of April he suffered a stress fracture in his right shoulder; two months later, when he re-entered the lineup as a pinch-runner, he aggravated the injury in a slide at home plate. The Phillies placed Bell on the disabled list for the rest of the season, but then failed to protect him in the minor-league draft. They sent him home to the Dominican Republic, where he could begin fall workouts with the unofficial Phillies' farm team at Escogido. In October, when Bell showed that he could throw and hit as well as ever, the Phillies realized their mistake: to prevent rival scouts from seeing him, they ordered the Escogido manager not to use Bell in any games. Al LaMacchia saw him anyway. LaMacchia was in the Dominican doing just such detective work, and he simply got out of bed early and spied on the morning practices at Escogido. The Blue Jays drafted Bell away from the Phillies that December, thus acquiring a twenty-one-year-old player with obvious major-league tools for a paltry $25,000.

To Bob Engle the theft of George Bell proved that scouting was still an honorable profession. "It's a little like the time the Pirate scouts stole Roberto Clemente from the Dodgers. Bell may not turn out to be *quite* that good, but the kind of scouting is the same, and it shows the chances there are to make a real dent in the game, to let 'em know you were here."

I wondered if Ed Katalinas would consider Engle "wedded to baseball." On the surface Engle seemed almost a prototype of the young scout. He had come into scouting from college ball (majoring in physical education at Colorado); he was good with numbers, didn't mind paperwork, and held no traditional bias against such technological aids as the radar gun ("just another tool"); he masked his enthusiasms, even his enjoyment in his work, with a dry wit and an apparent preoccupation with professional advancement. Inside, though, the scouting wheels kept turning and turning, even in his daydreams.

This kid Romagna, for example. The conventional wisdom says to forget about little right-hand pitchers, but the conventional wisdom is what Jim McLaughlin said you should always question. What about Juan Marichal? Howie Haak thought *he* was too small to risk three hundred bucks on. Romagna's about the same size as Marichal or Steve Stone, or Steve Blass, or Carl Erskine. How little is 5'10" and 180 pounds? And crowd or no crowd, the kid has two strong pitches and good control. If the Reds don't sign him by January, we could draft him out of that community college and offer him a healthy bonus. But what if a coach from a four-year school gets to him first?

And Shawon Dunston—an obvious blue chip for next June,

maybe even worth a six-figure bonus. He'll be nineteen by then. But suppose he graduates six months early. Just suppose for the sake of argument that he could, and that we talked him into becoming eligible on the sly in January, for a guaranteed bonus of, say, seventy-five thousand. It wouldn't be tampering, exactly. . . . It would just be good old-fashioned scouting.

13 ONE ON ONE

Apollo arrived as the night was falling, and knelt across from the ships, and let go an arrow. Terrible was the twang of his silver bow.

—*Iliad, Book I*

As the Phillies and Pirates played in the rain below, Jocko Collins sat in the Veterans Stadium press box and talked about basketball. He was at this Friday night game to do some late-season pro-scouting for the Milwaukee Brewers, his sixth employer in forty-two years in the baseball business. But in less than a month he was scheduled to begin his thirteenth season as a basketball scout for the Philadelphia '76ers.

All in all, Jocko said, it was a good life, a full year, for a man pushing seventy-five. "The dovetailing is nice. When one sport starts to wane, the other one comes in." But he explained that the two types of scouting require very different mental sets—what his early teachers, the Jesuits, might have called two distinct epistemologies.

"Baseball scouting is definitely harder, because you have to look so much further into the future. So you don't draft to cover some immediate need, say a shortstop, because you'd have to wait too long for the kid to develop, and even then he might never make the majors. But in basketball it's 'Can he help us next season?' Like the '76ers in the last draft—we took Franklin Edwards because we need a guy in backcourt who can control the game. Every great basketball team *must* have a guard like that to save the ball and set the tempo: he's the one who runs the stagecoach, the driver with a whip.

"When you scout basketball, you see a more mature boy,

talent-wise and body-wise, so you don't lean on intuition the way you do as a baseball scout. But you still try to see the rhythm of the mind and the body together, because you *cannot* put a ballplayer down on paper, I don't care what sport it is. He's a flesh-and-blood guy. A basketball scout might use a chart to break down a player's tools—speed, leaping ability, shooting, what kind of body he has, is he a hog or not a hog?— but a lot of that is just paper talk. You might as well use 'C.P.' or 'K.P.'—*can* play or *can't* play. I missed out on Mitch Kupchak because I didn't see what was in his heart. When he was at North Carolina, he couldn't catch a basketball sometimes. Stiff . . . he was awful. Now the guy's a star in the N.B.A., because he worked at it and worked at it and made himself a ballplayer. But Jack Sikma—I knew the '76ers should've drafted him. I saw him play in college, Illinois Wesleyan against Florida, and he had four fouls on him the first half, and in the second half he almost beat Florida by himself. You had to love a guy like that, team player, so great on defense.

"The defense is what wins for you in any sport. Your offense'll vary from game to game, night to night, but with the great defense you'll either win or stay close. In baseball the first line of defense is pitching: the pitchers control the game, and they make every ball that's hit easier or tougher to field. But baseball's not a team sport. Basketball's a team sport; football's a team sport—if I miss a shot or a tackle, somebody else can pick me up, cover for me, like actors in a play. Baseball may be more like writing—you succeed or you fail on your own. If I don't hit, my teammates can't help me hit. It's nine individuals. Baseball is one-on-one *all* the time.

"That's why people hold on to baseball. It's right out there: they can see it and understand it. And the rules haven't been tinkered with too much. We've had to tinker with basketball, like with the shot clock, but I think that the good Lord must have invented baseball—the ninety feet between bases, the bang-bang play at first base. Of all the sports I know, baseball's the most difficult to play. You remember George Mikan? He was named the Player of the Half Century in basketball, and he wore glasses that thick. He couldn't see the scoreboard. When I was a referee in the N.B.A., George would say, 'Jocko, what's the score?' Can you imagine a guy like that hittin' against Bob Feller?"

No. And I couldn't imagine George Mikan as a baseball scout either. That job requires an interesting mix of talents—patience, memory, self-confidence, political instincts, strength enough for all the lonely traveling—but good eyesight is an obvious priority. Scouting baseball, Ellis Clary says, is "like tryin' to be Kit Carson from a movin' train." Other scouts boast of being point men, able to read a pitch as well as the hitter does or able to isolate a hitch in the hitter's swing the way a military spotter might recognize the silhouette of an enemy plane flashed on a screen for a microsecond. Scouting begins with eyesight—and I was worried about Jocko's.

Jocko had been a first-class baseball man since 1940, but now he relied on other scouts to drive him to games, and he sometimes had trouble distinguishing things—or people—from close up. I wondered if he could be holding down major-league scouting jobs in two sports by substituting memory and intuition for physical perception. An interesting possibility—but I didn't want it to be true. I wanted his scouting to be as precise as his wit, and I preferred to think that his far-sightedness was literal, a case of hyperopia that allowed him to scout well enough from, say, thirty feet away.

Here in the big press box we were about two hundred feet from home plate. Most of the scouts had come in out of the soft rain to drink coffee, talk baseball, and squint down at the field. None of them wore glasses. Neither did Jocko: his intense blue eyes studied the diamond, the scoreboard, my face. He was taking no notes on the game, but he provided a thoughtful commentary on it—for both my benefit and that of the young Toronto scout, Mike McAlpin, who had given him a ride this evening.

Mark Davis, the left-handed pitcher the Phillies had recently called up from Triple A, walked the first two Pirate hitters on eight pitches. "He's aiming the ball," Jocko said, "like he wants to baby that arm, but he needs to air it out. There's no reason he shouldn't have control—his motion's smooth—but he has to turn the ball loose instead of pointing it."

Like most of Jocko's observations on the game, this one moved quickly from the specific to the general, offering a deeper reading of performance. "The real question you have to ask yourself is, why is this kid here? And the answer is—indirectly—the strike. Davis has Marty Bystrom's spot in the rotation. But where's Bystrom? I hear that during the seven weeks of the strike he gained forty pounds, and didn't pick up a baseball. Says his arm's tight now. So the Phillies ship Bystrom out and Davis in—but Davis needs more time at Oklahoma City. This is only his third pro season, and I think they've rushed him."

Going into tonight's game, Davis's major-league record was 0–3 with an earned-run average of 9.16. But he did look smooth on the mound, and he escaped the first inning with only one Pirate run. He settled down nicely after that, allowing no hits until the fourth inning, and he stayed ahead of Pirate hitters on the count. Then in the sixth inning Davis gave up three consecutive hits, including a Bill Madlock home run, on three consecutive pitches. He left the game, trailing 4–3.

The Phillie hitters were attacking Pirate pitching, but without real efficiency. After eight innings they had converted 13 hits and 2 walks into only 4 runs, and again Jocko looked for larger meaning in the situation: "Why should the Phillies be the best team in the division before the strike and have a record of 15-and-20 after the strike? They're just coastin'. They know that even if they won all their games, this split-season deal means that they still have to get through a playoff series with *somebody* just to win the division. Tug McGraw says these are just 'exhibition games.' Well, there's two things wrong with that. One is that you can't turn baseball on and off; you coast, then you reach back for what you need, and you find out it's not there. It's not inside you anymore. The other thing is that the Phillies are world champs—and that's not how world champs play. These guys look sluggish; they don't swagger. They should be aggressive on the bases, more in control on defense, the boss in the late innings, *daring* the other team to come at them."

After the Phillies gave up two more unearned runs in the top of the ninth, with two errors by Gary Matthews on the same play, and after their own ninth-inning rally fell one run short, Dallas Green fumed in the clubhouse. His diagnosis was the same as Jocko's, only expressed in blunter language: "You saw the 1981 post-strike Phillies epitomized in one game. You saw good pitching and good offense, then horseshit pitching, horseshit defense, and horseshit efforts at the plate—all in one game."

It didn't give Jocko real pleasure to be right. He wished the Phillies well. A half century ago they had signed him as an infielder, and he made it as high as Class B. Then he worked for the Phillies for the first twenty-seven seasons of his scouting career, until they fired him in a way that denied the value of those twenty-seven years. Maybe Jocko wished them well through sheer habit. Or maybe he just identified so strongly with the city iself. Philadelphia born and bred, out of the melting pot of Port Richmond, where in the days before World War I the Irish and Italian and Polish kids played endless games to make an American identity by acting out the city style, Jocko started out as Chocko, nicknamed for an ice-cream bar, Chocko-pick, that he used to buy every day near the baseball field. One guy from the neighborhood, Johnny Deegan, tried to turn Jocko on to chewing tobacco—Johnny, who chewed *all* the time, even in his sleep, even at Mass on Sunday. Jocko stayed with Chocko-picks and worked his way through St. Joseph's Prep, St. Joseph's College, then held down a job at the post office while coaching three sports at various schools in the Philadelphia area, and then began scouting for the Phillies. "A lot of my classmates at St. Joe's became lawyers, made a lot of money. But sports was always my thing. And the reward of findin' a ballplayer . . . it was like findin' uranium."

At one point in the game I asked this proud man a rude question. We were talking about Zinn Beck, the ninety-five-year-old Twins' scout who had died in March. Jocko liked and admired Zinn Beck but wanted to avoid sentimentality: "He was a great name in baseball, but I think for those last few years he might've been a scout from his rocking chair. They might've still paid him, but he couldn't get around to games on his own anymore."

"Jocko, how much longer do you think you'll be able to scout?"

Jocko kept looking toward the mound. "I'll do it for as long as I can do it. Your health and your eyes have to be good, but as far as I know mine're all right. Ira Thomas, Jack Doyle, Jack Coombs—they scouted all till the good Lord took 'em. The longer you scout, the more contacts you have, the smarter you get. It's like catchers. They last longer because they don't have any range to cover, so as long as they can catch and throw they're all right—and all that experience helps 'em call a good game. Right?"

Maybe, Jocko finally said, he'd get out of scouting the same way he'd got into it—by a fluke.

When I was a high-school coach in 1939, one of my players— kid named Frankie Hoerst, left-hand pitcher—was interested in pro ball. He got letters from Jimmy Dykes of the White Sox and Bill Terry of the Giants, and he says, "Will you handle me?" I didn't know anything, but I says, "The shortest trip to the big leagues right now is with the Phillies." I'd been a farm-hand in that organization, see, and so I took Frankie up to the Phillies' office and they signed him. He went away and did real well, and the next season they asked me if I wanted to scout. When I said yes, that brought their scouting staff up to two!

Gerry Nugent and his wife owned the ballclub then, and they had to operate it on a shoestring because the A's were the strong team in town, and the Phillies couldn't draw flies. Last place every year. Gerry had to borrow money to finance spring training, and he had to sell off his stars to stay in business. He sold Chuck Klein, Dolph Camilli, Bucky Walters, Claude Pas-seau, Kirby Higbe—he'd have had a hell of a ballclub if he could've kept those guys. And in 1940 he could only afford Cy

Morgan and me as the scouting staff. Cy was the farm director and I was the chief scout, and I wore out a couple of cars pilin' up the miles.

Clubs today want to hire young scouts, but when I came up the trend was older scouts and I was like a usurper. I finally made my mark, but it was a cutthroat business then. Those great older guys ahead of me—Paul Krichell, Charlie Barrett, Johnny Nee, Jack Doyle—they never relaxed, always competed. Very few guys ever gave you any tips, and if they did you had to figure they might be tellin' you a lie. You had to know who you were with, whether he was gonna bullshit you or not gonna bullshit you.

In those days the best prospects I saw were black kids. I saw oodles of 'em who could have played in the big leagues right away, if they'd been allowed to. Today the black kids head for basketball, and they're beautiful at it, but I wish I could move about half the ones I see when I scout basketball, move 'em off the courts and onto the diamonds.

I'll tell you a funny story that's not so funny. One day in 1942, September, I'm at the ballpark and a guy at the gate says, "Jocko, there's a colored kid here wants to see you." It was Roy Campanella, and he says, "Jocko, I want a tryout with the Phillies." I park him in the third-base dugout and go up to Gerry Nugent's office to explain it. "This kid's twenty, a great player. His father's Italian and his mother's a Negress." Gerry comes down to the field, and Roy says, "Mr. Nugent, I want a tryout. I think I'm a better catcher than anybody you got here right now"—which was true, because we had Mickey Livingston and Benny Warren—"and Jocko knows I can play. He's seen me lots of times. Right?"

I said, "He can play!" Gerry said, "All right, that's good enough for me. Roy, we'll sign you to a contract, but you have to start out in the Georgia-Florida League." Roy just stared at him; he knew what was what. Finally he said, "Jocko, thanks anyway." What could you do? When Roy was twenty-five, Branch Rickey signed him for Brooklyn, and he beat the hell out of us for the next dozen years.

My first big sign was Del Ennis. I went to Olney High School in Philly to look at a pitcher, who was okay, but here was this big outfielder hittin' balls out of the park. He knocked in twelve runs that day—two grand-slam homers, a bases-loaded

double, and a single. He was an overstrider, one of the biggest
I've ever seen, and you know what Branch Rickey said about
overstriders: "Walk away from 'em." To me Mr. Rickey was a
great man, but there's no simple rules in this game. A scout has
to be open to the great unorthodox hitter. Look at Mel Ott,
Stan Musial, Jose Cruz. And besides, Ennis didn't give his
hands up—he kept the bat back here, so even if he got fooled
on a pitch he could still hurt you, and over a ten-year span in
the big leagues he knocked in a thousand runs. He never got
the credit he deserved: good fielder, ran hard all the time. He
made his money on salary, but the fact is that I signed him for
a hundred-fifty a month, no bonus.

Kids didn't expect bonus money then. They were glad
enough to get off the farm, out of the mines, out of the factory. From hell to heaven. Minor-league ball was an adventure,
like goin' off to sea. Not that Gerry Nugent had any bonus
money to give anyway. Things got so bad he finally had to sell
the club, and a guy named Cox had it for the 1943 season
until Commissioner Landis kicked him out of baseball for
bettin' on games. And then the Carpenter family bought the
Phillies.

With the Carpenters money was no object. You got a player
and you like him? Okay, sign him! You always tried to get the
last shot in the bidding, because you could say to the mother
and father: "Talk to the other scouts. Get the best offer. And
whatever it is, we'll give you five thousand more." And that
used to always clinch the deal for you. Cy Morgan signed Curt
Simmons for sixty-five thousand and Bob Carpenter didn't
blink an eye.

Bob brought in Herb Pennock from Boston to build up the
system. That guy was a Hall-of-Famer on the field and a Hall-
of-Famer *off* the field. He let you do what you wanted to do,
because he had faith in the people that worked for him. Most
clubs cut down on their scouts during the war, but Herb added
on—said, "We're gonna scout extra hard." And that's how we
built the foundation for the Whiz Kids. I signed Granny Hamner. Johnny Nee, a great scout, came over from the Yankees
and signed Willie Jones out of South Carolina. Ben Chapman
signed Robin Roberts. Chappie had him work out in Chicago,
and Herb told him, "Call me when the workout's over." So
Chappie called and said, "I don't want to let this kid out of the

ballpark. He looks that good. But he wants twenty-five thousand." Herb said, "*Give* it to him."

To keep bonuses down, the owners got the idea of a four-thousand-dollar limit—anything higher than that, you had to put the kid on your major-league roster. Some ballclubs cheated. A few got caught, but it never came out in the open; they might give the kid a bonus of thirty-nine hundred, then slip him another ten thousand under the table. But when Ed Katalinas signed Al Kaline for the Tigers, he gave him thirty-five thousand up front, so the kid went to the majors right away. That one really hurt me because I'd had Kaline in my back pocket. We could have had him for the same money.

See, back in 1953 I got a tip from Charlie Eckman, who was a referee in the N.B.A. He said, "Jocko, I got a ballplayer for you. Boy in Baltimore named Kaline." So I went down to Baltimore to see him three different times, and each time he looked better. I said, "He can play centerfield right now. Put Ashburn in left and Ennis in right. He's skinny, but he's gonna fill out. He runs like DiMaggio." He loped in centerfield, and he could throw that ball on a line right to the pitcher's mound. Whoooosh! Great arm, good speed, nice level stroke—you knew he was gonna hit. . . . Well, it's too big a story to tell you, it would offend too many people, but somebody loused me up. We lost Kaline because somebody didn't do his job right. You know, later on we had Yastrzemski in the Philly ballpark and failed to sign him. We could've had Rusty Staub. But Kaline was the biggest disappointment of my life as a scout.

I don't have anybody but myself to blame for losin' Bobby Shantz. I just blew it. I saw him pitch many times, a block away from my own house! He was 5'6" and 135 pounds, and I said to myself: "How could that guy last in St. Louis on a hot summer day? He'd *melt* right there on the mound." He had a knuckle curve that was always a strike, and he hid the fastball. I didn't think the fastball was good enough. But his curveball made him a giant nine feet tall.

I still haven't figured out, after all these years, what it is about little lefties. Look at Shantz, Harry the Cat Brecheen, Harvey Haddix, Billy Pierce. They almost always have the curve—big curve, short curve, over the top—and they can get away with it. And their fastball, nobody can explain it. It seems the way they hold the ball, or whatever the hell they do, it's got that little tail on it, away from the right-hand hitter or comin' into the left-hand hitter's fists. A little lefty with just mediocre stuff can goose the ball up there and still get by, like Randy Jones. Or even Tommy Lasorda—I signed him out of Norristown High when he was about 160 pounds, a curve-ball guy, guts and not too much ability. But he made the big leagues.

Most scouts want *right*-hand pitchers to be big. The Phillies used to make a big deal of that, because Bob Carpenter wanted *all* his players big. So we wound up with some guys like Howie Schultz—Steeple Schultz, they called him—who were really bet-ter as basketball players. Or Dallas Green: he was one of my signs, and a hell of a power forward. Or Gene Conley: he played in the N.B.A. for the Celtics when the baseball season was over, and Bob Carpenter wanted him to quit that, thought he might get hurt. Gene says, "Will you pay me twenty thou-sand more not to play?" He got traded instead.

All this time I was in the N.B.A. too. I refereed high school and college games for about fifteen years, and then I reffed in the pros when the league formed in 1946. Did it eight years, and then I had to quit because of a bad foot, and Asa Bushnell made me the supervisor of the refs, which I did for seven years—until I got fired in 1961. The reason I got fired was that the owners got tired of hearing me defend the refs. I was like a buffer. I might give some ref hell in private, but when an owner said, "You've gotta fire this guy; he's costin' us ballgames," I'd say, "I can't fire him. Who're we gonna get to referee?" Hell, they only paid 'em fifty dollars a game and expenses. I wanted to take a fresh group of young guys to train as real pros, but the owners said that would cost too much.

It's murder in pro basketball today. Too much banging under the bucket and in the lane—if you wanted to, you could call a foul on every play. But you can't disrupt the game, you have to *control* it, so you try to get the big foul, and you try to assert yourself early. Then you can ease back, and if it gets too rough you come back again with the whistle. You should be less like a cop and more like the conductor of a symphony orchestra. The essence of reffing is judgment, not rules.

The N.B.A. refs have an excellent pension plan now. I'm not

part of it; it's not retroactive. And, of course, the baseball scouts aren't part of the big pension plan, because a few players vetoed the scouts and coaches. We don't have any protection. I've worked for six baseball clubs—and when they let you go, you can't transfer any benefits to your new job. When the Phillies fired me in 1966, I had to start all over. What happened was that our staff had just been reorganized, and they told me I had to go on a big trip to compare blue-chip prospects just before the draft. Nowadays they call it cross-check work. It happened that the day I was supposed to go was also my son's graduation day, so I told a guy at the office that I didn't want to leave that day, and he translated it to Bob Carpenter that I *refused* to leave. I was told to go to my son's graduation . . . and to look for another job.

That kind of thing is part of the business, but it's what makes me insist so hard about compensation for scouts. It's worse now, because all the money's up top—it's not there to recompense the people who find and develop the new talent. That's where the lifeblood of the game is, and that's where ball-clubs try to economize. Used to have fifteen farm clubs; now you have six. And it's tough for a kid to make a minor-league club anymore, to make a *rookie* club, because everything is condensed into one point. Old scouts used to say, "This kid looks marginal, but let's sign him up and send him to Class D. He'll play every day, maybe become a hell of a ballplayer." That kid doesn't get a chance in the 1980s.

Once it was a pyramid of talent, with the minors as a strong base. Now it's like the pyramid's inverted, because what you pay to run your whole farm system, plus all your scouts and their expenses, comes to about *half* what you pay to the twenty-five guys on the major-league roster. The players are ruinin' their own game, but they're too dumb to see it. I think they won the strike, don't you? But sooner or later that pyramid's gonna topple over.

The Brewers pulled their scouts off the road on June 12 and we were home seven weeks. It was frustrating, depressing, because when we started back we were scoutin' for 1982; 1981 was over. Harry Dalton didn't want to lay us off, but somebody higher up gave the order: "Got to cut down on expenses." Harry's a great guy for scouts, trusts his people—and I think he'd make a great commissioner of baseball. The thing is

that he's a baseball man, and there aren't enough of them in
the key jobs in the game. A baseball man is a guy who has the
game in his bones, and he has a feel for the people in it. He's a
guy who played the game as far as his talent took him, even if
that was just to the low minors, and then kept hanging around
ball diamonds after that, because there's no line anymore between him and the game, no point where baseball leaves off
and he begins.

The new guys have come out of some college program;
they're business managers, that kind of thing. Some are scout
directors, but they don't know how to read your reports and
they're afraid to trust your judgment. Instead of taking your
word on a player, they say, "Well, let's cross-check this kid."
And the cross-checkers find more faults. . . . They forget that
these kids are just babies, not experienced to play. That's why
you have to *project*. Rick Cerone—he was my first-place choice
for the draft one year when I was with the Mets. I didn't get
him. Mike Scioscia, catches for the Dodgers—next year he was
my first choice. Never got him. Cross-checkers gave both those
kids low grades. But you had to like Cerone: good arm, good
stick, some power. And Mike Scioscia was seventeen years old,
6'4", good left-hand hitter. How could you not like a guy like
that?

I got Bob Bailor for the Orioles, signed him for knick-
knacks. Larry Milbourne, I signed him for less than knick-
knacks. I was almost afraid to sign Milbourne; he looked like
he'd blow away in the wind. But I just had a hunch on both
those guys, and you should always play a hunch—if you don't,
you won't get a second chance, and you'll kick yourself. My
grading system is letters: *E, G, A, BA, P.* That means "excellent," "good," "average," "below average," and "poor"—and
average means a major-league standard. I can go with letters
better than I can with numbers. These younger scouts like numbers, but they wind up splittin' hairs: 47 or 48, what the hell's
the difference? And they can write an essay about a player,
with all the new words—velocity, location, rotation on the
curveball. Hey. Can he throw hard? Does his ball move? Is it
heavy? Does he have the good sharp curve? Can he get the ball
over the plate? These have been the baseball questions for over
a century. Why would you want to change 'em around today?
All this other stuff, this terminology, it's good for the newspa-

pers, but it sounds like we're talking about robots, not flesh-and-blood players.

You want to scout, you have to get a feeling for a *guy*. You get a feel, and you check it against your experience over the years, and you try to learn from your mistakes. Because you're gonna make a ton of mistakes. Johnny Nee used to say, "May all your mistakes be Triple A's." If a player made it to Triple A, see, the ballclub had gotten its investment back on him. But most of the guys you sign won't make it *that* far. And a few of the guys you said couldn't play might become stars, and you're happy for them; you feel like askin' them to bless you, because that's at the heart of scouting. Branch Rickey didn't like Sandy Koufax, said the kid would never throw strikes. I didn't like Bobby Shantz. So what the hell? It's like the Jesuits taught us: nobody's infallible but the Pope, and that's only on matters of faith and morals. Put him out to scout, he'd have as tough a time as any of us.

"Jocko," I said, "you're the fourth scout I've met this season who was educated by the Jesuits. You went to St. Joe's, Jim McLaughlin went to St. Louis U., Paul Florence and Ed Katalinas went to Georgetown. What does it mean?"

"What do *you* think it means?"

"Well, maybe all that training in logic is worth it after all. Aristotelian analysis? Could that help you break down a player's tools and put them back together in your mind?"

Jocko thought that was funny.

"Then how about rhetoric? Didn't the Jesuits keep stressing effective expression, make you take a lot of oral tests? I can see how that might help you persuade a prospect to sign, or persuade a ballclub to draft one of your prospects."

"You know what it might be, Kevin? The Latin and Greek! Yeah, they were both required in those days. They train your mind as well as anything—wake up your curiosity, give you some discipline in memory. I can still remember some of the *Iliad*, and it was 1927 when we did that." Then Jocko said something that sounded like "Dinay declangay yanet, agorayoyo biyoyo," and declaimed: "Apollo arrived as the night was falling, and knelt/across from the ships, and let go an arrow./Terrible was the twang of his silver bow."

In front of us, in the first row of the press box, two sportswriters had spun around in their chairs. Below us, the Phillies and the Pirates seemed tinier than before, their contest framed now by the Trojan War and by the words of a blind poet describing the falling darkness.

FALL

THE
FUTURE

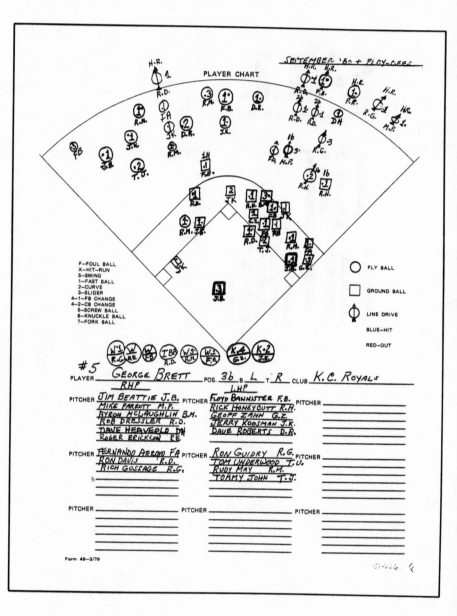

PLAYER CHART

SEPTEMBER '80 + PLAY-OFFS

F—FOUL BALL
X—HIT-RUN
S—SWING
1—FAST BALL
2—CURVE
3—SLIDER
4-1—FB CHANGE
4-2—CB CHANGE
5—SCREW BALL
6—KNUCKLE BALL
7—FORK BALL

○ FLY BALL

☐ GROUND BALL

⬥ LINE DRIVE

BLUE—HIT

RED—OUT

#5
PLAYER __George Brett__ POS. 3b B _L_ T _R_ CLUB _K.C. Royals_
RHP
LHP

PITCHER _Jim Beattie J.B._ PITCHER _Floyd Bannister F.B._ PITCHER ____
Mike Parrott M.P.   _Rick Honeycutt R.H._
Byron McLaughlin B.M.   _Geoff Zahn G.Z._
Rob Dressler R.D.   _Jerry Koosman J.K._
Dave Heaverlo DH   _Dave Roberts D.R._
Roger Erickson RE

PITCHER _Fernando Arroyo FA_ PITCHER _Ron Guidry R.G._ PITCHER ____
Ron Davis R.D.   _Tom Underwood T.U._
Rich Gossage R.G.   _Rudy May R.M._
   Tommy John T.J.

PITCHER ____ PITCHER ____ PITCHER ____

Form 49—3/79

14 DOLLAR SIGN ON THE MUSCLE

There's no such thing as an easy sign. I never remember throwin' a contract down on a table and somebody just grabbed it up and signed it.

—Hugh Alexander

The second symbol from the right at the top of the chart marks George Brett's home run in the final American League playoff game of 1980. It says that Brett lined a Rich Gossage fastball deep into the right field stands.

But Jim Baumer didn't believe that any scouting symbol could do justice to that hit. "It was gone as soon as Brett swung. He just *crunched* the ball, and I think it was still on the rise when it slammed into a post in the upper deck." Baumer had been part of the reconnaissance group preparing the Phillies' advance reports on the Royals and Yankees as possible World Series opponents, and he made a couple of deductions in the brief moment Brett's hit was in flight. "If he could pull Goose Gossage's fastball like that, it meant that he could pull anybody's. I saw for myself why he'd hit .390 that season, and I knew that the best our pitchers could do with him was to feed him slow stuff and keep the ball down. We could also use the chart to position our fielders. Most of all, though, we had to limit the damage Brett could do; we had to keep those guys in front of him off the bases. The biggest thing in our report was to have the pitchers go after Wilson, Washington, and White—to pen up the rabbits."

A year later Baumer glanced through the pages of the report, allowing this or that notation to trigger the image of a particular pitch or swing. He kept his copy as a souvenir of the contribution the scouts had made to the winning of a World Series. But the report had no further value as baseball intelligence, because in advance scouting no secret has meaning for much more than two weeks. If the challenge of scouting amateurs is to project young talent into a distant future, then the challenge of doing advance work is to appraise mature talent in the living moment—to be a scout in the sense that coaches and players are already scouts, thinking in ever-shifting terms about what a specific opponent is immediately able or likely to do. The George Brett of September 1981 would not be the George Brett of September 1980. "So when we still thought we might play in *this* year's Series," Baumer said, "we did a whole new set of reports, based on fresh observations. We started by forgetting what we thought we knew. We didn't waste time studying last year's charts."

The scouts' time was wasted anyway. In early October the Phillies lost a mini-playoff series to the Montreal Expos, who then became champions of the National League East. The 1981 major-league season was over, and the new reports were consigned to a dustbin. Nobody kept one as a souvenir.

But the scouting year has a rhythm of its own. Fall is the season for grabbing undrafted talent, especially junior-college players and Latins, through old-fashioned hustle and salesmanship. In October the Phillies signed two good-looking junior-college prospects, third baseman Chris James and outfielder Tony Brown, and dispatched Ruben Amaro to the Caribbean to cross-check players as young as fifteen.

Fall 1981 was also a season of departures that dramatically affected Philadelphia scouting. On the day after the major-league season ended, Dallas Green resigned as the Phillies' field manager to become general manager of the Chicago Cubs; he took three scouts and five minor-league coaches with him, and left town claiming that the Phillies' scouting and farm systems really hadn't been working right since *he'd* quit directing them.

Jim Baumer, in his first year as scouting and farm director, was then challenged to defend the general direction and recent results of the whole player-development program. The challenge came from new ownership. The Carpenter family's sale of the Philadelphia franchise became final on October 29, when a syndicate headed by Bill Giles made good on its bid of $31,000,000. The shift from family to syndicate ownership was a shift from old money to new money and, in scouting, from pure traditionalism to cost-consciousness. Further cuts in the staff were inevitable.

The fall season offered a set of lessons in the politics and economics of scouting, and Baumer was about to become a student as well as a teacher.

Education, Baumer said, wasn't something that somebody could give you. The values he followed as a scout, and now as a scouting director, had been learned and lived from the inside out, through the disappointments of his seventeen-year career as a professional player. The major-league portion of Baumer's record looked like this:

		G	AB	R	H	HR	RBI	SO	BA
1949	CHICAGO WHITE SOX	8	10	2	4	0	2	1	.400
1961	CINCINNATI REDS	10	24	0	3	0	0	9	.125

He was an eighteen-year-old bonus baby that first time up, and in fact his original signing typified the bonus era in scouting. At Baumer's high-school graduation in Broken Arrow, Oklahoma, fourteen of the sixteen major-league clubs had scouts in attendance. "And then they all went to my house, some of the best salesmen in the game—Freddie Hawn of the Cardinals, Hugh Alexander of the Indians, Tom Greenwade of the Yankees. The night I graduated was the same night Mickey Mantle graduated. And Greenwade, who ended up signing Mantle, was at *my* graduation. I was supposed to be a hot property, but hardly anybody knew about Mickey, so Greenwade told him to wait, that he'd get to Commerce to see him in a few days."

Of all the scouts who performed in the Baumers' living room that night, Hugh Alexander felt surest of having the inside track. Alexander's bid was $6,000 a year for three years, the most he could offer without crossing the bonus line; any greater amount would have required the Indians to protect Baumer on their major-league roster. "A few other scouts went to the limit," Alexander says, "but they weren't as tight with the family as I was. There was no way in the world they could beat me just by offerin' the same amount of money, because they'd come after him late, when he was a senior. I'd watched Jim Baumer since he was fifteen. I saw him turn into a real good player, a hell of a shortstop. He had major-league power, a major-league arm, and as good a pair of infielders' hands as I've ever seen. He didn't run real well, maybe because he was so big for his age. But he was mature, had a good head for baseball, always knew what he was doin' on a field. And I thought I had him signed.

"All at once he got a phone call from Chicago—Frank Lane wanted him to fly up there with his family and do a workout at Comiskey Park. It didn't bother me. I said, 'They're not gonna get in over me, because they don't know the kid.' And in a workout you're not gonna pay that kind of money, especially back in those days. But he went up there and put on a show, hit about twelve balls into the seats and a couple in the upper deck—and that's a big ballpark. Frank Lane finally gave Jim a contract for about forty-five thousand, so I was out of the game. I felt like a poker player who lost a good pot because some other guy bet more goddamn money on one card than I brought to the goddamn table."

Baumer was sent to the White Sox farm team in Waterloo, Iowa, where he performed well enough to be called up to Chicago in September. His ten major-league at-bats were the last he would get for the next dozen years. "My second year out, in Colorado Springs on a cold night, I came across second base on the double play, and when I turned the ball loose my arm went with it. Had no feeling in it. For about two weeks I couldn't throw a ball twenty feet, and when the arm finally came back it was never as strong, and they made me a second baseman. But I did have almost a Mike Schmidt arm before that."

Over the next decade Baumer toiled for six other organizations: the Pirates, the U.S. Army, the Tigers, the Braves, the Cardinals, and the Reds. With Cincinnati in 1961 he had his best spring training ever, and was named as the Reds' starting second baseman on opening day. "But a few days before we broke camp, I got hit hard by a pitch. It caught me on the left wrist, really messed it up, and for a while I couldn't get the bat around quick enough. After all those years, there was no way I wasn't gonna play. So I did start on opening day and just tried to play through it, but after ten games the Reds said they couldn't wait for me. They went on to win the pennant that year, but I was gone."

Even then Baumer didn't surrender the dream of a major-league connection. He played six more seasons—five of them in Japan, as a power-hitting shortstop for the Fukuoka Lions—before he accepted the fact that he could make the connection only through scouting.

After his long maturity from bonus baby to journeyman, Baumer brought to scouting a special insistence on psychological toughness as the first criterion of a professional player. *Meek* and *puss* were the most damning words in his reports. But as a member of the Houston Astros' staff, he soon learned more about the political and economic realities of scouting. The Astros had once been a hungry expansion franchise, ready to outhustle, outbid, or outscheme any other scouting force. In the years following the institution of the amateur draft, however, the Astros gave much lower priority to player development; they concentrated on wooing fans through special promotions, ballpark extravaganzas, and trades aimed at short-term improvement. In the process they got rid of Joe Morgan, Mike Cuellar, Rusty Staub, and half a dozen other young players, receiving mostly used-up talent in return. Baumer was only one of several Astros' scouts (Brandy Davis was another) who quit the staff in disgust.

He joined the Milwaukee Brewers as a special-assignment scout in 1972 and was promoted to scouting director the next year—just in time to make one of the best bets of his career. Two of his scouts told him that Robin Yount, a high-school shortstop in Danville, Illinois, was good enough to be a third-round draft pick. The dollar sign on the muscle was $25,000. "I went to Danville to see the kid myself, and I just liked everything about him. He had all the tools I had in high school—power, arm, hands—but the biggest difference was speed. There was no question he had the range of a major-league shortstop. He was aggressive, mature for his age, and you could tell that he wanted to play and was gonna play.

"But in order to sell Yount to the office as a first-round pick, I had to get the other scouts to bump their money up. I said, 'I want you to go look at him again, to be sure you've got him in the right place, because I like him a lot better than twenty-five.' So they both saw him again and put him in the Group One category, over fifty thousand. The Phillies had first pick in the draft that year and took John Stearns; we picked second and took Yount. We knew he wasn't a student, didn't want to go to college, so he was very signable. He's listed in the book as being signed by Gordon Goldsberry, but I could've sent Gordy's wife over to close the deal."

Baumer became the Brewers' general manager in 1975 and engineered some significant trades—George Scott and Bernie Carbo to Boston for Cecil Cooper; Gerry Pyka and Rick O'Keeffe to Cincinnati for Mike Caldwell—but when Milwaukee finished in last place again in 1977, Baumer was fired and replaced by Harry Dalton. Starting over at Philadelphia, he had moved up once again from special-assignment scout to director of the scouting and farm systems. This time he had more money to play with, at least until the new owners came in. The October signings of Chris James and Tony Brown brought the Phillies' bonus commitments for the year to a total of about $350,000.

And if Baumer had been able to sign a few more of his picks from the January and June drafts, that figure would have been close to $600,000.

Philadelphia's first round choice in the June draft, pitcher Jon Abrego, held out for a bonus of $70,000. Baumer approved it even though it was a notch higher than the Phillies' usual offer to a June first-round player; in the preceding nine years they had almost always signed that draft pick for about $55,000. In 1981, $55,000 was the exact amount they paid to their second-round choice, outfielder Charles Penigar. Neither player hired an agent. They and their families simply proved to be tough and intelligent bargainers, aware that the Mets' offer of $200,000 to Darryl Strawberry in 1980 had established new plateaus for baseball bonuses. As high-school players, both Abrego and Penigar were able to use college as an effective threat.

Baumer considered it a point of honor not to offer any bonus higher than the dollar sign on the muscle. It didn't matter how much money the Carpenters would let him spend, or how much an amateur player expected; what mattered was pricing the talent right. The Philadelphia tradition was to compute maximum bids in terms of an imaginary open market—"How much would I risk on this player if we were all scouting the old way, before the draft system began?" In practice Baumer used $50,000 as a convenient gauge: to merit more than that, to be a Group One player, a prospect should have "all the tools."

Baumer was conservative even about Group One players, and admitted that he had risen slightly above his principles in approving the bonuses for Abrego and Penigar. But with Charles Kerfeld he drew the line, and lost the ballplayer, at $50,000. He had selected Kerfeld as a chance draft in June, in the twenty-fourth round, because of an intriguing last-minute phone call from Eddie Bockman, who described a right-handed pitcher, 6'6" and 225 pounds, with a live arm and enough meanness to aim his good fastball at anyone, even umpires. "He wears big thick glasses," Bockman said, "and he has hair down to his ass." When the Phillies' scouts went to watch Kerfeld after the draft, they found that he had shaved his head and now looked like an executioner, especially when his fastball tailed in like a whip to right-handed hitters. "With those glasses of his," Baumer said, "and with the hitters diving for cover, he reminded some people of Ryne Duren—as a giant. I didn't care that he was a twenty-fourth round draft choice. I went by the talent, and there was enough there to go to fifty thousand. Then I stopped, because he still has some holes in his game—the breaking pitch, control, and maybe attitude. I like his aggressiveness, but he's a player you have to project too much into the future. You can't let scouting become guesswork. So at some point you just have to wish 'em luck and let 'em go."

Kerfeld turned down the $50,000 and enrolled at Yavapai Junior College, expecting to be drafted by another major-league team in January and offered more money. Baumer could shrug off that loss, but not the loss of three shortstops who rejected a total of $135,000 in bonuses. "We offered fifty thousand to Jerry Holtz, and fifty to Matt Shumake, and thirty-five to David Denny. All of 'em went to four-year colleges instead, and I guarantee you they'll never get offers that high when they're eligible again. They say, 'Yes, but I'll get a free education out of it'—like education was something that somebody could give you and not what you go and learn for yourself. And they assume, which they shouldn't, that the scholarship is automatic for four years. They don't realize that college coaches are businessmen, just like we are.

"It wasn't the money. None of those shortstops said, 'I want more money.' I think they were just afraid to go out, didn't want to leave the nest and deal with the cruel world. They turned out to be meek."

That sounded defensive to me, maybe because I was a teacher at a four-year college. Did wanting book knowledge, or just the social or athletic style of a certain school, make you a puss? "Why not criticize the scouts instead of the players?" I asked.

"Isn't it part of the job to judge signability and toughness *before* the draft?"

"We did know that Shumake and Denny would be hard to sign, and that's why we took them as late-round draft choices. Holtz was a special case. Joe Reilly didn't discover him till May, and then Holtz kept saying how he really wanted to play pro ball. After we took him in the fourth round, he was still friendly, but his uncle gave us some trouble. Finally the uncle came around, told him he should sign for fifty thousand, but Holtz had changed. He said baseball was secondary to getting an education. He said he wanted a school like Cornell—and when he turned us down, he also turned down some big baseball schools like Miami. You can read that as being sincere, but I came away with the feeling that he's just afraid of bigtime competition.

"We should have known about that sooner, just like we should have known about Whitt, our number-two pick in the secondary draft. He was away from home for two days and then he just turned around and went back. And the Reds should have known that a couple of their very top draft picks this year were problem guys; they sent them home the first week for doin' dope and other bad stuff. But so much of scouting today is coverage, not depth, that it's always a gamble. And you double the gamble when you go after high-school kids. The Dodgers have told their scouts to ease away from highschool prospects, because they're harder to sign and there's too much at that age that you can't know. Myself, I'd rather take chances on the younger players. It's more fun and the prizes are better."

Two of the biggest disappointments of the scouting year were Billy Irions and Vince Soreca, both college players. Irions was the Phillies' first pick in the secondary draft, a left-handed pitcher described by Tony Roig as part Indian and "a tough son of a bitch." He had once been drafted by the Brewers but turned down an offer of $35,000; the Phillies were able to sign him for $16,000, but when he joined the Northwest League farm team at Bend, Oregon, he was out of shape and not especially tough. He was able to pitch only 34 innings, compiling a dismal earned-run average of 7.68. Baumer wanted to be patient with Irions, though, because part of the conventional wisdom of scouting is that left-handed pitchers mature late.

Vince Soreca was a more doubtful case, with little future as a catcher and less as a hitter. He had been drafted in the third round and signed for $30,000. He then batted .178 in AA competition and was demoted to an A league, where he raised his average to .179. Since Soreca's arm was the only tool as good as it was supposed to be, there was talk in the farm system of converting him to a pitcher. But the draft choice used to obtain him had been earmarked for a catcher, so this one was an expensive mistake—especially since both of the Phillies' national cross-checkers had voted enthusiastically for another catcher, Phillip Lombardi, who was already off to a fine start in the Yankee farm system.

At the draft in June I had guessed that Baumer chose Vinnie Soreca in the third round for the same reason he chose Jerry Holtz in the fourth: to placate Joe Reilly, an area scout who considered cross-checkers his natural enemies and who lobbied endlessly to beat them. Now I saw that the issue was more complex and part of a continuing problem. Soreca was three years older than Lombardi and had therefore been expected to begin playing in the high minor leagues, where the Phillies' catching problems were most acute. A year earlier, in June 1980, their first and third draft choices had also been catchers—Lebo Powell and Doug Maggio. By October 1981 Powell had completed his second year of troubles both on and off the field, and Maggio was about to be given his unconditional release.

Baumer's good news was that Abrego and Penigar, the first two draft choices in June, were what their touts had promised. Abrego suffered an inflamed elbow at the end of the season, but until then he was challenging rookie-league hitters with a major-league fastball. Penigar was an all-around athlete who continued to progress as a switch-hitter. And there were some

impressive bargains among the lower-round draft choices—
like high-school outfielder James Olander, a seventh-round
pick who signed for $20,000; or college pitcher Charles Hud-
son, a twelfth-round pick who signed for $5,000. "Hudson
has a supple delivery off a real loose black body," Baumer
said. "And Olander wouldn't have embarrassed us as a num-
ber-one pick; our early scouting reports didn't do him justice.
After the draft is like a new scouting season, when you start
to find out about the talent that you bought. And the fall's
another season yet. But I'd say that this year, so far, is one to
be proud of."

He was even prouder when I told him that his scouts still
seemed to be the least popular men in the business. They were
famous for minor discourtesies to rival scouts, like refusing to
share a copy of a high-school team's baseball schedule, and
for affecting the tough-guy style that had been Dallas Green's
trademark as scouting director. Now it was Baumer's, and he
liked the image. "The attitude that keeps you from giving one
of your competitors a ride in your company car is the same
attitude that finally allows you to make a good surprise draft
choice, or to know *not* to draft someone, or to steal a kid off
a junior-college team. You shouldn't be in this line of work if
you're afraid the other guys might call you a prick. I don't
have time for this stuff about the 'fraternity' of scouting. I'm
more concerned about morale inside our own system, because
a scouting staff is kind of like an army."

Sometimes Baumer made scouting director seem like a rank
just below full colonel—and the impression was reinforced by
his close-cropped hair, slightly stiff bearing, and clipped style
of speech. At other times, when the discussion turned away
from baseball, he relaxed easily and his voice slowed toward
a southwestern drawl. The question for me wasn't whether
Baumer was playing a role, but whether the Phillies under Bill
Giles would still spend enough money on scouting to make
the role plausible. Giles's baseball values seemed to have been
shaped at Houston when he was the Astros' director of public

relations and promotions. He remained more interested in marketing the product than in building it, more committed to ballpark gimmicks and older players with name recognition than to the traditional path of player development. Ten years earlier Jim Baumer had resigned from the Astros' scouting staff to escape the dominance of such values.

"How will you be able to maintain staff morale," I asked, "if you have to start laying off a lot of scouts?"

"I don't expect to have that problem. We won't be adjusting to a real tight budget; we'll be adjusting to *having* a budget. Because under the Carpenters we could pretty much spend whatever we wanted on scouting."

In 1981, the final year of the Carpenter family's largesse, the Phillies led all major-league organizations in spending on player development. Their total expenditures—about $3,700,000, not counting administrative salaries and expenses—were divided almost evenly between the scouting and farm systems. When I was trying to get some sense of the Phillies' activity in Latin America, I drew up the following figures for Philadelphia scouting as a whole, based mostly on guesses by Baumer and his assistant, Jack Pastore.

SALARIES FOR SCOUTS
IN THE UNITED STATES $690,000
        special-assignment scout   (1)
        national cross-checkers   (2)
        regional supervisors   (3)
        area scouts   (20)
        part-time scouts   (60)
        retired consultant   (1)

TRAVEL EXPENSES
IN THE UNITED STATES 625,000
        airline and cab fares
        lodging and meals
        company cars and mileage allowances
        long-distance telephone charges

BONUSES IN THE UNITED STATES 355,000
    players from the January draft   (7)
    players from the June draft   (23)
    players from tryout camps   (5)
    other undrafted free-agents   (8)
    commission scouts

SALARIES FOR SCOUTS IN LATIN
AMERICA 85,000
    supervisor, part-time   (1)
    area scouts   (4)

TOTAL TRAVEL EXPENSES
IN (AND TO AND FROM) LATIN AMERICA 80,000

BONUSES IN LATIN AMERICA
(PREDICTED THROUGH THE FALL SEASON) . . . 25,000
    players paid directly   (4)
    players purchased from Latin teams (4)
    commission scouts

TOTAL $1,860,000

The money the Phillies spent in Latin America was just over 10 percent of their yearly outlay for all scouting, but it might have been their wisest investment. In the 1960s they signed a few good players like Manny Trillo and Willie Montanez by relying on occasional scouting trips to the Caribbean. In the 1970s they established a permanent presence in Latin America and began signing players in quantity from Puerto Rico, the Dominican Republic, Mexico, Panama, and Venezuela.

Not from Cuba, of course. The Phillies' supervisor of Latin scouting, Ruben Amaro, had played in Cuba in the early 1950s. He remembered how it was when Joe Cambria, smoking a big cigar and wearing a white linen suit, would arrive at tryouts in his limousine and survey hundreds of candidates, finally deigning to offer one or two of them a new baseball in exchange for a signature on a Washington Senators' contract.

"And he never had any trouble finding takers," Amaro said. "All those kids were *desperate* to sign. Cambria even turned Fidel Castro down twice. He could have changed history if he remembered that some pitchers just mature late.

"You have to scout different in Latin America now. Cambria had Cuba all to himself, so the Washington Senators monopolized the talent. Now the other major-league clubs have seventeen full-time scouts just in Puerto Rico, so there's competition. And that's healthy. I tell my scouts—Acevedo, Perrazza, Herrin, Maduro—that I don't want to hear any of them bragging: 'I signed a kid for one hundred dollars.' That's not the point. The number one thing in Latin scouting, just like it used to be in the States, is getting to know the family, winning their confidence, establishing a reputation. We can afford to offer a fair contract and look after the kids we sign. If we pay to get a kid's teeth fixed or to overcome what a bad diet did to him, and we make sure he gets eased into a whole different culture and language, then we're helping ourselves."

Amaro spoke with little trace of an accent. He was originally from Vera Cruz, Mexico, but had left at eighteen, in 1954, when the Cardinals offered him $3,900 to sign a professional contract. Playing for four major-league teams through the 1960s, he compiled a lifetime batting average of only .231, but I remembered him as a smooth and utterly dependable shortstop, a handsome fielder who made the hard plays look easy. He was still a handsome man, with strong, open features and tight skin the color of burnt gold, and he radiated optimism as he talked about "rescuing the year." The Phillies' major-league season, like the year of the strike itself, had been a bust. But now Amaro was freed from his coaching duties and could begin his scouting season, starting with an extended trip to the Dominican. "There's incredible talent there," he said, "especially in middle infielders."

In 1975 Amaro thought one middle infielder, Jorge Lebrun, was so good that he offered him a contract for $38,000 in bonus and benefits. One of the benefits was the hiring of a special tutor, because Lebrun was only fourteen years old. Partly as a result of this case, the Puerto Rican government later restricted American scouts from signing players younger than sixteen, but the Phillies' rivals were less critical about Lebrun's age than about the size of the contract. Other scouts complained that what Dallas Green called "aggressive" scouting would only drive up the price of Latin talent for everybody. The bidding war never quite materialized. Scouting expenses in Latin America remained quite reasonable by American standards, mainly because there was little competition from other pro sports or from colleges, and some players were obvious prospects when they were still young enough to be hidden from other baseball scouts. The average player selected in the first round of the June draft in the United States could expect to receive a bonus of $60,000; Latin American players with comparable tools were often signed, or purchased from a local team, for under $5,000.

In retrospect Amaro admitted that Lebrun was too young, that a premature professional contract had stunted his development. "When he first came to America, before we brought him into our minor-league system, he stayed at my house in Philadelphia. One day he was supposed to go to a workout at the ballpark, but he asked me: 'May I stay in the backyard and keep on playing with Ruben and David?' My two sons were about ten and twelve, and they were knocking a ball around with him or playing tag or something. And it hit me how much he was a child like them, and I had to wonder if he could keep his zest for baseball when he got into a professional setting. And the publicity of the signing hit his father, and Mr. Lebrun started thinking his son was worth more money, and he put a lot of negative thoughts into Jorge's mind. At the next spring training Jorge didn't want to do anything, wouldn't complete the conditioning program, and we almost had to push him out on the field. Then he started to gain weight. When I signed him, he was about 5'10" and 160 pounds. Four years later he weighed almost 200, and most of it was in his lower half. He lost all his range in the infield, and he hadn't improved any tools. So at the age of eighteen, when some bright kids are just starting out their careers in professional baseball, Jorge got his unconditional release.

"I would rather sign a player at eighteen or nineteen, because that kid can show me which way he's gonna go, with his bat and his body and his mind. But a lot of Latin players mature early, and if you wait too long you can lose them to the other scouts. We signed Orlando Isales at fifteen, and he was less of a projection than Lebrun; he was more polished. And when I saw Julio Franco at sixteen, I saw everything I needed to see.

"When Franco showed up for his first workout, he was a real skinny kid, about 5'11" and 150 pounds, with a small chest and not much maturity or hardness on his body. He was wearing an old pair of shoes that didn't fit, and in the sixty-yard dash he only ran 7.2. I projected him as about a 6.8 runner, because he had nice long legs and his actions were so fluid. In the field he showed me great hands and an outstanding arm, but what amazed me were his actions at bat. When I run a tryout, I pitch to the kids myself. Anytime I can't do that, I'm gonna quit scouting—because I can move the ball around, throw curveballs, change speeds, and I scout a hitter the way other players will. I couldn't fool Franco more than once with anything. He had a nice flat swing and he sprayed line drives to all the fields. Even at sixteen he knew how to throw a bat at the ball, so it was like pitching to some veteran in the minor leagues.

"He still baffles me. I played baseball more by being logical and intelligent about the ballgame than because of my tools. I didn't have a lot of speed, and my first year in professional baseball I made sixty-four errors at shortstop in sixty-two games. I finally played eleven seasons in the big leagues because I started to ask 'why?' all the time. I became a scout while I was still a player. I studied the strength of my pitchers; I studied the thinking of my pitchers; I studied how every player on the opposition hit my guys. Well, in extended spring training two years ago I had a chance to see Franco play seven straight days at shortstop, and I thought my mind must be playing tricks on me, because he remembered every hitter, every pitcher, even in a camp where the coaches were running new players in and out all the time. I couldn't believe he knew how to play the game that way, that early. Franco is still a little flashy right now, a little hot-doggish; he needs to learn to play ground balls *simpler*. But he shows you the kind of talent you can grab in Latin America."

The Phillies grabbed Franco for $4,500. Their Dominican scout, Francisco "Qui-Que" Acevedo, ran his own team, the Escogido Lions, and he signed Franco on speculation and then sold the contract to Philadelphia. A year later Acevedo sent Amaro a report on Juan Samuel, a second baseman with 6.2 speed and the kind of home-run power that second basemen aren't supposed to have. The prose section of the report said simply: "I like to sign him." Acevedo later sold Samuel's contract to the Phillies for $3,000.

Now Amaro had a new sheaf of reports from Acevedo and was about to fly down to cross-check the players. He would work his way slowly through the Dominican and Puerto Rico before heading down to Zulia, Venezuela, for winter ball. And if he only had some way to get in and out of Cuba on a hit-and-run scouting raid, he could rescue the year for sure.

"With enough commandos to cover me, I'd go get a second baseman named Juan Vicente Anglada. He's about 6'2" and *strong*, with even better power than Juan Samuel, and he was born to play. I'd get him and about a dozen others, because there are that many in Cuba who could play in the big leagues right now. I've seen some of them at tournaments like the Pan-American games, but there are others who never get to play outside of Cuba because Fidel is afraid they'd never come back. He's turned everything to *mierda*, to shit, but the baseball talent there is out of a scout's dream."

That fall I pursued the memory of a dream—by playing baseball on weekends for an amateur team whose manager was a scout. Leroy Hill opened the Chiefs' roster to a wide range of ages and talents. The catcher, Mike McCardell, had once played in the Cincinnati farm system and was still young enough and good enough to be a legitimate prospect; Hill planned to sign McCardell to a Pittsburgh Pirates' contract at the end of the season. At the other extreme were those of us who depended on the kindness of umpires. I was a thirty-nine-year-old relief pitcher whose nickname was "Batting Practice." Two of Hill's sons also played on the team; one of them had attended a Florida baseball school in the spring, and had returned absolutely unchanged except that he knew exactly how to insert a pinch of Skoal between cheek and gum.

Years ago, before he became a scout, Leroy Hill managed a town team that competed in three leagues in the same season. Later he managed an American Legion team that featured Ruly Carpenter as a pitcher and third baseman. "The first time I managed in order to win, and the second time it was more a way of scouting. But now I manage for the same reason this ballpark was built—for fun."

The ballpark, Doubleday Gardens in Newark, Delaware, was the whim of a rock musician, George Thorogood, who had spent about $200,000 so that he could always play baseball whenever he felt like it. Thorogood ultimately became so successful that he had to start worrying about what it might cost to get hurt playing a silly game. He moved out of town, to other whims. But he wanted that bright wedge of space to be used by "the people," and so he entrusted it to Leroy Hill's care. Hill was a retired Air Force colonel, a retired data-processing manager at the Chrysler plant, and a part-time scout for the Pirates. He spent much of his ample leisure time maintaining the field and its spirit; and to the equipment that Thorogood had donated, Hill added procurements from the Pirates and from scouting friends. The Chiefs' game balls were stamped "Pacific Coast League," and had already weathered a few batting practices in Portland, Oregon.

Hill had broken into scouting in 1950 under Jocko Collins, and together they signed such players as Chris Short and Johnny Briggs for the Phillies. He still regarded Jocko as his mentor, but he had no hard feelings against Bob Carpenter for firing Jocko in 1968 or for allowing Hill himself to be fired in 1975. He thought the Carpenters' sale of the Phillies was bad for baseball and especially for scouting.

"The new owners won't be underwriting four million a year for player development. They don't have a feeling for that side of the game. They won't just eliminate the Carpenters' little generosities, like giving extra pensions to loyal old scouts or taking a guy like Judy Johnson to spring training. They'll also fire some people—and that's gonna get political. It's why scouting's never a pure science; it's always affected by dollars and personalities. That's baseball."

But this was baseball, too: playing for just fun, as Hill said, on a field far away from the business side of the game. Occasionally I was able to apply some lesson of the scouting year, like using Tony Roig's discussion of full body looseness, extension, as a guide to warmups and the mechanics of hitting and throwing. My clearest lesson, though, had been that real ballplayers are born, not made. Any scout's list of tips for hopeful prospects would begin with the simple injunction to have plenty of God-given talent. And the disadvantage of having a scout for a manager is that, no matter how genial and constructive he is, you internalize some of his silent objectivity, so that even your greatest day on a baseball field can seem like something that happened to you instead of something you did.

One fluky, lucky Saturday I wound up as the winning pitcher in both games of a doubleheader. Our opponents were the Destroyers, mostly semi-pro players. One of them was Scum Lon, really named Lonny Hartnett, who always showered and shaved, trimmed his hair and shined his shoes, just before a game against the Chiefs. He thought Leroy Hill might discover and sign him, might disregard his old age (twenty-two) and cloudy reputation, if only he could *look* more like a prospect, and if only everybody would stop calling him Scum Lon. He was a lanky right-hander who occasionally announced the game while he was pitching it, in a low tone but still loud enough for the batter to hear something like "He winds and fires . . ." as Lonny wound and fired.

Lonny didn't get discovered that day. Neither did I, but I was able to make good use of another scouting tip. In the last inning of the second game, with one out and the tying run on second, I was pitching to Bert Talley, an excellent contact hitter. McCardell signaled for a fastball but I shook him off, remembering what Regie Otero had told me back in the spring: "The straight chonge is the most dongerous pitch in baseball, because the hitter's timing throws it off." And it worked. Talley read the pitch as a simple change-up only after his weight was all the way forward, and he swung under the ball and popped it softly to the first baseman. Then Leroy Hill called time and walked to the mound.

"Will you please," he asked, "please quit diddling around? Whatever you got left, just throw it. Even a bad fastball."

On the next pitch, a bad fastball, Mike Foraker drove a low liner to left that should have fallen for a hit, but Kenny Farrall made a beautiful diving catch to end the game. "It just goes to show," Hill said later, "that if you hang around ball diamonds long enough, if you play enough games and don't care what people think—"

"You might step in a hole and get hurt," Lonny said. His own pitching performance had put him in a bad mood, but when I left the field Lonny was still talking earnestly with Hill about the possibility of a pro career.

The next morning I bought two Sunday papers, cut the box scores out of one and circled the winning pitcher, and then sent the clipping to the Phillies' scouting office with a cover letter—

Dear Mr. Pastore:

Urgently urge you to check this boy out. Good face—looks mature. Soft hands (real soft). No puss. Outstanding straight chonge.

A Friend

Jack Pastore never followed up on that letter—maybe because he was so busy trying to save his job. Dallas Green's departure had triggered a chain reaction in the Phillies' scouting system, and nobody could tell where it might stop. Far from rescuing the year, the fall scouting season deteriorated into a sequence of political responses.

First, as soon as Green announced his resignation, Jim Baumer suspended the issuing of 1982 contracts to all scouts. "I needed time to see who was going to Chicago with Dallas Green and who wanted to stay with us. If anybody wanted to go with him, that was fine with me, only I wanted to be sure. I didn't want any scout working for me who wished he was over at Chicago."

Second, Baumer fired Brandy Davis. "He was frustrated as a cross-checker," Baumer explained, "because I didn't give him the authority he used to have. And I couldn't take it that he acted on his own—he went wherever he wanted, any time he wanted, to see the ball players he wanted. Sometimes we couldn't even find him." In addition, Davis was close to Dallas Green.

Third, Gordon Goldsberry and Gary Nickels resigned from the scouting staff under gentle pressure. "I could see the handwriting on the wall," Goldsberry said. Seven years earlier Baumer had released him from the Brewers' staff. Nickels simply had higher ambitions than Baumer wanted to encourage. "Gary had it in his mind that he should be the assistant scouting director. Maybe he would be better in an office—not this one—because I have a reservation about him as a scout. He never played pro baseball himself, so it's hard for him to size up a player's intangibles: dedication or teachability or toughness. A lot of young scouts have that problem."

Fourth, Dallas Green gave Davis, Goldsberry, and Nickels equivalent jobs with the Cubs and, on his last day in Philadelphia, he told Bill Giles that Baumer and Pastore were the ones who should be fired. He rehashed every problem in the player-development program since August of 1979 when he had left the director's post—the failure to protect George Bell in the minor-league draft, the wasting of high draft-choices on

mediocre catchers, the inability to sign three promising shortstops, the violation of scouting courtesy, maybe even scouting
ethics, in withholding so many contracts for so long.

"Dallas really stirred up some shit," Baumer said. "He put
a lot of bad thoughts in people's heads, and it was very unjust.
I told him face-to-face why I held up those contracts. He was
saying that Jack Pastore had too much authority, but when
Dallas was the director he had an extra guy, Howie Bedell,
helping to supervise the farm system. He finally fired *him*. So
this year we did the job with fewer people, just as well, except
that there wasn't as much back-stabbin' and stuff in the background."

Bill Giles ultimately supported Baumer and Pastore, but only
after some heavy lobbying and the promise of new economies
in scouting. The Phillies would not be hiring replacements for
Davis, Goldsberry, and Nickels; other scouts were simply going
to take on more work. And a few veterans, like Lou Kahn in
the south and Spider Jorgensen on the west coast, no longer
seemed indispensable.

In another year, it was rumored, Ruly Carpenter might return to baseball as a Phillies' scout, helping to take up some
of the slack in the mid-Atlantic area. It was an intriguing
thought—a young baseball man, tutored by Paul Owens, who
loved scouting so much that he'd do it for free—but it just
didn't figure. Ruly Carpenter now was a prince without a
throne. How could he be happy, or remain uninvolved, while
the new people made decisions their own way? Or what if
seeing an amateur game conflicted with a hunting trip? It was
hard to imagine a former owner with personal assets in eight
figures, maybe nine, becoming a scout. It would be like Jimmy
Carter becoming a county sheriff.

In December, just before the office Christmas party, Baumer
fired his own secretary, Liz Riordan. And skirmishing in the
Philadelphia office continued into the new year as other "Green
people," like Ruben Amaro, came under closer scrutiny. The
Phillies' scouting system was beginning to contract, while the
Cubs' system was on the verge of major expansion. Dallas

Green was already spending big money on the player-development approach that had worked so well before. He was adding another farm team, hiring more coaches and scouts, and getting ready to withdraw the Cubs from the Major League Scouting Bureau.

"Wouldn't it be ironic," Brandy Davis asked me, "after all these years of talk in Philadelphia about the Bureau being creeping socialism and the death of scouting—wouldn't it be ironic if, just when the Cubs were resigning from it, the Phillies were getting ready to join?"

The Phillies, Baumer said, were not about to join the Bureau—at least not any time soon. "The reason our cutbacks make sense," he said, "is that we already had the biggest scouting staff in the game."

The Phillies' cutbacks at the end of 1981 were the exception rather than the rule in scouting. Throughout the major leagues, for the second straight year, scouting was on the upswing as teams like the A's, the Braves, and even the Indians offered competitive salaries to build up their staffs. It was a good omen, indicating that most ballclubs in the 1980s would try to meet the challenge of the major-league players' new freedom by giving greater priority to homegrown talent.

Having lost on the main issue of the strike—the imposition of penalties against themselves for signing free agents—the owners could foresee players' salaries totaling about $130,000,000 in 1982. But instead of reducing spending in their scouting or minor-league systems, the owners were bringing player-development budgets to a new high of $65,000,000. That worked out to about $2,500,000 per team, half of it for scouting.

The reason the owners didn't invest even more heavily in scouting is that their own creation, the amateur draft system, imposed a law of diminishing returns. A team with a scouting budget of $1,800,000 might, just conceivably, double the results of a team with a scouting budget of $900,000. But the draft was a great equalizer, allowing an econo-scout organization like the Mariners to use its poor field record each October as a ticket to preferred amateur selections the following June. And to budget anything more than $1,800,000 for scouting seemed merely wasteful, because the quantity of available talent was finite and the best of it was locked up by drafting.

The majority of scouts I met believed that the draft system should be abolished, and their reasoning was compelling:

- The draft illegally constrains the young athlete's right to bargain. Only a very principled as well as talented amateur, a teen-aged Curt Flood, would ever force the issue all the way through the courts, but it was really the issue of the strike writ small—the worker's access to more than one potential employer in a monopoly system.
- Without a draft, the total of bonuses paid to all amateurs would rise very little, if at all; extra expenses would come primarily from hiring more and better scouts. The great dynasties of the pre-draft eras—the Giants under McGraw, the Yankees under Barrow and Weiss, the Cardinals and Dodgers under Rickey—had been built by outscouting other teams, not outbidding them. Open-checkbook owners, like Steinbrenner or Autry or Turner, would surely make some spectacular signings without a draft, perhaps even offering $400,000 (double the current record) to a premier high-school prospect. But for every such signing there would be twenty other players, currently drafted in the third round or below, who could be signed at well under their present market value—and several of them would be almost sure bets to outperform the $400,000 prospect.
- Abolishing the draft would invigorate player development at all levels, giving major-league organizations an incentive to increase, even double, their spending on the scouting and farm systems. In the process the

salaries of major-league players might level off naturally.

I had come to agree with the anti-draft scouts, but for a more personal reason. After spending the better part of a year with the forgotten men of baseball, I simply wanted to see what would happen if they were given *their* freedom, if they were turned loose to become full-fledged salesmen again and allowed to exercise all of their skills as mercenaries and visionaries.

Even working within a draft system, the scouts maintained their quirky individualism and penchant for intrigue. In the preceding twenty years they had been forced to cope not just with the draft but also with the Bureau, with competition from college coaches, with the drainage of talent, especially black talent, to other pro sports, and with the more unpredictable (but usually more relaxed) values of young American men. Their primary responsibility, putting the dollar sign on the muscle, was now trickier than ever. If the scouts were no longer real salesmen, they were still striving to be the most active kinds of investment analysts—detectives, touts, reconnaissance men, journalists, critics. Their business cards might as well have said: "Baseball Intelligence."

In the 1980s scouting had become timely again. But it would also remain timeless, transcending even the business side of the game. The scouts expressed their ultimate evaluations in the language of money, but their real language was more subtle, salty, funny, aesthetic, and even religious. In the year of the strike, while the owners and players traded recriminations, I listened to underpaid searchers talk about unspoiled kids, and what I heard seemed to get back to what made any of us care about professional sports in the first place: images of excellence, dreams of discovery, playfulness in the midst of rugged competition, and a readiness to see the extraordinary in the so-called commonplace. The voices of scouts were pathways to the past—to baseball history, to their own failed ambitions as athletes, and to the roots of the game in American life.

The wisdom of scouts is not science but *lore:* literally, what has been learned from experience. Their charts categorizing tools, makeup, and performance look objective enough, but the men who fill them in are the first to admit that they traffic in opinion—personal and hard-won opinion—rather than demonstrable fact. When they contrast themselves to scouts in other sports, baseball men point out that they have to judge young talent under more various circumstances and project it further into the future. But they do that by first traveling into the past. When Moose Johnson watched a high-school infielder named Walter "Bubby" Brister in 1981, he was reminded of Mike Schmidt; when Brandy Davis watched a college infielder named Mike Schmidt in 1971, he was reminded of Jim Fregosi. What both men call "intuition" may be simply the instantaneous scanning of images in well-stocked memory banks, but it's no less interesting for that. By the time a scout finishes looking at him, any given player is like the new writing on an old parchment, part of a palimpsest of talent that makes the lore of baseball continuous.

Scouts draw their logic from the structure of the game itself—a game demanding versatility more than specialization, looseness more than strength, and the ability to pay constant attention through long stretches of inactivity. Some scouts group these virtues under the general heading of "life," as in describing a player's live body or live reactions. Translated into psychological terms, they are the very virtues of breadth, extension, and depth that the scouts try to practice as spectators in their quest for talent. As a fellow spectator through a scouting year, I gained a fuller sense of life, both in and out of baseball.

All this led me, at the very end of the year, to the Great Unanswered Question of scouting. Not the good face—I'd given up on that one long before. The Great Unanswered Question was: What the hell is it about left-handed pitchers?

Do they really mature late? And if so, why? And why can they be little? At spring training, at the June draft, and at the Johnstown tournament I had heard scouts downgrade small right-handed pitchers, usually with the afterthought that the very same talents would be worth a lot of money if only the kids were left-handed. I thought about writing to Bill James, the dean of baseball statisticians, asking him to devote a few pages of his next *Baseball Abstract* to graphs of left-handed careers and formulas for left-handed mass. Instead, I posed the question to Jack Pastore, the Phillies' assistant scouting director, the man who—by his failure to respond to a letter he received in the fall—had, by implication, put a dollar sign of zero on my muscle.

"Would you have liked me any better as a lefty?" I asked.

"That wasn't the problem. Lefties don't mature *that* late."

"But why are they different? Why will scouts take a chance on a little lefty but not on a little righty with the same tools?"

"Little lefties have a much better track record—Billy Pierce, Bobby Shantz, Harvey Haddix, Randy Jones, Ron Guidry."

"But why should that be?"

"Well, lefties are rarer, so hitters—especially left-hand hitters—aren't as used to seeing them. And lefties usually have a better natural breaking pitch and more action on the fastball, because very few of them throw straight over the top. Most of them come three-quarters to sidearm, so they have a little more trouble with control. That's why they take longer to mature."

"Yes, but why don't they throw straight over the top?"

Pastore shrugged and gave as scientific an answer as any scout was ever likely to give to the Great Unanswered Question. "It could be the difference in the two different sides of the brain," he said. "Or maybe it's because of the way the earth tilts at its axis."

15 EPILOGUE

The baseball booby prize for 1982 belongs to Brewers General Manager Harry Dalton for suggesting that scouts be made eligible for Hall of Fame election. The Hall always should have been the sacred preserve of players and managers, period. . . . If scouts are allowed in, who's next? Groundskeepers and concessionaires?

—letter *to* The Sporting News *(January 10, 1983)*
from J. M. Murphy

Edward W. Stack, president of the Baseball Hall of Fame, noted recently that the eligibility rules for membership in the Hall had already been tinkered with several times in the 1970s, and so his board of directors was afraid that the average baseball fan would become confused if scouts were now made eligible. J. M. Murphy, whose letter is excerpted above, is probably the kind of fan who worries the board.

Murphy's letter is based on two unexamined assumptions: that scouts are simple menials whose work could be done by almost anybody; and that the Hall of Fame should be a "sacred preserve," as if its membership could be determined from on high instead of being subject to real-world special interests. The first assumption, I hope, has been abandoned by anyone who has read this far in the book. The second ought to be tested against the processes that actually influence the Hall's selection or rejection of players: elections achieved through family lobbying (Harry Hooper), elections delayed because of old grudges (Bill Terry), elections limited by convenient symbolism (ten black players representing all the decades of segregated baseball), or elections denied because of myopic attention to offensive statistics (catchers and shortstops in general).

Would it really dilute the recognition paid to Lou Gehrig if Paul Krichell were somehow honored in the same building? Or would it instead enhance Gehrig's memory by providing a fuller historical sense of the game? Does the Hall of Fame exist to legitimize the prejudices of the average fan or to correct those prejudices?

When I posed these questions to Harry Dalton, he thought that *prejudices* was too strong a word. "Scouts have never been in the limelight," he said, "and so most fans haven't had a way to understand the importance of scouts, much less to appreciate the incredible things they did in the eras before the draft. But general managers who've come up through scouting or farm systems, like me or like Hank Peters, see the inequity. The Hall of Fame honors executives and umpires as well as players and managers, but it hasn't found a way to honor men who gave themselves to the game, who *became* the game in order to find all that talent. I'm ready to help any way I can to make scouts eligible for the Hall. Right now, though, that battle is being fought single-handedly by Birdie Tebbetts."

Birdie Tebbetts is a former catcher, and—like Branch Rickey, Paul Krichell, Paul Florence, Paul Richards, and Howie Haak— he has brought a catcher's insights to bear on the recognition and evaluation of talent. He played in the major leagues for fourteen seasons and then managed major-league teams for another eleven, until a heart attack slowed him down. Since 1967 he has been a full-time scout, specializing in analysis at the major-league level but really covering all sides of the game. With the Yankees in the late 1970s he even negotiated on behalf of management to work out long-term contracts for players like Ron Guidry and Mickey Rivers. "What makes my job easier," Tebbetts says, "is that ballplayers know that I think like a ballplayer. And I'm regarded by baseball men as a baseball man."

Tebbetts is also a member of the Veterans' Committee of the Baseball Hall of Fame. At each of the committee's meetings since 1981 he has introduced a motion that the by-law on eligibility for selection be amended to include the word *scout*. Each year the committee has approved the motion emphatically, and each year the Hall's board of directors has simply tabled it without explanation.

"I really haven't tried to get press coverage on this," Tebbetts says, "because people don't understand. They see that I'm a scout and they figure that I'm thinking about myself. But I'm really thinking about the old scouts, the pre-war guys. Those scouts were a different breed, and there weren't many of them. They drove all over hell to find ballplayers, and they made final decisions *on their own* about how valuable the players were, and they competed to sign them. They weren't just leg men; they built ballclubs. And they never had a pension or a share in the things that other baseball people were given. I've been in every seat in baseball, and I'd have to say that the old-time scouts were the most important people I ever came in contact with."

One of those old scouts, Eddie Goostree, played a key role in Tebbetts's own career. Goostree was the Detroit Tigers' scout who found and signed such players as Schoolboy Rowe, Hub and Gee Walker, Tommy Bridges, Rudy York, Whitlow Wyatt, Claude Passeau, Virgil Trucks, and Dizzy Trout. In 1934 Goostree traveled to Beaumont, Texas, to size up a few of the Tigers' farmhands who were being considered for sale or trade. His report to the front office stated that catcher George Tebbetts should not be surrendered but should in fact be promoted toward the majors as soon as possible. In 1982 Goostree's widow wrote to Tebbetts expressing the hope that her husband, whose name remains unfamiliar even to knowledgeable older fans, might finally be honored in some way by major-league baseball.

But Tebbetts insists that he's not trying to get any single scout into the Hall of Fame. "If I were just fighting on behalf of Eddie Goostree, then the Cardinals would argue that it ought to be Charlie Barrett, and the Yankees would say it should be Paul Krichell. That's not my point. I'm not pushing any specific candidate. I just want to get the wording of the rule changed so that scouts *can* be recognized. Maybe the old scouts will ultimately be honored as a group, in the form of a single plaque. If that's the only way it can be done, then so be it. And if not that, then at least I'd like to hear somebody on that board of directors explain why the word *scout* shouldn't be added. I'd just like to hear that speech.

"Almost every general manager in baseball has offered to help put my proposal across, but I've been stubborn enough to say no. I'll just continue to do my job and place it before the board of directors each year until somebody sees the logic of what I'm talking about. Because I'm bound to win."

POSTSCRIPT, FALL 1988

At the end of the 1980s the world of baseball scouting seemed to have grown smaller. Frontiers were closing—every team was fishing in the Caribbean now—and team philosophies were less distinct. The job of scouting itself was a little more standardized, more narrowly defined by structures like the draft and the Bureau. And some of the giants of the game were gone. Baseball men who thought ahead to twenty-first-century scouting sometimes wondered what room would be left for the traditional values of the profession.

In the course of the decade scouts were tamed a little in Latin America and a lot on junior college campuses by new rules designed to curb "abuses" of the open market. It was no longer possible to grab players from the Dominican as freely as the Phillies had once grabbed Julio Franco and Juan Samuel, by using intermediaries to tie up sixteen-year-olds with small bonuses (like the Escogido club, run by scout Qui-Que Acevedo). And it was no longer possible to sign players out of junior-college programs in the fall, as the Phillies had once signed Marty Bystrom and Chris James. Responding to pressure from the NCAA, the major-league teams agreed that any boy entering a J.C. program would remain untouchable until the end of the following spring season. The January draft thus became unimportant enough to be dropped in 1987.

One result was that the annual June lottery ballooned in significance and size. In June 1981—in the draft reported here in Chapter 9—926 players were selected in 44 regular-phase rounds. In June 1988 a record 1,432 players were selected in 76 rounds. Ballclubs were doing more drafting partly to fill out the rosters of new farm clubs (the number of minor-league affiliates was up) and partly to gamble on high-school kids with academic difficulties (college entrance requirements had been stiffened by the NCAA's Proposition 48). But the main reason for all the drafting was a new determination to "control" prospects even while scouting them. In the absence of a January draft, a boy's freedom to bargain was constrained for a full year, so it now made more sense to stake claims on potential J.C. players before they even enrolled. For example, a raw high-school prospect could be drafted in June and scouted over the summer. If he then entered a J.C. program, he could be scouted in more depth through the fall and spring seasons, and perhaps finally be tendered a serious offer just before the next June draft.

The expansion of the draft was preceded by expansion of the Major League Scouting Bureau. In December 1983, at the baseball winter meetings in Nashville, general managers voted 15–11 to make Bureau membership mandatory. Each of the twenty-six teams was required, starting in September 1984, to pay $85,000 a year in return for a steady stream of computerized reports from the Bureau's sixty scouts. According to Dallas Green, then the Cubs' general manager, passage of the measure represented the tyranny of the majority. "All fifteen of the *Yes* votes came from teams that already belonged to the Bureau. They were saying: 'The rest of you have to subscribe to this service whether you think it's any good or not.' "

Mandatory membership was really a strategy for keeping the Bureau alive. In 1982 the Cubs and Giants had dropped out, and in 1983 the Royals and Yankees were thinking about leaving. If membership fell to thirteen teams (a mere half of the major-league clubs), then either the dues would become prohibitive or the quality of information would suffer. John Schuerholz, the Royals' general manager, thought that the dues were already too high, because Bureau information wasn't very confidential. "There's leakage of Bureau reports to non-member clubs," Schuerholz said, "so they get information for free that the rest of us are paying for."

Seattle general manager Hal Keller, sponsor of the measure, said that the problem of confidentiality was the fault not of the Bureau but of "burglary-minded scouts from non-member teams." In any case, Keller argued, mandatory membership would not only lower the dues; it would make confidentiality irrelevant.

Over the next few years some of the new Bureau teams came up with their $85,000 by cutting personnel. The Orioles, for example, fired four full-time scouts in areas where they regarded the Bureau's local scouts as above average. Other teams, like the Blue Jays, restricted their cuts to part-timers. And a few, like the Cubs, made it a point of honor to fire no one, to leave Bureau reports unread, and to stay on record as opposing "socialized scouting."

But the most striking trend was initiated by old Bureau teams, like the Tigers and Mets, who hired new scouts and allotted new money to back them up. Instead of fighting the Bureau, these teams supplemented it with fresh troops of their own. The Tigers' full-time staff, which had been slashed to five in the mid-1970s when the Bureau began operating, was rebuilt to eighteen in the mid-1980s. The Mets used extra manpower to zero in on high-school talent, always a more expensive commodity, and their scouts were among those who began to complain that the problem of confidentiality had surfaced in a new way. College coaches, the scouts' competitors for high-school prospects, now seemed to have an easy time acquiring Bureau information.

The trend toward hiring led Gerry Craft, an area scout for the Astros, to establish the Professional Baseball Scout School in 1987. In each of its twelve-day sessions, the PBSS provides about one hundred hours of classroom and on-field instruction: analysis of tools by position, systems of grading, actual evaluation of prospects, use of radar guns, determination of signability, scenarios of signing, and the legal and ethical limits of scouting. The faculty has included such scouting luminaries as George Genovese, Jesse Flores, and Al Kubski. Of the sixty-six PBSS graduates in 1987 and 1988, more than half had jobs with major-league organizations by 1989, and five had become full-time scouts. But the school has scaled back admissions until the next big hiring breakthrough: major-league expansion.

Salaries did not improve much in the 1980s, and most new area scouts were still under $20,000. So scouting directors, even while demanding thorough baseball backgrounds, looked for young recruits. Ellis Clary said, "Everybody wants a nineteen-year-old with twenty years' experience." In 1981 some of the young scouts, like Gary Nickels and Bob Engle, had hoped to move out of scouting and into executive roles. But like Nickels and Engle, those scouts were more likely by 1989 to have become regional cross-checkers, traveling even more than they had as area scouts. "I thought I wanted an office job," Engle said, "and I could've had a good one in Toronto. But after you've been on the road for a few years, you hate to give up the independence of it."

As the young scouts became middle-aged, they took on more and more of the mannerisms and attitudes of their veteran teachers. Talking to them, it was easy to believe that—despite all the changes—the heart and soul of scouting would never go out of style. Radar guns were here to stay; videotapes were now commonly used by cross-checkers to "pre-scout" and by scouting directors to settle disputes at draft meetings; portable equipment for testing bat speed would soon be on the market; the Mets were relying more heavily on psychological testing; and the Pirates were reviving some notions of physical testing from the old Royals' Academy. Sure, sure, the forty-year-old scouts would say, but all those are just *tools*. In the year 2081 some crusty old guy would still be behind a backstop trying to convert all the other numbers into dollars, and to do that he would have to draw on memories, feelings, and values. He might even chew tobacco, say "horseshit," and believe in the good face.

The saddest change in scouting during the 1980s was simply the disappearance of so many great individual baseball men. It was a changing of the guard, with fewer and fewer scouts still active who knew what it was like to operate without a draft. Some veterans, like Socko and Broadway Charlie, became semi-retired "consultants." Others retired because they had to: Spud Chandler, no longer able at seventy-eight to take the grueling travel; Al Campanis, an easy target after stating on national TV that blacks lacked the "necessities" to succeed as major-league managers and executives. Lou Kahn and Jim Russo retired happily. Leon Hamilton retired but kept one foot in the door, probably out of habit.

And there were the deaths: Paul Florence, who logged fifty-seven years in professional baseball, every single season a study in class; Ed Katalinas, who excelled in three different eras of scouting; and Jocko Collins, the first to leave, and most genuinely beloved by other scouts. "I never heard him utter a dishonest word," Joe Reilly said. Jocko had resigned from the Brewers' staff in 1982 to undergo eye surgery but later resumed basketball scouting as a consultant for the Philadelphia '76ers. At a testimonial dinner in January 1984, about a year before Jocko's death, Tom Lasorda began the festivities by toasting the man who had signed him many years before: "To one of the greatest scouts in the history of baseball."

Ellis Clary, still working tirelessly, said, "I ain't goin'. I done been." The last active member of The Underground had taken a new job as all-purpose scout and instructor for the Blue Jays. When he hired Clary, Toronto vice-president Bobby Mattick explained, "I needed help in knocking down a lot of these theories the younger guys have come up with." Earlier, Clary had left the Twins when the Griffith family sold control of the franchise, and he was one of several scouts who had to forge new baseball loyalties after turning seventy. Just before Howie Haak was to begin his thirty-eighth season with the Pirates, he was bounced out by Syd Thrift and then quickly hired by the Astros. In March 1988, on his way from California to spring training in Florida, he heard that another baseball man had referred to him as "old." Haak was 77. For the next day and a half he drove his Cadillac (spittoon and all) without a break from Phoenix, Arizona to Perry, Florida—2,028 miles— then camped at a cheap motel in Bradenton and began driving all over the state on baseball day trips.

Some shifts of individual allegiance were directly related to shifts in team scouting strength. During Dallas Green's tenure as general manager (1981–87), the Cubs hired half a dozen scouts from the Phillies' 1981 staff: Hugh Alexander, Ruben Amaro, Brandy Davis, Gordon Goldsberry, Lou Kahn, and Gary Nickels. "It wasn't just personnel that got transplanted," Brandy Davis said. "It was an idea." Davis believed that a whole crop of home-grown talent (Dunston, Grace, Lancaster, Maddux, Moyer, Palmiero) was the result of that transplant. At the end of the 1988 season, however, the Cubs fired Gordon Goldsberry and Gary Nickels.

The Phillies themselves represented an even more dramatic shift of strength. They had dominated the N.L. East from 1976 to 1983 by following the path of player development. By 1988 the Phillies were a second-division ballclub with a depleted farm system. When publications like *Baseball America* evaluated development programs, the Phillies were routinely ranked near the bottom. To make matters worse, in such rankings five of the top ten slots were usually occupied by the other teams in the N.L. East: the Cubs, Mets, Cardinals, Pirates, and Expos.

In Philadelphia it was fashionable to blame Bill Giles, principal owner in the consortium that bought the team in 1981. In the first three years of the Giles era, the Phillies traded away two dozen prospects, including Ryne Sandberg, Julio Franco, and Lance McCullers. Then they announced a commitment to youth, just as the pipeline of talent was running dry. As late as July 1987 Giles claimed that the Philadelphia farm system was teeming with future major-leaguers. "We have more than anybody," he said. Then in June 1988 he demoted Jim Baumer from scouting and farm director to just plain scout. At the same time new general manager Woody Woodward, Baumer's biggest critic, was fired.

But even before the Giles era began, some glimmers of future failure may have been evident and may, by chance, be preserved in the pages of this book—some confusion in the chain of command, for example, with wonderfully detailed reports coming in from the field but no consistent channeling of that information. In 1980 the Phillies' national cross-checker said that one player was not even a prospect; however, that player then became the club's first-round draft choice. And in hindsight, the 1981 draft was an almost total washout; by 1988 only one Philadelphia selection was in the majors (Charles Hudson of the Yankees), and only one was still in the Philadelphia organization (Jim Olander at Class AAA).

Maybe the Phillies disliked the draft so much that they just weren't very good at drafting. Even in Dallas Green's heyday as scouting director, the club's first-round picks were rarely successful. The Phillies were great spokesmen for free enterprise and seemed to have excellent luck with undrafted players, all the way from Larry Bowa to Marty Bystrom, Don Carman, and Jeff Stone. In 1981 the undrafted find was Chris James, signed by Doug Gassaway, the area scout for Texas and Oklahoma. Until 1985 Gassaway, a protégé of Hugh Alexander, was given the lion's share of picks in the January and June drafts. Among his winners were Keith Moreland and Bruce Ruffin, but the Phillies had committed themselves so heavily to sunbelt talent that the most productive scout in the organization, Tony Lucadello in the midwest, might as well have put his draft list in a time capsule. Philadelphia sportswriter Bill Conlin offered this composite description of an early-round Philadelphia pick: "Billy Bob Crewcut from Cradle of Liberty Junior College in True Grit, Oklahoma—somebody who will go out and hit .212 at Batavia, .190 in the Florida Instructional League, .235 at Spartanburg, and be quietly released."

In 1986 Gassaway was gone too. He quit after a series of arguments with Baumer, then signed a better contract with the Texas Rangers. Hugh Alexander made his own dissatisfaction public, then quit to join the Chicago Cubs and begin his second half-century as a baseball scout. Maybe a student of management would have seen the Phillies' organization in the 1980s as an ongoing power vacuum, or as an executive analogue to all the wheeling and dealing with players. Rich Ashburn, who knew the organization as well as anyone, thought that the scouting program was a case study in the Peter Principle: "The line on Baumer always has been that he is a great judge of talent while working in the system, but not so great sitting behind a desk trying to run the system."

The Baltimore Orioles were another strong player-development team that hit bottom at the end of the decade. A change in philosophy was evident in 1984 when the Orioles signed three established free agents (Fred Lynn, Lee Lacy, Don Aase), and then had to abstain from the first three rounds of the June 1985 draft. The organization had been respected for its brainpower since the days of Jim McLaughlin, but its scouts and executives were too easily hired away by other clubs. And even as the Orioles were sinking, four of the strongest player-development teams in baseball were being run by ex-Baltimore men: Frank Cashen (Mets), Harry Dalton (Brewers), John Schuerholz (Royals), and Lou Gorman (Red Sox).

General managers accorded greater recognition to scouts in the 1980s and were almost unanimous in supporting Birdie Tebbetts's efforts to make scouts eligible for the Hall of Fame. (In 1988 Tebbetts still thought that victory was just a question of time. While he waited, he was relaxed enough to joke. "You know who should *really* be in the Hall of Fame? Scouts' wives.") By contrast, owners' attitudes toward scouts varied enormously. When Marge Schott took over the Cincinnati Reds, one of the most tradition-minded organizations in the game, she suggested saving money by cutting the scouting staff in half. "Scouts don't do anything but watch baseball games," Schott said. And in New York, when one sportswriter studied the Yankees' media guides and announced that twenty scouts had been let go over three years, that organization took its major-league revenge by omitting any reference to scouts in subsequent guides.

In 1984 the scouts themselves created the Scout-of-the-Year Award. It was conceived by Tony Pacheco and Jim Russo, promoted by general manager Al Rosen, and sponsored by Topps gum and Coors beer. When Howie Haak was honored as the first recipient of the award, some baseball men suggested that Red Man tobacco should have been a cosponsor.

Beginning in 1985 three awards were given each year—for the eastern, central, and western U.S.—in order to recognize area scouts whose achievements had transcended their own territories and their own ballclubs. Among these recipients was Tony Lucadello, the midwestern legend, whose endless quest for talent by 1986 had led to 2,000,000 career auto miles (four round trips to the moon) and forty-nine major-league signees. Another award winner was Dale McReynolds of the Dodgers, who had broken into scouting under Jim McLaughlin and then patrolled the north-central U.S. for thirty-five seasons. Mc-Reynolds was the author of *The Baseball Scout's Handbook*, a forty-five page typescript distilling the lessons of a lifetime. After all the advice on coverage, judgment, and signing, the manual concluded: "There is no starting point in your job as a scout, nor is there an end. *The season is always.* You just dive in and no matter where or when you enter, you just keep going. Somewhere out there is a player you will seek and find and sign and he'll make it all worthwhile."

In the late 1980s McReynolds believed more than ever in looking at a prospect in terms of Jim McLaughlin's chart, "The Whole Ball Player." What couldn't be seen with the eye, but what absolutely needed to be determined, was whether a boy had the inner qualities to survive and learn from the rigors of minor-league baseball. The path of professional ball was arduous, and at the end of the decade some of the most promising players of 1981 were still at class AA or AAA. A 1987 article in *Baseball America* reported on Vance Lovelace and Charles

Penigar, high drafts in 1981, who had been released by two other clubs before signing with the Angels' organization. After seven pro seasons each player was still trying to gain a firm foothold. The headline read: "Last Chance for Failed Prospects."

Stories like that remain compelling to me, because I have been trying in a general way to keep track of the players mentioned in this book. Charting their destinies provides another set of perspectives on a scouting year. The perspectives are incomplete, of course. Because of my limited space and intuition, a few of the most successful draftees from 1981 are nowhere to be found in the preceding pages: Mark Langston (drafted number 35 overall), Frank Viola (37), Tony Gwynn (58), Sid Fernandez (74), David Cone (75), John Franco (126), Mike Pagliarulo (156), Lenny Dykstra (316), and Danny Cox (320). Player number 200, drafted by the Expos on the eighth round, was a high-school *pitcher* named Mark McGwire from Claremont, California. He didn't sign. He went to Southern Cal, the Oakland A's, and first base.

Scouting requires and sometimes breeds humility. Frank Viola of St. John's, for example, did not surface as a Group One pitcher for most scouts until just before the 1981 June draft when he outdueled Ron Darling of Yale in a twelve-inning championship game. Darling pitched a no-hitter for eleven innings, but Viola won 1–0. Most cross-checkers who saw that game, like Brandy Davis of the Phillies and Bill Werle of the Orioles, tried to boost Viola's stock at the last minute— whereas Herb Stein, the Twins' scout who eventually signed Viola, had been touting that stock to the organization for almost three years.

And Tony Gwynn may represent the success of a third-round pick whom a ballclub is able to scout thoroughly in its own city over the course of a college career. Gwynn starred in both baseball and basketball at San Diego State; he was even selected in the NBA draft by another hometown team, the San Diego Clippers. Brandy Davis's only report on Gwynn (dated April 25, 1981) included these notes: "Competitor, athletic, mature.

Husky, barrel-chested, strong body and legs, Gary Matthews lookalike." Davis liked Gwynn $32,000—in the money range for a third-round pick—but he rated the arm below average and projected the player as "American League DH–type."

As college prospects, both Viola and Gwynn were supposed to advance quickly if at all, and both zipped to the majors in a season and a half. Gwynn was a success from the start. Viola was a late-maturing lefty who had to learn how to throw a changeup and how to control his temper.

Those two stories are happy and thus atypical. All of the first ten players drafted in 1981 went on to play in the majors, but the majority of prospects in this book have had no such luck. Many of the paragraphs below tell of hitters who topped out at Class AA, or pitchers who were betrayed by their own arms. What cannot really be told here is the quality of mind and heart those players brought to the game. The paragraphs are impossibly condensed—any of them could conceivably be a chapter in itself—but together they may provide a mosaic of one year's talent. For all players like these, and for the scouts who follow them, here's hoping that the season is always.

High-school pitcher *Jon Abrego* (Chapters 8, 9) was the Phillies' first-round draft (number 20 overall) in June 1981. He was signed by scout Eddie Bockman for a bonus of $70,000. The story of Abrego's pro career is a chronicle of arm problems. After a promising first year, he underwent reconstructive elbow surgery and then sat out all of 1982. In December 1983, when he was still recuperating, the Cubs claimed him for $25,000 in the minor-league draft. Abrego had a cup of coffee in the majors in September 1985: 1–1 with a 6.38 ERA in six games. His one big-league victory came against the Phillies. He toiled through four more minor-league seasons—and a shoulder operation—before being released, at age 25, out of spring training in 1988.

High-school pitcher *Bill Babcock* (Chapter 9) was a premium prospect who told some scouts that he wanted a bonus of

$90,000. Most put a lower dollar sign on Babcock, and Brandy Davis used the old line "Pitchers are like racehorses" to explain why he was nervous about ever recommending big bonuses for young arms. Babcock was drafted by the White Sox on the third round (number 59 overall) and was signed by scouts Larry Monroe and Walter Widmayer. He turned out to be a racehorse who broke down early, missing an entire season with arms problems in 1983, pitching 27 innings in 1984, and getting his release in 1985. Babcock's highest minor-league level was Class AA.

Major-league outfielder *Harold Baines* (Chapter 11) became an A.L. all-star in 1983, and until 1988 his "average" season was about .290 with 23 home runs and 99 RBI. But a series of knee injuries and operations at the end of 1987 turned Baines into a designated hitter, and in 1988 (age 29) he fell to .277 with 13 home runs and 81 RBI. Baines was originally selected by the White Sox as the number one player in the 1977 June draft. He was signed by scouts Benny Huffman, Walt Widmayer, and Paul Richards for around $50,000, about half what the premier player in the June draft usually received in the 1970s. The first person to "discover" Baines was Bill Veeck, former president of the White Sox, who saw him as a Little-Leaguer in 1971, two years before Baines showed up as an illegal fourteen-year-old at one of Joe Reilly's tryout camps.

High-school pitcher *Ricky Barlow* (Chapter 9) was one of Tony Roig's "loosy-goosy" black players in 1981. That June he was the Tigers' first-round draft (number 17 overall) and was signed by scout Hoot Evers. Despite a fluid motion, Barlow was yet another young pitcher plagued with arm trouble in the minors, and his record over seven years was 23–55. Barlow became a free agent in 1988 and went to spring training with the Chicago White Sox. Five weeks later he was given his unconditional release.

Minor-league outfielder *George Bell* (Chapter 12) became an established major-leaguer in 1984. In 1987 he was named the A.L.'s Most Valuable Player, hitting .308 with 47 home runs and 134 RBI. In 1988, after challenging an attempt by management to convert him from a leftfielder to a designated hitter, he slipped to .264 with 24 home runs and 97 RBI. From the very birth of its franchise, three main targets of Toronto scouting have been Latins, all-around athletes, and minor-leaguers in other organizations. In acquiring Bell in 1980, the Blue Jays hit the trifecta.

College outfielder *Terry Blocker* (Chapters 8, 9) was the Mets' first-round draft in June 1981 and was signed by scout Joe Mason. Blocker was fourth player chosen, and as such he is the biggest disappointment so far. In over seven seasons in the Mets organization he had only fifteen major-league at-bats (one hit) and was traded to Atlanta in 1988 at age twenty-seven. In spring training the Braves' centerfield job was his to lose, and he lost it. A week into the 1988 season Blocker was demoted to Richmond for a sixth year at AAA, and in late May he became so frustrated that he quit the team. He returned two weeks later for "one more shot." Promoted to the majors for the last two months of the season, Blocker hit .212 with 2 home runs and 10 RBI.

College pitcher *Greg Brake* (Chapter 12) was an outstanding performer at the 1981 AAABA tournament in Johnstown. Scouts described him as the classic example of "a little lefty with stuff." Brake was not selected in baseball's amateur draft until 1984, after his senior season at Western Michigan University, when the Oakland A's selected him on the ninth round. He was signed by scout Del Wilber. That summer Brake pitched at Medford, Oregon (Class A), where he simply overmatched younger hitters and ended the season 12–0 with a 1.76 ERA. It was all downhill from there, and over the next two years he had progressively less success with hitters his own age. In July 1986 the A's gave Brake his unconditional release.

High-school shortstop *Walter "Bubby" Brister* (Chapter 9) was cited by scout Moose Johnson in 1981 as the prime example of a prospect with a great body. Brister was the Tigers' fourth-round draft in June (number 95 overall) and was signed by scouts Johnny Young and Bill Lajoie, who had to compete against Alabama football coach Bear Bryant. In his first pro season Brister hit .208 against rookie-league pitching. Then he joined the Tigers' winter-league team at Lakeland and broke his hand on the first pitch of his first game. The hand healed in time for spring training in 1982, but Brister chose not to report. "I had trouble adjusting to the style of life in the minor leagues," he says, "and I decided that my future was in football after all." Brister went on to play football at Northeast Louisiana University in his hometown of Monroe, and he is now a quarterback for the Pittsburgh Steelers.

High-school outfielder *Tony Brown* (Chapter 14) was not drafted in 1981 but was signed that October by Philadelphia scout George Farson for a bonus of $10,000. In seven minor-league seasons (through 1988) Brown has averaged almost .300 with fair power and above-average speed. In 1989, at age twenty-seven, he figures to be promoted to Class AAA for a full season.

Minor-league pitcher *Don Carman* (Chapters 3, 11) stood out at spring training in 1981 simply by winning so often at games of "Flip." He was gangly but coordinated, a lefty whose breaking pitch disassembled the swings of lefty hitters. Carman had been undrafted in 1978, but Philadelphia scouts Don Williams and Doug Gassaway signed him that August on the basis of his performance at a tryout camp. In 1984, his sixth professional season, Carman broke into the majors as a relief pitcher. He is now an established starter with a career record of 42–35 (through 1988) and two near-no-hitters. Scouts say that Carman is erratic but still improving at age twenty-nine, and he has trade value.

College outfielder *Joe Carter* (Chapters 8, 9) was the Cubs' first-round draft in June 1981 (number 2 overall) and was signed by scout Buck O'Neil. In 1984, after three impressive minor-league seasons, Carter was traded to Cleveland and was immediately promoted to the majors. From 1986 through 1988 he averaged about .278 with 29 home runs and 108 RBI a season. Carter is an all-around athlete who starred in three sports in high school—and before that, at age thirteen, he lied about his age in order to attend major-league tryout camps.

High-school outfielder *David Cochrane* (Chapter 9) was cited by scout Gordon Goldsberry in 1981 as a prime example of a prospect with "the good face." That June he was the Mets' fourth-round draft (number 82 overall) and was signed by scout Roger Jongewaard. Cochrane is a switch-hitter with power from both sides, but his shot at the majors has been delayed by too many strikeouts and by uncertainty about where to play him. In eight minor-league seasons (through 1988) Cochrane has rotated from third base to first base to designated hitter— and in 1987 at Hawaii he even pitched occasionally. He was traded to the Mariners in 1988, and at Calgary (Class AAA) he hit .286 with 15 home runs and 61 RBI. Most scouts no longer regard Cochrane as a major-league prospect.

College outfielder *Vince Coleman* (Chapter 9) was the Phillies' twentieth-round draft in June 1981 (number 514 overall). Philadelphia scout Andy Seminick wrote: "This boy runs better than anyone I have seen since I began scouting." Coleman turned down the Phillies' $10,000 offer and returned to Florida A & M for his senior season. In 1982 the Cardinals drafted him on the tenth round (he was signed by scout Marty Maier) and began converting him into a switch-hitter. Coleman became one of George Kissell's projects. In 1983, his second pro season, he batted .352 at Macon (Class A) and stole 145 bases, a pro baseball record, despite missing 32 games with a leg injury. He broke into the major leagues in 1985 and set a new rookie record with 110 stolen bases. By 1988 he was still the league's preeminent speedster but had become a multi-dimensional player, with steady improvement at the plate and in the outfield. Branch Rickey might say that Coleman had traveled "over the horizon."

College outfielder *Willard Currier* (Chapter 9) was the mystery player who became the Phillies' sixth-round draft in June 1981 (number 150 overall). He was signed by scout Dick Lawlor for a bonus of $12,000. In 1981 and 1982 Currier played in Class A, averaging .228 each season. His other tools—power, speed, arm—were slightly poorer than described in Lawlor's initial report. In May 1983 the Phillies gave Currier his unconditional release.

College pitcher *Ron Darling* (Chapters 5, 8, 9), a junior at Yale in 1981, was rated by many scouts as the best pitcher eligible in the June draft. But in the first round he was chosen behind two other pitchers, Mike Moore and Matt Williams; the Rangers took Darling as number 9 overall. His stock had dropped after he hired an agent. His signing with Texas required high-level negotiations and is officially credited to the general manager, Eddie Robinson, rather than a scout. In 1982 Darling was traded to the Mets; in 1984 he became a regular major-league starter. In his first five seasons he has lived up to what the scouts envisioned, although Howie Haak claims that Darling is "consistent in an erratic sort of way." Darling has lots of no-decisions, but through 1988 his career record was 73–41. He is an excellent fielding pitcher and still swings a good bat.

Major-league pitcher *Mark Davis* (Chapter 13) contracted tendinitis in 1981 and finished his short rookie season at 1–4 with a 7.74 ERA. He had originally been drafted in January 1979 and signed by scout Eddie Bockman. Eventually Davis was traded to San Francisco, where he was an unsuccessful starter (5–17 in 1984); and then to San Diego, where he was used strictly as a relief pitcher. In 1988, at age twenty-seven,

Davis became one of the top relievers in the N.L., with 28 saves and a 2.01 ERA. He has lost a couple of feet off the fastball but has gained command of a wicked curve, and he now thinks in terms of ground balls more than strikeouts.

High-school shortstop *David Denny* (Chapters 9, 14) was the Phillies' seventeenth-round draft in June 1981 (number 436 overall). Instead of signing, he enrolled at the University of Texas. As he grew heavier and stronger, and a step slower, Denny was converted to a third baseman. He was a power hitter with a high percentage of strikeouts. In June 1984 he was drafted by the A's on the tenth round, but again he chose not to sign. In his senior year at Texas he remained undrafted. That summer the Phillies, who had offered Denny a $35,000 bonus four years earlier, signed him for $1,000. At age twenty-two he played an unimpressive year at Class A, adjusting with difficulty to the use of a wooden bat, and in 1986 he was given his unconditional release.

High-school infielder *Shawon Dunston* (Chapter 12) was not yet signable in 1981, but the scouts at Johnstown daydreamed about him anyway. By the spring of 1982 Dunston was the most coveted baseball prospect in America. At Thomas Jefferson High in Brooklyn, he hit .790 and stole 37 bases in 37 attempts. In June the Cubs drafted Dunston as the number one prospect in the nation, and he was signed by scout Gary Nickels for a bonus of $135,000. In 1986, his first complete major-league season, Dunston hit 17 home runs. In 1988 he became a leadoff hitter but drew only 16 walks all season. He hit .249 with fair power and great speed; afield he was spectacular but inconsistent. At the end of the season Dunston seemed likely to be traded.

College outfielder *John Elway* (Chapter 9) was the Yankee's second-round draft in June 1981 (number 52 overall). Although he signed with scout Gary Hughes for a bonus of $125,000, he retained eligibility for two more seasons of football at Stanford. Elway became an All-America quarterback, and in spring 1983 the Baltimore Colts drafted him as the number one football player in the country. He refused to consider any offers from the Colts and, using his baseball career as a threat, forced a trade to the Denver Broncos. It seems obvious that Elway made the right career choice. In summer 1982, his last season in baseball, he batted .318 in 42 games at Oneonta (Class A), but today it is hard to find a baseball man outside the Yankee organization who admits to having taken Elway seriously as a major-league candidate.

High-school outfielder *Charles Faucette* (Chapter 9) was the Blue Jays' twelfth-round draft in June 1981 (number 291 overall). He was signed by scout Bob Engle, who came up with enough bonus money to outbid the football coaches at UCLA. But Faucette didn't take minor-league life very seriously—especially at Medicine Hat (Class A), where he played only 29 games in 1982 and hit .130. In 1983 he chose not to report to spring training. By that time, he was on a football scholarship at the University of Maryland. In 1987 Faucette was drafted as a defensive specialist by the New York Giants; he failed to make the team, but then played three games for the Giants as a "replacement player" during the NFL strike.

Minor-league shortstop *Julio Franco* (Chapter 14) was originally signed in 1976 by Qui-Que Acevedo, the Phillies' Dominican scout, for a bonus of $4,500. In five minor-league seasons he hit with good power and great consistency, but several Philadelphia scouts and coaches thought his fielding and his behavior were too erratic. In 1982 he was traded to Cleveland as the key figure in the "five for one" acquisition of Von Hayes. Franco broke into the majors for good in 1983 and played five solid seasons at shortstop, then made a successful conversion to second base in 1988. At the plate, despite a radically coiled stance and "wrapped" bat, he has surprising bat speed and discipline. At the start of the 1989 season Franco, still only twenty-seven, had 1059 career hits and a .295 career average.

Minor-league pitcher *Richie Gaynor* (Chapter 3) was originally scouted as a high-school outfielder. The Phillies drafted him on the sixth round in June 1980, and he was signed by scout Eddie Bockman. At spring training in 1981, when Gaynor began his conversion to pitching, most scouts wrote him off as a "little righty" (5'10" and 170 pounds) who, by definition, had no future. He did his best to prove them wrong—at Class AA in 1983, for example, when he was 13–3 with a 2.48 ERA. But after Gaynor struggled at Class AAA and then underwent knee surgery, the Phillies gave up on him. In 1987 he joined the White Sox organization, became a relief pitcher, and developed a very effective knuckleball. When he reinjured his knee during a bench-clearing brawl in June 1988, Gaynor was once again released. In retrospect, he thinks that baseball men may have penalized him because of his size, even though he filled out to 185 pounds. "Or maybe," he says, "the problem was that I wasn't *supposed* to make it, so no scout or executive had much of a stake in my success."

Amateur pitcher *Hertford Gibbs* (Chapter 11) threw impressively at a tryout camp in 1981, but he turned out to be no prospect at all. He was scouted by one of the Phillies' part-timers, Aldie Livingston, who drove to Houston, Delaware, to see Gibbs pitch in the Atlantic Coast League, a small and almost exclusively black amateur circuit. Gibbs gave up five hits and six walks in less than two innings. But when Livingston tried to leave, he was forcibly detained by a dozen fans who made him drink cold beer, eat some of the best fried chicken in the Delmarva region, and scout the game instead of the player.

High-school pitcher *Dwight Gooden* (Chapter 6) was just a junior in 1981, and was only a name to most scouts when Leon Hamilton cited him as a better pitching prospect than

Vance Lovelace, his much-heralded teammate. In June 1982 Gooden was the Mets' first-round draft (number 5 overall) and was signed by scout Carlos Pascual. Gooden's progress was meteoric. In 1984 he jumped to the majors at age nineteen and became the N.L. Rookie of the Year. In 1985 he won the N.L. Cy Young Award. Veteran scouts, trying to find a precedent for such early success by a big right-hander with great poise and the overpowering fastball, repeatedly compared Gooden with Bob Feller. He underwent treatment for a drug problem in 1987 and emerged as still a great, if no longer transcendent, pitcher. His breaking pitches have lost a little bite, but a 95 mph fastball takes up some of the slack. At the end of the 1988 season Gooden had a career record of 91–36 (.717) with 1067 strikeouts. He was not yet twenty-five.

High-school pitcher *Mark Grant* (Chapters 8, 9) was the Giants' first-round draft in June 1981 (number 10 overall) and was signed by scout Marty Miller. In three partial seasons at San Francisco, Grant was used both as a starter and reliever. Traded to San Diego in 1987, he became a regular starter—but through the 1988 season he was still showing only glimpses of the talent that had led many scouts in 1981, like Brandy Davis, to call him the best high-school pitcher in the nation. "It's like he goes two steps forward, one step back," said San Diego pitching coach Pat Dobson. Grant finished in 1988 at 2–8 with a 3.69 ERA. In 1989 he may once again be headed for the bullpen.

High-school pitcher *Chris Graves* (Chapter 11) performed well at one of Joe Reilly's tryout camps in 1981. He later enrolled at Towson State, where in 1984 his record was 9–0 with a 1.22 ERA. That summer he played for Johnny's Auto Sales, the perennially strong amateur team managed by Brewer scout Walter Youse, and he pitched successfully in the AAABA tournament at Johnstown. Graves was never offered a professional contract.

High-school shortstop *Jerry Holtz* (Chapters 9, 11, 14) was the Phillies' fourth-round draft in June 1981 (number 98 overall), but he turned down a $50,000 bonus and went to college. In three years at Villanova, Holtz set a school career record for home runs, but he was moved from shortstop to second base because of occasional bursitis in his throwing arm. "If I could go back and do it all over again," Holtz said in his junior year, "I guess I would've signed with the Phillies. But who the heck knew about starting a pro career out of high school? I didn't. I was eighteen and I'd been away from home about twice in my whole life. Joe Reilly and Jim Baumer thought that I let them down. They said they were 'baseball men' and that was all they lived for, but it blew my mind that neither one of them had ever been to college. They said, 'Look at us. We did all right without a college education. And you'll come out of college, Jerry, and the way the economy is now you're not gonna get a job anyway.' That was a valid point, but all my coaches were telling me not to sign, to get an education instead. And something inside me just said no, because at that time I doubted my own ability. But in college I've grown a lot, and now I'm pretty confident about my future."

Holtz was drafted by the Orioles on the fourth round in June 1984 and was signed by scout John Hagemann. In five minor-league seasons (through 1988) Holtz has not advanced above Class AA. He has shown good speed but little power, and is now an outfielder—and a longshot.

College pitcher *Charles Hudson* (Chapters 9, 14) was another of Tony Roig's "loosy-goosy" black pitchers in 1981. That June he was the Phillies's twelfth-round draft (number 306 overall) and was signed by scout Doug Gassaway for a bonus of $5,000. In four seasons with the Phillies (1983–86) Hudson was 32–42 with a 3.98 ERA. He was traded to the Yankees before the 1987 season and has since shuttled between starting and relieving. His two-year A.L. record is 17–13. At the end of the 1988 season, Hudson was the only Philadelphia draftee from 1981 on any major-league roster.

Junior-college pitcher *Billy Irions* (Chapters 9, 14) was the Phillies' first selection in the secondary phase of the 1981 June draft. He was signed by scout Doug Gassaway for a bonus of $16,000. Irions' two pro seasons were marred by poor physical conditioning and proneness to injury—and when he arrived for spring training in 1983 still out of shape, the Phillies gave him his unconditional release.

High-school infielder *Chris James* (Chapter 14) was not drafted in June 1981. That fall he enrolled at Blinn Junior College in Texas, where he was scouted by the Phillies' Doug Gassaway. James dropped out of school and signed for a bonus of $10,000. He was converted to the outfield in the minors. Since breaking into the majors for good in 1987, James has hit with good power and fair consistency. He has also shown all-around athletic skill and should still be improving in 1989. He is the brother of pro football running back Craig James.

High-school infielder *John Kanter* (Chapter 9) was the Phillies' fifth-round draft in June 1981 (number 124 overall) and was signed by scout Scott Reid. In three minor-league seasons Kanter showed good power for a second baseman, but his highest batting average was .227. He was described as a "teaser" by the Phillies' Jack Pastore: "Some days he looks like a major-leaguer, and other days you wonder how he got signed." In June 1984 at Peninsula (Class A), when his average was .175 in 32 games, Kanter was given his unconditional release.

High-school pitcher *Charles Kerfeld* (Chapters 9, 14) was the Phillies' twenty-fourth round draft in June 1981 (number 618 overall). West coast scout Eddie Bockman saw him as a big flaky kid with the right kind of aggressiveness on the mound, and the Phillies later offered him a $50,000 bonus. Kerfeld rejected it and enrolled at Yavapai Junior College. The Mariners drafted him that January; he turned them down too. He finally signed with the Astros (scout Bob Kennedy) after being selected in the secondary phase of the June 1982 draft. Kerfeld made the majors in 1985 and quickly established himself as a formidable reliever—listed at 6′6″ and 245 pounds and looking every ounce of it. In 1986 he was 11–2 with 7 saves and a 2.52 ERA. After the Astros lost the N.L. playoff series to the Mets that fall, Kerfeld said: "People in New York have black teeth and their breath smells of beer. And the men are even worse." Kerfeld did not work out at all over the winter and he started to put on some *real* weight. He spent part of 1987 and all of 1988 in the minors, first rehabilitating an elbow and then trying to regain his form. End-of-season scouting reports on Kerfeld were very favorable.

High-school catcher *Phillip Lombardi* (Chapter 9) was the Yankees' third-round draft in June 1981 (number 78 overall) and was signed by scout Don Lindeberg. In the minors he has also played first base, third base, and outfield, because cartilage problems in the left knee have threatened his future as a catcher. Lombardi played a total of twenty-five major-league games in 1986 and 1987 (hitting .250, 11 for 44) and then was traded to the Mets. At Class AAA in 1988 he hit .308 with good power. At age twenty-five he still stood a reasonable chance of making a major-league roster.

High-school pitcher *Vance Lovelace* (Chapters 6, 8) was the Cubs' first-round draft in June 1981 (number 16 overall) and was signed by scout Bob Hartsfield. In eight minor-league seasons (through 1988), Lovelace has not improved appreciably beyond the scouts' original description of a "big left-handed thrower." He was traded to the Dodgers in 1983, released in 1986, and then picked up by the Angels. Using a shorter stride and quicker release, he had some success as a power reliever, but in 1988 at Class AAA he reverted to his wild ways. At the end of the season he appeared briefly in three major-league games recording an ERA of 13.50. Lovelace, who will turn twenty-six in 1989, is more likely to be released again than to mature into a major-league pitcher.

Semi-pro catcher *Mike McCardell* (Chapter 14), previously released by the Cincinnati Reds, was signed by Pittsburgh scout Leroy Hill in November 1981 for a bonus of $500. After a good spring training in 1982, McCardell was sent to Greenwood (Class A). In the first month of the season, while sleeping on the team bus, he was awakened by a Pirates coach who made the mistake of pulling him by the hair. McCardell came up swinging, flattened the coach, and was given his unconditional release the next day. From 1983 to 1987 McCardell played semi-pro ball in Wilmington, Delaware for $100 a week.

College outfielder *Kevin McReynolds* (Chapters 8, 9) was regarded by many scouts as the best all-around prospect in the June 1981 draft. But because of a knee injury, he was selected behind Joe Carter, Dick Schofield, and Terry Blocker. The Padres drafted him as number 6 overall, and he was signed by scout Al Heist. In 1983 McReynolds was named MVP in the Pacific Coast League, and in 1984 he became an established major-leaguer. He was traded to the Mets after the 1986 season and has since achieved a kind of quiet stardom, solid on both offense and defense despite recurrent knee problems. His motionless hitting stance is a good example of what Branch Rickey called a "quiet bat." In 1988 McReynolds hit .288 with 27 home runs, 97 RBI, and 21 stolen bases in 21 attempts.

High-school first baseman *Joey Meyer* (Chapter 9) was so overweight in 1981 that several teams, like the Phillies, did not consider him a serious prospect. That June he was drafted by the Angels on the eighth round but he enrolled at the University of Hawaii; in June 1983 he was drafted by the Brewers on the fifth round and was signed by scouts Jyun Hirota and Ray Poitevint. In the minors Meyer hit with consistency and tape-measure power (one home run in 1987 was launched 582 feet into the third deck at Mile High Stadium in Denver), but his weight was a continuing problem. Meyer went home when his wife had a baby, and in four days he went from 270 pounds to 290. When he made the majors in 1988, Meyer stayed below

260 pounds by following a diet based on chicken, fish, and "some" beer twice a week. Used mostly as a designated hitter, Meyer batted .263 with 11 home runs and 45 RBI. His nickname is "Blue Demon."

College outfielder *Lemmie Miller* (Chapter 9) was the Dodgers' second-round draft in June 1981 (number 50 overall) and was signed by scouts Dennis Haren and Dick Halon. At Arizona State Miller had been used mainly as a DH, but in the minors he became a good defensive outfielder. The problem was his bat. In 1983 and 1984 he hit over .300 at Class AAA, but he seemed to lack aggressiveness as well as power and was released after the 1985 season. Then he was picked up by the Orioles and dropped to Class AA, where in 1986 he hit .235 in seven games. His final stop was the Mexican League. The highlight of Miller's career was a brief major-league stint at the end of 1984; he went 2 for 12.

College pitcher *Mike Moore* (Chapters 8, 9) was drafted by the Mariners as the number one player in the country in June 1981 and was signed by scouts Bob Harrison and Steve Vrablik. Moore was allowed one season at Class AA before being rushed to Seattle in 1982. His best year was 1985 (17–10 with a 3.46 ERA), but his career shows no consistent development beyond the power pitching that worked for him in college. In 1987 Moore lost 19 games; in 1988 he was temporarily relegated to the bullpen. After seven major-league seasons his record was 66–96. At the end of the 1988 season Moore became eligible for free agency.

Minor-league pitcher *Scott Munninghoff* (Chapter 3) was traded from Philadelphia to Cleveland in December 1981. Originally, he was the Phillies' first-round draft in June 1977 and was signed by scout Tony Lucadello for a bonus of $40,000. He pitched briefly in the majors in 1980 and then was demoted to Class AAA, where he struggled more and more with the mechanics of his pitching motion. When the Indians acquired

Munninghoff, they dropped him to Class AA and continued to modify his delivery. At spring training in 1983 Munninghoff was given his unconditional release.

College outfielder *Ricky Nelson* (Chapter 8) was the Mariners' fourth-round draft in June 1981 (number 79 overall) and was signed by scout Bob Harrison. Despite a problem with shin splints, Nelson played seven pro seasons, most of them at Class AAA. His only sustained major-league tour of duty was in 1983, when he hit .257 with five home runs. In 1987 Nelson was given his unconditional release.

High-school outfielder *James Olander* (Chapters 9, 14) was the Phillies' seventh-round draft in June 1981 (number 176 overall) and was signed by scout Scott Reid for a bonus of $20,000. In his first six minor-league seasons, through Class AA, Olander averaged over .300 with fair power, good speed, and a strong arm. But at Class AAA his career was short-circuited by one injury after another, and he spent most of 1987 and 1988 on the disabled list. Spring training in 1989 will be make-or-break time for Olander.

College pitcher *Arby Oswell* (Chapter 9) was the Phillies' twenty-third round draft in June 1981 (number 591 overall) and was signed by scout Doug Gassaway. Oswell pitched poorly at Helena (rookie league) and was given his unconditional release at the end of the 1981 season. Rollie DeArmas, his manager, noted that Oswell had a below-average fastball, poor pitching mechanics, and no real competitive energy. It's also possible that he ruined his chances by insisting on the nickname "Ace." Arby Oswell is a baseball name with magic in it. Ace Oswell is the name of a tow-truck operator.

High-school outfielder *Charles Penigar* (Chapters 9, 14) was the Phillies' second-round draft in June 1981 (number 46 over-all) and was signed by scout Spider Jorgensen for a bonus of $55,000. Traded to San Francisco in 1983, he struggled for two seasons at Class AA before the Giants tried to convert him into a pitcher. In 1986, after a Class A season of 4–5 with a 4.48 ERA, Penigar was released. When the Angels picked him up, they turned him back into an outfielder—and at Class AA in 1988 he hit .269 and stole 47 bases. Penigar is a switch-hitter with fine speed, but most scouts consider him a doubtful prospect because he lacks power. Despite his size (6'5", 185 pounds), he has averaged only three home runs a year in the minors. Penigar will turn twenty-six in 1989.

Minor-league catcher *Lebo Powell* (Chapter 8) was given his unconditional release by the Phillies in January 1983. He had been originally drafted on the first round in June 1980 and signed by scout Andy Seminick for a bonus of $55,000. Powell played three mediocre seasons, all at Class A. But if not for his "lack of coachability" and his troubles off the field, he probably would have been invited to spring training in 1983. After receiving an inquiry from the Florida Bureau of Unemployment Compensation, the Phillies responded: "This employee was released because we did not feel he was major-league material."

High-school infielder *Leon "Bip" Roberts* (Chapter 9) was the Pirates' fifth-round draft in June 1981 (number 118 overall). Many scouts thought he was too small—barely 5'8" and 160 pounds—to be a baseball prospect. Ironically, Roberts at that time was more interested in football and he enrolled at UNLV. The Pirates drafted him again in June 1982 and scout Earl Silverthorn signed him. In the minors Roberts progressed quickly and was drafted away by the Padres. He spent all of 1986 in the majors as a platoon second baseman, hitting .253. At Class AAA in 1987 and 1988, Roberts hit over .300 with impressive speed and was versatile enough to play third base, shortstop, and outfield. He may not get another major-league shot with the Padres, at least in 1989, but at age twenty-five he is still a legitimate prospect.

Junior-college pitcher *Randy Romagna* (Chapter 12) was the Blue Jays' first-round draft in January 1982. He had previously been drafted twice by the Reds but had turned down their bonus offers, which were said to be low because of the prevailing scouting prejudice against small right-handed pitchers. (Romagna was 5'10" and 180 pounds.) The Blue Jays drafted Romagna on the strength of Bob Engle's report on the 1981 Johnstown tournament, and scout Dave Yoakum signed him. In 1982 and 1983 he pitched fair seasons at Class A with a cumulative record of 15–14 and a 4.06 ERA, but at spring training in 1984 he began his conversion into a third baseman. Most switches in the minors are the other way around: weak-hitting position players being converted to pitchers, as in the case of Rich Gaynor. In 1984 at Class A Romagna hit .250 with three home runs. He went downhill from there and in 1985 he was given his unconditional release.

College infielder *Chris Sabo* (Chapter 12) was the Reds' second-round draft in June 1983 and was signed by Gene Bennett, the scout who expressed a wistful hope in 1981 at Johnstown that the Reds might someday have a shot at him. Sabo broke a collarbone in that tournament when he tried to bowl over a catcher at home plate, and he has shown the same kind of aggressiveness in his pro career. After five uneven seasons in the minors, he broke into the majors in 1988 and became Rookie of the Year in the N.L. He hit .271 with 40 doubles and 46 stolen bases, and generally displayed a hell-for-leather style that reminded manager Pete Rose of himself. "I think Chris Sabo was put on this earth to play baseball," Rose said.

Minor-league infielder *Juan Samuel* (Chapters 3, 14) made the majors in 1984 and finished second to Dwight Gooden in the voting for N.L. Rookie of the Year. His original signing in 1979—by Qui-Que Acevedo for a bonus of $3,000—helped to draw dozens of new scouts to the Dominican, eventually diluting the Phillies' advantage there. (They have signed no major Dominican talent in the 1980s.) In five major-league seasons (through 1988) Samuel has averaged .264 with both speed and power, and in 1987 he had a total of 80 extra-base hits. (Rogers Hornsby and Charlie Gehringer are the only other second basemen to accomplish this feat.) But he still chases bad pitches, and Richie Ashburn says that the low-and-away slider may keep Samuel out of the Hall of Fame. Samuel is likely to become an outfielder in 1989.

Minor-league pitcher *Ed Sanford* (Chapter 3) was signed by the Cardinals in 1979 after being released by the Royals; he had been originally signed by scouts Al Diez and Ed Dunn. Sanford made slow progress in professional ball. In 1982 when he was finally promoted to Class AA at age twenty-five, he was 0–5 with a 6.39 ERA; he finished that season at Class A where his statistics reflected undeniable talent: 5–4 with a 2.58 ERA. But in 1983, after his weak showing at spring training, the Cardinals gave Sanford his unconditional release.

High-school shortstop *Dick Schofield* (Chapters 8, 9) was the Angels' first-round draft in June 1981 (number three overall) and was signed by scout Nick Kamzic. In 1983, near the end of his third pro season, Schofield was promoted to the majors at age twenty. Through 1988 he has averaged .231 with fair power and speed. One of his biggest boosters from 1981, cross-check scout Brandy Davis, is disappointed by Schofield's hitting but points out that he has matured into one of the best short-stops in the A.L.

High-school shortstop *Matt Shumake* (Chapters 9, 14) was the Phillies' eighteenth-round draft in June 1981 (number 462 overall). He was a chance draft because he had already an-nounced his intention to accept a scholarship to Clemson, and in fact he turned down a bonus offer of $50,000 just before the fall term began. In June 1984 Shumake was drafted by the Reds on the fifth round and was signed by scouts Cam Bonifay and Julian Mock. In four minor-league seasons (through 1987) Shumake averaged .255 with fair power, but he had to be

moved to the outfield and he could not establish himself above
Class A. In spring 1988 the Reds gave Shumake his unconditional release.

College pitcher *Bill Shuta* (Chapter 12) attracted the interest
of many scouts at Johnstown in 1981, but had undistinguished
junior and senior seasons at the University of Michigan in 1983
and 1984. He had dropped down from his overhand motion
in order to get more action on the fastball, but the result was
a serious control problem. Shuta was finally drafted in June
1984 by the Tigers in the thirty-fourth round. Ed Katalinas
then tried to sign him to a Detroit contract: "I said, 'I have
faith in you. You have the arm and the body, and you just
have to put your delivery together again.' He told me he had
a chance to get into the meat business in Chicago. I said, 'You
can sell meat when you're fifty! Take a chance on baseball
now.' But he was such a late draft pick that I couldn't come
up with enough money to sign him."

College third baseman *Michael Sodders* (Chapters 9, 10) was
the Twins' first-round draft in June 1981 (number 11 overall)
and was signed by scout Jess Flores, Jr., after seven weeks of
bargaining over bonus money. As the sportswriters' "College
Player of the Year," Sodders expected more than the $40,000
he finally received. The Twins had drafted him that high only
because he was a college senior and thus without bargaining
leverage. After his late signing, Sodders began at Class A, against
younger players, and in his first at-bat he hit a grand slam.
But he finished that season at .179, and he spent the rest of
his career in the mid-minors. His bat was his only tool, and
after college he never proved that he could use it consistently.
In 1985, now in the White Sox system, Sodders was given his
unconditional release.

College catcher *Vince Soreca* (Chapters 9, 14) was the Phillies'
third-round draft in June 1981 (number 72 overall) and was
signed by scout Joe Reilly for a bonus of $30,000. Soreca was

drafted where he was because the Phillies wanted a catcher, but after a disastrous first year he was converted to a pitcher. In two seasons at Class A he had a cumulative record of 12–12 with a 4.60 ERA. Soreca had a weak spring training in 1984: he showed a live fastball but was still struggling with the rudiments of pitching at age twenty-three. That April the Phillies gave him his unconditional release.

Minor-league outfielder *Darryl Strawberry* (Chapter 2) was Hugh Alexander's best example in 1981 of a prospect with all five tools. He had been drafted by the Mets in June 1980 as the number one player in the country and signed by scout Roger Jongewaard for $200,000—the highest bonus awarded in the draft era. Strawberry was promoted to the majors in June 1983. He finished that season at .257 with 26 homers, 74 RBI, and 19 stolen bases, and was named N.L. Rookie of the Year. In 1988 he hit .269 with 39 homers, 101 RBI, and 29 stolen bases. The leap from one level of performance to another came in July 1987, when Strawberry was installed as the Mets' cleanup hitter. Since then, one sportswriter says, "He has disciplined all of his frightening ability into a consistent, fundamentally sound superstar package." The one hole in his game is fielding, perhaps highlighting a problem of attention and attitude. But at the plate Strawberry's trademark has become a quick bat uncoiling through a long swing, meeting the ball with a soft wrist flick reminiscent of Hank Aaron's.

College catcher *John Thornton* (Chapter 12) dropped out of school in 1981 and was selected by the Indians in the second round of the 1982 January draft; he was signed by scout Bobby Malkmus. That summer at Class A he suffered several injuries, played in only 26 games, and hit .193. The Indians released Thornton out of spring training in 1983, and he was later signed to a Brewers' contract by Walter Youse, his manager on the Johnny's Auto Sales Team. In 1984 at Class A Thornton hit .284 with 14 home runs. But he had become a first baseman, a less valuable commodity than a catcher, and he progressed only as far as his hitting took him—which was short of Class AA. In 1985 Thornton received his unconditional release.

College pitcher *Lee Tunnell* (Chapter 9) was the Pirates' second-round draft in June 1981 (number 40 overall) and was signed by scout Buzzy Keller. Tunnell broke into the majors late in 1982 and established himself in one dramatic game in Los Angeles; named as the starting pitcher only fifteen minutes before game time, Tunnell proceeded to outduel Fernando Valenzuela for a 1–0 victory. As a starting pitcher in 1983, Tunnell was 11–6 with a 3.54 ERA. As a relief pitcher in 1984, he had to deal with a sore arm whenever he threw two days in a row; he finished the season at 1–7 with 1 save and a 5.27 ERA. Tunnell's career has continued to be up and down. In 1987 his contract was purchased by the Cardinals, but he has spent more time in Louisville than in St. Louis. At age twenty-eight in 1989, Tunnell probably has more major-league seasons ahead.

College pitcher *Matt Williams* (Chapter 9) was the Blue Jays' first-round draft in June 1981 (number five overall) and was signed by scout Jim Hughes. He was a mature, aggressive prospect whose career was shortened by arm problems. After two full seasons at Class AAA, Williams was traded to the Texas Rangers in 1985 and pitched briefly but impressively at the major-league level: 2–1 with a 2.42 ERA. But in 1986 he was limited to appearances in eleven games at Class AAA (1–4 with a 5.70 ERA), and in January 1987 he voluntarily retired at age twenty-eight.

College outfielder *Mel Williams* (Chapter 9) was the Phillies' tenth-round draft in June 1981 (number 254 overall) and was signed by scouts George Farson and Gary Nickels. His best tool was speed, but in 1982 and 1983 Williams was hampered by ankle and knee injuries and had serious trouble making the jump from Class A (where he hit .285) to Class AA (.232). After being demoted back to Class A in mid-season 1983,

Williams hired a lawyer to challenge the Phillies' handling of his career. He played 25 more games and hit .180, and in September the Phillies gave him his unconditional release.

College pitcher *James Winn* (Chapters 8, 9) was the Pirates' first-round draft in June 1981 (number fourteen overall) and was signed by scout Buzzy Keller. Elbow and lower back problems slowed Winn's progress, and even after he made the majors he was shuttled several times to Class AAA. Winn became a relief pitcher and was traded to the White Sox in 1987 and then to the Twins in 1988. In 1988 he pitched 21 major-league innings and went 1–0 (no saves) with a 6.00 ERA.

Player X was scouted in 1981 but remained undrafted and unsigned. He showed enough talent to be noticed but not enough to justify a real dollar sign on the muscle. He was Pat Seeney (Chapter 11), who arrived at a tryout camp with only one tool: the ability to rope line drives to all fields. He was Craig Humbert (Chapter 12), who pitched bravely for the home team at Johnstown when his fielders gave him minimal support. He was Lonny Hartnett (Chapter 14), who tried to will a professional career into being by doing low-volume sportscasting of his own performance even while he was performing. Maybe each of these players had been born thirty years too late. If the year had been 1951 instead of 1981, if huge minor-league systems still allowed scouts to follow their whims as well as their critical faculties, Player X might have spent part of the 1980s on a team bus riding from Keokuk to Dubuque. But Keokuk and Dubuque no longer have minor-league teams, and the accelerated pace of modern farm systems requires more immediate results even from the chosen few (less than 1 percent of all the eligible amateurs in a given season) who do receive pro contracts.

Today Player X may play semi-pro ball or amateur ball or softball, or he may just watch the games on TV. The intense dream of 1981 has already faded toward nostalgia. And the scout who noticed him then, who paused for a moment to catch the glint of something God-given but not given fully enough, has now forgotten Player X's face (even if it was a good one) and his name. All that remains is an image of a swing or a pitching motion—a purified form of one isolated talent, to be used as another guide for judgment when he looks at the new boys next season.

INDEX